BATTLE FOR PARIS 1815

BATTLE FOR PARIS 1815

THE UNTOLD STORY OF THE FIGHTING AFTER WATERLOO

by

Paul L Dawson

FRONTLINE
BOOKS

Battle for Paris 1815

Published in 2019 by
FRONTLINE BOOKS
www.frontline-books.com

An imprint of
Pen & Sword Books Ltd
47 Church Street, Barnsley, S. Yorkshire, S70 2AS

ISBN: 978 1 52674 927 7

CIP data records for this title are available from the British Library

Typeset in by

Printed and bound by
TJ International Ltd, Padstow, Cornwall
Typeset by Donald Sommerville

Pen & Sword Books Ltd incorporates the imprints of Pen & Sword Archaeology,
Atlas, Aviation, Battleground, Discovery, Family History, History, Maritime,
Military, Naval, Politics, Social History, Transport, True Crime, Claymore Press,
Frontline Books, Praetorian Press, Seaforth Publishing and White Owl

For a complete list of Pen and Sword titles please contact

PEN & SWORD LTD
47 Church Street, Barnsley, South Yorkshire, S70 2AS, England
E-mail: enquiries@pen-and-sword.co.uk
Or
PEN AND SWORD BOOKS
1950 Lawrence Rd, Havertown, PA 19083, USA
E-mail: Uspen-and-sword@casematepublishers.com

Contents

Dedication

To David W Paget. Thank you for over twenty years of friendship and excellent company.

Acknowledgements

In the preparation of this book I would like to thank all those who have offered advice and support. I would like to thank all those who have helped me with my research. I never planned to write on Waterloo, and at long last this is my fourth, but possibly not my last volume, on those intriguing and fateful days of 200 summers ago.

Thank you to Captain Sbrava of Service historique de la Défense for granting me unique access to regimental muster lists that have been off limits to researchers due to the poor condition of these documents. Permission was granted at the time of *Waterloo Truth at Last* going to press, so the details of these documents are presented in this work, along with comments on the fate of the men at Waterloo.

Furthermore, I am indebted to Jean Charles Lair and his partner Hélène who must be singled out for compiling the casualty data for the 1st and 2nd cavalry corps from the regimental muster lists housed at Service Historique de la Défence Armée du Tére, in Paris. Without their help, this book could not have been written. We have spent many hundreds of hours in Paris, and without their help, the work in collecting the research material would have taken far longer than the four years it has taken already.

I must also acknowledge the tremendous and most generous assistance in the provision of research material by Ronald Pawly and Yves Martin of digital images of material at Archives Nationales and Service Historique de la Défence Armée du Tére, in Paris. Ronald has been of great help in our many hours of discussion and debate on the campaign and sources available to researchers. Bravo gentlemen.

Pierre de Wit needs to be thanked for his assistance, and I urge readers to his excellent online study of the campaign. Professor A. Pollard needs to be thanked for his friendship and ongoing support of my work on Waterloo.

Lastly, the long-suffering staff at Service Historique de la Défence Armée du Tére, in Paris need to be thanked for answering questions and locating items of research that have made this the fourth volume in my series of books on the campaign of Waterloo possible.

Paul Dawson BSc Hons MA FINS
Wakefield 30 October 2018

Introduction: Waterloo again?

Not another book on the Waterloo campaign? Well yes and no. Most histories of the Hundred Days Campaign stop with Waterloo. Yet the French Army fought on until 3 July 1815. This book seeks to describe these events and show how the most maligned of Napoleon's marshals saved his army and that of Napoleon's beaten at Waterloo. Using archive material that has never been published in French or English before, the details of what occurred after Waterloo are presented, with episodes discussed for the first time since they occurred over 200 years.

Grouchy was the last of Napoléon's marshals. Emmanuel, Second Marquis de Grouchy, walked with a limp and was nearly 50-years-old. A career soldier, with a service record of thirty-six years, having served King, Revolution, Consulate and Empire; he originally enlisted in the Corps Royal d'Artillerie in 1779. Perhaps thanks to his intellectual mother, Gilberte Freteau de Peny, and his sister, the early feminist, Sophie de Condorcet, Emmanuel Grouchy, became an ardent supporter of the youthful French Republic. His military record shows that he fought in many of the major battles of the Republic and early years of the Empire. His service history shows that Grouchy was an able divisional and corps commander, had taken field commands in the campaign of 1806 and 1807, had served in Spain briefly as a governor, and led Prince Eugene's cavalry in the 1809 campaign. He took command of the 3rd Cavalry corps in 1812 and served with distinction in the 1814. Following Waterloo, whilst in exile in America, he struck up a remarkable friendship with Thomas Jefferson.

Yet for many, primarily due to the Dino de Laurentis film *Waterloo*, Grouchy is the bumbling buffoon strawberry eater who failed to march to Waterloo. This vision of an incompetent man, promoted beyond his abilities, has stuck to Grouchy. The film *Waterloo* has done more harm to his reputation than any other. This image has stuck on the public imagination. Grouchy lost Waterloo.

Despite what many historians suggests, Grouchy acquitted himself marvellously during the campaign. He was an excellent administrator, and the truth of the matter is, he was an excellent choice to command the right wing of Napoleon's army. His retreat to Paris is a text book fighting retreat, yet few remember him for this. This book traces what Grouchy did after Waterloo was lost, until he was stripped of command by Davout on 30 June 1815.

Inevitably, in looking at the events after 18 June, we have to re-visit many episodes of the campaign covered in my book on Grouchy. I make no apologies for that, as in order to discuss the events from 19 June onwards for the right wing of the Armée du Nord, ground already covered has be to be revisited briefly to set the events into context. Indeed, in some cases new information is presented. Where this material challenges my earlier thesis, I put my hands up and say I got this wrong in the light of new information, but overall, particularly on Grouchy's culpability, the more documents we find from those fateful days, the more innocent Grouchy becomes of the crimes he supposedly committed. The discovery of a letter dated 20 June 1815 concerning the cannonade of Waterloo being heard by Grouchy, enables us to demolish a lot of myths about that episode. General Exelmans, seen for 200 years as a critic of Grouchy, suddenly becomes his supporter, it is also conclusive proof that Exelmans did not suggest alternative routes to Waterloo – this was merely him after the event trying to paint his own actions in the most favourable light possible, and to slander Grouchy. As an author, I have a bias, but what I have done my best to do, is to present all the information from the pro- and anti-Grouchy factions, to show the reader how I came to my conclusions. The nature of historical research means, that as critical and evaluative historians, we are also desiring to critique our own work and progress the study of our chosen field. Since writing my book on Grouchy for Frontline, my research has been on-going. The discovery of a huge tranche of material in the French Army Archives has added greatly to my understanding of what happened for the right wing of the Armée du Nord.

Note on the sources

With this book, as far as has been possible, I have sought primarily to use documents written during the period of 18 June to 4 July 1815. Grouchy and his part in the fateful days of June 1815 have, ever since they happened, become dominated by two factions, either for or against Grouchy. In their arguments both sides narration of the events of June 1815 are dominated by hindsight and above by personal and political interests. Grouchy has been accused of being one of the determining causes, if not the cause, of the defeat of the Emperor at Waterloo. As a result of this, it is very hard to get down to the nub of the issues at hand due to complex self-interest of the men from 1815, and from later historians. What I aim to do with this book is to judge Grouchy as far as possible, from his actions as they happened in 1815 and where needed, to expose aspects of those events as either truth or lies. This is only possible with a thorough examination of all the original documents from 1815 that can be located in archives in Europe. By original, I mean documents that were written in June 1815, and not decades later, or are copies of lost originals – but more of that later.

The events of those fateful days are so charged politically, and those who took part in these events, who wrote their stories down in later years, did so for a single reason, to curry favour with who was in power at the time. For example, General Kellerman wrote his memoires down in 1817 in such a style that if the text was ever read by a monarchist, then Kellerman had always been such, and he goes out of his way to damn Napoléon. General Gérard wrote to curry favour with the Orleanists regime, whilst others wrote at a time, the 1840s, when being a Bonpartist was permissible, and officers pour out book after book of how devoted they were to the Emperor. It is very easy to write a book about the events of the Hundred Days from these sources. In fact, many do. Indeed, for some, translating published eye-witness testimony, without offering any critique on hermeneutics (Hermeneutics addresses the relationship between the interpreter and the interpreted; viz: What does it mean? What were the author's intentions? Is the source authentic?), and above all when and why the officer was writing, appears to count as ground-breaking and cutting-edge history.

Sadly, many armchair historians have no language skills, yet French and German are not dead languages like Latin, but for many published materials are not accessible because of a failure to study a language beyond English. Making these sources accessible is very laudable, but these authors don't present the backstory behind a particular source, and indeed cherry-pick the bits of the source they wish to publish, rather than present the entire text in toto. Of course, the sources one chooses dramatically affects the conclusion one comes to. Indeed, in recent years, the campaign has been the subject of a plethora of books claiming to unlock new sources on Waterloo; yet for many students of the battle, these are not new sources if you can read French! The self-same books present no new material at all to students of French and German, and yet are lauded by many, when in fact these books contain no new material, and indeed suffer from the lack of original archive research and rigorous methodology. Populist and military history tends to be dominated by amateur historians with little or no academic training, no language skills (a barrier to both reading texts not in English but also in visiting archives that are not English) or by ex-army officers who conflate their own military experience as somehow being a key device in unlocking the military experience of a soldier from 200 years ago. Yes, this is partially true, as being under enemy fire and the feelings it generates is the same regardless of when you were fighting, being on campaign one worries about mostly about the next meal, the next mouthful of water, where the enemy is, etc. The same thought processes transcend time, but it does not give the writer a grounding in the theory of history that comes through academia.

Because published memoires have been so commonly used in the creation of narratives on the campaign, and also to try and overcome the inherit bias in using material written after the fact, by and large I have restricted my study to documents that can be verifiably proved to have been written the day the events took place. These documents, the vast majority of which, have never been published in French, let alone used to study the campaign, which I present here, often for the first time, offer genuinely new material (well not exactly new as it has been sat in the French Army Archives there to be consulted by anyone interested since 1815), and genuine scholarly research.

The documents that exist in 2018, are by their very nature 'freaks', the whys and wherefores of their survival marks them out as special. We cannot be certain how many hundreds of documents are missing. All we have in 2018 are those documents deposited into archive storage at some point in 1815, that survived the Siege of Paris in 1870 when we know thousands of documents were destroyed, were accessioned into the Army Archives in the 1880s, and above all are those documents not stolen from the archives, which sadly is an ongoing concern. Unscrupulous researches steal documents away, more than likely for sale for personal gain, or fortune hunters come along and cut out signatures for sale on the open market, again for money. We are not dealing with a complete data set. But it is all we have, and all we have is far more reliable as source material than an officer writing thirty or forty years later when what he thinks he remembers is contaminated by his life and times since the event, both in their politics and ambitions in life, as well as by what they have read and been told about the events that they took part in. Yet, despite all this, the French Army Archive possess thousands of documents from 18 June to 4 July 1815 that so far have never been used in the systematic study of the Waterloo campaign. These documents are official government papers, orders sent from corps commanders, as well as dispatches sent on the day of battle to senior officers. The paperwork provides a largely bias

4

free data set. The officers writing the orders and dispatches were not doing so with a weather eye for posterity, they were writing down in the heat of battle the most important points about what they had witnessed, free of political judgement or personal bias. Even so, a letter written in the midst of battle, still has bias. Neuroscientist John Coates conducted research into memory; his study undertaken between 2004 and 2012 found that what is recalled from memory is what the mind believes happened rather than what actually happened. This effect is often referred to as 'false memory'.[1] Thus a quickly written dispatch will be a report of what the writer assumes was important, and not what may have actually been important. A memoir, letter or other material used to help create a narrative of events is of limited value in terms of historical interpretation without context.[2] The closeness of the written narrative to the events that took place will affect what is recorded.[3] The further the written narrative shifts away from the day the event took place, the closer the written narrative becomes to a figurative fiction. The recollection of crucial events will be re-evaluated and re-contextualised throughout the life of the author to the point of creating the written record – personal memoires become influenced by the socio-political, socio-economic environment, and experiences of the author will have an impact on how they recall and event.[4] A group of First World War veterans were interviewed in the 1960s and 1970s. They talked about the generals being lions leading lions, and not once complained about the conditions they lived in. Scroll on twenty or thirty years and these same men, based on what they have seen on TV, read or been told, change their recollections so much that they bemoan the generals that they formerly praised, and often broke down in tears about the same living conditions they did not complain about. As public, or collective memory changes, so too does personal memory.[5] Therefore, we must test these sources against independent and ideally verifiable sources. Which returns us to the statement of Paul Fussell, that memoires occupy a place between auto-biography and fiction.[6]

What I present in the narration is an interpretation of events based upon the experiences of those involved. Using documents written the day the event happened rather than relying upon secondary sources such as published memoires. It should be seen as *a* version of events and not *the* version of events. Waterloo was the beginning of the end, not the end in itself. What follows is a reassessment of what happened using that surviving archive material.

Chapter 1

Politics and Paris

In the words of Gregor Dallas, Napoléon's position in spring 1815 was built on 'wobbly foundations'. There was the very real prospect of a more widespread civil war.[1] Napoléon no longer possessed the means to re-impose a dictatorship, and no single political faction was dominant; he presided over political and domestic chaos of his own making.[2] In 1815, Napoléon did not represent national will, and had the support from, it is estimated, just 3 per cent of the nation.[3]

Revolt in the spring of 1815 was not just limited to France. In London, riots against the government and its punitive corn laws came to an end in mid-March.[4] Nationalist riots broke out in the former French Confederation of the Rhine states against the Prussians.

Paris in spring 1815 was restless with rising unemployment and increasing taxation. The Congress of Vienna was busy endeavouring to re-draw the map of Europe, a process that was far from easy. France, backed by her Allies, Austria and Great Britain, was on the verge of declaring war against Prussia over the fate of Saxony, one of Napoléonic France's allies. To face this crisis the French army needed to be brought up to a war footing and brought up to strength. One of the last acts of the Monarchy in the spring of 1815 was, on the 9 March 1815, to call up 12,000 half-pay officers and 30,000 half-pay men, of which it seems some 8,952 returned to the army.[5]

Myth tells us that the Napoléon returned to France on a wave of hatred from the Bourbons by the army, mainly officers and men on half-pay, a force that numbered perhaps 40,00 malcontents, most of whom had been paid but felt they had been badly treated by being placed on half-pay and did not recognise the need to reduce the strength of the army to a peace-time footing. The call-up of men to face the Saxony crisis returned many of these unemployed soldiers back to the army, diluting the opposition to the monarchy. But we accept that the resentment generated by what appeared to be indiscriminate selection of those placed on

6

half-pay was perhaps the primary grievance former soldiers had with King Louis, as opposed to being die-hard Bonapartists. Opposition to Louis was not solely restricted to Bonapartists, many were Republicans, die hard Jacobins, Orleanists and Liberalists, all of whom had their own agenda on how France should be governed. For Napoléon to succeed in rallying France behind him, he had to appeal to the disparate opposition groups, which led fundamentally to his own downfall as he had no single power base. Napoléon had to win over key sections of society to support his new government in a coalition, as opposed to the virtual dictatorship he had enjoyed since 1799.

So divided was France, that Napoléon faced Civil War: Generals Grouchy and Lamarque were dispatched from Paris to crush the rebellion in the Vendee. Vandamme and d'Erlon headed to quell rebellion in the north. Historian Charles Esdaile notes, the desire for Napoléon to return was far less than to remove the Bourbons, and as soon as war returned to the political agenda, popular and political support rapidly fell away from the new regime. He ruled not by consent of the people but the desire of the army.[6]

Yet despite the worrying developments on the home front, Napoléon was determined to take the inevitable war to the Allies before they could attack France. On the 3 June, Napoléon informed marshals Soult and Davout that Marshal Grouchy had been named commander-in-chief of the cavalry of the Armée du Nord. Grouchy joined the Imperial Headquarters at Laon on 5 June and began to work with Soult on establishing the movement orders for the forthcoming campaign.

The Imperial Guard left Paris on 8 June 1815. Napoléon left Paris on 12 June for Soissons to join headquarters. On the Belgian border were the two Allied armies; a force of 116,000 Prussians and Saxons, led by the Prussian Field Marshal Gebhard Leberecht von Blücher, was based at Namur, and a force of 93,000 British, Dutch, and German troops based at Brussels, commanded by the Duke of Wellington. Leading elements of the Allied armies were at Charleroi and Gilly on the evening of 14 June 1815. Inconclusive actions at Ligny and Quatre-Bras on 16 June resulted in by the Armée du Nord being divided into two parts on 17 June, which ultimately led to the battles of Wavre and Waterloo on 18 June. Faulty intelligence reports, and a breakdown in communication from Napoléon to Grouchy on 17 and 18 June, compounded the catastrophic failure of issuing orders too late on 17 June for Grouchy to catch Blücher's men and prevent him linking with Wellington. This was the final nail in the coffin for Napoléon's plans to march into Brussels.

Waterloo was not the last battle of the Hundred Days but the events after 18 June have seldom been studied. What happened next in the build up to the Battle of Paris is what follows.

Chapter 2

The Campaign Begins

An unlikely supporter of the Revolution, the Marquis de Grouchy had eagerly joined the Revolutionary armies and the those of the Empire, making a name for himself as a solid and competent cavalry officer. Thus, it is little wonder that Grouchy was named commander-in-chief of the cavalry reserve on 4 June 1815.

At the start of April 1815, a call went out to all former Guards of Honour who were on half pay or no pay to return to the eagles. They were to act as 'Officiers Ordonnance' to Marshal Grouchy.[1] Of the four cavalry corps under Grouchy, the 1st was headed by Pajol, the 2nd by Exelmans, the 3rd by Kellerman the younger and the 4th by Milhaud, one-time politician and regicide. Pajol and Exelmans are key players in our story.

The 1st Cavalry Corps was led by the exuberant Claude Pierre Pajol. In the French Army Archives can be found an incredibly detailed account of 14 and 15 June, complete with maps, as well as copies of orders received and sent to the 1st Cavalry Corps. Alas it stops on 15 June, the rest of the document has been torn out.

Général de Division François Remy Isidor Exelmans was appointed commanding officer of the 2nd Cavalry Corps on 5 June. His career began on 6 September 1791 when he joined the Volunteer Battalion of the Meuse aged just 16. Promotion to sergeant came on 1 January 1792 and to sous-lieutenant on 22 October 1796. He was promoted to lieutenant on 19 June 1798 and became on 22 October 1798 aide-de-camp to General Eblé. He quickly passed to the 16th Dragoons as a captain on 13 April 1799, and after a matter of months was made aide-de-camp to General Broufies on 21 July 1799. Promoted to captain aide-de-camp on 8 July 1800, and thence aide-de-camp to General Joachim Murat on 21 May 1801. Promotion to squadron commander came on 3 October 1803, and with no experience at all of regimental command, let alone company command, was named Colonel of the 1st Chasseurs à Cheval on 27 December 1805. He remained in command of the Chasseurs à Cheval for two years, when he was recalled to Murat's service as Général de Brigade aide de Camp on 14 May 1807. He was transferred as Major of the Chasseurs à Cheval of the Imperial Guard on 24 December 1811 and was named Major of the Grenadiers à Cheval of the Imperial Guard some seven months later on 9 July 1812. With no experience of brigade or divisional command, he was named commanding officer of the 2nd Cavalry Corps on 15 February 1813, a post he retained through to 12 June 1814 when he was appointed Inspector General of Cavalry.

He clearly had the ability, we assume, to rapidly learn the duties of corps commander with on the job training during the 1813 campaign – but how capable was he? Following Waterloo, he was dismissed on 24 July 1815. Recalled to the army staff on 1 September 1819, he served under General Monthion. Named Inspector General of Cavalry on 7 May 1828, he was later named Marshal of France 10 March 1851.

He did not enjoy the title long as he died on 22 July 1852.[2] His military career is one of competence. He was an excellent staff flunky, of that there is no doubt, but of his capabilities as a corps commander, we are left with rather vague images of him as a tactician capable of independent command. Copious material can be found generated by him during the 100 Days in the French Army archives, but from it, one gets the feeling his corps was run by his staff. The bazaar permutations of his corps on 17 June, its haphazard performance, and bungled night time cantonments, make us wonder as to his competence or at least that of his brigade and regimental commanders.

His divisional commanders were Jean Baptiste Strolz and Louis Pierre Aime Chastel. Chastel had been appointed to field command on 16 April 1815 and was attached to 1st Corps. Of the brigade commanders, at the head of 1st Brigade of Strolz's 9th Division was Général de Brigade Baron André Burthe. He had been on half pay since 1814 and had begged Davout for employment on 31 March 1815. According to his police file, he had had been watched since returning to Paris on 1 March 1815. Against the terms of his parole, he took a field command in April 1815 and was recommended for promotion to Général de Division by Exelmans on 3 July 1815. His file also states on 26 July he refused to wear the white cockade and is recorded as an ardent republican. He enlisted in the 2nd Dragoons on 11 April 1791 and was made sous-lieutenant on 13 April 1793 in the 10th Dragoons. Made adjutant to General Solignac 23 February 1796, he became aide-de-camp to General Massena 15 October 1798. Promoted to Colonel of the 4th Hussars 1 February 1805, he was made Général de Brigade on 30 December 1810. On half pay till 25 December 1811, when he took a field command, in charge of a light cavalry brigade in the 2nd Cavalry Corps during the Russian campaign. On the in-active list from 1 September 1814, he officially took a field command on 15 May 1815. Placed under observation after Waterloo, he was given a staff appointment under General Monthion on 30 December 1818 and retired 6 January 1825.[3]

Commanding the 1st Brigade of Chastel's 10th Division was Général de Brigade Baron Pierre Bonnemains. Bonnemains wrote a grovelling letter to Soult on 23 May 1815 outlining his career and merits as an officer, begging for a place in the Armée du Nord. He had been promoted to Général de Brigade on 6 August 1811, had served under Eugene in 1813. Two days later Prince Eugene sent a glowing reference to Soult. We don't have a date for his appointment to the Armée du Nord, but on 2 July, Exelmans recommended General Vallin's and Bonnemains to be promoted to lieutenant general for their distinguished and good conduct in the 100 Days campaign. Marshal Grouchy also requested promotion for him on a glowing letter of praise dated 3 July 1815, as did General Vallin and Louis Marchant, secretary of state, on 5 July 1815. Bonnemains wrote to Marshal Victor on 23 October 1815 asking about his back pay and promotion and again in May 1816, and yet again on 1 December 1816, Victor wrote to Bonnemains on 24 December 1816 saying he was owed no back pay or promotion. Naturally, Bonnemains challenged this in a letter dated 26 December 1816. For his truculence, he was placed on the at watched list on 30 December 1815. He did not let the matter drop and petitioned the King on 4 December 1820. At last he was granted his long overdue promotion on 26 January 1821. His claim for back pay was still ongoing, and he petitioned the government again on 22 January 1822, finally granted on 11 February 1822.[4] He would play a key role in the campaign of 1815. He died in 1850 aged 77.

In the early hours of 15 June, the French army began to cross the frontier; an army that was enthusiastic in their support of their 'Great Captain', who, like them, was confident of the expected outcome. The order of the day, issued on 14 June, proclaimed:[5]

> Soldiers, today is the anniversary of Marengo and Friedland, places where the destiny of Europe was decided on two occasions. Accordingly, like after Austerlitz and Wagram, we believed the arguments and the oaths of the princes that we left on their thrones! Today, however, in their coalition against us they take offence at the independence and at the most sacred rights of France. They started

their aggressions on a precise manner: let us therefore march to meet them; them and us, are we not the same men?

Soldiers, at Jena, against those same Prussians, who are today so arrogant, you were one against three, and at Montmirail, one against six.

That those of you who were prisoners of the English tell you their stories of their pontoons and of the horrible evils that they suffered.

The Saxons, the Belgians, the Hanoverians, the soldiers of the Rhine Confederation, groan at their obligations to help the cause of the princes who are enemies of the justice and the rights of all people. They know that this coalition is insatiable. After destroying twelve million Italians, one million Saxons, and six million Belgians, it will devour the smaller States of Germany.

The fools! One moment of good fortune blinds them. The oppression and the humiliation of the French people are above their power! If they move into France, they will find their graves.

Soldiers! We have to make forced marches, give battles, take risks; but, with steadiness, victory will be ours: the rights, the honour and the welfare of our country will be retaken.

For each Frenchmen who has the courage, the moment has come to win or to die!'

Napoléon's plans called for a concentric advance of three columns onto Charleroi. Reille's 2nd Corps and d'Erlon's 1st Corps formed the left wing of the army, and were to march from Solre-sur-Sambre, via Thuin, to Marchienne-au-Pont, a short distance outside of Charleroi. Pajol's cavalry in the centre, supported by Domon's cavalry, was to advance from Beaumont to Charleroi, with General Vandamme's 3rd Corps to follow under the protective screen cavalry. At the rear were Lobau's 6th Corps and the Imperial Guard. The right wing comprised General Gérard's 4th Corps, protected by one of Milhaud's cuirassier divisions.

Napoléon's plan was that if the army left its positions at 03.00 hours, some 60,000 men would be at Charleroi by midday. However, things went very wrong before the campaign really began, as at 07.00 hours Général de Division de Ghaisnes, Comte de Bourmont, who commanded the 14th Infantry Division, along with his staff, deserted their posts and headed off to join the Prussians. No doubt this caused widespread alarm among the division. General Hulot was named the new divisional commander by General Gérard.

Be that as it may, despite this set back and other, by the early afternoon Charleroi had fallen to the French, Marshal Ney was head to Frasnés with 1st and 2nd Corps, with Grouchy's cavalry champing at the bit to see action. With the French across the River Sambre in ever increasing numbers, Prussian General Pirch withdrew his troops from the line of the river and concentrated his troops at Gilly. Pirch had around 10,000 men at his disposal. Following the action at Gilly, Sombreffe had become the concentration point for Blücher's army. At first light, just a few minutes before 04.00 hours, Napoléon was on horseback. He was seemingly in good spirits, intending to reach Brussels as soon as possible. By daybreak he had had no news of Wellington's movements, or of Blücher, but considered that in all probability the Anglo-Belgian Army would take ground in front of Brussels to make a stand. In this scenario he would push them back to Antwerp, along their lines of communication, causing them to be separated still further from their Prussian allies. Before this plan could be put into operation however, Napoléon had to be sure that Blücher could not come to their assistance.

Winning early victories at Charleroi and Gilly, two battles were fought on 16 June, both of which were inconclusive; indeed, Ney's paralysis at Quatre-Bras was the main reason for the victory at Ligny being partial. The scene was therefore set for the fateful events of 18 June as Fleury de Chaboulon explains:[6]

Marshal Grouchy, with the 3d and 4th corps, and the cavalry of Generals Pajol, Excelmanns [sic], and Milhaud, was placed on the heights of Fleurus, and in advance of them. The 6th corps and the guard were in échélon between Fleurus and Charleroi. The same day the army of Marshal Blücher, ninety thousand strong, collected together with great skill, was posted on the heights of Bry and Sombreffe, and occupied the villages of Ligny and St. Amand, which protected his front. His cavalry extended far in advance on the road to Namur. The army of the Duke of Wellington, which this general had not yet had time to collect, was composed of about a hundred thousand men scattered between, Nivelles, Genappe, and Brussels. The Emperor went in person, to reconnoitre Blücher's position; and penetrating his intentions, resolved to give him battle, before his reserves, and the English army, for which he was endeavouring to wait, should have time to unite, and come and join him.

He immediately sent orders to Marshal Ney, whom he supposed to have been on the march for Quatre Bras, where he would have found very few forces, to drive the English briskly before him, and then fall with his main force on the rear of the Prussian army. At the same time, he made a change in the front of the imperial army: General Grouchy advanced toward Sombreffe, General Gérard toward Ligny, and General Vandamme toward St. Amand. General Gérard, with his division, five thousand strong, was detached from the 2d corps, and placed in the rear of General Vandamme's left, so as to support him, and at the same time form a communication between Marshal Ney's army and that of Napoléon. The guard, and Milhaud's cuirassiers, were disposed as a reserve in advance of Fleurus. At three o'clock the 3d corps reached St. Amand and carried it. The Prussians, rallied by Blücher, retook the village. The French, entrenched in the churchyard, defended themselves there with obstinacy; but, overpowered by numbers, they were about to give way, when General Drouot, who has more than once decided the fate of a battle, galloped up with four batteries of the guard, took the enemy in the rear, and stopped his career.

At the same moment Marshal Grouchy was fighting successfully at Sombreffe, and General Gérard made an impetuous attack on the village of Ligny. Its embattled walls, and a long ravine, rendered the approaches to it not less difficult than dangerous: but these obstacles did not intimidate General Lefol, or the brave fellows under his command; they advanced with the bayonet, and in a few minutes the Prussians, repulsed and annihilated, quitted the ground. Marshal Blücher, conscious that the possession of Ligny rendered us masters of the event of the battle, returned to the charge with chosen troops: and here, to use his own words, 'commenced a battle, that may be considered as one of the most obstinate mentioned in history'.

For five hours two hundred pieces of ordnance deluged the field with slaughter, blood, and death. For five hours the French and Prussians, alternately vanquished and victors, disputed this ensanguined post hand to hand, and foot to foot, and seven times in succession was it taken and lost. The Emperor expected every instant, that Marshal Ney was coming to take part in the action. From the commencement of the affair, he had reiterated his orders to him, to manoeuvre so as to surround the right of the Prussians; and he considered this diversion of such high importance, as to write to the marshal, and cause him to be repeatedly told, that the fate of France was in his hands. Ney answered, that 'he had the whole of the English army to encounter, yet he would promise him, to hold out the whole day, but nothing more'. The Emperor ordered him anew, 'to beat back the English, and make himself master of Quatre Bras, cost what it might.'

The marshal persisted in his fatal error. Napoléon, deeply impressed with the importance of the movement, that Marshal Ney refused to comprehend and execute, sent directly to the first corps an order, to move with all speed on the right of the Prussians; but, after having lost much valuable time in waiting for it, he judged, that the battle could not be prolonged without danger, and directed General Gérard, who had with him but five thousand men, to undertake the movement, which should have been accomplished by the twenty thousand men of Count Erlon; namely, to turn St. Amand, and fall on the rear of the enemy. This manoeuvre, ably executed, and seconded by the guard attacking in front, and by a brilliant charge of the cuirassiers of General Delort's brigade and of the horse grenadier guards, decided the victory. The Prussians, weakened in every part, retired in disorder, and left us, with the field of battle, forty cannons and several standards. On the left, Marshal Ney, instead of rushing rapidly on Quatre Bras, and effecting the diversion, that had been recommended to him, had spent twelve hours in useless attempts, and given time to the Prince of Orange to reinforce his advanced guard. The pressing orders of Napoléon not allowing him to remain meditating any longer; and desirous, no doubt, of repairing the time he had lost; he did not cause either the position or the forces of the enemy to be thoroughly reconnoitred, and rushed on them headlong.

After Ligny the Prussians withdrew north-east, and Wellington north. Marshal Grouchy was sent on the early afternoon on 17 June, to chase the Prussians, and the Emperor headed north with the left wing of the army towards Brussels. Fleury de Chaboulon noted that the victory at Ligny was important because:[7]

It separated the English army from the Prussians and left us hopes of being able to vanquish it in its turn. The Emperor, without losing time, was for attacking the English on one side at daybreak and pursuing Blücher's army without respite on the other. It was objected to him, that the English army was intact, and ready to accept battle; while our troops, harassed by the conflicts and fatigue of Ligny, would not perhaps be in a condition to fight with the necessary vigour. In fine, such numerous objections were made, that he consented to let the army take rest.

Ill success inspires timidity. If Napoléon, as of old, had listened only to the suggestions of his own audacity, it is probable, it is certain, and I have heard General Drouot say it, that he might, according to his plan, have led his troops to Brussels on the 17th; and who can calculate what would have been the consequences of his occupying that capital. On the 17th therefore, the Emperor contented himself with forming his army into two columns; one of sixty-five thousand men, headed by the Emperor, after having joined to it the left wing, followed the steps of the English. The light artillery, the lancers of General Alphonse Colbert, and of the intrepid Colonel Sourd, kept close after them to the entrance of the forest of Soignes, where the Duke of Wellington took up his position. The other, thirty-six thousand strong, was detached under the orders of Marshal Grouchy, to observe and pursue the Prussians. It did not proceed beyond Gembloux.

The night of the 17th was dreadful and seemed to presage the calamities of the day. A violent and incessant rain did not allow the army, to take a single moment's rest. To increase our misfortunes, the bad state of the roads retarded the arrival of our provision, and most of the soldiers were without food: however, they gaily endured this double ill luck; and at daybreak announced to Napoléon by repeated acclamations, that they were ready to fly to a fresh victory. The Emperor had thought, that Lord Wellington, separated from the Prussians, and foreseeing the march of General Grouchy, who, on passing the Dyle, might fall on his flank, or on his rear, would not venture to maintain his position, but would retire to Brussels. He was surprised, when daylight discovered to him, that the English army had not quitted its positions, and appeared disposed, to accept battle. He made several generals reconnoitre these positions; and, to use the words of one of them, he learned, that they were defended "by an army of cannons, and mountains of infantry". Napoléon immediately sent advice to Marshal Grouchy, that he was probably about to engage in a grand battle with the English, and ordered him to push the Prussians briskly, to approach the grand army as speedily as possible, and to direct his movements so as to be able to connect his operations with it. He then sent for his principal officers, to give them his instructions. Some of them, confident and daring, asserted, that the enemy's position should be attacked and carried by main force. Others, not less brave, but more prudent, remonstrated, that the ground was deluged by the rain; that the troops, the cavalry in particular, could not manoeuvre without much difficulty and fatigue; that the English army would have the immense advantage of awaiting us on firm ground in its intrenchments; and that it would be better, to endeavour to turn these. All did justice to the valour of our troops, and promised that they would perform prodigies; but they differed in opinion with regard to the resistance, that the English would make. Their cavalry, said the generals who had fought in Spain, are not equal to ours; but their infantry are more formidable, than is supposed. When intrenched, they are dangerous from their skill in firing: in the open field, they stand firm, and, if broken, rally again within a hundred yards, and return to the charge.

Fresh disputes arose; and, what is remarkable, it never entered into any one's head, that the Prussians, pretty numerous parties of whom had been seen towards Moustier, might be in a situation to make a serious diversion on our right. The Emperor, after having heard and debated the opinions of all, determined, on considerations to which all assented, to attack the English in front.

The battle of Waterloo began sometime around 11.30 hours. This was Napoléon's last battle. The fate of Napoléonic France hung in the balance.

15

Chapter 3

The Guns of Waterloo

At about 11.30 hours, the guns of General Reille's 2nd Corps opened fire, and therein lies one of the great myths of 1815. Received wisdom implies that Grouchy failed to march to the sound of the guns of Waterloo. Myth says the guns were heard at Sart-à-Walhain, and a confrontation took place between Grouchy and his senior officers over what to do. Establishing exactly what happened in that garden at Sart-à-Walhain on 18 June 1815 is of great importance when we look at what happened after Waterloo.

Yes, the cannonade of Waterloo is important, but the whereabouts of Exelmans and what he did or did not say is of more immediate concern. Locating him on the first half of 18 June is key to answering other much deeper questions about the campaign. The traditional story has Exelmans at Sart-à-Walhain with Gérard, both men telling Grouchy to march to the sound of the guns.

Can we find sources from 1815 and crucially from June 1815 to support this view? Since writing on Grouchy [Paul L. Dawson (2017) *Napoléon and Grouchy*, Frontline] new research has found a document about these events written, at most, forty-eight hours after the discussion at Sart-à-Walhain took place. The discovery of this letter has made me change some of my own previous ideas on the subject. An anonymous writer in a letter dated 20 June 1815 presents a very different eye-witness account of the event taking place. We have retained the original spelling of names:[1]

20 Juin 1815

Vaterlo

The 16th during the attack on the village of Ligny General Gérard did not have his cavalry, 2,000 strong, that General Grouchi had taken on the morning.

The 18th in the garden of Sart-à-Walhain, the sound of cannonade was heard, Gérard said he thought it was coming from the left, and that in consequence they had to march to support the army, and it would be a decisive day, Grouchi said it was coming from the right. Gnl Exelmans elbowed his way between the two men and said that he [Grouchi] had no time to waste and were headed in that direction to the right.

Gnl Grouchi also said that he had orders to put himself astride the road to Louvain where he was expected to arrive at 7PM.

The 18th around 4PM an officer names P[illegible] sent by the Emperor came to Gnl Grouchi carrying orders for him [illegible].

The letter is of great importance in unlocking what happened that June day both at Wavres and Sart-à-Walhain. Did Grouchy hold a council of war at Sart-à-Walhain, or was Grouchy experiencing option paralysis? Torn between instincts of marching to battle and carrying out his written orders, what was the best course to adopt? Should he heed the advice of Gérard and head to the guns, or follow his orders and advice of Exelmans and heads to Wavre? Who made the decision to march to Wavre? Did Grouchy provide dynamic leadership or did he go along with the brusque bullyboy tactics of Exelmans? But before we address these questions, we need to interrogate the letter.

The first paragraph speaks of Gérard at Ligny. The writer states that General Maurin and the 7th Cavalry Division were not with 4th Corps and Grouchy had deployed them elsewhere. Does this match reality? Given Gérard's aide-de-camp Rumigny[2] states that the headquarters of 4th Corps was accompanied by the 6th Hussars, we wonder how much faith we can place in this letter. Rumigny, aide-de-camp to General Gérard noted:[3]

> General Gérard set off on the right of the village of Ligny, the Prussians gathered their forces, and he observed the Namur road, whilst waiting for the infantry to arrive. Soon after, he moved forward, with his staff, but he became spotted by a squadron of Prussian lancers and a few sharpshooters. The Chasseurs à Cheval who escorted the General opened fire, and during an exchange of musketry with the sharpshooters, the General who was always at our head, showed no concern of being without a strong escort.
>
> Colonel de Carignan, with the 6th Hussars stood with him. Suddenly, a Prussian lancer Officer with his squadron launched themselves into a gallop and charged us.
>
> The General and his small escort made a brave stand until the approach of the enemy squadron, which overthrew eight or ten of our Chasseurs à Cheval.

The General and his Chief of Staff, wanting to escape found themselves in a sunken road, and their horses fell. They were caught by a Prussian lancer, who galloped after them into the sunken road. Finding himself in front of the General, he gave five to six lance thrust to Saint-Rémy. When we arrived the Prussian prudently withdrew, leaving his two opponents on the ground. General Saint-Rémy[4] escaped with relatively light injuries, and General Gérard from mild bruising to his leg. I went to call the cavalry. They arrived at the trot, and in turn crushed the Prussian squadron, who fell back on Ligny.

Rumigny mentions both Chasseurs à Cheval and Hussars, ergo the 6th Hussars and 8th Hussars? Yet we know from Colonel Grouchy that he was here also with the 12th Chasseurs à Cheval:[5]

During the charge in the afternoon a single squadron repulsed the charge of three squadrons of Prussian Uhlans. Distinguished in the action were Chasseurs à Cheval Schneiblein and Ferrad, who saved General Gérard[6] and his chief of staff who had become dismounted in the action.

General Berton commanding the 14th and 17th Dragoons under the orders of General Chastel, who commanded the 10th Cavalry Division states Maurin's Division accompanied the attack of 4th Corps.[7] But the same writer states:[8]

We said above that the 4th and the 2nd Divisions of the corps was placed on the evening of the 15th at Heppignies and was united with the 3rd Corps to attack Saint-Amand. A division of the Young Guard was sent to be in reserve to the left of this village, along with the light cavalry of General Domon. A brigade of lancers, commanded by Marshal-du-Camp Colbert, was placed beyond these troops, to maintain communication with the left wing.

So Domon, commanding the 4th, 9th and 12th Chasseurs à Cheval, was nowhere near 4th Corps. Yet we know part of the division was at some point. Was Berton mistaken? Given that the 12th Chasseurs à Cheval suffered the highest losses of the division, did Domon send the 4th and 9th on detachment and keep the 12th Chasseurs à Cheval with him at Ligny? Very possible. So where was Maurin? Why was 4th Corps saved by General Vandammes attached cavalry? If the 6th Hussars and 8th Chasseurs à Cheval were with Gérard, why did the 12th Chasseurs à Cheval rescue him? Or was only a single squadron of the 6th with the headquarters? This seems very plausible indeed, that the bulk of the division were elsewhere, hence the need for the 12th Chasseurs à Cheval to come to the rescue. Losses in the division were as follows:

Regiment	Killed		Wounded		Missing		Total
	Officers	Men	Officers	Men	Officers	Men	
6th Hussars[9]	0	1	0	1	0	11	13
8th Chasseurs à Cheval[10]	0	1	0	2	0	0	3
6th Dragoons[11]	0	4	0	16	0	10	30
16th Dragoons[12]	No meaningful data recorded						
Total	0	6	0	19	0	21	46

So, is it possible that the dragoons were sent off with Exelmans elsewhere, leaving just the light cavalry brigade? Perhaps. Rumigny clearly mentions the first brigade. Arguably therefore the dragoons were elsewhere. Were only detachments of the 6th Hussars and 8th Chasseurs à Cheval with Gérard? The very low losses of the 8th Chasseurs à Cheval may imply that the Chasseurs à Cheval Rumigny mentioned were in reality the 12th. We don't know. But, as we mentioned earlier, it is possible that the bulk of Gérard's cavalry was elsewhere, which resulted in bitterness and resentment from Gérard to Grouchy. Did Gérard feel let down by Grouchy? Was his brush with death or being taken prisoner totally preventable to his mind if he had all his cavalry force and did not have to rely upon Grouchy junior? Clearly the 6th Dragoons were in action, but where? With Exelmans? Perhaps. Why did the 8th Chasseurs à Cheval sit out 16 June? Either way we cannot fully answer the claim that 7th Cavalry Division was not with 4th Corps, but the distinct possibility exists that only the 1st Brigade under Vallin was with 4th Corps and 2nd Brigade commanded Pierre Marie Auguste Berruyer were under Grouchy elsewhere on the field. At Ligny, General Antoine Maurin took a musket ball to the chest and was relieved of his command by General Vallin. Alas we don't know how or when – was it while leading the 6th Hussars against the Prussians?

The second paragraph deals with the guns of Waterloo. In getting back on message regarding the letter of 20 June, we need to assess the document under scrutiny concerning Exelmans. In order to test the authenticity of the document, we need to compare it to the events that took place that day:

1. Was a cannonade heard?
2. Was Exelmans present?
3. What did Exelmans say?
4. Which officer arrived?
5. What order arrived at 16.00?

So, we start with the first point. Our first witness is Marie Theodore Gueulluy, Comte de Rumigny aide-de-camp to General Gérard related:[13]

Worried that our leaders sat down to dinner in an isolated farm, without troops to guard them, I left the room and walked to the garden, which was surrounded by a wall, with a kind of clerestory, painted green, at the end. Some distance to the west, was a wood, which I was looking at, when I heard the thud of a gun. This explosion was followed by several others, I put my ear against the wall to better distinguish the sounds. I was alone, and I heard many shots of various calibres. This might be the fighting of the vanguard. I returned hastily into the farm ... 'Mr. Marshal,' I said, 'there is in the direction where the Emperor is, a fierce battle – It may be a battle of the vanguard – Let me go with you Mr. Marshal down to the garden to judge.' I conducted myself, the Marshal and General Gérard to the end of the garden, where first we heard nothing ... I then put my ear to the ground, and I distinctly heard the cannonade. The Marshal was then convinced and ordered us to mount. We executed the order, and we moved onto the road to Wavre. At the head of the column, I heard the beginning of lively discussion between Marshal Grouchy and General Gérard.

By the time, we reached the rear-guard General of Vandamme, our two leaders entered a peasant's house, in which was a tiled stove. Everyone was outside, except for Mr. Pontbelanger, aide of Marshal Grouchy, and me. We were both against the front door to prevent anyone coming to distract or interrupt them. I was, you know, Colonel, aide to General Gérard, and therefore the first of his officers. The General and Marshal held open a map of a captain, and the marshal had supported his right hand on this map, suspended against the stove, the General supported it with his left hand.

The crux of the discussion was concerning the direction to give the army. Gérard wanted to move to the Emperor, and Grouchy on the contrary, push the Prussians before him. The point where we were, there was no more to doubt that the fight was an intense, a real battle – we saw the shells burst in the air again. It was clear the sounds of the fighting came from the left...the left wing of the Prussian army had moved westward without our knowledge. It was now clear as day. But the Marshal hesitated, refused, piling on the reasons why. Finally, we heard General Gérard say with the utmost animation: 'Monsieur le Maréchal, it is an axiom in war that we should march on the guns when you hear the cannon.' 'General,' the Marshal replied, 'you have to follow orders, not to interpret them.' After these words, followed by a reflection that I did not hear, and some sharp words of the Marshal, they separated. On reaching me, General Gérard was exasperated, he said, 'There is nothing to do, it's awful!'.

This account from an intimate of Gérard is rather exaggerated. It is highly doubtful that over a distance, in a direct line from Waterloo to Sart-à-Walhain of around nine miles, that howitzer shells could be seen, especially given the direct line of site from Sart-à-Walhain to Waterloo is blocked by Mont-Saint Gilbert. The account was written in the 1840s, decades after the event so it is by its very nature going to be highly informed by what Rumigny has read, particularly the various writings of General, later Marshal, Gérard, and will be biased in favour of Gérard. But of interest, the scene of the disagreement between Grouchy and his officers took place not at Sart-à-Walhain but near to Wavre. However, Gérard was not at Wavre until 17.00 hours, as Adjutant-major to the Artillery of the 4th Corps Louis Etienne Thouvenin narrated on 21 May 1840, concerning the actions of 4th Corps on the 18 June:[14]

> We could not consistently follow the marshal to Wavre, and when we arrived about five o'clock, the troops of the 3rd Corps had already been for some time, without success, engaged in the attack on the bridge of Wavre. These troops occupied the portion of the town which is on the right bank of the Dyle: we were told that the bridge was cut. The Prussian artillery on the left bank occupied positions that dominated ours, but at a relatively great distance (12 to 1600 meters.)

So, if the cannonade was heard and Gérard and Grouchy met at Wavre, it cannot have been till late afternoon assuming Gérard remained with his men, as a good commander should have done. Or did Gérard and his staff ride with Grouchy and not remain with his corps? This seems very likely, and he left command and control of his corps to subordinates.

Another witnesses, the aide-de-camp to General Etienne Nicholas Lefol, wrote that Grouchy heard the cannonade at Sart-à-Walhain:[15]

> that hearing the sound of guns to our left, my General sent me thereby directly to Vandamme who, in turn, ordered me to leave, and

gallop to Marshal Grouchy to inform him of these circumstances. I found the Marshal at Sart-à-Walhain, in a castle belonging to Mr. ***, and when I reached him, he was at a table, consulting maps, while the officers of his staff ate strawberries. I do not know if the Marshal had already been advised of the news I brought him, but what I can say is that immediately after hearing me, he gave the order to ride out. I remember that several officers ran into the garden and applied their ears to the earth to try and ascertain the direction of the cannon fire for a moment after the cannonade of Waterloo was heard then with such force that the earth seemed to be shaken.

We followed the marshal, who stood at the head of his army, and I re-joined our division which at that time, was engaged with a large party of Prussians at a place called La Baraque between Sart-à-Walhain and Wavre.

We did not know which corps of enemy we faced, and neither did we know the number of our opponents, when a soldier told us that a man had fallen close to us. We proceeded immediately to the spot indicated, and we found a young Prussian officer, who had terrible wound in the thigh. He was hidden in the corn, which was very high at this time of the year. The General Lefol asked him in German about the forces that were against us, and we were fully informed. We left this young man, having directed him to the ambulance. I remained a little behind our staff to throw him my handkerchief which he seemed to accept with gratitude, and he used immediately to bandage his wound. What will become of this poor child? Was he found when the passed through the place the next day in this place, or will he die without aid? This is what I know.

In this account Vandamme was not present when Gérard and Grouchy had their altercation, which if true, casts more doubt on what we think actually occurred in the house and gardens that day. The Chief of Staff of 4th Corps from 17 June, after the wounding of General Saint-Remy at Ligny, was Simon Loriere. He wrote about the movements of 4th Corps as follows:[16]

The next day June 18, the fourth corps left its position at seven in the morning, and although it had to go through all the long defile of Gembloux, we were obliged to halt in front of this city, to give time to the third corps to move through it (because, as before, we marched again on a single column). I do not know the reasons which had determined the Marshal to put General Vandamme at the head, but and at nine o'clock we were all marching to Wavre. At eleven, the 3rd corps was fully deployed at Walin [sic]. Count Gérard, which preceded the march of his corps, learned that Marshal Grouchy was stopped in a house in this village (belonging to Mr. Hollaert) he went with the officers of his staff, he ordered me to follow: we found ourselves there for lunch.

I was walking around the garden of this house, when I thought I heard (at about half past eleven o'clock) the detonation of artillery on my left, the sound was muffled because the rain was falling heavily, yet I could not misunderstand this, and indeed, hastened to go and inform my general. He went immediately with the Marshal to a high place in the garden, where I heard the noise; many officers were present, including the marshal, Count Gérard, the aid-de-camp and orderly officers of generals Vandamme and Exelmans, and Mr. Denniee, our chief inspector of review. Everyone was convinced that I was not mistaken. The rain had stopped for a quarter of an hour, and the shots could be heard so distinctly, that the earth trembled. The Marshal himself supposed it to be another battle of Wagram.

Mr. Hollaert, owner of the house where we were, was summoned by the marshal, who asked him where he supposed that terrible cannonade took place, he indicated the forest of Soignes, remote from the point where we were about three and a half leagues. General Gérard then opened the view to march immediately to the canon, to put us promptly in connection with operations of the Emperor. He suggested to the Marshal to execute this movement with his corps and division of light cavalry of General Valin, observing that what we had before us could not do us much harm, because, since daybreak, we were informed that all we had before us was the Army Corps of Thielemann, responsible for supporting the retirement of the Prussian army that had gathered to Wavre; and in any case, our junction with the Emperor became meaningful to both. The marshal did not seem to agree. He climbed immediately onto his horse to follow the road to Wavre.

This account is very different indeed to what Rumigny states. However, we must note that Grouchy did not know, based on his report to Napoléon, that he only had Thielemann's Army Corps in front of him. As the report states, Grouchy believed that all the Prussians were heading to Brussels. Therefore, the comment that 4th Corps could be detached, and most of 3rd Corps bar a small corps of observation to watch Thielemann, is informed by what the writer has learned subsequent to the actual event, ergo it seems unlikely that Grouchy would have willingly divided his force, when he believed that he had in front of him at least 30,000 Prussians. Grouchy did not know Waterloo was to be fought, thus, the Prussians were heading to Brussels to link with Wellington there, and a move to the west made no sense, other than to gain the Brussels road at Waterloo.

From this account we have Exelmans' orderly officers present. This is clearly not d'Estourmel as he was not in the army, but who was it, other than the general himself? Captain François of the 30th Regiment of Line Infantry, who we have noted already is far from a reliable eye-witness, has this to say:[17]

> June 18th. General Gérard's division (to which I belonged), under the orders of Marshal Grouchy, left Gembloux, with the other divisions, at 10. a.m. The soldiers were impatient to engage the enemy. About 1 o'clock in the afternoon, we arrived at Walhain, a village situated about half-way between Gembloux and Wavre, where we heard a brisk cannonade on our left, in the direction of Mont Saint Jean and Waterloo, and we felt certain that the Emperor was engaged with the enemy. Marshal Grouchy called a halt (we of the 30th were at the head of the column). He seemed anxious, and did not know what to do, whether to cross the Dyle, or march in the direction of the cannon, leaving one or two divisions on the left bank of the river, which they could cross, the bridge not having been cut, and the neighbouring positions of no importance, or the town itself either, which was surrounded by mud. Marshal Grouchy called a Council of War. General Gérard voted for marching at once in the direction of the cannon; leaving a corps of observation on the right bank of the Dyle. This opinion did not prevail.

We must ask, though, what guns were actually heard. The Battle of Waterloo began about 11.30 hours with the first moves of 2nd Corps against Hougoumont. The total number of French guns in action, would be twenty-two, coming from the batteries of General Piré, Foy and Jerome. This is not the sound of a great battle, more as Grouchy is said to have noted, the sound of a rear-guard action. The grand battery did not get into action till around 13.00 hours or later, and it is this famous cannonade that the supporters of General Gérard state that Grouchy heard and ignored. By this time Grouchy was at Wavre.

So, to answer the first point, it does seem that yes, artillery fire was heard. But at 11.00 was it Waterloo? Or was it Vandamme and Exelmans vanguard in action at Baraque? Arguably the latter, as 2nd Cavalry Corps was there with its artillery at 10.00 hours with Vandamme not far behind. Vandamme attacked at midday into Wavre. Could 2nd Cavalry Corps' six guns have been heard? Baraque is six miles from Sart-à-Walhain, Hougoumont is eighteen miles away. It seems more likely that an exchange of artillery fire from French and Prussian guns, coupled with carbine and musket fire, would have been heard six miles away, rather than from a much greater distance. So yes, gunfire was heard, but not the guns of Waterloo. It was the opening shots of the action that would contain the Prussians at Wavre and prevent the defeat at Waterloo from becoming a total massacre.

Chapter 4

Order and Confusion

On the balance of evidence, it was the guns of Wavre that were heard by Grouchy and his staff. Yet, we still need to examine the letter of 20 June 1815. Where was Exelmans and what did he say? Received history has Exelmans being a censor of Grouchy.

According to the letter dated 20 June 1815, he was present and agreed with Grouchy. However other supposed eyewitnesses state the opposite view, decades after the episode took place.

The letter of 20 June is clear in what Exelmans said, yet every other eye-witness, albeit writing years or decades later, directly contradict this first and perhaps most reliable account. Captain François had this to say about Exelmans censoring Grouchy:[1]

> General Exelmans, who was much excited, said to the Marshal: 'The Emperor is fighting the English army, there can be no doubt about that. Marshal, we must march towards the firing. I am an old soldier of the army of Italy, and I have heard Bonaparte lay down that principle a hundred times. If we keep to the left, we shall be on the field of battle in an hour.'
>
> 'I believe you are right,' replied the Marshal, 'but if Blücher comes out of Wavre and takes me in flank, I shall be blamed for not having obeyed my orders, which are to march against Blücher.'
>
> General Gérard, who was glad to find General Exelmans of his opinion, said to the Marshal: 'Your orders state you are to be on the field of battle. Blücher has gained a march on you. He was yesterday at Wavre when you were at Gembloux; and who knows where he is now? If he has joined Wellington, we shall find him on the battle-field, and then you have executed your orders to the letter. If he is not there, your arrival will decide the battle. In two hours, we can be taking part in the fight, and if we have destroyed the English army, what can Blücher, who is already beaten, do?'

> If Marshal Grouchy had followed the advice of these two brave men, the battle would have been won. I attribute the disaster of this unfortunate day to him.

This is a clear case of false memory. Written decades later this testimony is totally at odds to the letter of 20 June. François was not an eye-witness to the events and is reporting what he has read and been told about the event. He is not a reliable witness as he was not present at the events he claims he was at. Yet his testimony is used as proof positive about Exelmans being opposed to Grouchy, when in fact he agreed with the Marshal.

Secretary to the Emperor, Fleury de Chaboulon, reported in 1820, no doubt from gossip, as he most certainly was not present, that:[2]

> On the 18th, at nine in the morning only, he quitted his cantonments to march to Wavres [sic]: when he reached Walhain, he heard the cannonading at Mont St. Jean. Its continually increasing briskness left no doubt, that it was an extremely serious affair. General Excelmanns [sic] proposed, to march to the guns by the right bank of the Dyle. 'Do you not feel,' said he to the marshal, 'that the firing makes the ground tremble under our feet? let us march straight to the spot where they are fighting.'
>
> This advice, had it been followed up, would have saved the army: but it was not. The marshal slowly continued his movements: at two o'clock he arrived before Wavres. The corps of General Vandamme and that of Gérard endeavoured to open a passage and wasted time and men to no purpose. At seven o'clock he received, according to his own declaration, the order from the major-general, to march to St. Lambert and attack Bülow; which step ought to have been suggested to him before that time by the tremendous cannonading at Waterloo, and by the order given in the first despatch received in the morning.

The writings are in direct contradiction to the eye-witness reports given, at most, forty-eight hours after the events took place. Yet these later writers are believed, as in doing so, the blame for the loss of Waterloo is passed from the Emperor to Grouchy.

Furthermore, given no news had come from the Emperor, how did Exelmans and Grouchy know that morning that Napoléon was fighting at Waterloo? Grouchy only received word of the major battle once the cannonade had or had not been heard. Indeed, the grand battery on the French right wing only opened fire around 13.00 hours, two hours or more after the supposed guns of Waterloo had been heard, which must have been Reille's guns bombarding Hougoumont as we commented earlier.

Therefore, a lot of hindsight has been added to all the accounts, presenting in most cases the view that valiant and capable officers were let down by an imbecile i.e., Grouchy. Gérard, Exelmans *et al* all wanted their side of the story presented, and it could not be simpler than to damn Grouchy who had been censored by Drouot on 26 June 1815 and ever since. Drouot's censor does not overtly condemn Grouchy. Drouot seemed to be totally convinced that Grouchy would arrive. But since that day, Grouchy has become the villain of Waterloo. The facts presented by Gérard, Exelmans, and their supporters were seen as hard unquestionable truth, when in fact they were based on falsehoods. This brings us back to the question of the reliability of our source material.

The closer a letter is written to the time of the events it talks about, the more reliable is can be judged to be. François is writing decades later when what he has read and been told has impacted on what he thinks he remembers. It does look on balance of evidence that Grouchy and Gérard had a disagreement, but Exelmans backed Grouchy.

With hindsight Exelmans clearly had a change of heart and it seems he did his best to change the facts of the situation. Exelmans edited the day's events to censor Grouchy and present himself as a man of action who could have changed the outcome of Waterloo. So good was Exelmans' PR machine that his biographers copied wholesale his take on the events of that day. Both Thoumas and Andre in their biographies of Exelmans state that Exelmans demanded he march his Corps via Moustier Ottignies to Waterloo based on reconnaissance reports and talking to local inhabitants.

No documents from 18 June 1815 confirm this was ever an option. Fleury de Chaboulon was not even present at Sart-à-Walhain, but as his testimony supports the paradigm that Grouchy was a buffoon who lost Waterloo, and it aligns with Exelmans' biographers, it has to be true doesn't it?

Towards the close of the letter, the stand out phrase for me is the comment that Grouchy was to be astride the Louvain road. Where was this? Consulting the Ferraris map of the 1770s, we see that Louvain is due east of Brussels, and the Louvain road must surely be that heading north from Namur. So Grouchy in theory was heading east and not north west to Waterloo? Where was he going? Was he ordered to head east? The reality is, that yes, Grouchy on 17 June had been sent off towards Maastricht, by an order timed at 13.00:[3]

> Repair to Gembloux with the cavalry corps of Pajol and Excelmanns, [sic] the light cavalry of the 4th Corps, Teste's division, and the 3rd and 4th Corps of Infantry. You will send out scouts in the direction of Namur and Maastricht, and you will pursue the enemy.

Reconnoitre his line march, and tell me of his movements, that I may penetrate his designs.

I shall move my headquarters to Quatre-Bras, where the English still were this morning; our communication will then be directed via the Namur road.

Should the enemy have evacuated Namur, write to the general in command of the 2nd Military Division at Charlemont to occupy this town with a few battalions of National Guards.

It is important to discover what Wellington and Blücher mean to do, and whether they meditate uniting their armies to cover Brussels and Liège by risking the fate of a battle.

At all events, keep your two-infantry corps continually together, within a mile of each other, reserving several ways of retreat place detachments of cavalry between, so as to be able to communicate with headquarters.

If Grouchy was heading to Maastricht as ordered, as we know he was, and had troops on the Louvain road, the writer of the letter of 20 June was clearly aware of which direction Grouchy was heading. On getting to Louvain, he could gain a main road to Maastricht. Grouchy was ordered to go in totally the wrong direction – but we only know that with hindsight. On 17 June 1815, neither Grouchy nor Napoléon had any idea where the Prussians were. Pajol had been ordered out on reconnaissance around midnight on 16 June. Pajol reported in at 03.00 hours and again later in the day. Only then, once the Prussians had been found, could orders be given. With hindsight, we know where the Prussians were, but on 17 June 1815 the French headquarters had no idea. Even Grouchy falls into the trap of using hindsight to verify his line of argument, noting he asked for orders at daybreak to catch the Prussians—thus writing in 1818 he knew where the Prussians were, and tries to back-date this information to 1815. Yet, unless a now lost report from Pajol timed at 03.00 emerges, based on archive evidence, no orders could be given until the Prussians were found.

Only later on did Grouchy disregard his instructions in order to actually follow the movements of the Prussians. Furthermore, the order sent Grouchy's forces off in the wrong direction. Yes, the Prussians were heading north-east, but Maastricht was altogether in the wrong direction, as this would entail a more easterly line of march. So, the letter passes the first test. Getting to the Louvain road was clearly a key objective in heading east.

With hindsight, we know the Prussians were heading to Brussels. But, based on the information that was known at 13.00 hours on 17 June 1815, all that the French headquarters knew was that Pajol, had found some Prussians at Namur and Abbey of Argenton. Had Grouchy not taken the initiative, which many historians claim he was not capable of, and sent out scouts both north and north-east, he would have happily marched to Namur or Maastricht and have been of no use at all on 18 June. In such a scenario, the defeat at Waterloo would have been even more total, as it would have freed up 19,000 Prussian troops. One cannot begin to imagine the impact that these troops could have had if Grouchy, who most historians like Hooper, A.F. Becke, Codman Ropes and Stephen Millar tell us lacked the vital skills for independent command and was mission-blind, had actually followed his orders! In reality, Grouchy was a far better field commander than historians allow him to be. Rather than rely upon a) Pajol's dispatch, and b) his orders, Grouchy did the obvious thing and sent out cavalry patrols to find the Prussians. We don't know who sent off Pajol south-east, but in doing so it meant that all future reconnaissance patrols had to be undertaken by Exelmans dragoons — troops not ideally suited for this task – nor was it a task that many had experience of. Picket and patrol work were light cavalry duties, as Exelmans himself critiqued his commander for at the end of 17 June. Grouchy had no choice but to use Exelmans. Vandamme's light cavalry had been sent off to join Ney, and half of Pajol's command and Subervie's 5th Cavalry Division had also trotted off to Waterloo. Pajol's three remaining regiments had been sent off in the early hours of 17 June and would not be seen again until late on 18 June. So, for twenty-four hours or more, Grouchy was robbed of his 'eyes and ears' provided by light cavalry. Little wonder then that Gérard's cavalry, commanded by Maurin, which had two chasseur regiments, was seconded to Exelmans.

While being common sense to send the cavalry out on patrol, this had a major drawback. It meant both Vandamme and Gérard had no 'eyes and ears' of their own. We know where the Prussians were, but on 17 June the field commanders had no idea at all. For all Vandamme and Gérard knew, the cavalry screen could have missed a pocket of Prussians, who at any moment could attack their columns on line of march when the men were at their most vulnerable. Little wonder that Gérard, at the end of the vast column that would eventually move to Wavre, was slow. All he knew was that the Prussians were out there, and he had no idea where; proceeding with caution was the most sensible thing to do. But this meant that when Grouchy needed a quick victory by concentrating his troops, Gérard was four hours behind Vandamme. Napoléon, in robbing Grouchy of his vitally important light cavalry, had made the Marshal's task even harder. Napoléon, and no other, is to blame in not giving Grouchy orders until after midday, twelve hours after the battle ended. In sending Grouchy in the wrong direction and robbing him of his light cavalry, Napoléon gave Grouchy an impossible task to perform.

Grouchy was acting upon the Emperor's orders based on the reports he was receiving from men like Pajol, Vallin, Chastel, Vandamme and others. In hindsight, it is easy to say what Grouchy should have done. However, we must judge Grouchy's actions on the information he had to hand on 17 to 20 June 1815. His mission was vague, and in the first instance wrong. It is entirely due to his initiative that he found the Prussians heading to Wavre, and that he had to question his orders and also to ask critical questions about the reconnaissance reports sent to him. Pajol had found Prussians at Namur, but Grouchy was adroit enough to realise that the body of Prussian troops Pajol had found could not be the bulk of the army for Ligny, which he reasoned correctly was not heading to Namur or Maastricht as the Emperor had told him but must be heading towards Brussels.

Yet Grouchy is always painted by historians as lacking this vital judgement so crucial in field commanders. He had the skill and ability to be a Marshal of France, and indeed had more ability than Victor or Jordan than either Marshal had shown for years. Grouchy was ordered to find the Prussians and give battle. In this he was obeying orders, and at least one other senior officer agreed with him, Exelmans. As we commented upon in my previous book, when at long last Napoléon reported a troop presence at Wavre, Grouchy assumed these were the same troops that Vandamme had spotted and were the troops from Gembloux. At no stage did Grouchy ever think otherwise. When General Domon found the Prussians at Moustier on the night of 17 June, and Marbot found the place deserted early on 18 June, Napoléon assumed that the Prussians were not heading to link with Wellington, but were making for the Namur to Louvain road, which was correct. He failed to grasp that the Prussians could pass through Wavre and then turn west to join Wellington, because he felt in his own mind that the Prussians were undoubtedly heading to Louvain. The appearance of the Prussian 4th Corps in no way changed his thinking, as Grouchy had reported the whereabouts of the 1st, 2nd and 3rd Prussian Corps. Where Napoléon thought the 4th Corps had come from we can only guess. Did he assume it was the troops that Milhaud and Domon had spotted? Perhaps. This lulled him into a false sense of security that the only Prussians he would confront were those of the Prussian 4th Corps. It was a logical assumption to make. The truth was Grouchy had pursued only the Prussian 3rd and 4th Corps. He was not aware of the major Prussian troop concentration between him and the Emperor.

He could not act offensively against troops he did not know existed heading from Gentinnes. He cannot be blamed for the Emperor not sending him intelligence reports bout this major body of troops that Milhaud and Domon observed on 17 June until the morning of 18 June, when the it was far too late to act upon. If Grouchy had known a large body of Prussians was heading to Wavre on 17 June, as a separate body to those moving back from Gembloux, the obvious answer was 'here are the Prussians'. Yet, Napoléon failed to inform him of this fact. When Berton and Exelmans reported to headquarters 'here be 30,000 Prussians' at Gembloux, Napoléon did not react immediately-this command decision lost the campaign. What could Dragoons realistically achieve against infantry, artillery and cavalry, other than to observe? What did the Emperor think would happen if he did not send infantry immediately, backed by artillery? Imagine if Grouchy had been at Gembloux in force 8 hours earlier, and had caught the bulk of the Prussian Army? It was not to be. Four hours were wasted, and in those four hours the Prussians got away from Grouchy, the Prussian 1st and 2nd Corps slipping away north. Not giving Grouchy vital intelligence data and not sending infantry forward when it was needed at 09:00 on 17 June were catastrophic errors. The third mistake was the Emperor became mission-blind in that the Prussians could not fight and could not get to Wellington. Napoléon was not betrayed by Soult, nor by Grouchy—he alone bears responsibility for his actions on 17 June.

Not having been in action on 16 June, the Prussian IV Corps, commanded by General Bülow, was the strongest of the four Prussian Corps in the field. Due to this, it was the first Prussian force sent to Waterloo. However, getting to Waterloo was not straightforward. No major road went from Wavre to Mont-Saint-Jean, and because of the heavy rain from the previous two nights, the roads towards the battlefield were in poor condition; in essence they were little more than a morass of ankle-deep cloying mud. Making matters worse, the men of Bülow's command had had to pass through the congested and narrow streets of Wavre which took time. Indeed, the last elements of the Corps did not leave Wavre until around 10.00 hours. It had taken a full six hours for the Corps to cross through Wavre. Behind IV Corps came the Prussian I and II Corps under Pirch and Zieten. Sensibly enough, the Prussians left a strong rear guard at Wavre to hold back the French pursuit conducted by Marshal Grouchy. In the fighting at Wavre, the Prussian commander Thielman was so concerned that he may be overwhelmed he begged for reinforcements. By the time Zieten's command began to reach Waterloo, the fighting at Papelotte

31

and Frischermont had reached another a crisis point. So serious was the situation, that when General Zieten approached the battlefield, he was concerned at the sight of stragglers and casualties coming from Wellington's left that he stopped his advance. No doubt, from Zieten's point of view, these troops heading to the rear, appeared to be withdrawing. Fearing that his own troops could be caught up in a general panic, after assessing the situation, Zieten started to head away from Wellington's left flank and to link up with Thielemann at Wavre. A major crisis point in the battle had been reached. The French were close to neutralising the Prussian IV Corps and preventing the Prussians joining Wellington's threatened left flank.

It was crucial that immediate and decisive action be taken to prevent a French breakout. About the same time, General Thielemann was in desperate need of reinforcements to fend off Grouchy. If Zieten fell back to aid Thielemann, as seemed possible, for the allies, the battle was lost.

The Prussian Army Liaison officer to Wellington, General Muffling, seeing Zieten's command and its subsequent about face, galloped over to find the general, and persuaded him to support Wellington's left flank.[4] The outcome of the battle, thanks to Muffling, was now in the favour of the allies.

Prussian General Gneisenau narrated:[5]

> Towards six o'clock in the evening, we received the news that General Thelmann [sic], with the third Corps, was attacked near Wavre by a very considerable Corps of the enemy, and that they were already disputing the possession of the town. The Field-Marshal, however, did not suffer himself to be disturbed by this news: it was on the spot where he was, and nowhere else, that the affair was to be decided. A conflict, continually supported by the same obstinacy, and kept up by fresh troops, could alone ensure the victory, and if it were obtained here, any reverse sustained near Wavre was of little consequence. The columns, therefore, continued their movements. It was half an hour past seven, and the issue of the battle was still uncertain. The whole of the fourth Corps, and a part of the second, under General Pvich [Pirch] had successively come up. The French troops fought with desperate fury: however, some uncertainty was perceived in their movements, and it was observed that some pieces of cannon were retreating. At this moment, the first columns of the Corps of General Zieten arrived on the points of attack, near the village of Smouhen [Smohain], on the enemy's right flank, and instantly charged. This moment decided the defeat of the enemy. His right wing was broken in three places; he abandoned his positions. Our troops rushed forward at the pas de charge, and attacked him on all sides, while, at the same time, the whole English line advanced.

If Zieten had gone back to Wavre, the Prussian attack at Waterloo could have been contained, and Grouchy no doubt would have been remembered for his action on the right wing, much as Davout is for Auerstädt. Just imagine, if one-third of the Prussians at Waterloo had not been there, the outcome of the day could have been different. But again, imagine if Grouchy had headed to Waterloo across country. Who would have stopped the Prussian 3rd Corps getting to Waterloo and totally crushing Napoléon? As it was Grouchy held in check a quarter of the Prussian army. If he had not been present to do so, the consequences would have been even more catastrophic. Grouchy and Exelmans collectively made the right decision.

The contemporaneous writing of 20 June shows clearly that Exelmans and Grouchy were in the same mind of heading to the plains of Louvain. Grouchy recalled:[6]

> I informed the Emperor that at break of day we were marching to Sart-à-Walhain. Indeed, at sunrise, Vandamme's corps was moving in this direction, following the cavalry of General Exelmans. Successive reports confirmed that several Prussian columns had passed in the area of Sart-à-Walhain.
>
> At this village so I wrote again to Napoléon, to tell him that I thought at the time we had reached the Prussian rear-guard, and I sent my dispatch by Major Frênaie.[7] The officer was perfectly well aware of what I had collected about the enemy's movements, and reported promptly as ordered, as they were to give me. The opinion of a former soldier decorated with the Legion of Honour, in whose house which I stopped at Sart-à-Walhain to write the letter reporting that the Prussians were concentrated in the plains of Louvain'

Grouchy's 1819 recollections are perfectly correct. He sent a dispatch to the Emperor between 10.00 and 10.30 hours:[8]

> Sire
>
> I will not lose a moment in sending you the information I have gathered here. I regard it as definitive, and so that Your Majesty receives it soonest, I am sending Major de la Frênaie with it.
>
> Blücher's 1st, 2nd and 3rd Corps are marching in the direction of Brussels. Two of these corps marched either through Sart-à-Walhain or just to the right of it. They are marching in three columns more or less abreast. Their march through here lasted six hours without interruption. Those troops passing through Sart-à-Walhain are estimated as being at least thirty thousand men with fifty to sixty cannon. An army corps came from Liège and has joined up with these corps that fought at Fleurus. Enclosed is a requisition form which proves this. Some of the Prussian troops in front of me have

headed in the direction of the plains of Chyse, which is on the road to Louvain, that is north of Wavre, and two and a half leagues from that town. They seem to want to mass there, either to offer battle to any troops that pursue them there, or to join with Wellington—a plan about which their officers spoke. With their usual boasting, they maintain they only left the battlefield of the 16th to join up with the English army in Brussels.

This evening I will be standing before Wavre en masse, and in this way, be situated between Wellington, whom I assume is falling back before Your Majesty, and the Prussian army. I require further instructions, whatever Your Majesty chooses to order, as to what I should do. The terrain between Wavre and the plain of Chyse is difficult to pass; it is broken ground and boggy. I will be able to get to Brussels easily along the Vilvoorde road quicker than any troops who go over the plain of Chyse, especially if the Prussians make a stop there. If Your Majesty wishes to send me orders, I can still receive them before starting my movement tomorrow.

Most of the information in this letter came from the owner of this house where I have stopped to write to Your Majesty. He is an officer who served in the French army and has been decorated and seems to support your interests. I attach some notes:

The rear of the corps that marches through Sart-à-Walhain is in Corroy. The entire army is moving on Wavre. The best route to Wavre is via Nil-Pierreux, Corbais, Baraque and Lauzelle. The wounded have been sent to Liège and Maastricht. The reserves and troops that did not participate in the Battle of Fleurus are marching to Wavre, some to Tirlemont. The bulk of the Prussian army is camping on the plain of Chyse. This is confirmed, and they seem to be massing there.

The plain of Chyse and the plain of Louvain are one and the same thing. Officer d'Ordonnance La Frênaie agreed that he took the dispatch to Soult:[9]

I know that on the 18th we reached the head of the column of General Vandamme about a league from Gembloux. When we arrived at Sart-à-Walhain, a decorated officer came near you and informed you that Prussian columns were moving on Wavre, although he thought the army of Blücher was moving on Louvain. With this news, you [Grouchy] then wrote to Napoléon, and I was charged by you to carry your dispatches, orders and reports.

I departed the place immediately, at the time when a cannonade that did not sound like a general engagement, was heard. I went to the sound of cannon, and after travelling for two long hours and a half at trot and canter, I found Napoléon on the battlefield of Waterloo. I handed him the report you had entrusted to me, he read it, asked the point where you were and told me to stay with him. I remained there until evening. No orders were given to me to bring you, and it is not to my knowledge that other officers have been shipped.

The time of writing the order is awkward. The original is lost and is variously stated to be written at 10.00 or 11.00. Either way, it did not arrive with headquarters at Waterloo until after 13.00. La Frênaie says it took him two and a half hours to get to Waterloo from Sart-à-Walhain—departing at 10.30 would make for an arrival at 13.00 or thereabouts. If at about 11.30 the cannonade was heard, then arrival would be closer to 14.00. In either case, the dispatch did not arrive until the 13.00 order had been sent to Grouchy, as Napoléon never seems to have replied to it. La Frênaie seems adamant that he delivered the dispatch, so on balance it seems to have arrived with headquarters. Its contents, as we shall see, left Napoléon in no doubt whatsoever that Grouchy was not heading to Waterloo.

General Thoumas, in his glowing biography of Exelmans, names this man as Chevallier Rossy.[10] Searching the records of the Legion of Honour we find two candidates:

Alexandre Hyacinthe Rossy[11]

Pierre Joseph Marie Reigner Rossy[12]

The first man, Alexander Hyacinthe Rossy was at Waterloo on 18 June as a serving officer in the 21st Line[13]. The second man had been discharged as a captain from the 6th Regiment of Lancers on 20 August 1814 but was living in the Department of the Dole in 1815. A further seventy-five men with the surname Rossi were awarded the Legion of Honour. Of those awarded the decoration before 1800, all were Italians, none living in Belgium. Is this a case of making up facts to suit the agenda of the authors to exonerate Exelmans?

The story of M. Rossy and d'Estourmel does not appear until 1891, seventy or so years after the event. As a Marshal of France, Exelmans had lots of political cache to gain by blaming Grouchy and others for the loss of Waterloo and making his own actions above reproach. If d'Estourmel had served in the army, and sent such an important dispatch why did it take seventy years for the story to emerge? Surely all of Grouchy's distractors would have leaped on the bandwagon of more evidence to damn Grouchy? None do. Exelmans in 1830 does not even mention the episode! Did it happen? I suspect we are dealing with false memory – facts being changed after the event to cover up mistakes. A memoir, letter or other material used to help create a narrative of events is of limited value in terms of historical interpretation without context.

The letters cited in this narrative were written down by combatants or by family members long after the events had taken place, and are not necessarily an accurate reflection of events that happened. Each of the writers of the letters included in this work had a personal and unique view of Waterloo – what they experienced will be different from participant to participant. The letters left by the participants recorded what was important to them. However, the closeness of the written narrative to the events that took place will affect what is recorded.[14] This is the reason why the police take statements immediately from as many eye-witnesses as possible without allowing the eye-witnesses to hear what others are saying. They then tease out the facts from this jumble of data.

But the biggest issue with memory recall after time is almost always that the person recalling the event has been influenced by other memories (their own and from other people) which have combined to create a new version of the event. Similar issues arise with personal letters. Soldiers writing home are doing so with self-imposed censorship and the stories told differ according to the recipient of the letter; they include what the writer deems important and also what the writer thinks the reader will think is important and how the writer understands those events/facts. They are more objective and more reliable than memoirs because they are a 'snapshot' and are immediate, unlike memoirs, but have already passed through one level of perception filter: the writer. It is only by collating data from various accounts that something approaching a balanced view of an event can be created. One must also bear in mind that what might be reported as 'fact' by the writer is in all actuality 'perception'.

According to Houssaye, copied directly from Thoumas biography of Exelmans, it was at Sart-á-Walhain that Exelmans' Aide-de-Camp, Major d'Estourmel[15], arrived with Exelmans' situation report from Neuf-Sart:[16]

> He announced that a strong Prussian rear-guard was posted before Wavre. This officer was also charged to say that, according to all indications, the enemy's army had passed the bridge of Wavre during the night and morning, in order to get nearer the English Army, and, consequently, that General Exelmans contemplated proceeding to the left bank of the Dyle via Ottignies. This fresh information and the opinion expressed by Exelmans, furnished additional reasons in favour of Gérard's opinions. However, to Grouchy, who was as convinced as ever that the Prussians

had gained Wavre in order to retreat towards the Chyse, the presence of their rear-guard in this town only confirmed him in his presumptions. He congratulated himself that he had resisted Gérard, because the Emperor's orders were to follow the Prussian Army, and that at last he seemed on the point of reaching this army that had hitherto baffled him. He told d'Estourmel that he would himself give orders to General Exelmans and called for his horses.

There are a number of major problems with this account. Firstly, Grouchy stated that it was not Exelmans who headed to Waterloo, but Pajol, as Exelmans himself was at Wavre heading to Louvain:[17]

At sunrise, Vandamme's corps was in motion in that direction, following the cavalry of Exelmans: successive reports confirmed that several Prussian columns had passed by Saravalain and its environs, and from that village he wrote again, to announce to Napoléon, that he expected every moment to join the rear-guard of the enemy, sending the despatch by major La Frênaie, an officer perfectly capable of giving an account of what had been gathered of the movements of the enemy, and of bringing back orders, if any should be given. He re-joined Exelmans, who, since the morning, had been on the heels of the extreme rear-guard of the Prussian cavalry, and at half-past 11, at about a league and a half from Wavres, they discovered a rear-guard of infantry, with cannon. The cannonade began immediately, and Vandamme arriving with the head of his infantry, marched upon the Prussians, who took a position in the wood of Limilette, from which they were immediately driven upon Wavres. The enemy was vigorously pursued, and between one and two o'clock, Grouchy was master of the part of the town situated on the left bank of the Dyle.

During the affair near the wood of Limilette, a cannonade was heard at a distance on the left. Grouchy rode in that direction and had no doubt but that it was from Napoléon's attack on the English army. Having reached the Prussians, whom he was ordered to pursue, and being already engaged with them, his duty was not to abandon them, but to attack them vigorously at Wavres, to prevent their undertaking anything on the side of Waterloo. He was not then, nor could he be, informed, that at the break of day, two of Blücher's corps had quitted Wavres, directing their march towards the British army, or that at about that moment the head of these corps were reaching the heights of St. Lambert, in sight of the French troops at Waterloo. Moreover, having but 32,000 men, and having reason to believe the Prussian force of 95,000 concentrated before him, Grouchy was too weak to divide his forces, and would have run the risk of being cut to pieces had he done so. Nevertheless, a little after, general Pajol, who was in the rear, had orders to move upon the village of Limale, and in the direction of the cannonade that was heard … The cavalry of Exelmans was at Lower Wavres, and Pajol had been directed, as before mentioned, to Limale, in order to put Grouchy in communication with Napoléon, and to be ready to cut off the retreat of the Prussians, if they should retire on Brussels, after being driven from the position of Wavres—Pajol would have been before them on that route and must have greatly harassed their movement.

Grouchy gives a very different version of events, one which matches the eye-witness letter of 20 June, whereby Exelmans was heading to Louvain and not advocating getting to Waterloo. Indeed, about separating his force, Grouchy commented:[18]

> Part of Gérard's corps was engaged at the mill, which had not yet been captured; but about half of the latter corps was in the rear, and nearer to St. Lambert than the troops at Wavres. Accompanied by Gérard, Grouchy went to meet that portion of his corps, intending to direct it by Limale towards St. Lambert.
>
> This corps was in a state of partial disorganization, and its movements were slow, and without precision, in consequence of the impression made upon them by the desertion to the enemy of Lieutenant-General Bourmont, and some other officers, and different causes. The evening before, it had taken an enormous time in leaving the plains of Fleurus, and on this morning, it was much too late in leaving Gembloux. The arrival of these troops, the only force really disposable and capable of being marched immediately towards St. Lambert, occasioned great delay. They at last appeared, but the want of guides, the difficulty of the roads, and divers secondary circumstances, retarded greatly the movement which had been ordered.

Grouchy was perfectly correct about the dis-organisation of the Corps. Into this we need to factor the horrific losses the 4th Corps took on 16 June. The 111th Line lost a minimum of 20 per cent of its effective strength.[19] Losses in 4th Corps as a whole were somewhere between 20 and 30 per cent i.e. almost a third of the Corps were dead or wounded. This would have had a massive impact on regimental organisation and cohesion. Lack of officers and key sub-officers – just as Grouchy relates in 1819 – would have greatly affected the effectiveness of the corps. Therefore, it does seem that Grouchy's comments about 4th Corps were based on facts gathered from other sources other than Grouchy, notably regimental muster lists and casualty records prepared by divisional commanders on 17 June and sent to Marshal Soult. Therefore, Grouchy's recollections do seem credible.

But we need to examine Grouchy's other assertion that some of the 4th Corps was to be sent to Saint-Lambert. Did this happen? Did Grouchy really plan to send 4th Corps to Waterloo in response to Napoléon's order about catching Bülow in the rear? One eye-witness suggests this did happen. Captain J. M. J. Deville[20], of the 111th Regiment of Line Infantry, gives the following narration which suggests that his regiment took no part in the fighting on 18 June, and was the only one of Grouchy's regiments to try and march to Waterloo as Napoléon had wished:[21]

> 18 June, in the morning an orderly officer arrived from the Imperial Headquarters of the emperor on the left of our regiment, and asked where he could find Marshal Grouchy, for whom he carried orders. We indicated where he could be found and he went in that direction. During our movement at the moment when the cannonade shook the earth, a second orderly officer arrived from the same place escorted by some lancers and turned to me and said 'I bring an order to the marshal, to tell him to march to his left. Send this order to your colonel to commence this movement to be followed and executed without delay by the other corps until I can talk to the marshal'.
>
> I went immediately to Colonel Sauzet and I passed the order to him that I had received. Colonel Sauzet left the line of battle and ordered his column to march to its left. Whether the other corps had followed us or had received a counter-order I do not know exactly, but the movement was stopped. We remained immobile in this position until three, four or five o'clock. We then decided to march, albeit hesitantly, moving towards the gunfire, which had greatly decreased, after an hour of marching we stopped and after half an hour later we occupied the positions we had done during the day, and where we spent the night.

It seems the regiment was sent east to Saint Lambert but oddly the order for the movement is said to have come from the Emperor and not Grouchy. Did the courier carrying the famous 'you will catch Bülow in the rear' order somehow get to 4th Corps before getting to Grouchy? Is it possible that the 111th headed off to Saint Lambert? This makes any notion that Exelmans wanted to send his cavalry force to Saint Lambert null and void, as it does seem that Grouchy did make preparations to get troops to Waterloo. We know some elements of the 22nd regiment of Line got close to the battlefield of Waterloo.

We also know from Gérard's aide-de-camp on 19 June, that Grouchy did indeed send troops to Saint-Lambert:[22]

> The aide-de-camp told me that Marshal Grouchy having found the enemy in position on the heights of Wavres and had attacked, but had met strong resistance, but that he believed, however, that our troops had entered the city during the night. Another attack had taken place at the same time in front of St.-Lambert.

On balance of evidence, Grouchy did indeed send men to Waterloo via Saint Lambert. But the whereabouts of the 111th is debatable. The regiment lost just one man on 18 June[23] whereas the other regiments in the 14th Division took more losses. Does this indicate that the regiment was tied down uselessly marching from place to place? Seemingly so. Who sent the counter order? Grouchy? Gérard? Did such an order exist? Grouchy again:[24]

> While these matters were in progress, Grouchy returned with Gérard to Wavres; hoping that Vandamme could have passed the Dyle, and that he might direct his corps towards St. Lambert, by the left bank—he found things in the state in which he had left them, and after alighting from his horse to conduct himself, a new attack on the mill, in which Gérard was wounded, and the object not accomplished, finding there could be no success at Wavres and Bierge, and wishing, at all hazards, to move towards Napoléon, he then determined, whatever inconveniences might result, to leave only the corps of Vandamme, and the cavalry of Exelmans, before an army, the strength of which was not well known, and to have the troops of Gérard parallel with the Dyle, towards Limilette, to unite them with the rest of that corps which had marched thither. Grouchy himself repaired to that place with all haste: unhappily the country on the right of the Dyle is intersected with ravines and streams, which fall into the river, and the practicable and customary road between Wavres and St. Lambert is by the left bank, so that the movement of these troops required much time.
>
> Meanwhile, Pajol's cavalry, and a division of infantry, crossed the Dyle, and at night they were masters of the first heights on the other side; within cannon shot of which the Prussians had posted themselves —a rough and steep road affords the only passage from the valley, through which the river flows, to the plain, on which the villages of Limale and Limilette are situated. The darkness of the night rendered this ascent slow and difficult, and the space above was not sufficient to enable the troops to deploy: the enemy also was so near that his balls reached the head of the defile—it is probable that had Grouchy been vigorously pushed, he would have been driven, with loss, to the other side of the Dyle. Thus,

it was important to drive the enemy on this point, since it would enable him to remove the Prussians opposed to Vandamme, and to accomplish his junction with Napoléon, respecting whom, however, he was not uneasy, the letter of Soult giving him to understand that the battle was gained at Waterloo: —he was, however, surprised at hearing nothing more from him, officers and parties having been despatched to procure intelligence.

Let's look at what Grouchy says. Grouchy's comments on the topography between Waterloo and Wavre is perfectly correct. Secondly, if the 111th were detached, it seems Grouchy issued a recall order to unite all his force at Limalette. Thirdly, Grouchy is quite correct in thinking Waterloo was won based on the dispatch from Soult. The dispatch states:[25]

> At this moment, the battle is won on the line of Waterloo, in front of the Soignes Forest; the centre of the enemy is at Mont-Saint-Jean, and manoeuvre to reach our right.

Grouchy clearly received the order, as he reports both the content of the letter concerning the victory at Waterloo, and he sent portions of 4th Corps to Saint-Lambert as ordered, supported by Pajol's cavalry. So far so good. On the balance of evidence, Grouchy did obey the order to send troops to Saint-Lambert, the 111th Line, and had planned to send 4th Corps, just as Gérard had argued for earlier in the day:[26]

> General Gérard then suggested that we should march immediately to the cannon, to put us promptly in connection with operations of the emperor. He suggested to the marshal to execute this movement with his corps and division of light cavalry of General Walin, observing that what we had before us could not do us much harm, because, since daybreak, we were informed that all we had before us was the army corps of Thielemann, responsible for supporting the retirement of the Prussian army that had gathered at Wavre; and in any case, our junction with the emperor became meaningful to both. The marshal did not seem to agree. He climbed immediately onto his horse to follow the road to Wavre.

Is Grouchy in 1819 writing to explain away his actions? Yes, very much so. His writings could be easily dismissed as the ravings of a man trying to save his reputation and dig himself out of a hole, to use modern parlance. Yet if he made this up, what then do we make of the 111th Line and its apparent move to Saint-Lambert? Both writers were working independently, and Deville is at pains to paint a bad image of Grouchy, so did he invent the episode he recalls? I don't think

41

so, and instead we need to see that Grouchy did his best to obey the orders he received.

The trouble with the events of 18 June is that the subjects are so emotive for French writers. Many of the participants wrote down their accounts of the day, with a heavy helping of hindsight. Grouchy's subordinates broke into two camps 1) Gérard's: that Grouchy was incompetent, 2) Grouchy's supporters.

A third camp can be Bonapartists who blame Grouchy no matter what because this is what the Emperor did. If the Emperor blames Grouchy for the loss of Waterloo, and as the Emperor is a demi-god who could do no wrong, Grouchy is at fault. This view was common in 1815 as much as it is in 2018. These three factors all colour and cloud the events of that day, which makes unpicking what happened very difficult indeed.

This is why the letters and orders from 18 June and the immediate day or days after the events are of such vital importance. We have to check and check again what writers say, the motives of the writer, and also if named individuals actually were at the places historians and writers say they were.

This is especially the case concerning Exelmans.

The other major problem with the Thoumas-Houssaye argument, that Exelmans wanted to go to Saint-Lambert, is that Major d'Estourmel who carried this dispatch to Grouchy did not serve in the Armée du Nord. He was a Royalist and was with the King in Ghent on 18 June 1815. There is no way that any of this story is true. In the biography of Exelmans by Eugene Andre the same story is repeated.[27] Furthermore as we have seen, Exelmans was not at Neuf-Sart.

Therefore, this entire episode is a fabrication. The fact that this story appears in both the biographies of Exelmans served to reinforce the notion that this episode happened. It was very likely to be Exelmans issuing falsehoods to cover his own tracks. Exelmans, by presenting this information, was saying to the world 'look I did my best, it was Grouchy's fault Waterloo was lost'.

Historian Tim Clayton agrees with this view and presents no new evidence beyond Exelmans writing to Gérard in 1830 about heading to cross the bridge to the west.[28] It was clear he has done no archive research to check Houssaye's claim about Exelmans or about Major d'Estourmel. This letter from Exelmans to Gérard is a case of what should have happened rather than what did happen. Exelmans is covering up for agreeing with Grouchy to keep heading east, and moreover for his Corps, seemingly doing nothing whatsoever on 18 June.

Exelmans as a Marshal of France was presenting his own past in the most glorious way possible whilst slandering Grouchy. If the letter of 20 June is correct, Exelmans forced the issue to keep heading to Louvain. We must recall here the second order sent to Grouchy on 17 June which reads as follows:[29]

> Repair to Gembloux with the Cavalry Corps of Pajol and Exelmans, the Light Cavalry of the Fourth Corps, Teste's Division, and the Third and Fourth Corps of Infantry. You will send out scouts in the direction of Namur and Maestricht, and you will pursue the enemy.

To get to Maestricht, Grouchy had to head to Louvain. Therefore, both Grouchy and Exelmans were obeying direct Imperial Orders to head to the right, to Louvain.

So, on balance of probability, Exelmans was at Sart-à-Walhain, and rather than censoring Grouchy, supported his decision to move to Wavre. We also have established that Grouchy sent troops to Saint-Lambert but recalled them later on the same day when he realised he needed more troops at Wavre, which fits neatly into the assessment of the last paragraph of the letter.

Chapter 5

Confusion and More Confusion

During the course of 18 June, Grouchy received two orders from the Emperor; the first sent around 10.00 hours, the second sent around 14.30. For ease of reference, we call these the Zenowicz order i.e. 10.00 and the Poirot order i.e. the 14.30 order. In returning to the letter of 20 June.

The anonymous writer states the order which arrived about 16:00 was carried by an officer with the name beginning with P. Two officers on Napoléons staff had surnames beginning with P, Planat de la Faye, an Officer d'Ordonnance, and Aide-de-Camp Pierre Antoine Poirot, who served on Soult's staff.[1]

So far so good, it is likely Poirot carried an order to Grouchy. So which order was carried? The order sent from the Emperor to Grouchy at 10.00 hours on 18 June, carried by Zenowicz reads:[2]

> Monsieur Marshal, the Emperor has received your last report dated six o'clock in the morning at Gembloux.
>
> You speak to the Emperor of only two columns of Prussians, which have passed at Sauvenière s and Sart-à-Walhain. Nevertheless, reports say a third column, which was a pretty strong one, had passed by Géry and Gentinnes, directed on Wavre, reported by Milhaud's cavalry before they left.
>
> The Emperor instructs me to tell you that at this moment His Majesty has decided to attack the English army in its position at Waterloo in front of the forest of Soignes. Thus, His Majesty desires that you are to continue your movement to Wavre, in order to approach us, to put you in our sphere of operations, and to make your communications with us, pushing before you those portions of the Prussian Army which have taken this direction, and which may have stopped at Wavre, where you ought to arrive as soon as possible.

> You will follow the enemy columns which are on your right side with light troops, in order to observe their movements and pick up their stragglers. Instruct me immediately as to your dispositions and your march, as also to the news which you have of the enemy; and do not neglect to keep your communications with us. The Emperor desires to have news from you very often.

The order is frustratingly vague, but how ever one reads it, Grouchy was not ordered to Waterloo. Indeed, we suppose that the order from the Emperor further confirmed in Grouchy's mind that the Prussians were making for Brussels. Poirot's order reads: [3]

> Monsieur marshal, you wrote to the emperor this morning at six o'clock, saying that you were marching on Sart-à-Walhain, and that you planned then to move to Corbaix and to Wavre. This movement conforms with the dispositions of the emperor which have been communicated to you.
>
> However, the emperor orders me that you should manoeuvre in our direction and try to get closer to the army, so that you can link with us before another corps can come between us. I do not indicate a direction of movement. It is for you to see the place where we are, to govern yourself accordingly and link with our communications, and to always be prepared to fall upon any of the enemy's troops who seek to annoy our right and crush them.
>
> At this moment, the battle is won on the line of Waterloo, in front of the Soignes Forest; the centre of the enemy is at Mont-Saint-Jean, and manoeuvre to reach our right.
>
> Marshal Duc de Dalmatie.
>
> P. S. A letter which has just been intercepted, which says General Bülow is about to attack our right flank, we believe that we see his corps on the height of Saint-Lambert. Lose not an instant in moving towards us to join us, in order to crush Bülow, whom you will catch in the very act.

We have the two orders. We now need to discuss who carried the letters and when they arrived with Grouchy. The writer of the 20 June letter states that the order carried by Poirot arrived at 16.00. Did it?

Zenowicz

This officer's own recollections add some more details regarding when the order he carried arrived: [4]

> Marshal Soult gave me the order that the emperor had told me. I departed and I arrived there, between three and four o'clock in the afternoon, at a division of the rear-guard which was part

of the army corps I had been sent to locate. A quarter of an hour later, I joined Comte Grouchy; he was with General Gérard in a small room of a house where an ambulance had been established. I presented my dispatches to the marshal, and even told him verbally what I was charged with. After browsing through what I had given him, Marshal Grouchy communicated it to General Gérard, who after reading it cried, animated with energetic emotion, apostrophising Grouchy: 'I've always told you if we are f... it's your fault'.

This order arrived, it seems, after Gérard was wounded. When was that? None of the accounts of the wounding of Gérard give a time. Grouchy states it took place between 16.00 and 19.00 hours, between the arrival of the two dispatches from Soult. Gérard said he did not arrive at Wavre till well after 16.00 hours:[5]

> The first attack made on the mill Bièrge was by the troops of the 3rd Corps, but it was not until half past four or five o'clock in the evening that the Count Grouchy ordered me to replace the troops General Vandamme had at the Mill of Bièrge with some battalions of my troops.

Therefore, Zenowicz must have arrived later, as Gérard himself makes clear. Comte de Rumigny, aide-de-camp to General Gérard, further details Vandamme's movements and notes he was wounded with an attack carried out by the 30th Regiment of Line Infantry, under the orders of General Rome:[6]

> Suddenly a bullet, which was in striking range, laid down the general.
> We seized him and, wrapping him in my coat, we took him back and placed him on a farm wagon. There we waited anxiously for the prognosis of Dr Cuttinger, chief surgeon of the corps. The bullet had hit the third button of his coat and had taken with it a part of the frill from his shirt in the wound and then had lodged in the left lung.
> The news of the day did not reassure us. We knew the attack on Wavre by Vandamme had been repulsed and he remained on the left bank. We could no longer hear the cannonade in the direction of the emperor.
> At eight o'clock, General Gérard called me. Here are his words, I wrote them in my diary which I kept because of the importance of the subject. After a few words uttered with difficulty, the general, drawing me near his bed, said 'my dear Rumigny, it is likely that I will die, my heart fills with blood, but before I die I want to make a last service to the emperor. Go to Brussels where he should be

now, tell him that I neither hate nor have ill-will against Grouchy, but every single corps left in his hands are lost for the French army'.

This places Gérard in an ambulance, like Zenowicz states, but much later in day sometime after 20.00 hours. The time Zenowicz gives is vastly compromised by the date at which he is writing, decades and decades after the event, when what he thinks he remembers is grossly contaminated by what he has read and been told after the event, and of course without standardised time – one officer's watch could be different from another's with no certainty that either was correct. Fleury de Chaboulon suggests that the courier took the long way around to avoid the enemy and thus arrived much too late for Grouchy to act on his orders.[7] Rumigny did indeed head off to find the Emperor as Soult makes clear in a letter of 20 June 1815:[8]

At the time I was leaving Philippeville an aide-de-camp of Lieutenant-General Count Gérard arrived, and told me that he preceded general Heuresson who was wounded the night before yesterday at the attack of Wavres. The aide-de-camp told me that Marshal Grouchy having found the enemy in position on the heights of Wavres had attacked but had met strong resistance. However, he believed that our troops had entered the town during the night. Another attack had taken place at the same time in front of St.-Lambert. The aide de-camp was not aware of the outcome; It was led by General in Chief Vandamme, who appeared to gain ground...[illegible]. Marshal Grouchy had made arrangements to join the army as he had been ordered to do so. M. de Beauveau[9], aide-de-camp of General Gérard, who arrives at this very moment and confirms everything that the first said, and even adds that yesterday evening, being near Mr. Marshal Grouchy, he asked him if he had news of the Army of the emperor, that the Marshal replied that he did not know anything.

This is game-changing information on the role of Grouchy. Here we have two aides-de-camp confirming that Grouchy did move to Saint-Lambert and Waterloo, in a letter of 20 June 1815. Incredible! Here is first-hand evidence that totally exonerates Grouchy. Furthermore, it confirms to my mind that the 111th Line had headed off to Saint-Lambert, perhaps supported with other troops, along with elements from the 22nd Line. Therefore, based on eye-witness testimony from an officer of the 111th Line, the casualty records of the 22nd Line, eye-witness statements from Rumigny and de Beauveau, regardless of what all other books on the subject have reported, beyond all reasonable doubt Grouchy did attack towards Saint-Lambert. Furthermore, again contrary to myth, we do know that Soult had sent out patrols to link

47

with Grouchy on 17 and 18 June, and no doubt to establish the nature of the Prussian threat:[10]

> Since Quatre-Bras, the division of Domon was detached to scout along the left bank of the Dyle, along to the Brussels road; the 4th Regiment of Chasseurs à Cheval passed the bridge at Moustier, where his skirmishers opened fire with their carbines at the Prussian cavalry. With the onset of night, the division returned and bivouacked to the right of Headquarters.

Major Tissot, with the 2nd Corps at Waterloo, recalled that:[11]

> General Domont was sent with is division of cavalry to search for and communicate with the troops from the Corps of Marshal Grouchy.

We also know that early on the 18 June, a second patrol was sent out towards Wavre and Moustier. It comprised the 7th Hussars and the 3rd Battalion of the 13th Regiment of Light Infantry.[12] Therefore, it does seem that Soult did his best to communicate with Grouchy, and that factors beyond his control prevented this.

But we are getting somewhat off message here, and we need to return to our narrative of events, and to try and corroborate the letter of 20 June. Regarding any orders and what time they arrived or did not arrive with Grouchy, we have the words of an eye-witness who stated that:[13]

> Several officers were sent before midday by Napoléon to search for Marshal Grouchy, but only one of them, Col Zenowicz, arrived at Wavre, and not until about six o'clock in the evening. The marshal then resolved to pass the Dyle at Limale with a part of his army, but it was then too late.

So, beyond reasonable doubt Zenowicz arrived with Grouchy in the evening, three or more hours after Poirot had done.

Poirot

On balance, it seems that Zenowicz arrived with Grouchy around 19.00 hours, ergo the order carried by Poirot arrived before 19.00 hours. In his testimony, Grouchy agrees with this.[14] Indeed, since 16.00 hours Grouchy felt that Waterloo was won, the Emperor had said so. Now with the second order, written as with the earlier order in response again to Grouchy's early morning dispatch, Grouchy headed off back to Maestricht or Brussels and recalled the 111th Line.

Therefore, Grouchy and the writer of the 20 June letter both agree that the 14.30 hours order, which we know was carried by Poirot arrived at 16.00 hours, and the 10.00 hours order carried by Zenowicz did indeed arrive about 19.00 hours. The orders arrived the wrong way around! This inversion of the sequence of arrival, as we shall comment, had tremendous implications for the outcome of Waterloo and Grouchy's movements. Furthermore, given that the Emperor referred back to the 06.00 hours dispatch, how was Grouchy to know that the orders arrived the wrong way around? He issued orders based on the first order that arrived with him, and then issued new orders in obeisance to the most recent order he received from the Emperor. Grouchy could not have known that the orders got mixed up until the second order arrived – did he ever realise this? Only by comparing the times that the two orders were written could Grouchy observe the inversion of sequence. In the heat of action, checking times on orders may not have been the number one priority for Grouchy. Further, who was he to question to the Emperor? The Emperor ordered him to head east again, and obey he must.

Thus, the contents of the 20 June letter do seem to be very reliable indeed and must therefore be the first and most reliably document concerning the cannonade of Waterloo and what happened at Sart-à-Walhain. But of interest, it means the sequence in which the orders were sent was reversed. The 10.00 hours order told him not to march to Waterloo BUT to head to Wavre. This totally transforms our understanding of Grouchy's actions.

With the arrival of the 14.30 hours order, Grouchy it seems prepared to head to Saint-Lambert with elements of 4th Corps and Pajol's corps. The very late arrival of the 10.00 hours order, which ordered Grouchy to Wavre and back east, changed this. The 4th Corps was recalled, and all forces were concentrated at Limalette. Both orders were sent in response to Grouchy's 06.00 hours order, and no reply ever came in relation to the 10.00 dispatch Grouchy had sent. This order was to keep heading to Grouchy's right i.e. towards Louvain. The arrival sequence of these orders means that at Waterloo Napoléon may have believed that Grouchy was expected at Waterloo, when in reality, the most recent order Grouchy had from him was to head to Wavre and towards Louvain! Grouchy, by recommitting to the action at Wavre, was obeying Imperial orders. At no stage did Grouchy disobey his orders to march to Waterloo, he was specifically ordered to Wavre when he got the second order. The spasmodic courier services from Imperial Headquarters and inversion of order arrival with Grouchy had a huge impact on the outcome of the battle of Waterloo. Grouchy had been vaguely ordered to Waterloo, where no doubt he was expected, his none arrival resulted in him being branded a traitor, when in reality he was obeying orders to switch his operations back to Wavre. If anyone deserves blame its Zenowicz. Poirot took at most two hours to get to Grouchy, Zenowicz a good nine hours. Clearly, he knew this, hence his elaborate back story about Soult and the staff being imbeciles:[15]

> June 18, 1815, the day of the battle of Waterloo, I was on duty as a senior officer in the imperial headquarters, and I was not allowed to leave for a moment Napoléon. About nine o'clock, the Emperor mounted his horse, and I followed him.
>
> Approaching to the lines of the army's right flank, after talking to a few moments to Count Erlon, he left his suite and returned, accompanied only by the Major General [Soult], he ascended a slight elevation, from hence we easily discovered various positions of the two armies. After reviewing some time with his glass without changing his position, he addressed a few words to the General Staff, and then when he came down from the plateau, the Emperor beckoned me to come near to him I obeyed. He then addressed those assembled near to him saying 'this is the Count of Erlon, on our right', pointing to the Corps of the general and continuing, after describing a circle with his hand to the right of the line, he added: 'Grouchy is marching in that direction, go to him, pass through Gembloux, follow in his footsteps, the Major-General will give you even a written order.' I wanted to point out to the Emperor whilst he was talking to me that the road was too long, but without giving me time to finish, he said: 'It does not matter, you would be taken following the shortest route,' and then pointing to the end of the right side of the line, he said: 'Come back here and join me, where Grouchy will debouch on the line. It cannot wait; he must be in direct communication with us and come into the line of battle with us. Go, go!'
>
> Immediately after I had received this order, I ran after the Major General who at that time was at the farm of Caillou, where the imperial head-quarters had spent the night. We arrived at ten o'clock at the farm. The Major General went to his room and sent for his secretary. The first thing to do is to log the date and time. It is easy to see that this time cannot be that for the departure of the dispatch, because before one leaves, it takes time to write it down, and it is also necessary to enter in the order register of the Major-General. All this requires sufficient time and in an ordinary service, where the hours and minutes have no role to play, this observation is of no importance, but in a particular case, when counting the hours and minutes when we take a wrong bearer of an order, it must be possible to restore the facts as they occurred. I repeat, the

time of the order which I was carrying was ten o'clock. I retired to the orderly's room. After half an hour of waiting, I joined the General Staff.

Nothing yet other than the date was written, the Major General observed the map, and his secretary amused himself in cutting a feather. I returned to the living room, where I found Mr. Regnault, chief officer of the 1st Army Corps who, learning that I had for twenty-four hours been in the saddle and had not had anything to eat. He kindly sent from his wagon a piece of bread and water mixed with spirits. After my meal, I went back to the General Staff, he was busy dictating the order I expected, I went again to the orderly's room.

After half an hour, I was asked for. Marshal Soult gave me the order, that the Emperor had told me.

Making Soult out to be dilatory plays neatly into the thesis that Soult was a royalist spy who deliberately sabotaged the campaign, muddled orders and made more mistakes in ten days than Berthier had in twenty years. With Berthier struck off the list of Marshals, his replacement in the function of Major-General was Marshal Soult. Soult was named Major-General on 9 May 1815 with General Bailly de Monthion as Chief of Staff.[16]

The appointment was not confirmed till 13 May 1815.[17] In the same letter, Davout asked for the service papers of the members of the staff to be sent to him for approval.

Soult was a capable field commander. His service in Spain for four years from 1808 to 1813 had given him ample experience at commanding a large army. In March 1813 he was at the head if 4th Corps, fighting at Lutzen and Bautzen, but in the summer returned once more to Spain, where his actions in the closing months of the Peninsular War clearly showed his tactical abilities. His re-organising of King Joseph's Army after Vittoria was a masterpiece of staff work. Yet Soult is castigated for not being Berthier and being one of the main reasons for defeat at Waterloo. Indeed, popular novelist (rather than historian) Bernard Cornwell goes as far to say that Soult's orders to Grouchy were 'Intelligible nonsense'[18] and thus Soult lost the campaign, which is far from the truth.[19] Soult, like Grouchy, is made the scapegoat for the disaster that befell the army: Napoléon did not lose the battle because he was betrayed by Soult, or Ney or Grouchy, but this is the traditional view of Waterloo from Napoléon lovers, blaming anyone other than Napoléon.

The simple truth is, Soult was a very capable tactician and superb workaholic administrator as his career in Spain, and later as Minister of War and Prime minister of France demonstrates. Yes, Soult was not Berthier, but he had operated as a commander and chief of an army comparable to the Armée du Nord for four years and was probably the best candidate for the job of Major-General.

Soult, admittedly, other than for a brief period in 1813, had never served directly under Napoléon and had to do a lot of 'on-the-job-training' to understand Napoléon and his way of working. Berthier, after being with Napoléon since the days of the Republic, knew exactly how Napoléon worked, how he thought, and how he gave orders. This day-to-day experience was invaluable in interpreting the wishes of Napoléon. However capable Soult was at staff work, he did not have the working knowledge of how Napoléon operated. Few men did beyond Duroc, Bertrand, and Berthier, two of whom were dead.

Soult was handicapped not by being a poor staff officer, but by his lack of experience of working under Napoléon, whereas the Emperor no doubt treated him as he did Berthier. Yet Soult was learning on the job how to interpret the wishes of the Emperor and translating the outpourings of the Emperor into orders that worked. No one, not even Davout, could have filled Berthier's boots. This is the point many who condemn Soult miss – no one could replace the working partnership Napoléon and Berthier had developed.

Napoléon and Berthier had worked as a unit for over fifteen years, creating vital bonds of understanding. Soult was dropped into a Berthier-shaped hole. He could do the staff work admirably, but what he could not be was Berthier, who knew exactly what the Emperor wanted. The pairing was unique and impossible to replace. Napoléon probably did not realise this. He gave orders the way he had always done, treating Soult like Berthier, and expecting the same results. Berthier knew what the Emperor desired from decades of working with him, Soult did not. Any other Marshal given the role of Major-General would have had the same problems, including the person often stated as being the better man, Marshal Davout.

Davout had no direct experience of working under the Emperor, and he had sat out much of 1813 and 1814 in garrisons. He also had no independent field command since Jena in 1806.

What were Soult's mistakes? The many hundreds of books on Waterloo all state Soult made mistakes, but they never list them. As far as can be ascertained from hard facts from June 1815, Soult's one error was in bungling orders on 10 June.[20] However, the orders would have been prepared by the staff themselves headed by Monthion and then signed off by Soult. Berthier bungled orders in 1809 yet is never described as a traitor. Why? Because to go back to the old argument, someone other than Napoléon lost Waterloo. Soult is branded by Beckett as an arch-traitor, a Royalist plant to lose the campaign.[21] Yet, Soult was more a realist than a royalist. Soult, as Major-General, was assisted primarily by the chief of staff General Bailly de Monthion[22], Adjutant-Commandants Michal La Bretonniere[23], Babut[24], Petiet[25] and Fourier d'Hincourt.[26] His aides-des-camp included Marie Guillaume Eli Baudus[27] and Jean Alexandre les Pays de Bourjolly.[28]

François-Gédéon Bailly de Monthion had joined the army in 1793. He was a highly capable staff officer. In the 1805 campaign he served on the staff of the Grande Armée under Marshal Berthier, serving again in 1806, was his chief of staff in 1809, and deputy chief of staff to the Grande Armée in 1812 and 1813. He was Berthier's talented understudy.

In his 17 June orders, Grouchy had to head to Louvain to gain Maastricht, and on 18 June, the Emperor notes the Prussians were at Chyse, which when we consult the 1777 Map is vis a vis the Plain of Louvain. This was where Exelmans would head. Therefore, whoever wrote the 20 June letter knew the contents of Grouchy's orders, and it is clear that Exelmans and Grouchy obeyed the written letter of the orders, as failure to obey direct Imperial Orders was to face the wrath of the Emperor. It is also very clear that Grouchy never received recall orders, if they ever existed.

If the Emperor had ordered Grouchy to march to Waterloo on 17 June, then the 10.00 hours order to Grouchy makes no sense at all as it clearly sends Grouchy to Wavre. Was this a 'fake order' issued by Soult to send Grouchy away from Waterloo and thus sabotage the Emperor? Some historians, like Beckett, would support such an idea. But all evidence written on 17 to 20 June 1815 points to Grouchy never being ordered to Waterloo till it was far too late for him to get to Waterloo. Was the sending of the first order deliberately sabotaged by Soult? Was the wording of the orders so vague as to be meaningless indicative of yet more treachery by Soult? No. Beckett argues that because the content of the 10.00 hours order as it exists is so different to the contents reported by Zenowicz, it's proof positive that Soult deliberately issued wrong orders. Yet Zenowicz did not write his account until 1848, over thirty years later, when no doubt his own recollections of the day had been greatly influenced by false memory. The written order of 1815 is of more value than a memoire of 1848. But what are we to make of it? Zenowicz correctly names the *Ordonnateur en Chef* of 1st Corps as Regnault. This was without doubt Louis Regnault.[29] Just because he names an officer who was at Waterloo, does not mean that what he says about the Emperor expressing the 10.00 order to be a recall order for Grouchy is what the Emperor actually desired. As with Exelmans and the case of d'Estourmel, Zenowicz is writing what he thinks should have happened, rather than what did, in order to shift blame to Soult or Grouchy, i.e. anyone other than the Emperor, the line Beckett takes. Houssaye discounted Zenowicz's description of the contents of the order, as I do, but some take this to be a cover-up to shift the blame from Soult. This argument is very dubious at best when assessed from documents written on 18 June 1815 and not by the Emperor in exile, who re-wrote history to suit his own ends. The Emperor had always done this with his bulletins, as had apologists for the Emperor or officers in need of rehabilitating their careers post the revolution of 1830. We also forget that Berthier nearly lost the 1809 campaign due to his bungling of orders.

The orders sent to Grouchy were no more vague than any other sent in the campaign, regardless of Cornwell's accusations. What we are missing though is the verbal portion of the orders which no doubt elaborated upon the written word to make the order and its contents crystal clear. Thus, we are at a major disadvantage and can only work on the written word.

In returning to the discussion of the 20 June letter, we conclude this document is a genuine document written 20 June 1815. It is of importance as it tells us that:

1. Exelmans was at Sart-à-Walhain and not Neuf Sart.
2. Exelmans agreed with Grouchy marching to Wavre and Louvain.
3. Pierre Antoine Poirot arrived around 16.00 hours, carrying the 14.30 hours order to march to Waterloo. In response troops were sent to Saint Lambert.
4. Zenowicz arrived with the 10.00 hours order much later with orders to head to Wavre.

No recall orders were issued to Grouchy. Exelmans and Grouchy both chose to follow written orders rather than to incur Imperial wrath. Grouchy has oft been seen as disregarding the advice of his subordinates, being high-handed and arrogant. Here we have an eye-witness that speaks of unity of opinion between Grouchy, Exelmans, and we suppose Vandamme, placing irascible Gérard as a trouble maker, overruled by his colleagues during a council of war. Thus, the great mystery of Waterloo is now finally solved. Napoléon expected Grouchy at Waterloo, as he had sent word to Grouchy to do so at 14.30 hours. Sadly, the order was nullified by the disastrously late arrival of the 10.00 order sending Grouchy to Wavre.

Comment

How was this possible that such chaos could reign in the head-quarters staff? Who was to blame? The staff had had faced many issues. In order to carry out their duties, the staff needed large numbers of horses. However, the hastily improvised nature of the *Etat-Major* in 1815 resulted in many officers having only one horse, and often of a mediocre sort. It was not until the morning of 16 June that the deficiency in horse flesh was felt. Soult in Charleroi had trouble making contact with corps and divisional commanders. Grouchy reported to Soult that he had no idea where Kellerman and 3rd Cavalry Corps were on 15 June. Early on 16 June Soult issued the following order to Napoléon:[30]

> Charleroi, 16 June 1815
>> Sire,
>> The daily active service of the staff officers requires more horses, which most of them are unable to procure for want of pecuniary means.
>> I have the honour, therefore, to propose to Your Majesty, as an extraordinary gratuity, the sum of eight hundred francs for Adjutant-Commandants and 600 francs to the officers of the army staff. I beg Your Majesty to inform me of his decision on this subject.

Having to find mounts whilst on active service on campaign was too little too late, as it would be impossible for officers to have time and funds to buy horses. The Emperor had known about this issue since the middle weeks of May, and yet had done nothing about it. Soult, often seen as the traitor, was hampered by Davout. Indeed, so aware of the need for funds to establish the headquarters and the need to buy good horses for the staff, Soult had petitioned the Minister of War, Marshal Davout, for funds to establish the *Grande-Quartier-General* on 19 May 1815 requesting:[31]

> 80,000 francs to buy 60 horses to move wagons, to buy harness and waggons, to clothe 30 domestic servants and establish the headquarters office 20,000 francs to buy horses for couriers and *officers en mission.*

Soult, furthermore, requested twelve secretaries be sent from the War Ministry and more funds be allowed to buy a further sixty horses for officers on the staff. Soult in the same letter notes he had been made Major-General to replace 'the Prince of Wagram' i.e. Berthier.[32] Davout wrote the same day to the Emperor complaining about Soult and his demand for money, which he viewed as unreasonable. He awarded

Soult: '40,000 francs to establish his household and the *Grand-Quartier-General* 10,000 francs to buy horses for couriers.'[33]

This left a huge shortfall in funds to buy mounts. Soult was awarded 50 per cent of the money needed to buy horses for couriers. A good horse in 1815 cost around 600 francs; 10,000 francs was therefore enough for sixteen horses, not even half the number of horses he needed. For the additional sixty horses, Soult needed 40,000 francs, none of which he obtained. Davout had hamstrung the staff in not releasing funds to mount the staff. Davout kept rigidly to regulations. Admittedly no new regulations had been issued since 1804, but clearly Davout was in no mood to be pragmatic and accept that costs had increased in ten years, coupled with hyperinflation as the economy stagnated. What were his motives? Was he so wedded to regulations that he could not be flexible, or was he working for another agenda? Had he realised already before the campaign began that the fate of the Emperor was already lost and the return of his master only temporary? His immediate shift from Bonapartism to Realism on 22 June, seems to suggest he may already have been of the realist camp. Nevertheless, his loathing for Soult, and using regulations as an excuse, he did his best to hamstring Soult. All rather pathetic really, but the history of the Marshallate and their non-cooperation with each other for the previous decade shows that the Marshals as collective group were rather petty and self centered individuals.

Davout hampered Soult in rebuilding the staff, and the staff were sent to war lacking men and horses due to his interference. Soult complained to the Emperor on 21 May, and on 23 May Davout awarded 6,000 francs a month pay to the staff but payable only from 1 June.[34] Soult replied the same day to the Emperor complaining about Davout not living in the real world and that the cost of the staff had changed since the regulation of An 12 was issued, and he had to build from scratch the office of the *Grand-Quartier-General*.[35] The Emperor ultimately agreed with Soult, and awarded 80,000 Francs to establish the equipment train of the headquarters, 3,600 francs pay for the office for the month of May, and 6,000 francs pay for the month of June, paid in advance payable from 1 June.[36] By June, it was too late to buy enough horses, it was too late to get the man power that was desperately needed for the staff to function. Davout takes the blame for poor performance of the staff and not Soult. Davout, as well as being jealous of Soult taking a field command, detested General Bailly Monthion and did his best to get him removed from post.[37] Does this antithapy to both men help explain his petty snubbing of

Soult until overruled by the Emperor? Perhaps. Indeed, Davout states Monthion was a total failure as Major General in 1812, 1813, 1814 and that he was hated by the Army. Given Davout had not taken part in the campaign of 1813 and 1814, his comments were not based on experience but on his own opinion, which is very different to fact. Yet for many, Davout was a Bonpartist saint who could do no wrong, whereas Soult, Grouchy, and Monthion were all branded traitors and failures. Davout, however, sold out the army and advocated for the return of the King from the point the Emperor abdicated. If any Marshal was a traitor, it was Davout. Soult is blamed for bungling orders on 4 and 10 June – a comment which seems credible.[38] Men make mistakes, to err is human. To withhold funds to establish the headquarters staff was this a mistake or a deliberate act? Be that as it may, whatever Davout's motives, the lack of good horses probably cost the French the outcome of the Battle of Waterloo.

Getting back to the events of 18 June, it is only from the anonymous letter of 20 June 1815, that the true sequence of orders arriving with Grouchy has been confirmed, which exonerates Grouchy and makes Exelmans into an officer who generated falsehoods to hide his own past. When faced with subordinates who clearly lied to him, no wonder Grouchy felt victimised and marginalised until the day he died. This is why the anonymous letter of 20 June is so important. It shows what happened that day, and how a delayed courier changed the course of history. Empires are built and lost on fate:[39]

Even so, it is unlikely that Grouchy could have reached Waterloo in time to affect the outcome of the battle, something Grouchy knew very well:[40]

> I have just shown that the late hour of the arrival of my troops at Gembloux, and the weather, still more than my slender information as to the real movements of the Prussians, had hindered me from pushing my infantry beyond that town, on the 17th. But on the 18th, before sunrise, it was in motion in the direction of Saravalain and Wavres, which latter place, the head of the column did not reach, until between one and two o'clock, though it marched without halting an instant. To assert that then I could have paralyzed, by a flank movement, which my proximity to the enemy did not permit me to make, the attack of general Bülow on the right wing of the French at Waterloo, shows ignorance of the position of the Prussian army, which was at this time in echellons, between Napoléon and me—and shows a forgetfulness of distances, of the state of the roads, and the nature of the country; for the Prussian corps which decided the fate of the battle had marched from Wavres at day-light,

and were on the march from four in the morning until one in the afternoon, before they reached the head of the defile of St. Lambert. (See the report of M. Blücher). Thus then, *unless I could have given wings to my soldiers*, it was impossible that they could have arrived in time to be useful at Waterloo.

To hold in check, as it is asserted I could have done, an army 95,000 strong, with a corps of 32,000 men, was a very difficult task, and it is publishing an erroneous opinion to advance that I could have accomplished it. On the evening of the 17th, my troops had scarcely reached Gembloux. On the evening of the 17th, marshal Blücher had all his army, except a rear-guard, collected near Wavres—at sunrise on the 18th, Blücher detached from Wavres a part of his troops, for the purpose of forming a junction with the duke of Wellington. At sunrise on the 18th, I was seven hours' march from thence. How could I hinder the detachment, and prevent the junction?

It cannot be said, with more justice, that marshal Blücher had deceived me, or had concealed from me the movement of a part of his army, as some writers have advanced. —

1st. Because, not only I was not in position before M. Blücher, when he commenced his movement towards the left of the English army, with the design of turning the right of the French at Waterloo, but, as I have remarked, my troops were at a great distance when this movement was executed.

2d. Because I did not reach the Prussian rear-guard till the 18th, about noon, a league and a half from Wavres, that town having been occupied during the night by the enemy's corps, which effected, at break of day, the movement in question.'

Historian George Hooper comments: 'The truth is that on the morning of the 18th, the facts of the situation, if we may be allowed the phrase, rendered it impossible for Grouchy to prevent the junction of Wellington and Blücher. One fact alone ought to settle the question forever. Grouchy, at Gembloux, was separated from Napoléon at La-Belle-Alliance by more than twice the distance which separated Blücher from Wellington. No manoeuvring could have made the lines of march shorter. Four Prussian army corps were nearer to Wellington than two French army corps were to Napoléon ... Turn it which way we may, consider it a question of generalship, or one of time and distance, and we arrive at the same conclusion. It was, on the morning of the 18th, beyond the power of Grouchy to alter materially the Battle of Waterloo.'[41]

Chapter 6

Waterloo

After nearly ten hours fighting Napoléon had lost Waterloo. In a last desperate gamble to win, he had ordered the Imperial Guard to attack around 20.00 hours supported by whatever troops were still capable of fighting. In the midst of this very crisis, the French high command took a few measures to save what could be saved. Firstly, the division of Girard, stationed at Fleurus, was summoned to take up a position at Quatre Bras as a cover for what was now the inevitable retreat of the army. Soult ordered Girard's division to take up a defensive position at Quatre-Bras. A *commissaire des guerres* was sent by General D'Aure to Charleroi to organise the artillery reserve and parc to cross back over the river Sambre. At about 19.00 hours, according to Bellina Kupieski[1], general Monthion had set things in motion to clear the main road south of obstacles:[2]

> At half past 7 o'clock, His Majesty, to save the material of the army, manoeuvred the artillery so as to guard and protect the retreat to Genappes, this place being designated by the Imperial Head-quarters to fall back upon, which was commanded by Marshal du Camp Le Bel[3], but there was much disorder and we had great trouble in reaching this place.
>
> Two hours before the retreat commenced, the Lieutenant-General Monthion received an order from an officer on the Imperial Head-quarters Staff (I believe this to have been Battalion Commander Gérard) who commanded that the Imperial Headquarters and the Gendarmes were to evacuate their carriages, wagons and baggage so that the road way would be free of obstruction. A half hour after, the Marshal Duke of Dalmatia repeated the same order, carried by Colonel Raoul.[4]
>
> By what fatality prevented the execution for this order on which depends the salvation of the army and which save the material!

> The army arrived at Genappes, the route being totally blocked, and our infantry only passed with great difficulty.
>
> The Emperor arrived with his Staff and tried in vain to clear the road. The soldiers were filled with terror that they were being pursued, and were concerned only with their escape, the cry was heard 'save yourself, save yourself, we have been betrayed!'

Checked by the 3rd Netherlands Division, the Imperial Guard fell back. On his right wing the Prussians over ran Plancenoit, Maison du Roi and almost gained La Haie Sainte. Under enormous pressure the French army broke. By midnight 18 June 1815, Napoléon was at Genappe. Waterloo had been lost. Just under twenty-four hours earlier, Napoléon had planned for victory and his entry into Brussels. Fate however, had had other plans. Napoléon had fought and lost his last battle.

The French army had known defeat before. In previous years, the Emperor had regrouped his forces, and taken the fight back to the allies. If the army could be rallied, then potentially the set-back of Waterloo could be reversed.

Unlike 1814 however, the Armée du Nord was far from being completely loyal to Napoléon's cause. The army of 1815 was fragile and was not the army that Napoléon had commanded in previous years. The rank and file were enthusiastic for war, a feeling not shared by some senior officers and the public at large in France. France was war-weary and bankrupt and needed stability not more conflict. At the other end of the scale, none of the higher-level formations had any operational experience as formations and had conducted no brigade or divisional exercises. Commanders and staff were still joining their divisions as the campaign started, indeed General Alllix did not get to Paris in time to take up his appointment with 1 Corps and so did not participate in the campaign at all.

Napoléon's top table of officers were hardly a dream team, indeed, Charles Esdaile remarks that the Armée du Nord was nothing like the Grande Armée had been in the years before 1813 and was less likely to win battles or to be able to sustain defeat.[5]

Regarding the chaos of the route of the retreat, Marshall Ney recounted on 26 June 1815 that:[6]

> As for myself, constantly in the rear-guard, which I followed on foot, having all my horses killed, worn out with fatigue, covered with contusions, and having no longer the strength to march, I owe my life to a corporal who supported me on the road, and did not abandon me during the retreat. At eleven at night I found Lieutenant

General Lefebvre Desnoëttes, and one of his officers, Major Schmidt, had the generosity to give me the only horse which remained to him. In this manner I arrived at Marchienne-au-Pont at four o'clock in the morning, alone, without any officers of my staff, ignorant of what had become of the Emperor, who before the end of the battle had entirely disappeared, and who I was allowed to believe might be either killed or taken prisoner.

General Pamphile Lacroix, chief of staff of the second corps, whom I found in this city, having told me that the Emperor was at Charleroi, I was led to suppose that his Majesty was going to put himself at the head of Marshal Grouchy's corps, to cover the Sambre, and to facilitate to the troops the means of rallying towards Avesnes, and with this persuasion I went to Beaumont; but parties of cavalry following us too near, and having already intercepted the roads of Mauberge and Philippeville, I became sensible of the impossibility of arresting a single soldier on that point to oppose the progress of the victorious enemy. I continued my march upon Avesnes, where I could obtain no intelligence of what had become of the Emperor.

In this state of matters, having no knowledge of his Majesty nor of the Major-General, confusion increasing every moment, and with the exception of some fragments of regiments of the guard and of the line, everyone following his own inclination, I determined immediately to go to Paris by St. Quentin, to disclose as quickly as possible the true state of affairs to the Minister of War; that he might send to the army some fresh troops, and take the measures which circumstances rendered necessary. At my arrival at Bourget, 3 leagues from Paris, I learned that the Emperor had passed there at nine o'clock in the morning.

Chapter 7

19 June 1815

Soult

The Armée du Nord was fleeing south with the Prussians hot on its heels. The army fled in whatever direction it could. 2nd Corps headed back to Quatre-Bras, whilst other elements headed to Philippeville. No command and control existed for at least twenty-four hours or more to direct where the army was to go to. In this chaos hundreds of men quit the ranks and fled. If the retreat had been properly managed, maybe some vestige of order could have been maintained and the Armée du Nord may not have been as grossly compromised as it was. Napoléon fled to Paris, abandoning his army, just as he did in Egypt, Russia and Germany in 1813.

Rather than try and organise resistance and the army, Napoléon planned for a new campaign with a new army in July. He seems to have made no plans whatsoever about what was to happen next. He had not counted on defeat in his meticulous planning, so no plan B existed. It was Soult who had to initiate this second plan. The army headquarters had disintegrated in the rout. Key personnel were missing, either dead or prisoners. Soult had to rebuild the headquarters staff before any planning could take place. Without officers to transmit messages Soult could not issue orders or manage the situation.

Early on the 19th Soult and Napoléon arrived at Philippeville. One of the first acts of Soult was to write to Marshal Davout the minister of war in Paris:[1]

> Monsieur the Marshal, I have the honour to write to you for the first time since I wrote to you on the field of battle of Waterloo at half past two o'clock when the battle was begun and we had experienced great success, however at 7 o'clock a false movement was carried out with the orders of the Emperor, all was changed,

62

the combat continued until night fell, and a retreat was effected, but it was in disorder.

The Emperor rallied the army at Philippeville and Avesnes and began to organise the corps and to tend to their needs. You can well imagine that the disaster is immense.

Napoléon, via Soult, then issued orders to General Reille in the name of the Emperor:[2]

> Mr. lieutenant-general Reille.
>
> Count, the Emperor gives you command of all Corps from the Army of the North which are successively arriving on the glacis Philippeville and it is of the utmost importance that we work on at their rallying and reorganization.
>
> To this end, we must take care to ensure each regiment is reformed as are the brigades, regiments and companies. MM. general officers, staff officers, administrators, etc. should resume their duties and are immediately placed under your command. In this way we reform our army promptly as well as its equipment, but this needs organization.
>
> The intention of the Emperor is that you distribute during the day to every soldier, food in the following proportion: two rations of bread, a single ration each of water-of-life, meat and rice. There will also be distributed thirty cartridges to every infantryman, and ten to each cavalry trooper. The Commander of Philippeville has been informed of your needs and has been ordered to aid you.

Orders were sent to General Dumonceaux commanding the 2nd Military Division. He was told that the army had been defeated and was returning to France and was totally dispersed. He was ordered to place the 16th Military Division on alert and mobilise the National Guard. Napoléon left for Paris later the same day. Soult informed Grouchy that the 1st, 2nd and 6th Corps were commanded now by General Reille, and that the 1st Cavalry Division was heading to Marle, the 2nd to Saint-Quentin, the 3rd to Rhetel, 5th to Hervins, with Milhaud and Kellerman to Rennes. Headquarters was to be at Laon.

Grouchy

On the morning of 19 June Grouchy, who was still ignorant of Napoléon's defeat, prepared an attack to finally push the Prussians back and open the way to Brussels. About the operations planned for the day, Grouchy wrote:[3]

> I spent most of the night to get everything ready for an attack at daybreak, and yet I had few troops and resources united. When the

dawn appeared, the enemy saved me the trouble of marching to them, and advanced against me. They were pushed back and as the number of my troops available to me was increasing, I ordered Teste's division to take the village of Bièrges. This attack forced the Prussians to evacuate, as well as the part of Wavre that they occupied. General Vandamme then passed the Dyle without obstacles and the enemy was pursued to Rosierne in the drection of Brussels, as I was convinced that Napoléon, victorious yesterday, was already master of this city.

At 09.00 hours, Bièrges and the troublesome mill had fallen. General Teste had had a very hard task to drive out the two Prussian battalions defending the place. The capture of this point was a serious blow to the Prussians, as Grouchy's forces had now broken through Thielemann's defensive line in two places: the centre was broken and the right was now seriously threatened by overwhelming numbers. Thielemann had no other option other than to withdraw. Grouchy's objective for the previous evening had been gained, but over twelve hours later than planned. The way was now open at long last to march to Napoléon at Waterloo.

As soon as Zeppelin withdrew from Wavre, Vandamme pushed his men across the Dyle, both at Bièrges and Wavre, and advanced up the Brussels road which runs north out of Wavre. Two battalions of the 4th Kurmärk Landwehr Regiment fell back to La Bavette. Upon reaching a small wood to the east of La Bavette, the Prussians re-formed and opened fire against the squadron of pursuing French cavalry.

It was now the turn of Marwitz's cavalry to advance and it pushed the French cavalry back towards Wavre. Vandamme's infantry was moving up both the Brussels road (having forded the Dyle to the northeast) and moved men up from Bièrges, and by sheer weight of numbers forced the Prussian infantry to retreat towards Louvain, through the villages of St Achtenrode and Ottenberg. But behind Saint-Achtenrode, Thielemann halted and took up a defensive position.[4] To the north of Limale stood Neuf Cabaret, where General Borcke's brigade of Prussians was stationed; they had taken no part in the fighting on 18 June. He notes that he witnessesed the French cross the River Dyle and, at some point after daybreak on 19 June, observed a strong column of French cavalry heading towards Genappe. Against the French he deployed his artillery, which resulted in the French retreating back to Limale, crossing the river as they did so. However, his aide-de-camp contradicts this account, saying Borcke's men confronted the French at Neuf Cabaret, that the cavalry took little notice of the artillery, that the French moved off to Chambre, and that it was only at 17.00 hours that the French abandoned Limale. The truth was no doubt part-way between the two accounts. This body of cavalry could have been one of four formations, but is likely to have either been Maurin, from 4th Corps, or Pajol.[5] On balance, the troops were likely to be the latter. About the movements of the cavalry reserve, Biot, aide-de-camp to General Pajol (commanding the 1st Reserve Cavalry Corps), relates that:[6]

> The following day, 19 June, as dawn broke, the bivouacs of the 1st Hussars were rained upon by a hail of bullets. It was the Prussian corps of Tauentzin, forming the rear-guard of Blücher, who had been left there to defend the bridges and Limale and Wavre; we appeared to be cut off by them and we sought to join the main body. At first shot, I went directly to the attacked party, and returned to warn General Pajol of what had happened: he went himself to the scene. Our troops were already formed, but not across the river.
>
> There was a danger that they would strongly advance down the defile and fall onto the divisions of Gérard and stop their line of retreat. General Pajol instructed me to express these thoughts to the marshal, and I asked him to pass immediately, in front of the 4th Corps, which was done. We also recalled the 3rd Corps, which had forced the bridge of Wavre. The latter came to pass the River Dyle at Limale. When the reinforcements arrived where we were, the enemy decided to retire, but then abandoning his first line at the defiles of Saint-Lambert, we began marching towards the woods of Rixensart, leading to Rosierne. In this clash, we had the misfortune to lose General Penne, of Teste's division, carried away by a cannonball. This general officer had received a shot in the leg at the Battle of Ligny. I was ordered to accompany General Ameil, charged with 4th and 5th Hussars, to pursue the enemy and to accelerate his retirement, by passing through the Rixensart Wood.

Confirming this report, the 1st Hussars lost one man wounded and one man missing on 18/19 June. In comparison, at Quatre-Bras on 15 June, the regiment had three men wounded, one killed and one missing.[7] Clearly the fighting for 1st Hussars on 18 and 19 June was of a much lesser intensity than a few days earlier. The brigaded 4th Hussars however lost eleven men on 18-19 June. They had lost two men on 15 June, two on 16 June and two on 17 June.[8] Clearly whatever happened on 18/19 June to the regiment was different to the previous days. General Berton narrates the day as follows:[9]

> 19th, at three o'clock in the morning, General Thielemann wanted to restore communication with Brussels, attacked the French troops at Rosierne and Bièrges; the small force he used was easily repulsed,

Vandamme then proceeded to advance one of his divisions by the mill of Bièrges, the enemy had to stand and defend his right. It was the same day, on the heights of the village of Bièrges, that General Penne, who commanded a brigade of Teste's division, found a glorious death: it was regretted by all the braves. The corps of dragoons had also crossed in front of Limale.

At Wavre around 10.00 hours, General Thielemann ordered the retreat. Thielemann knew that Grouchy must himself either attack or retreat sooner or later, but to hold on to Wavre too long would mean his own destruction. By retreating, he would gain time, and when the opportunity arose he would again advance, and possibly convert Grouchy's retirement into a rout. Under the protection of Marwitz's cavalry, which comprised the 7th and 8th Uhlans and the 3rd and 6th Landwehr Cavalry with three batteries of horse artillery, the infantry retired, and Zeppelin evacuated Wavre. Grouchy was poised to fall on Brussels or head west to find the Emperor. At the very moment that his success seemed certain, At about 11.00 hours on 19 June, Grouchy received word of the Emperor's defeat. He wrote as follows about this event:[10]

> About eleven o'clock, an officer sent by the major-general announced the disaster of Waterloo. His report was only verbal; he was carrying no orders or instructions that indicated the points on which Napoléon withdrew, nor where I should direct myself. However, the details he gave were so explicit that it cast no doubt on the inevitability of events of the day: my first thought was to march on the rear of the enemy, but with too few troops for such a movement in which I would have been followed by the Prussian troops I had in front of me, I decided to retire on the Sambre and the Meuse, where based on that information I would judge my movement to be the most useful in difficult circumstances. I effected my retreat in two columns, in the directions of Temploux and Namur, with my light cavalry at Marc-Saint-Denis, and my dragoons on the last of these towns.

Aide-de-Camp de Blocqueville wrote:[11]

> The 19th, at ten o'clock in the morning, the marshal, having learned of the disasters of Waterloo, informed his generals, and that this fatal event forced him to retreat.

Soult and Napoléon had arrived at Philippeville in the morning of 19 June. The officer who carried the dispatch was Pierre Jean Baptiste Aube Dumonceaux.[12] The news of Napoléon's defeat at Waterloo must have come as a shock for everyone, but for Grouchy most of all. The dispatch read as follows:[13]

> Dear Comte,
> There has been fought a great battle at Waterloo in the front of the Soignes Forest, the army was not favoured, and the army is retiring to France.

History tells us that the fighting capacity of the remnants of the Armée du Nord with Marshal Soult was nil in the immediate aftermath of the battle. The men only regained something of their former vigour and enthusiasm as they got closer to the walls of Paris. Marshal Soult was in command of a spent military force that could no longer defend itself. All that was left were Grouchy's forces and at about 12.00, Soult's second messenger brought orders for Grouchy to retreat towards Laon:[14]

> Marshal,
> I give you the state of the location of the various army corps which formed the column commanded by the emperor in person.
> The army corps under your orders is not listed. His Majesty wishes, but does not give you a destination, that you are to arrive at either Philippeville or Givet. I am instructed to inform you that as soon as you arrive at one or the other of these places you will operate in the direction of Laon to join the army and inform me immediately so that I can send commands: the headquarters are moving to Laon.

Hot on the heels of the courier was a third aide-de-camp with more orders:[15]

> Philippeville 19 June 1815
> Marshal Duc de Dalmatie, the major-general to Marshal Grouchy.
> The army is withdrawing on numerous places, this evening we will be crossing the Sambre, you are to execute a movement, despite the bad weather, so that you will move via Philippeville to Givet, where we shall be reunited.
> In the name of the emperor
> Duc de Dalmatie.

The order outlined that General Reille was commanding 1st, 2nd and 6th Corps and was heading to Laon, the artillery was to move to La Fère, the engineers to Laon, the 1st Cavalry Division to Marie, the 2nd Cavalry Division to Saint-Quentin, the 3rd Cavalry Division to Rhefel and the 5th Cavalry Division to Hervins. The Imperial Guard was to march to Soissons.[16]

About this movement to retreat, Fantin des Odoards, of the 22nd Regiment of Line Infantry, wrote:[17]

> About eleven o'clock, our commander-in-chief finally learned the fatal news by a staff officer who had miraculously escaped the enemy.

The retreat from Wavre

Grouchy had to do to three things, and do them quickly:

1. Break contact with the Prussians. Knowing Bülow and a large Prussian force was now at Waterloo and would be heading to pursue the Armée du Nord, he had to break off contact with the Prussians, and leave a sufficiently large rear-guard so as not to get overwhelmed by them.
2. Draw in his scattered forces.
3. Hurriedly draw up a plan of action for a retreat to join the main body of the Armée du Nord.

Given the main Brussels Charleroi road would be blocked by the Armée du Nord and above all by the Prussians, Grouchy clearly could not head back to Charleroi to cross the River Sambre. Heading to Namur seemed the safest option open to him.

In order to secure the line of retreat, General Exelmans was ordered by Grouchy to march to Namur and occupy the vital bridges over the Sambre as quickly as possible. He set off just after midday. Pajol's cavalry and Teste's infantry division were to act as the rear-guard to give time for 3rd and 4th Corps to break off action and head south. General Vichery, who had been placed in command of 4th Corps, was ordered by Grouchy:[18]

> At Nil-Perreux 19 June 1815
>
> Marshal Grouchy to General [Baron de] Vichery, commandant of the 4th Corps of the army
>
> My dear general,
>
> The disorder is great at this point in the march, making it necessary that you take your position with the rear-guard for some time at La Baraque, to let pass your artillery park and other vehicles. I first wanted you at the front, but I prefer you now to follow the column, to try to overcome the disadvantages of the march.
>
> General Vandamme will keep Wavre until ten o'clock at night, so it is necessary that you take the position of La Baraque (by

carefully monitoring the defile at Limale) long enough so that the enemy cannot stand between you and him.

Put in your centre your artillery divisions and they are to be kept close and at a distance, so that the 4th Corps can give a new proof of the good spirit that animates it, deploying a lot of energy in these difficult circumstances.

My intention is that we push without stopping until Temploux and Gembloux have been passed: you will only make stops from time to time.

I ordered one of your divisions to move to Baraque so it can support the cavalry and is head of the column.

Be reassured, general, of my high consideration of yourself

Signed. Grouchy.

Grouchy began his retreat. His troops had reached the line La-Bavette-Rosierne in their pursuit of Thielemann, and now Exelmans' cavalry was sent off with orders to make all speed to Namur and secure the bridges over the Sambre at that place. Exelmans reached Namur at around 16.30 hours, a little more than five hours to cover thirty miles by devious lanes and byways in a terrible condition after the rains. General Bonnemains' report notes:[19]

The 19th at nine o'clock in the morning, Marshal Grouchy, being master of the defiles, made the corps of Exelmans, with the brigade of General Bonnemains forming the head of column, to debouch and to charge the enemy. It was at this moment when the commander-in-chief received the sad news of the loss of the Battle of Waterloo. He ordered the movement to be stopped and ordered General Bonnemains to move with the 4th and 12th Regiments of Dragoons and two batteries of light artillery to Namur and leave no stone unturned to get there and hold the place before the enemy could. Passing near Gembloux, General Bonnemains learned that beyond the city a column of enemy cavalry had appeared, headed to Genappe onto Namur.

It was here that General Bonnemains deployed his ten squadrons. General Bonnemains, after a reconnaissance, with some men hastened to gain Namur where he was welcomed by all the people and authorities of this city. He asked them to prepare for our wounded and provide emergency supplies for the army. General Bonnemains, having been relieved in the evening by the other brigades from the corps of Exelmans, marched for the same purpose on to Dinan [sic] ... and was happy to get there before the enemy did, which was that night about a league off in the direction of Charleroi on the 20th.

The 4th corps, preceded by the 7th Cavalry Division (six squadrons under Vallin, who had taken Maurin's place), re-crossed the Dyle by the bridge at Limale, and moved by a narrow lane to the main Namur-Brussels road. Vandamme's corps withdrew from La Bavette and marched through Wavre, Dion-le-Mont, Chaumont, Tourrinnes, Sart-à-Walhain, Grand Leez, Saint-Denis and then to Temploux on the Namur-Nivelles road, where it arrived at 23.00 hours. Gérard's corps had reached Temploux an hour earlier. In the action Vallin suffered the following losses:

Regiment	Killed		Wounded		Missing		Total
	Officers	Men	Officers	Men	Officers	Men	
6th Hussars[20]	0	3	0	0	0	10	13
8th Chasseurs à Cheval [21]	0	0	0	0	0	0	0
6th Dragoons[22]	0	0	0	1	0	0	1
16th Dragoons[23]	No meaningful data recorded						
Total	0	3	0	1	0	10	14

Pajol, in command of the rear-guard, which was composed of the 4th Cavalry Division — twelve squadrons under Baron Soult — and Teste's infantry division operated against Thielemann to keep him occupied until Wavre had been cleared, and then retreated by Corbaix, Sart-à-Walhain, Sauvenière to Gembloux, where he bivouacked for the night.

This retreat was largely unhindered by General Thielemann's Prussians, many of whom had been routed after Grouchy's action at Wavre. But General Pirch's 2nd Corps was on its way to cut of Grouchy's line of retreat. He arrived at Mellery at about 11.00 hours, however his troops were so exhausted that he had to let them rest. Namur was not gained until the early hours of 20 June.

Chapter 8

Grouchy's Action at Namur

At daybreak on 20 June, Grouchy's rear-guard left Gembloux and marched on Namur via Saint-Denis and La Fallise; his infantry left Temploux about 09.00 hours. A short distance beyond Temploux, the column was attacked by Prussian cavalry which had been sent off in pursuit by Thielemann at first light that morning.

More mundane matters occupied Grouchy. He sent orders to Vandamme to send all the walking wounded from Namur to Chaumont, transport where possible was to be organised for these unlucky men. Namur was ordered to furnish 100,000 rations of bread. Charlemont was to be the next destination for the army once it had passed through Namur. To cover the line of retreat, Pajol was ordered to scout the right flank of the army.[1]

At the same time, more cavalry was seen coming against the rear, along the Nivelles-Namur road. Grouchy recorded that:[2]

> The 4th Corps was to take the road from Namur to Charleroi, the 3rd on the direct route to Temploux, but at this moment, the two columns were attacked, that of the right was obliged to conduct a retrograde movement and unite with the left-hand column. The 20th Dragoons under the command of Colonel Briqueville captured to field guns and a howitzer from the enemy. The weak squares of [missing] regiment were charged by a strong force of cavalry and would have sustained huge losses had it not been for the good disposition, calm attitude and accurate musketry. The enemy cavalry was charged by the 1st Hussars under the orders of Maréchal-de-Camp Clary who took several prisoners. The movement continued without further loss to Namur. We were forced to march in a single long column which much embarrassed the transportation of the wounded which I always conveyed with the army, which meant it took a long time to pass through the town across the single bridge. I charged General Vandamme with the defence of Namur.

As Grouchy notes, upon arriving near the village of La Fallise, about three miles from Namur, the Prussians found Vandamme's rear-guard posted on the brow of the hill, below which lay the town in the valley of the Meuse. About this, Charles Philippe Lefol, aide-de-camp to General Lefol, wrote:[3]

> About three-quarters of a league from Namur, close to a village called Fallise, the general, suspecting that we would be charged by a strong column of cavalry which followed us closely, immediately made the regiments form square in the midst of which we took refuge, but the square was barely formed when the cavalry attacked with great advantage. If it had not been for the small wood close at hand, into which our disordered troops ran for safety, although we were slashed by sabres severely, the Prussians would have had far more success.
>
> By rallying on the other side of the wood, we realised we had abandoned two cannons in our flight, and we were left stuck in the middle of a thicket. The general immediately ordered that we should recover them, and I was appointed to accompany the men called to this expedition. After strenuous efforts, despite the Prussian cavalry firing their pistols at us, we were able to return these two pieces to the cries of joy from our brave soldiers.
>
> We always fought, and the resistance was obstinate, we were pursued at the point of the bayonet to Namur, where the engagement was very fierce, and where we lost a lot of people. Forced to defend ourselves we were pushed into the suburbs with great vigour until we reached the gate of the city, this was more a flight than a retreat. They had surrounded the gate with huge chunks of wood as well as with straw and coated with pitch, which was set on fire at the arrival of the Prussians.

Exelmans' Dragoons

Exelmans' corps was the vanguard for Grouchy's retreat. His corps was the strongest command Grouchy had. Yet frustratingly, we know very little about what Exelmans did in the campaign after the battle of Ligny. His command drops out of history for more than twenty-four hours, into which vacuum, many historians had endeavoured to fill with half-truths, myth and rumour.

What the archive documents do show, is that Exelmans' men were the 'eyes and ears' for Grouchy on 17 June, and on 18 June, whilst Grouchy's infantry was toiling through the mud, Exelmans' cavalry had overtaken the Prussian rear-guard not very far from Wavre itself. Reporting this to Grouchy, General Exelmans noted that:[4]

On 18 June, my troops were ordered to march in the morning. I was
ready to move at about half-past seven o'clock, but with no light
cavalry it was not until about nine o'clock I found behind Mazy
the rear-guard of the Prussian army, on the road to Wavre at the
height of Moustier, and almost simultaneously observed a convoy
escorted by a few thousand men near the tavern *A Tous Vents*,
which appeared to be heading towards Louvain, but I was moving
as to bring concentrate my force on the Dyle. I formed my troops
in a wooded ravine to the left, near the farm of Plaquerie, and the
right on Neufsar.

Some of Exelmans' dragoons were spotted at Mont-Saint-Guibert by
the Prussians and were driven off. von Falckenhausen's men of the 3rd
Regiment of Silesian Landwehr Cavalry took twenty-eight prisoners.[5]
However, a wood and village would have blocked Exelmans' view of
Cabaret A Tout Vent, so clearly it seems this information was passed
to him from Bonnemains, as we shall see later. Berton's brigade was
deployed on the Namur to Louvain road, with the 17 June chasing
Bülow's rear-guard.[6]

Grouchy without light cavalry, had to rely on Exelmans' Dragoons
for reconnaissance. What Grouchy needed for the task at hand was
light cavalry, but the Emperor had robbed him of the vast majority
of his light cavalry. Mazy, in theory, is situated about six miles south
of Gembloux. Did Exelmans really swing that far south? 'Neufsar' is
Neuf Sart and has hardly changed since 18 June 1815. Moustier, or
Mousty, based on the Ferraris map, is just south of Ottignies. *Cabaret
A Tout Vent* is on the outskirts of Dion-le-Mont, on its eastern side at
the crossroads of the chemin de Tout Vent and Chaussée de Huy. The
building no longer stands. There is no wood to the right (east) of Neuf
Sart, assuming he was heading north, when we look at the Ferraris
map of 1777. So, we assume he was on the flat ground between Vieux-
Sart and the Sarats Wood. Louvain is to the north of Wavre and the
Louvain road heads to Louvain, and thence heads west to Brussels.
It also seems that Louvain-la-Neuve, which appears on the 1777 map
as Louvrange, which is south-east of Wavre, was the most logical
direction for the troops at *Cabaret A Tout Vent*. But for Exelmans, the
Prussians were seemingly heading north to Brussels or west to Wavre.
He must have observed that last element of Bülow's command heading
off to Waterloo.

The farm of La Plaquerie was due east of Ottignies by less than a
mile and is clearly shown on the 1777 Ferraris map. Thus, it seems
that Exelmans headed north through Helliers and Mont-Saint-Guibert,
so to have the farm of La Plaquerie to his left and Neuf Sart to the

right. Perhaps he stood at the farm of De Biereux which a few hundred metres due south of where La Baraque was.

Historian Tim Clayton states that it was at this point that Exelmans suggested to cross the Dyle there and advance to Saint-Lambert. He presents no new evidence.[7] The endless repetition of the same myths of Waterloo does not make the study of those fateful days of June 1815 any easier for the historian. Exelmans is not only writing fifteen years later, but also seems to be writing the case for what should have been done, rather than what was done. His recollections are coloured by misgivings and hindsight that cannot be corroborated by any other source, seemingly yet more 'false memory'. The issue of Grouchy not getting to Waterloo is still so emotive for many historians that, as we have seen, moving away from the current paradigm is impossible for many. Hyde-Kelly[8] and A. F. Becke[9] failed in their analysis of Grouchy as they wrote tempered by hindsight and overtly influenced by the propaganda of the Emperor. It is easy to say, in 2017 (or 1830 for that matter), what Grouchy should have done, but we must judge him on what he knew on 18 June 1815 and how he acted upon what he knew.

It seems Exelmans only had with him Strolz's division, as Bonnemains seems to have been sent off to Perwez. Clearly Strolz's division had headed north from Gembloux and Bonnemains had headed to Perwez. Berton had headed even further north-east. General Berton claims the corps were initially sent to the Namur-Louvain road via Nil-Saint-Vincent and that they approached the farm at 14.00 hours.[10] General Bonnemains' report notes:[11]

> The 18th, the corps of dragoons of General Exelmans was united at seven o'clock in the morning at Valhain [*sic*] and took the road to Wavre. Around nine o'clock he found himself in the presence of many Prussian advance guards composed of all arms and we set in motion a movement to reconnoitre them. We had to withdraw about a league from the place and wait for the arrival of Marshal Grouchy with the army corps of Pajol, Vandamme and Gérard. They joined us between one or two o'clock in the afternoon. At this moment, we heard a terrible cannonade from the direction of Waterloo before the Prussian avant-garde was attacked by the army corps of Vandamme that chased them into Wavre and beyond the Dyle. From that moment, and for the rest of the day, the corps of Exelmans remained in reserve.

However, another eyewitness states:[12]

> The 2nd Corps of cavalry, consisting of 4,000 men commanded by General Exelmans, discovered the rear-guard of the Prussians

74

near a place called Baraque at about ten o'clock in the morning. General Exelmans brought his cavalry to the Dyle, ready to pass that river when, at about twelve, the marshal arrived with General Vandamme's corps and gave orders to march upon Wavre; this he did, after Exelmans had defeated the rear-guard of the Prussian army, which were from 8,000 to 10,000 men.

To the east were Vandamme and 3rd Corps, which we assume now swung north-west to head to Wavre once Grouchy had been made aware of this news. Clearly, Grouchy correctly now assumed that the Prussians that had been at Perwez had gone via Wavre to join Wellington instead of heading to Brussels. With the true line of Prussian movements only discovered towards midday, if not later, he could not have headed off to Wavre at daybreak, as all he knew for fact was of a body of Prussians at Wavre, some at Perwez and others moving from Namur. Grouchy headed off with his staff to join Exelmans. He then described his own subsequent movements as follows:[13]

> I joined General Exelmans, who since morning had been close behind the extreme rear-guard of the Prussian cavalry, and at half-past eleven, a league and a half from Wavre, finally we found a rear-guard consisting of infantry with cannon. As soon as I had carried out my reconnaissance the cannonade began, and General Vandamme, arriving with the head of his infantry, marched to the Prussians, pushed them back, took the position of Limalette Wood, and there they were immediately attacked and overthrown: the cavalry of General Exelmans, by turning to the right and passing the wood, pushed on to Bas-Wavre. We followed the enemy strongly, and between one and two o'clock in the afternoon we were masters of that part of the town on the left bank of the Dyle.

This is corroborated by de Blocqueville, one of Grouchy's aide-de-camps:[14]

> The marshal, having joined the dragoons of General Exelmans, who were in the presence of a Prussian rear-guard, began the attack, pushed them back and they were forced to retreat to Wavre.

Another eye-witness stated:[15]

> The orders of the Marshal were; to march upon the army of the enemy, so as to prevent the junction between Wellington and Blücher. He arrived, to carry that object into effect, at Gembloux on the 17, which the Prussian army had quitted about twelve noon for Wavre. The Marshal left Gembloux with his army on the morning of the 18th, to find out the Prussians, and to fight

them. The second corps of cavalry, consisting of 4,000 men, commanded by General Exelmans, discovered the rear guard of the Prussians, near a place called Baraque, at about ten o'clock in the morning. General Exelmans brought his cavalry to the Dyle, ready to pass that river, when at about twelve the Marshal arrived with General Vandamme's corps and gave orders to march upon Wavre; this he did, after Exelmans had defeated the rear-guard of the Prussian army, which were from eight to ten thousand men.

But after midday where was Exelmans? He had attacked at La Baraque around mid-day on 18 June, and by morning 19 June was at Limale. Seemingly Bonnemains' brigade had reached as far north as Ottenbourg by morning of 19 June. General Berton caustically noted about the failure of the attacks at Wavre as follows:[16]

> We all marched on Wavre, without even acknowledging the bridge of Moustier, we remained for a part of the day to throw ourselves back and forth, against a formidable position beyond a river, where anywhere else we should have already been able to cross without having to fire a single shot. But we led successive attacks of infantry against the bridge of Wavre and the mill of Bièrge, where we lost a lot of people unnecessarily against the only two points that the enemy could defend with advantage. Four-fifths of our infantry could not be brought into action before Wavre, and eighteen regiments of cavalry were doing nothing, and partly thrown to the rear right where there was nobody, because, independently of the corps of Pajol which was in Tourrinnes, I received orders to send a regiment of my brigade (the 17th of dragons, Colonel Labiffe), to reconnoitre the road from Louvain to Namur, and the means to properly ensure that the right and rear of this Prussian corps had crossed the Dyle.

Yet where was the rest of Exelmans' Corps? Why had Grouchy issued him no orders? Why had Exelmans not shown initiative and asked for orders? This was the biggest failing of Grouchy on 18 June – not using his resources more effectively. Clearly some of the dragoons had been at Chyse, where they reported Prussian troops, which was in reality the Prussian IV Corps, which we know the French followed towards Ottenberg.

Berton's brigade may still have been on the Namur to Louvain road. What Exelmans' corps did in the intervening period we have no information. Without further research, we simply do not know.

Exelmans is also to blame for not taking the initiative, the key may well lie in the muster lists for the officers and men of Exelmans' Corps. The big question is, where was Exelmans? Grouchy's failure on the 18 June was in not using his resources as well as he could have done in relation to his cavalry force. Can casualty data shed more light on what happened?

Losses in the 1st Division were as follows:

Regiment	Killed		Wounded		Missing		Total
	Officers	Men	Officers	Men	Officers	Men	
5th Dragoons[17]	1	0	2	0	0	1	4
13th Dragoons[18]	0	0	4	0	0	0	4
15th Dragoons[19]	0	0	0	0	0	0	0
20th Dragoons[20]	0	0	0	1	0	1	2
Total	1	0	6	1	0	2	10

What is striking in the above, is that four officers in the 13th Dragoons were wounded. Were they picked off by Prussian snipers? If so, where was the regiment? Captain Pierre Quinton suffered a gunshot wound to the left leg.[21] Arguably the 5th and 13th at some stage got involved with Prussians, likeswise the 20th. The very low losses suggest clashes of scouting parties rather than an any major fighting.

Losses in the 2nd Division were as follows:

Regiment	Killed		Wounded		Missing		Total
	Officers	Men	Officers	Men	Officers	Men	
4th Dragoons[22]	0	0	0	0	0	0	0
12th Dragoons[23]	0	0	0	0	0	1	1
14th Dragoons[24]	0	0	0	0	0	1	1
17th Dragoons[25]	0	0	0	0	0	0	0
Total	0	0	0	0	0	2	2

The loss of just two men missing, MAT No. 656 Joseph Godeffe of the 12th dragoons and POW MAT No. 481 Jean Baptiste Lemaitre, 6th Company 14th Dragoons, suggests that for the bulk of 18 June, Exelmans' dragoons did nothing. Not utilising this cavalry force was a massive blunder by Grouchy and Exelmans. The cavalry could have headed along the Louvain road pursing the Prussians, or as Exelmans says in hindsight, got to Waterloo by other means. Be that is it may, it seems Exelmans contented himself with letting his men rest after their exertions of the previous seventy-two hours. Losses were very light indeed for the cavalry. When we compare the losses to Ligny, the difference is all the more marked. Losses in the division were as follows:

Regiment	Killed		Wounded		Missing		Total
	Officers	Men	Officers	Men	Officers	Men	
5th Dragoons[26]	0	8	7	9	0	1	25
13th Dragoons[27]	0	0	0	3	0	4	7
15th Dragoons[28]	0	0	0	0	0	0	0
20th Dragoons[29]	0	0	0	2	0	0	2
Total	0	8	7	14	0	5	34

From the table it is clear that the 5th Dragoons took the brunt of the fighting in the 1st Brigade and the 15th Dragoons seem, for whatever reason, to have sat out the fighting. Perhaps also the 20th Dragoons did not fight? Why did Strolz not commit all his command? Was he ordered not to do so by Exelmans? Was he being cautious in not wanting to commit all his men and kept back a reserve? Possibly, as we remember only half of the 3rd Cavalry Corps was in action on 16 June, but perhaps for a very different reason, one of reliability and loyalty. In previous years Exelmans had a reputation as a bold and aggressive field commander but, for whatever reason, his performance in 1815 was markedly more tentative and more cautious. It is, however, fair to say he lacked tactical aptitude. Losses in 2nd Division were:

Regiment	Killed		Wounded		Missing		Total
	Officers	Men	Officers	Men	Officers	Men	
4th Dragoons[30]	0	7	12	7	0	5	31
12th Dragoons[31]	0	1	9	6	0	1	17
14th Dragoons[32]	0	0	5	0	0	0	5
17th Dragoons[33]	1	0	7	0	0	0	8
Total	1	8	33	13	0	6	61

By the morning of 19 June, Exelmans' men were widely dispersed along the River Dyle. The dragoons formed the van-guard and rear-guard of the retreat to Namur. About the retreat, as he remembered it, General Berton wrote:[34]

> Seven regiments of dragoons from Exelmans' corps, with the wounded and the reserve artillery, marched quickly to capture the bridge at Namur, over the River Sambre, and entered the city the same day at four o'clock. The infantry had remained in position in front of Wavre until midnight, supported on his right by the cavalry corps of General Pajol, on his left by the division under General Vallin; the 20th Regiment of Dragoons, from the corps of Exelmans, marched with the central columns.
>
> The infantry reached Namur on the 20th in the morning, after having fought several bloody battles with the very Prussians who were following them with ardour, and against which the 20th Dragoons, commanded by Colonel Bricqueville, had made some fine charges, captured two guns which had been abandoned and had been for some time been in enemy hands, and also took a howitzer.
>
> Teste's division remained in charge of defending the city, which they did without cannon until six in the evening against the 3rd Prussian Corps, which lost in vain nearly three thousand men. Teste did not leave until everyone in Namur had been evacuated and that the heights of Bouvigne and Dinant had been occupied by our troops.

Berton clearly identifies the 20th Dragoons and six more regiments. The 2nd Cavalry Corps had eight regiments. Which regiment was not with the corps? Seemingly the 12th were the advanced-guard. Certainly the 20th Dragoons headed to Namur, but it seems others headed off in different directions.

Strung out far in front, as Grouchy's advance guard, were General Bonnemains and his dragoons. He was tasked with securing the line of retreat. From Dinant, he sent the following dispatch:[35]

> General Dumonceau, Commander of the 2nd Military District.
>
> I write to you with agreeable news. My troops will arrive in front of Dinant about midday, where we shall be joined by Marshal Grouchy and the corps under his orders which arrived from Namur. It is important that from this position we try and contact the Emperors headquarters and the location of his army.

Bonnemains with the 4th and 12th Dragoons was heading to Givet, and he sent the following dispatch to General Bourke who was placed in command of Givet-Charlemont at the start of the Hundred Days.[36]

> Dinant 20 June 1815
>> M. General
>> [mostly illegible] I arrived at Dinant about midday, where I was joined by Marshal Grouchy and his corps under his orders which arrived from Namur. It is important that from this position we try and contact the Emperor's headquarters and the location of his army. [illegible] please send any news have you received to the Marshal and also of their movements and orders.

General Bonnemains, in his report to General Chastel, wrote:[37]

> General Bonnemains, being charged by Marshal Grouchy and General Exelmans to use all means to get information on the progress of the Emperor and the army, could not get anything positive in the immediate area. He formed small parties to send messengers to Philippeville and Givet.
> The first was intercepted by the enemy and the second was not and resulted in the response of the general commanding Givet and from the Duc de Dalmatie for rallying the various corps.
> Everyone in France believed Grouchy had lost his army. General Dumonceau, commanding Givet, sent the letter from General Bonnemains to the Minister of War without delay, where the news was read to the Chamber and made a great sensation.

Alas we don't have Chastel's reply, but some of it was clearly about enemy troop positions as General Bonnemains sent the following dispatch to General Chastel from Dinant on 20 June:[38]

> I received your news and I passed around the flank with a troop of cavalry to arrive in front of Dinant, arriving there about midday, where Marshal Comte de Grouchy will also be with the army corps under his command from Namur, and where he will establish his headquarters, and will send to the Emperor the dispositions of the army.

Clearly, Bonnemains had headed south from Namur, via Profondeville, and thence to Dinant, and was moving onwards to Givet. Bonnemains, writing from Dinant, sent the following dispatch to General Bourke, commanding the garrison at Givet, advising him of the arrival of Grouchy's forces:[39]

> I am informing you that my troops arrived at Dinant sometime after midday, and that Marshal Comte de Grouchy is at Namur with the army cops under his orders. [Illegible] I will send you news concerning the arrival of the marshal and the movements he had ordered.

General Vincent, at Givet no doubt with the 15th and 20th dragoons, sent the following dispatch to the Emperor at 21.00 hours:[40]

> I have the pleasure to inform Your Majesty that General Exelmans had departed Namur at midday and his head of column is heading to Givet. These comprise the dragoons, the corps of General Pajol, as well as the 3rd and 4th Infantry Corps, which have been ordered to debouch from Namur. The enemy pursued General Vandamme to Namur. At the moment of his departure from that town, a part of his artillery and dragoons passed through a defile with the division of Abert [sic], they have not sustained any great loss, but a good number are wounded.
>
> Generals Abert and Gérard are wounded; they were in the rear and are prisoners.

So, we know Vincent was at Namur, as was Berton with the 14th and 17th Dragoons, Bonnemains was heading south, this leaves Burthe's command, the 5th and 13th Dragoons unaccounted for. Losses in the 1st Division for the fighting at Namur, were as follows:

Regiment	Killed		Wounded		Missing		Total
	Officers	Men	Officers	Men	Officers	Men	
5th Dragoons[41]	0	0	0	1	0	2	3
13th Dragoons[42]	0	0	0	2	0	8	10
15th Dragoons[43]	0	0	0	0	0	0	0
20th Dragoons[44]	0	3	0	6	0	17	26
Total	0	3	0	9	0	27	39

The 2nd Division lost:

Regiment	Killed		Wounded		Missing		Total
	Officers	Men	Officers	Men	Officers	Men	
4th Dragoons[45]	0	0	0	0	0	0	0
12th Dragoons[46]	0	0	0	0	0	2	2
14th Dragoons[47]	0	0	0	0	0	1	1
17th Dragoons[48]	No meaningful data recorded						
Total	0	0	0	0	0	3	3

Losses were very light indeed for the cavalry at Namur.

Namur

The local population of Namur were not immune to the fighting that was taking place. One resident wrote:[49]

> For two days we have been here in a precarious situation, which is hard to describe. After the battle, which had been lost by the French, the army corps which had directed itself towards Wavre saw itself cut off and forced to lay down its arms, or to cut itself a path, which latter it chose to do. On the 19th in the afternoon, the French 12th Dragoons Regiment arrived in front of our gates and asked to pass through to Givet. Due to the civilians lacking any troops, they were obliged to receive it. This regiment was followed by a great number of dispersed soldiers and, above all, the wounded. On the 20th, the entire army corps successively arrived. Among the generals in command, it was noticed was: Marshal Grouchy, Vandamme, Exelmans, Bonnet, Vincent and some others; all these troops were made up of old soldiers. Towards one o'clock they began to defile across the Sambre bridge, during which a very lively cannonade and musketry fire took place at the Brussels gate. The enemy placed several guns on the ramparts and positioned three battalions to cover the retreat; there the enemy defended himself until the evening. Towards eight o'clock the Pomeranians forced a breakthrough and attacked the French within our walls; from the Brussels Gate up to the Sambre bridge one fought ferociously in the streets, which were covered with dead and wounded. One is bound by justice to mention that General Vandamme on this occasion spared our city. But the following event needs to be made public: during the heat of the battle, the Prussians urged General Pirck [*sic*] to attack the town and take it by force, but the brave general replied he loved the inhabitants too much to befall this terrible disaster upon them. His Pomeranians, who had been in garrison there, cheered for the generous decision of their general. It is thus that one receives the reward if one treats brave soldiers with esteem. The French took all the letters and the newspapers from the post with them, before leaving us.

As General Berton notes, on the march from Wavre to Namur the 22nd Regiment of Line Infantry and other elements of 3rd Corps did not arrive until the very early hours of 20 June. Namur was not gained without a fight, as Colonel Fantin des Odoards wrote:[50]

> Already we could see the heights of Namur, which would offer us a good stronghold, when suddenly two cannon shots were heard in our rear. This sound pleases the soldier when he attacks the enemy and it brightens every face, but in retreat, and in the state of mind that we had since the loss of Waterloo, which was no longer a

mystery to our subordinates, it produced an effect exactly opposite: 'There they are!' anxiously said the same men who three days before had faced the Prussians with ardour. The rear-guard, after two shots had been fired against them, was charged impetuosity and was at first thrown into disorder and the two cannon they had were captured.

Luckily the panic did not spread and was soon repaired. Part of our column arrived, who moved to Namur at the run, and the troops who were at the rear about-faced. A brilliant charge by our cavalry on the Prussian advance guard tumbled it back and not only captured the canon that we had lost, but also took one of their howitzers. The beginning was a good omen. Surprised by an unexpected resistance, the Prussians stopped to reinforce those who followed them, and we used their hesitation to take strong positions in Namur and to place the artillery wherever it could be used. We barricaded the bridges, the gates and then did everything to stop the enemy.

Captain Jean Marie Putigny, of 2nd Battalion 33rd Regiment of Line Infantry (part of 3rd Corps), narrated:[51]

Our corps moved to a position in front of Namur to protect the retreat of Comte Gérard, who passed through our lines and entered into the town. We followed progressively after we had sustained an attack from the enemy. My battalion was at the extremity of the rear-guard, placed on a road that passed through the orchards and gardens of the suburbs. The English [sic Prussians] charged with great obstinacy.

The battalion commander was killed, the captain, an old soldier, also. I took command and I remained so until the end. A spent ball hit me in my right leg. Limping, and with my left arm in a sling, I was isolated by the charge, and was stuck in a hollow by the walls. I was fighting against two redcoats who were impossible to break. I defended myself and fought furiously. The larger of the two was a lieutenant of the Guards, he sneered, his boot just missed me and gathering all my remaining strength, thrust at his face, and sent this insolent subject of His Gracious Majesty to God's heaven. He was the last of the enemy that I had killed with my hands on the field of battle. My grenadiers dragged me off, and we closed the heavy gates of Namur in the face of the attackers.

In the early hours of 20 June, the 30th Regiment of Line Infantry arrived at Namur, as Captain François reported:

In the night we crossed Gembloux. At five o'clock in the morning, we stopped on the road from Charleroi to Namur, dying of hunger and fatigue and pursued by the Prussians. The sappers of the 30th found three cattle on a farm, but when they were about to distribute the meat, our generals learned that the Prussians had passed the Sambre. Marshal Grouchy Instructed General Bonnemains to stand fast against them with two regiments of dragoons, and we resumed our march on Namur.

The 30th formed the rear-guard and we had not yet left the scene of the halt when we were attacked. We were forced to abandon our meat, we upturned our cooking pots and we formed into line of battle. The Prussians departed, seeing our defensive movements, but they returned and closely followed us as we marched forward, and they began to bombard us with artillery when we reached the heights, which were about three-quarters of a league from Namur. We answered their artillery with our own.

We, as well as the 96th, formed into squares, and we continued our march towards Namur, alone on the road. The 30th is no stronger than three platoons which were formed into two squares. The Prussian cavalry charged us three times … We marched slowly, often stopping and facing the front until the Prussian cavalry were between ten and fifteen paces away, then stopped and fired in two ranks. In this manner, we gained Namur, where the other regiments of the division were formed. Here, we were selected to support the retirement of the division of General Teste. After various manoeuvres in columns of attack, we entered the city, while General Teste prepared its defences to stop the enemy at the gates of Namur. We camped on the road to Dinant.

Sub-Lieutenant Gerbet, of the 37th Regiment of Line Infantry, notes that at Namur Marshal Grouchy advantageously placed his artillery and advance guard to defend the town. The 37th Regiment of Line Infantry was formed in square to receive the enemy cavalry charges, which attacked, but without success and left many dead on the field of battle. Vandamme's command, he noted, entered and passed through Namur, and the rear-guard was formed from General Teste's command, which fended off the Prussians and forced them to abandon the attack.[52]

Wounded with 4th Corps that day, under General Pecheaux, were officers of the 30th Regiment of Line Infantry. In the attacks, the regiment lost one officer killed (Captain Villeminot) and two wounded (Captain Plancon and Lieutenant-Adjutant-Major Pierre Charles Desfontaines). At Ligny, Desfontaines took a musket ball to the right leg, as well as a bruise to the kidneys. He had recovered from these wounds sufficiently to remain with the regiment and fought at Namur, where he suffered a contusion from a canister shot to the right leg.[53]

In terms of other ranks lost, five men were wounded and four were taken prisoner.[54] The brigaded 96th Regiment of Line Infantry lost two officers killed (Captain Ozenne and Lieutenant Fauville) and two officers wounded (Lieutenants Lefort and Ollivero de Rubianca). The regiment had ten men wounded.[55]

Grouchy had conducted a textbook withdrawal from Wavre. A vigorous defence of the town by General Teste enabled Grouchy to withdraw the majority of his command. From Namur, he endeavoured to link up with Marshal Soult and the remnants of the Armée du Nord.

Grouchy still held Namur on the afternoon of 20 June. Sometime that day, he issued the following order to General Vandamme about the evacuation of the place:[56]

> When you evacuate Namur, my dear general, I want you to come to take a position on the side of the suburb of Dinant, and that you stay here long enough for the town to be evacuated. I intend to push up tomorrow to Charlemont, and if denied, the outer edges of Namur and Dinant, where you will easily stop the enemy who has only cavalry, and I hope that, without significant loss, we will win Charlemont.
>
> I ordered the cavalry of General Pajol keep our right flank, and to gather news about what is going on in Charleroi, if possible.
>
> If the troops are too tired, they will take a halt before arriving at Charlemont.
>
> Do not forget to give orders to the division of Teste.
>
> Marshal Grouchy.
>
> P. S. There are three gates in Namur, please send infantry sentries and order them that the gates are held as long as necessary.
>
> I've barricaded the bridges over the Meuse and Sambre, which should also be defended before leaving the city.

Franz Lieber, of the Prussian Kohlberg Regiment, was part of the attacking force:[57]

> Half our army corps, to which I belonged, received orders to pursue Vanamere [sic], who had thrown himself into Namur. We marched the whole of the 19th; the heat was excessive, and our exhaustion and thirst so great that two men of our regiment became deranged in consequence. At four in the afternoon we went into bivouac; we started early again, and now my strength forsook me, I could not keep up with the troops, and began to lag behind. Suddenly, at about noon, I head the first guns. The Battle of Namur had begun. When I arrived where my regiment stood, or, as I should rather say, the little band representing it, I dropped down; but fortunately, one

of my comrades had some eggs, one of which he gave me, gave me great strength.

Our colonel came up to us saying: 'Riflemen, you have twice fought like the oldest of soldiers, I have no more to say. This wood is to be cleared; be steady bugler, the signa!' and off we went with a great hurrah! Driving off the French before us down a hill toward Namur, which lay on our front.

When I saw our men rushing too fast down the hill, I was afraid that the same enemies might be hid under the precipice to receive them. Holding onto a tree with my left hand, I looked over the precipice and saw about seven Frenchmen. They will hit me, I thought, and, turning around to call to our solders, I suddenly experienced a sensation as if my whole body was compressed into my head; the feeling overwhelmed me. It was a most painful sensation. After some time, I was able to open my eyes, or to see again with them. I found myself on the ground; over me stood a soldier firing at the enemy. I strained every nerve to ask, though in broken words, whether I was wounded and if so, where. 'You are shot through the neck.' I begged him to shoot me; the idea of dying miserably of hunger, half of my wounds, alone in the wood overpowered me. He of course, refused, spoke a word of comfort that perhaps I might be saved, and soon after he received a shot through both knees, in consequence he died in hospital…

My thirst was beyond description; it was a feverish burning. I thought I should die and prayed for … a speedy end of my sufferings. I received a second ball, which, entering my chest, gave me more local pain than the first; I thought God had granted my fervent prayer. I perceived, as I supposed, that the ball had pierced my lung and tried to breathe to hasten my death. A week afterward, while I still lay with my two wounds in a house in Liège, one of my brothers was in the hospital in Brussels and another at Aix-le-Chapelle.

About the evacuation of Namur, General Teste reported to Marshal Grouchy on 20 June 1815 as follows:[58]

In accordance with the orders that you gave me on the 19th, before leaving Namur, to hold with my division, this place until six o'clock the next day to allow time for the army and its equipment to operate, without being harassed by the enemy, their retirement through the valley of the Meuse, via Civet, I hastened to be informed of the condition of this important position and that before and during the night, I was told that I was to close and barricade, where possible, the gaps and openings of the square, so as to defend the access with the men under my command.

My arrangements were hardly completed when on the morning of the 20th, a Prussian corps of 12,000 to 15,000 men appeared before Namur to seize it by force. This attack, made with vigour, mainly on the iron gate where I had two companies of grenadiers of the 75th, was repulsed; the enemy left many dead in ditches. It was bombarded [by the enemy's artillery] from afar, until noon, when another attempt was made by the Prussians, and had the same result.

At three o'clock the enemy appeared more and more fierce; the men seemed to have drunk a lot of spirits, even the officers, who threw themselves on our bayonets at our barricades. The attackers retreated at half-past four, leaving the approaches to the place littered with their dead.

Instead of starting my retreat at six o'clock, I delayed until eight, and disputing the ground inch-by-inch, I waited for the enemy on the other side of the Sambre, where I had placed in houses which I had loopholed, my two companies of sappers ... At half-past eight, I occupied the position that I had prepared at the gate of France, under which I had placed a pile of faggots, which was set on fire, to impede the move of artillery to this point, and further delay the enemy.

I write this letter from the bivouacs of Profondeville, having marched very slowly and without being pursued by the enemy.

The Prussians must have had, in the deadly day of yesterday, 4,000 to 5,000 men out of action: we had only thirteen killed and forty-seven wounded.

General Teste had held back the Prussians to allow 3rd and 4th Corps to evacuate the place. Later the same day, Marshal Grouchy sent his formal report to Napoléon about his operations:[59]

Temploux 19 June 1815
Marshal Grouchy to the Emperor

It was not until after seven in the evening of 18 June that I received the letter of the Duc de Dalmatie, which directed me to march on to Saint-Lambert, and to attack General Bülow. I fell in with the enemy as I was marching on Wavre. He was immediately driven into Wavre, and General Vandamme's corps attacked that town, and was warmly engaged. The portion of Wavre, on the right of the Dyle, was carried, but much difficulty was experienced in debouching on the other side. General Girard was wounded by a ball in the breast while endeavouring to carry the mill of Bièrges in order to pass the river, but in which he did not succeed, and Lieutenant-General Aix had been killed in the attack on the town.

In this state of things, being impatient to co-operate with Your Majesty's army on that important day, I detached several corps to force the passage of the Dyle and march against Bülow. The corps of Vandamme, in the meantime, maintained the attack on Wavre and on the mill, whence the enemy showed an intention to debouch, but which I did not conceive he was capable of effecting. I arrived at Limale, passed the river, and the division of Vichery and the cavalry carried the heights. Night did not permit us to advance farther, and I no longer heard the cannon on the side where Your Majesty was engaged.

I halted in this situation until daylight. Both Wavre and Bièrges were occupied by the Prussians, who, at three in the morning of the 18th, attacked in their turn, wishing to take advantage of the difficult position in which I was, and expecting to drive me into the defile and take the artillery which had debouched, and make me re-pass the Dyle. Their efforts were fruitless. The Prussians were repulsed, and the village of Bièrges taken. The brave General Penne was killed.

General Vandamme then passed one of his divisions by Bièrges, and carried with ease the heights of Wavre, and along the whole of my line the success was complete. I was in front of Rosierne, preparing to march on Brussels, when I received the sad intelligence of the loss of the Battle of Waterloo. The officer who brought it informed me that Your Majesty was retreating on the Sambre, without being able to indicate any particular point on which I should direct my march.

I ceased to pursue and began my retrograde movement. The retreating enemy did not think of following me. Learning that the enemy had already passed the Sambre, and was on my flank, and not being sufficiently strong to make a diversion in favour of Your Majesty, without compromising that which I commanded, I marched on Namur. At this moment, the rear of the columns was attacked. That of the left made a retrograde movement sooner than was expected, which endangered for a moment the retreat of the left, but good dispositions soon repaired everything, and two pieces which had been taken were recovered by the brave 20th Dragoons, who besides took a howitzer from the enemy.

We entered Namur without loss. The long defile which extends from this place to Dinant, in which only a single column can march, and the embarrassment arising from the numerous transports of the wounded, rendered it necessary to hold for a considerable time the town in which I had not the means of blowing up the bridge. I entrusted the defence of Namur to General Vandamme, who, with his usual intrepidity, maintained himself there until eight in the evening; so that nothing was left behind, and I occupied Dinant.

The enemy has lost some thousands of men in the attack on Namur, where the contest was very obstinate; the troops have performed their duty in a manner worthy of praise.

The retreat of Grouchy from Wavre, via Namur, upon Dinant was executed in a skilful and masterly manner, as was the defence of Namur by General Teste.[60] At 23.00 hours on the 20th, Grouchy issued the following movement orders for the next day:[61]

Dinant, 20 June, eleven o'clock in the evening.

I am sending herewith, my dear general, the order of march for tomorrow, and ask you to give consideration those that concern you and give orders as necessary.

I also recommend that you keep, if possible, clear of the village of Rouvines, I expect that there would be a great congestion here, for almost all day tomorrow would be required to pass through it.

Movement Orders:

At 2 in the morning on the 21st, all the waggons which contain the wounded are to depart for Charlemont, where under the care of the *ordannateurs* of 3rd and 4th Corps and the *ordannateur* of the cavalry they will be admitted to hospital. If insufficient hospitals exist, then the wounded are to be lodged in private houses, where they will be afforded all the help that their suffering for the Fatherland demands.

All other vehicles are to march behind them and the park is to be established on the glacis of Givet. Any other vehicle that has not left Dinant by 3 in the morning and is found in the columns, is to be turned over and made unusable.

General Exelmans' cavalry is to leave the village that it occupied near Dinant at 6 in the morning and to take up cantonments around Givet on the right bank of the Meuse. If these villages need infantry for their defence due to their location, it is to be provided. The villages in the rear of Givet are to be allocated to General Exelmans' corps.

General Pajol's cavalry is to depart at 7 in the morning from the cantonments they occupied since last night and are to take up position behind Lelle stream. They are not to deploy in line until the column head of 4th Corps has arrived; then it is to deploy to Givet, which it will pass through to occupy the left bank of the Meuse.

The 4th Corps will start at five in the morning to make the banks of the stream of Lelle, where it will continue its movement until Givet, and their make camp.

The 3rd Corps, of which Teste's division is part, is to continue to be the rear-guard. It will hold as well as possible the village of Rouvines and at the entrance to Dinant and will defend the approaches as well as it can. It will be important to keep the defensible positions between Dinant and Givet, disputing the ground inch-by-inch, to ensure in this way the return of the wounded of the army into the fortress.

At night, the 3rd Corps will also occupy the camp. M. General-in-Chief Vandamme will appoint one or two regiments of his corps to form the garrison of the city.

All parks and artillery of each corps, other than that belonging to each division, will start at four o'clock, and will not stop at Givet.

Sometime the same day, Dumonceau wrote to Davout in Paris:[62]

Mezieres 20 June
In executing the orders of the Emperor, Marshal Count Grouchy has left here at 9 o'clock in the morning heading to Givet with around 1,000 National Guardsmen and 2 pieces of artillery to occupy Namur, not long after an officer arrived from Charleroi with news from the army about the disaster that has occurred,

I am determined to hold Mezieres with the two battalions of National Guard that the Emperor ordered to remain here … I received at 10 o'clock this morning a letter, a copy of which I attach to this letter to your excellency, concerning the emplacement and movements of the soldiers to Launay, Rhetel and Reims on the orders of the Major-General … Since around 3 o'clock this morning a considerable number of cavalry has passed here … General [Baron Martin-Alexis] Gobrecht is amongst the wounded and 200 to 300 cavalrymen have been rallied.

On 1 July Gobrecht sent word to Davout:[63]

I have the honour to write to your excellency to refute the accusation that has been expressed for my absence from Paris that I am a traitor: It is for reasons of my health and no other reason, having been trapped under my horse when it was killed at the battle of Mont-Saint-Jean.

Colonel Decaster, who is with me, also suffers still. I realise I am absent from my brigade without obtaining permission from your excellency.

Chapter 9

20 June 1815: Soult rallies the Armée du Nord

The scattered remains of the French army that had fought at Waterloo was fleeing along the various roads from Charleroi, moving towards Avesnes, Laon and Philippeville. Marshal Soult wrote to Napoléon on 20 June from Rocroy, informing him of the strength of the army:[1]

> When I departed from Philippeville, yesterday evening, I had with me 1,200 men from the Old Guard, 5 or 600 men from the infantry of the army, and 800 cavalry, Chasseurs à Cheval, dragoons and cuirassiers, and there remained in the environs of the town around 10,000 men, part of which headed to Mezieres and part to Rocroy via Laon, and part of the troops were headed in the direction of Beaumont. In the rear of the second column are 1,000 to 1,200 men of the infantry of the Old Guard, I estimate that there are 3,000 men from the Old Guard.
> I have not seen any men from the cavalry of the Guard.

Soult continues, noting:[2]

> Many of the soldiers are without arms, a great number of cavalry men are without horses. I also attest that a great number of horses for the artillery train are missing.

Here at Rocroi, Soult began to concentrate the wreck of the army. The troops were still widely dispersed, and still no orders had been sent to 1st Corps, 6th Corps or the Cavalry. Theobald Puvis, nevertheless, narrates the scene on the following day with some positivity:[3]

> The 20th, some order is beginning to appear. The evening with my captain, taking advantage of the neighbourhood where there was a big farm where we had spent several days during the cantonments

which preceded the opening of the campaign, we rested overnight in the farm, and on the 21st we re-joined the regiment, which had stopped near a village on the road. In our gathering, some officers of the 93rd reviewed the events of recent days. How we missed our comrades who had fallen on the battlefield on the morning of 18th? We had an effective strength of more than two thousand men in our four battalions, we found ourselves with only twelve hundred men and the strongest portion was our fourth battalion, which had suffered the least because of its service with the park reserve artillery.

An un-known French general – thought to be Baron Albert Louis Emmanuel Fouler Comte de Relinque, Grand Equerry to the Emperor – wrote the following report to Marshal Davout, dated Avesnes, 20 June 1815:[4]

On the 18th, the Emperor attacked with the 2nd, 1st and 6th corps without success. In the evening a Prussian corps presented its self on our right and eventually seized the village of Plancenoit, while the Emperor, instead of evacuating the battlefield and taking a position by withdrawing his right, threw all his guard recklessly on the centre of the enemy in an operation which was unsuccessful and resulted in the rout being more complete because there were no troops that had not been in action. The rout continued until Laon and some of the soldiers returned to their homes.

The loss of our army in these four days is between 30 to 40,000 men and 200 guns. All the 2nd, 1st and 6th corps, as well as the guard, cannot present no more than 6,000 men and 20 cannons, and the cavalry, has barely 2,000 horses. There yet remains the 3rd and 4th Corps but they have suffered greatly at Fleurus. We cannot say as usual, that the consequences of this defeat is incalculable, but on the contrary, they must lead to the loss of the Emperor's throne and the annihilation of France.

He adds more about the state of the army in the following message to Davout:[5]

The ties of discipline are absolutely destroyed between the soldier and officers, and between the officers and their generals .... The stroke of the cane is not used in the army, so there is no way to punish the soldiers and it is necessary to remedy the inadequacy by means of the laws of the picket etc. There is much talk of honour and sentiment, but they are purely imaginary beings and so rare that no legislation should rely on them.

Looting has become so general that the soldiers see it as one of their rights. The General Officers are unable to prevent this even if they had wanted to. This is what has produced the habit of stampeding in the French army and what makes us rightly the object of scorn and hatred across Europe.

My job does not allow me to approach the Emperor, but I had the courage to present to him several times the vices of his army, but without success. It should not be that France should perish with him, we need to take prompt and vigorous measures to re-organise the army, and restore military honour otherwise, all is lost.

The Armée du Nord had collapsed. Soult moved off from Philippeville on the night of 19 June and arrived at Rocroy in the morning of the 20th. Clausewitz pointedly notes the following in his summary of the retreat and dissolution of the Armée du Nord:[6]

An army like the French, glorified by a string of victories over more than twenty years, which originally displayed the compact structure, the indestructibility, and, one could even say, the brilliance of a gem, whose courage and order were not dissolved or dissipated by mere danger in the blazing fire of battle, such an army, if the ennobling forces that gave it its crystalline structure are broken – its faith in its commander, in itself, and the sacred discipline of service – such an army flies in breathless terror before the sound of a drum, before a threat from its opponent that bordered on a joke.

The fighting capacity of the remains of the Armée du Nord with Marshal Soult and Prince Jerome was nil. The men only regained something of their former vigour and enthusiasm as they got closer to the walls of Paris. Marshal Soult was in command of a spent military force that could no longer defend itself.

Chapter 10

21 June 1815

Soult

The British Army under Wellington began its move onto Paris on 21 June, and at 02.00 hours, Soult wrote to Marshal Davout:[1]

> I have the honour to address Your Excellency with the locations where the rallying of the various corps must take place. Orders were given and sent off in in all directions to gather the troops and make them come together, but so far we have achieved only very limited success. Men escape as we rally them and they avoid places where they know they will be quartered. The cavalry is more docile, but in the infantry the lack of discipline is at its peak.
>
> Officers of various ranks do almost nothing to restore order, and perhaps they are acting in the opposite direction, and the word is spread among the soldiers, and I feared that after these considerations, it was required to take a point farther from the border to rally the army.

The Armée du Nord under Soult's command was demoralised and dis-organised. He informed Napoléon that:[2]

> The soldiers disappear in all directions. It was reported a column of these fugitives was heading to Mezieres and I ordered it to move to Laon. Since leaving Rocroy to move to Laon, I have encountered a lot of fugitives, and I expected to find in the latter place a large gathering of fugitives, but General Langeron, told me he had the same frustrations, that the men disappeared. However, General Flahaut told me that he had encountered a body of men on the road to Avesnes, and that they were to move to Soissons and Laon.

Colonel Kupieski, noted in a dispatch to Marshal Davout dated 23 June 1815, that:[3]

> The Major General arrived at Rocroi with the troops he had rallied and had marched on to Vervins, where he united them with the

94

men rallied by Prince Jerome. They were to re-join the Headquarters Staff at Laon, where there has already been assembled 400 horses for the Imperial Guard, the Grenadiers and Dragoons, Chasseurs à Cheval, Lancers and Gendarmes gathered from the cantonments in the environs of Laon. About 600 cuirassiers have been assembled from many places and are to move to Rheims, along with all the light cavalry at Vervins. All the infantry and dismounted troopers on the roads to Mauberge and Chimai are to be sent to Laon, where it is expected about 3,00 will arrive on the 22nd. A great number of the draught horses for the artillery train and horse artillery have been marched to La Fère.'

Clearly, Soult had ordered horses be seized from immediate areas where the army was passing through, both from civilians and the Gendarmes, to act as remounts for the cavalry. Unknown to Soult, Napoléon's aides-de-camp were assessing the state of the army, reporting directly to the Emperor. About the state of the cavalry, aide-de-camp to the Emperor Dejean, reported to Davout that:[4]

The Emperor has ordered me to Guise to unite the cavalry as far as possible. Here is my report on the troops in this place:

The Division of Piré, is commanded at this moment in time by General Wattier, and comprises the 1st and 6th Chasseurs à Cheval, the 5th and 6th Lancers, totalling around nine hundred horse. The division is camped around Guise, and I have ordered it to move to Saint Quentin, where it will be united with General Piré and also General Reille.

The Brigade of General Bruno which comprises the 7th Hussars and 3rd Chasseurs à Cheval, numbers around 400 horses, and in addition many men from other cavalry regiments have gathered here. I have sent the brigade to Saints[?]

In the immediate area are around 400 men from the different divisions of Cuirassiers commanded by General Roussel d'Hurbal, they are to be placed at Origny.

Where was the rest of the cavalry? What had happened to the rest of Jacquinot's command as only General Bruno's brigade is mentioned? Tancarville, Kellerman's chief-of-staff, stated that the 3rd Cavalry Corps was at Rheims and that Milhaud was at Soissons.[5] Why had Lhéritier with Kellerman headed one direction and Roussel d'Hurbal gone in another? Had command and control broken down so much that the 3rd Cavalry Corps went in two different directions? Seemingly so.

More bad news came into headquarters. General Foy resigned his command, but in his letter of resignation he did boast he had rallied 2,000 men.[6]

Elements of 2nd Corps were moving to Laon, as Puvis of the 93rd Line notes:[7] 'That day of the 21st, we were advanced towards Vervins where we stopped for the night around the city.' Parts of the Imperial Guard were at Soissons by 21 June 1815. The parc of the Guard Artillery had at this time twelve 12-pounder caissons, seven 6-pounder caissons, four 6.4 howitzer caissons, four 24-pounder howitzer caissons, five infantry munition caissons, one munition wagon and one field forge. The convoy was moved by the 8th company of the 8th squadron of the Line artillery train. In addition, the 9th and 10th companies of 8th Squadron were sent to move the materiel of the guard artillery. Three new batteries of materiel were brought up from La Fère.[8]

Grouchy

Grouchy at Givet sent orders to Vandamme to retreat. He informed him that he would now command Teste's division. Vandamme was also assigned a cavalry regiment and to begin the retreat to Namur.[9] We must remember his own cavalry force had been taken from him on 17 June. Vandamme sent orders accordingly:[10]

> The 10th and 11th Divisions which are between Sauveniere and Gembloux are to repair to Namur, the left column in front, passing Argenton, Bovesse and Risnes. General Berthezene is to keep his equipment with the two divisions.
> The 8th Chasseurs à Cheval which are cantoned close to Sauveniere are to hasten their march with the two divisions to Namur.
> The 8th Division and 20th Dragoons are to be united at Gembloux with immediate effect to take the same route.
> Insist that the Generals maintain the greatest order whilst carrying out their movements. The 20th Dragoons are to form the rear-guard.

Clearly the movement from Namur was in two stages. Chastel's 10th Cavalry Division was evidently the vanguard of Grouchy's column with Strolz's brigade bringing up the rear. We are missing some correspondence between Vandamme and Grouchy and a dispatch from Vandamme to Grouchy. We have, however, the reply:[11]

> I think it best for the tired troops you command, for them to rest at Charlemont, part at the entrenched camp at Mont d'Ore where a regiment can be placed in the barracks and another in the houses of the inhabitants, and finally in the village of Charlemont itself and also Mont d'Ore. There is bread, we still have cattle and I shall issue water to them. Come to my headquarters as soon as possible. My intention is to hold a meeting with all corps commanders, so that I can take their advice as to our next operations as I have had no orders from the Emperor with regards this.

I have put General Teste and his division under your orders, I trust this is satisfactory to you that he will be part of 3rd Corps.

After tomorrow, I hope to be able to assign you a cavalry regiment or perhaps a division. Early this evening you will receive tomorrow's movement orders. We cannot re-supply our munitions here, and we are running out. It is necessary to be patient on the subject.

Clearly Grouchy was well aware of how tired his army was and made plans accordingly for the men to rest. He was also painfully aware about the lack of ammunition. At Givet, Bourke wrote to Davout that:[12]

On the night of the 20th current, there began to enter this place the army corps of Lieutenant General Vandamme and Gérard as well as the Corps of Cavalry commanded by the lieutenant generals Excelmanns [sic]and Pajol under the orders of Marshal Comte Grouchi [sic]. Their passage continued throughout the 21st. I also received their artillery, their wounded and also the prisoners which they made at the affair of Namur [illegible] ... the retreat of these troops has had an ill effect on the National Guard and citizens.

At some time on 21 June, Grouchy wrote to Marshal Soult from Dinant about his operations:[13]

I have the honour to inform you that we have had no news from His Majesty and have received no orders since the verbal announcement of the loss of the Battle of Waterloo, which was given to me by an officer of staff. While I was struggling with the enemy I fought and pushed back beyond Rosierne, moving from Wavre to Brussels, and I made my retreat on the Sambre, and there onto Charlemont where I will arrive tonight. Every day of my retreat has been marked by bloody battles, but they have been glorious to the French army.

I bring back the corps that were placed under my command, though weakened, forming a total of about twenty-five thousand men, but without losing a single military trophy or cannon, and having beaten off the enemy, we have killed three times more of his men, than the losses I have experienced myself.

I will address His Majesty this evening with the ratio of daily battles that I had to fight and the losses that the army has sustained.

It is essential after long marches that my corps has done, that these troops take at least one day of rest. The 3rd and 4th Corps and Teste's division are camping in Givet.

Late on 21 June, Grouchy's undefeated troops entered Charlemont. He had managed to escape destruction or capture with 25,000 men, most of his wounded, and all his artillery.

Chapter 11

22 June 1815

Grouchy

At 06.00 hours on 22 June, Marshal Soult sent orders (the first since 19 June) ordering Grouchy to move to Mézières, and then to move on to Soissons or Laon and Rheims, depending on the movements of the Prussian fotrces.[1] Grouchy's movement orders for the day noted that Pajol was to move out at 06.00 hours from cantonments near Givet and move to Rocroy, keeping him informed of the British patrols that had been spotted. Exelmans was to leave at 07.00 hours to move to Rocroy, one part of his corps moving via the brigade at Houssou, and the other via Roigny. The 4th Corps, under Vichery, was to move out at 08.00 hours to head to Rocroy and occupy the villages of d'Irauremont, Galichet and Petit-Hougreaux. Vandamme, with 3rd Corps, was to leave at 10.00 hours, and the 5th Hussars was also to operate under his orders.[2] According to Fantin des Odoards, of the 22nd Regiment of Line Infantry, the 3rd Corps was at Givet on 22 June, from where it moved to the town of Maubert-Fontaine on 23 June, in appallingly wet weather.

That same day, General Bonnemains' dispatch had arrived in Paris from Dinant with news that Grouchy's army had not been destroyed or defected to the allies, as Marshal Ney had claimed the previous day and which had directly led to the abdication of the Emperor. In response to Bonnemains' dispatch, Marshal Davout wrote to Grouchy at 20.00 hours on the 22nd, conveying new orders and informing the marshal of the rapidly changing political situation:[3]

> I just learned from a letter from General Bonnemains, passed to me by Dumonceau, which states you were in Dinant and Namur with your cavalry and the 4th and 3rd Corps of Generals Vandamme and Gérard. This is an event of very great importance for our country. Because, after the unfortunate events near Genappe

concerning 1st, 2nd and 6th Corps and the Guards, there was the greatest concern. The certainty that your corps is not destroyed is an incalculable advantage in the current circumstances. I am ignorant of the orders of the Duc de Dalmatie could have given you, but here are the ones you need to focus upon now.

You must move with the 3rd and 4th Cavalry Corps and artillery to Laon, via Mézières. If you learn in a positive way that the enemy is between you and Laon with a large force, you will direct your march onto Rheims and from there onto Soissons. You are to send to me frequently your news; take all necessary steps to maintain good order in your troops, you must inform them about the latest events in Paris. The Emperor has abdicated, wanting to remove any pretext for foreign powers to wage war against us, because by all their statements, they announced that it was to him that they were at war and not France.

The Chambers have just appointed a provisional government, commissioners will be sent to all the Allied powers to announce this event which should remove any pretext for war. If the Allied powers, as we hope to have acted in good faith in their statements, in a few days, peace shall be restored to the world.

If you feel, M. Marshal, in the event that this declaration would be an illusion, it is important for the service of the country to take all measures to prevent malicious rumours, to prevent disorganisation and desertion among the troops. You can even say that you have knowledge of these events to the Allied generals in your neighbourhood, inviting them to suspend all hostilities until they received orders from their sovereigns.

Write to all the prefects and all commanding generals of garrisons to announce these events and invite them to take action to arrest all deserters, to reach those who have abandoned their posts, either soldiers of the line or National Guards. Talk about these events to all generals and implore them in the name of the country to take all measures in order to keep all the troops with their regiments and remind them of all the duties of the French soldier.

France is counting on you, General Vandamme and General Gérard, and all the generals and officers in this important circumstance. I repeat, the arrival of your body made the biggest impression in Paris. Please accept, M. Marshal, the assurance of my highest consideration.

We cannot be sure when Grouchy received the order, but one can see that Marshal Davout was clearly among those wanting an immediate ceasefire following the abdication of Napoléon. How the news was received by Grouchy and the officers and men under his command we can only guess. He, presumably, gained the news the same day and prepared a proclamation to be read to the army on 23 June.

Grouchy sent orders to Vandamme, by his aide-de-camp Le Sénécal to lodge the wounded at Givet and to make sure the best horse teams and vehicles were retained for later use.[4] Grouchy's movements orders for the 23rd, were to move the army via Rhetel. His motive for this was simple enough – he was marching in a wide eastern ark to avoid any possible contact with the Prussian army, whereas the Prussians were heading west along the Oise river to cut Soult off from Paris.

Soult

At 07.00 hours on 22 June, Soult wrote to Napoléon informing him that contact had been established with Grouchy:[5]

> Sire, I am sending you a copy of the report we have received from Marshal-de-Camp Bonnemains, dated Dinant, about the movement of marshal Grouchy.
>
> I immediately sent an officer to Marshal Grouchy with the order to move with all his troops to Mezieres, where he was to continue his movement from to Soissons, Laon or Rheims.

Soult also informed Napoléon about the mood of the army.[6]

> Your Majesty,
> I asked M. Lieutenant-General Dejean to go immediately to your Majesty and inform you of the insurrection that is fermenting in the army, especially amongst the leaders and generals, it is so common that they no longer conceal their feelings. General Piré told me today that in 15 days the government would be changed, this seems a general opinion and I am sure that of twenty generals, there are eighteen who share the view.
> General Piré left a few hours ago to go to Paris with a letter from Prince Jerome. I stopped him as he had no authority to do so, other generals have also left the army to go to Paris. Generals Kellerman, Trommelin and Rogniat are among them, and I was told there was still more that had left. The example is contagious, and it is likely to be imitated by the corps commanders and officers who talk to individuals, especially if the Minister of War does not leave within twenty-four hours, to return to the army.
> Everyone is talking about the public interest and the troops are beginning to question the orders that are being issued. It has been reported to me that when the 11th Chasseurs à Cheval received the orders of General Subervie to halt at Vervins with the remainder of the 5th Cavalry Division, the officers of the corps replied that: 'they would do nothing, that the position is bad and they had been betrayed' and withdrew!
> I have also been informed that the leading agitators voiced the opinion that I should be forced to carry out their projects ...

There may be exaggeration in all of this, but it is nonetheless true that there is a very great agitation in the army and that the troops have never been more poorly deposed. The name of [the Duke of] Orleans is in the mouth and minds of most generals.

Soult also noted that Reille had rallied 6,000 men and hoped to gather a further 2,000 men from the 6th Corps. General Morand had rallied 5,000 infantry of the Imperial Guard, and General Lefebvre-Desnoëttes had rallied 1,800 cavalry of the Imperial Guard. The same day, Soult ordered General Ruty, who was, it seems, also temporarily in command of the Guard artillery as well as the artillery of the Armée du Nord, to send to La Fère all the artillery draught horses he could assemble along with all field guns and vehicles in need of repair. Once completed, the commander was to return to Soissons along with all surplus personnel to await further orders. General Neigre had formed three batteries of artillery from the guns and personnel that had been originally destined to join the Young Guard.[7]

Colonel Kupieski wrote in his optimistic dispatch to Marshal Davout of 23 June, that:[8]

Dispatched to La Fère from Laon were 2 or 3 companies with fifteen ammunition caissons and wagons.

All the Old and Young Guard have been assembled at Soissons and arrived on various roads, except those at Vervins. In total they number between four or five thousand. The Gendarmes have surrendered about 150 horses and are based at Laon.

Monseigneur, below is the number of men who have returned to the colours:

Line Cavalry, 6,000
Old Guard, 3,000
Guard Cavalry, 1,000
Artillery Train, 300
Young Guard, 1,000
Line Infantry, 10,000
Gendarmes and horses, 150
Horses, 400
Total men: 21,300

The number of men marching to the place to be assembled will take this number to about 36,000, however the bulk of the infantry is without ammunition boxes and muskets. I am not aware of the corps of Generals Gérard and Vandamme and of Marshal Grouchy, I have had no information about them since crossing the banks of the Givet.

I must also observe that a great number of soldiers are returning to their villages or to their parents and are no longer of use.

That, Monseigneur, is the state of the army. We have been pursued at every point by the enemy. On the 22nd he pushed out a reconnaissance on the road to Chimai and that of Avesnes a force between 4 or 5 squadrons, which the same day passed the frontier. It is easy to judge by their delay that they have suffered considerably, and they need time to re-organise.

Laon was a concentration point for the army. It was here that Marshal Soult began re-organising the shattered regiments. General Morand commanded the Guard infantry marching to Laon, which mustered 5,211 men.[9] It had numbered 12,314 men on the morning of the 18 June. Having lost 7,103 men over the previous four days, it had suffered a loss of 57 per cent of its effective strength. General Lefebvre-Desnoëttes commanded the cavalry which mustered 1,887 men – a loss of 47 per cent. Adjutant Dominic Fleuret of the 55th Line notes that he too headed for Laon:[10]

> After marching all night, I arrived at Laon, where I was reunited with the rest of the regiment along with the major, who was very satisfied with me and my thirty men.

Elements of the 2nd Corps were also moving to Laon, as Puvis of the 93rd Line notes:[11]

> The 22nd, we arrived to Marle.
>
> The 23rd, two battalions were grouped at the foot of the hill of Laon to track the movement of the army, our other two battalions occupied the place.
>
> Besieged in Laon.
>
> The city of Laon, sitting on an isolated mountain in the middle of a plain that stretches out of sight … is a fairly extensive chain of mountains. This position was of such importance it could not be ignored. So, we detached some battalions of infantry to occupy the place, and two battalions of the 93rd were among them. These two battalions had a strength of seven to eight hundred men, with those provided by other regiments (84th, and 100th Line and the 12th Light Infantry) you could count perhaps three thousand men, with batteries of field artillery. No doubt it was enough to defend this position, but no defence works had been prepared and they were cast up in a hurry, our position was therefore critical.
>
> Fortunately, the slowness of the enemy to approach the place after the departure of our army, and a thick fog which came for two

days and spread around us on all the plain, acted as cover. This allowed us to start some work to make us safe from any surprise, and we put ourselves into a position to make a long and serious resistance. Housed among the inhabitants, whom we found in their houses, their awakened the utmost national sentiment, and they feared that we were not strong enough to protect their city from falling into enemy hands.

Chapter 12

Abdication!

Napoléon had hoped to gather a fresh army of 150,000, from the Army of Rhine, Grouchy's troops, and the National Guards, and told the Chamber of Deputies on 21 June 1815 that he would meet the allies behind the River Somme from the 1 of July 1815.

This, however, did not happen and Napoleon decided to abdicate. The events that led up to this momentous decision are detailed below:[1]

On the arrival of the news, that the French had gained a decisive victory at Ligny sous Fleurus, although that news was conveyed in a manner which could scarcely be called official in its details, the Parisians delivered themselves to the most extravagant rejoicings; and on Sunday the 19th, 101 cannon were fired to announce the glorious intelligence. However, no bulletin arrived on that day, a circumstance which was almost overlooked in the general joy; but which, when none appeared the following day, gave rise to a thousand surmises, and an agitation that became visible in all the places of public resort.

On the morning of the 21st, it was found that no news had reached the capital during the night; but, about an hour before midday, an arrival at the Elysee Bourbon gave rise to a report which changed the general alarm into exultation. It was said the Empress had returned. An English lady told me, that, on receiving the news, she paid a visit to General Ornano, Napoléon's cousin, who was laid up with a wound received in a duel, and asked him if he had heard the good news. 'The good news?' replied the general. 'Yes, the Empress is come back'. 'The Empress!' returned the other, shaking his head, and holding up a note he had just received from the palace, 'the Emperor, you mean. All is over!'

In an hour the return of Napoléon had spread over the whole capital. It was known to every member of the two chambers, which assembled; the peers at half past one, and the representatives at a quarter past twelve. After hearing the proceedings of the former, moved at once to consider the immediate necessities of the country. After the first tumult of the meeting, and the tales which everyone told, had subsided, General Lafayette mounted the tribune, and delivered these words:

'Gentlemen, when, for the first time since many years, I raise a voice which the ancient friends of liberty will even yet recognise, I feel myself called upon to speak to you of the danger of our country, which you alone, at this juncture, have the power to save. Sinister rumours have gone abroad: unfortunately, they are all confirmed. Now, then, is the time to rally round the old tricoloured standard, the standard of eighty-nine; the standard of liberty, of equality, of public order; the standard which alone we have to defend against foreign pretensions, and internal treason. Permit, gentlemen, a veteran in this sacred cause ... to submit to you some preliminary resolutions, of which you will appreciate I hope, the necessity:

'Article 1. The chamber of representatives declares, that the independence of the nation is menaced.

'2dly. The chamber declares its sitting permanent. All attempts to dissolve it is a crime of high treason: whoever shall show himself capable of this attempt shall be regarded as a traitor to his country and be arraigned as such.

'3dly. The army of the line and the national guards who have fought, and still fight, to defend the liberty, the independence, and the territory of France, have deserved well of their country.

'4thly. The minister of the interior is invited to call together the general staff, the commanders and legionary majors of the national guard of Paris, to advise on the means of arming and completing that urban guard, whose patriotism and approved zeal, for six and twenty years, offer a sure guarantee to the liberty, the prosperity, and tranquillity of the capital, and to the inviolability of the representatives of the nation.

'5thly. The ministers, of war, of foreign affairs, of police, and of the interior, are invited to present themselves instantly to the assembly.'

The propositions of General Lafayette were listened to in profound silence and received at the end with applause. The three first were immediately adopted, the fourth was considered premature, but the fifth received the unanimous support of the chamber, as a measure which the urgency of the case demanded. One of the members went so far as to say that these steps must be taken without delay in case the chamber was dissolved. It was ordered, moreover, that Lafayette's declaration, with the exception of the first article, should be posted up in the capital, and sent to the departments; also, that it should be immediately transmitted to the Chamber of Peers and to the Emperor.

M. Regnault de St. Jean d'Angely then entered the house and read the following bulletin:

> The Emperor arrived at 11 o'clock; he has called a council of ministers; he has announced that the army, after a signal victory in the plains of Fleurus, in which the flower of the Prussian forces was destroyed, fought a great battle two days afterwards, four leagues from Brussels. The English army was beaten during the whole day and obliged to give up the field of battle. We had taken six English colours, and the day was decided, when, at night, some malcontents spread an alarm, and occasioned a disorder which the presence of his majesty could not allay, on account of the darkness. The consequence has been a disaster which nothing could immediately repair. The army is rallying under the walls of Avesnes and Philippeville. His majesty passed by Laon; and there gave orders that a *levée en masse* of the national guards of the departments should stop the fugitives. He has returned to Paris to confer with his ministers on the means of re-establishing the materiel of the army. The intention of his majesty is also to concert with the chamber those legislative measures which circumstances require. His majesty is, at this moment, occupied in framing propositions for the consideration of the chamber.

M. Regnault proposed to also read a supplement to *Le Moniteur* of the 21st, containing an account of the fatal battle of Mont St. Jean, in which no attempt was made to conceal that the defeat had been decisive. But the chamber passed to the immediate nomination of a commission of administration to provide for the reception of the national guard, which would provide their protection.

After further discussions and proposals, four ministers and Prince Lucien Bonaparte entered the hall. The latter informed the chamber that he had been named extraordinary commissary by the Emperor and required that a secret committee of the whole house should be formed, to give audience to the ministers. The galleries were emptied, and a message was then read from the Emperor, informing the Chamber of the loss of the battle in all its extent, and of the nomination of the dukes of Vicenza and Otranto, and Count Carnot as commissaries, to open peace negotiations with the allies.

For a moment there was complete silence. Then, one member addressed himself to the minister for foreign affairs:

> You talk of peace. What new means of communication have you in your power? What new basis do you give to your negotiations? The nations of Europe have declared war against Napoléon. Do you henceforward separate the chief from the nation? As to myself,

I distinctly declare that I hear no voice but that of the nation; that I see nothing but one man between us and peace. In the name of the public safety, unveil the secrets of your new policy; show us all the depth of the abyss, and perchance there may be still left in our courage some resources, and our country will be saved.

The applause from all parts of the hall left Prince Lucien with no doubt that the fate of his brother was decided. He made one last desperate effort, appealing to the representatives' 'honour, to their love of glory, to their generosity, to their oaths'. But he was interrupted by Lafayette, who exclaimed: 'We have followed your brother to the sands of Africa – to the deserts of Russia: the bones of Frenchmen, scattered in every region, bear witness to our fidelity.' Though Lucien continued to try and cajole the members to support Napoléon, the house unanimously opposed to his arguments. They then had to consider their next move, and this came in the form of compiling a new interim government. A president and five vice-presidents were consequently selected and with that the assembly adjourned until 08.00 hours the next morning.

Meanwhile, the Chamber of Peers met at 13.30 hours, the Arch-Chancellor presiding. The Minister of the Interior read the same bulletin which had been communicated by M. Regnault to the House of Representatives and named 16.00 hours as the time at which a message would arrive from the Emperor. After some discussion, the three first articles were adopted, nearly in the same terms as those used by Lafayette. The chamber then adjourned, first until 15.30 hours, then until 20.30 hours, when Prince Lucien appeared as commissary extraordinary of the Emperor with a message. The contents of the message were discussed for more than an hour but nothing in the message changed the decision of the representatives. After further speeches, it was agreed that that the chamber had but one step to take – to persuade the Emperor, 'in the name of the public safety, in the name of their suffering country,' to declare his abdication.

The house adjourned, meeting again at 09.30 hours on the 22nd. Rather than wait for Napoléon to offer his abdication, some members urged that a commission of five members should go to the Emperor and demand his immediate abdication.

Marshal Davout then appeared and read an extract from a dispatch from Soult which stated that the Imperial Guard had rallied at Avesnes, and that Marshal Grouchy had beaten the remainder of the Prussian army on the 18th; so that the forces on the frontier amounted to 60,00 men, to which might be added 10,000 more, with some cavalry, and 100 pieces of cannon. He continued, by saying, 'that a declaration of treason against every national guard, or soldier of the line, who should desert his colours, might yet save the country.' A member asked if it was true that the light troops of the allies had advanced as far as Laon. This, the Marshal denied.

Marshal Ney, back in Paris, denounced any plan to continue the war in a statement to the Chamber of Peers on the 22 June. He clearly realised that the cause of Napoléon was ended:[2]

> What you have heard is false, as false can be. Marshal Grouchy and the Duke of Dalmatia cannot collect sixty thousand men. That number cannot be brought together on the northern frontier. Marshal Grouchy, for his part, has been able to rally only seven or eight thousand men. The Duke of Dalmatia has not been able to make any stand at Rocroy. You have no other means of saving your country but by negotiation.

The words Ney spoke were part exaggeration and part the truth. Soult had rallied some 21,656 men by 21 June, which when added to the 25,000 or so men with Grouchy made a force of around 46,000. Ney, it seems, was not aware of the true strength of the army, or deliberately set out to undermine both General Carnot and Marshal Davout, and to agitate for peace and cessation of hostilities.

At 11.00 hours the sitting adjourned but was resumed at 12.00 hours. At 13.00 hours, the dukes of Otranto and Vicenza, Marshal Davout and Count Carnot were introduced. The president then arose, and, looking towards the galleries, said, 'I am about to read an important act, which is communicated to me by his majesty's ministers. I beg to remind you of the regulation, which forbids all sign of disapproval or approbation.' He then read the following:

> Declaration to the French People.
>
> Frenchmen! In beginning the war to sustain the national independence, I reckoned upon the union of all efforts and of all inclinations, and upon the concurrence of all the national authorities. I had sufficient foundation in hoping for success, and I braved all the declarations of the potentates against me. Circumstances appear to me to be changed. I offer myself as a sacrifice to the hate of the enemies of France. I pray that their declarations may prove sincere, and that their real object of attack has been myself alone. My political life is come to a close, and I proclaim my son, under the title of Napoléon the Second, Emperor of the French. The present ministers will form provisionally a council of government. The interest which I feel for my son induces me to invite the chambers to organize a regency, by a law, and without delay. Unite all of you, if you would consider the public safety, and if you would remain an independent nation. (Signed) Napoléon.

The abdication of Napoléon was heard with respectful silence, but with heartfelt relief. A few generous speeches were then given, after which a declaration was made that: 'The chamber of representatives accepts the abdication of Napoléon Bonaparte and declares the throne vacant until the declaration of the will of the nation. The chamber places his person under the safeguard of the national honour. The chamber of representatives declares itself a constituent assembly to form a constitution. The chamber will form commissioners out of its body to treat with the allies. The provisional government is to be composed of the present ministers and a commission chosen in the chamber. Marshal Macdonald is named generalissimo, provisionally, of the army and navy; General Lafayette commander-in-chief of the national guard of Paris, and Marshal Oudinot second in command.

Flotard of the 4th Regiment of Lancers notes the impact of Napoléon's abdication had on the army:[3]

> The news of Napoléon's abdication resulted in disorganizing the army, it had arrived at Laon on the evening of June 25 and spread with lightning speed in all the remnants of the regiments which rallied in this city and carried into all minds a terrible depression far more contagious and incurable than had been the terrible distress which had befallen us in the disaster of Waterloo.

With Napoléon gone, hundreds of men left the ranks and deserted, believing that the war was over. At Chaumont, the 3rd Battalion of the 102nd regiment of Line Infantry was assembled. It had occupied the place since 14 June, hoping to join the 1st and 2nd Battalions of the regiment to fight the allies, but instead found themselves retreating, as Captain Leon-Michel Routier explains:[4]

> we aspired to re-join the regiment which had already entered the field, when we heard with inexpressible pain about the disaster of Waterloo and its aftermath. Our army was destroyed or dispersed, the invading coalition for the second time was on the sacred soil of the Fatherland, betrayal reared its ugly head to assist in their efforts, and terror sown everywhere purposely, such was the general situation after losing this battle.

The same day, peace negotiations commended.

Chapter 13

23 June 1815

Soult

The army left Laon during the morning of 23 June. Marshal Soult ordered that General Morand with all of the infantry of the Imperial Guard, supported with two batteries of horse artillery, was to move through the wood of Mally and cross the river at the bridge of Etouvelle, keeping communications with Laon. In addition, the Guard cavalry was to march on the Laon-to-Soissons road parallel to the Guard infantry.

Marshal Soult ordered Colonel Hoffmayer to determine what each regiment of the Guard cavalry required, and to get those items sent from the depots to the fighting squadrons, as well as sending whatever horses and the depots contained, and to be sent to the army under the orders of a superior officer.[1]

Soult also instructed the 2nd and 6th corps, commanded by General Reille, to march at 10.00 hours to Etouvelle on the Laon-to-Soissons road. Reille was ordered to ensure that his men had all their allocation of cartridges and that muskets were to be taken from men who were no longer capable of using them and given to men who lacked arms. Troops were to be taken from 1st, 2nd and 6th corps along with Fédérés (the Fédérés or federates, were men who volunteered to join the National Guard) to help form the garrison of Laon under the orders of Marshal du Camp Langeron.[2]

General d'Erlon was ordered to march to Soissons along the Mons-to-Laon road via Clacy, leaving at midday.[3] General Wattier was placed in command of the 2nd Cavalry Corps and placed at the disposal of Reille. He had left Saint-Quentin at 03.00 hours on 23 June to move to Soissons.[4] Soult reported to Davout that the 4th Hussars had been in action at Vervins, and furthermore he noted that the powder magazine had been destroyed at Avesnes before it could fall into the hands of the British. He remarked to Reille that Grouchy had retired with the

110

3rd and 4th corps, with four regiments of Hussars and a Division of Dragoons, from Namur towards Givet in perfect order and without loss. General Wathiez reported to Grouchy that Guise had fallen to the enemy at 16.00 hours on 22 June. Wathiez further remarked that he had with him 120 men from the 6th Lancers and 240 from the 5th, noting that their dress and discipline was impeccable.[5]

Furthermore, Soult ordered that Rheims was to be garrisoned by the National Guard as well as men from the army held in the depots on the left bank of the river Marne. Artillery material was moved from Vincennes and Soissons to defend La Fère.[6]

Marshal Soult informed Marshal Davout that he would establish his headquarters at Soissons on the evening of 23 June. He noted with caution though, that the allies had a far superior force of cavalry.[7] To offset this deficit, he ordered General Watier at the head of the 2nd Cavalry Corps to operate with generals Kellerman and Milhaud in the area of Craonne and Corbeny, and to move in the direction of Soissons. If a body of Allies threatened the line of communication the 2nd Division was to contain them in front of Laon.[8] At 08.00 hours Soult wrote to Kellerman:[9]

> M. General, I hereby give you orders as General Commanding the 3rd Cavalry Division, to move to Rhetel via Craonne and Corbeny.
> Reports have to come that the enemy is at Vervins, and it is possible that they will head to Laon, therefore as General Commanding the 3rd Cavalry Division, you will send a strong force in the direction of Notre Dame de Liesse and send news of any enemy troops that you may observe in front of you. If it is not then possible to move via Craonne and Corbeny, you are to change your line of march to be via Soissons, where you will cross the river Aisne and you till take up position at the bridge of Orei [?].

At Craonne was General Domon, who sent the following dispatch to Soult:[10]

> Conforming to the orders of your excellency, we left this morning, the 23, for Rhetel ... General Curely moved in the direction of Signy and then re-joined the route to Rhetel with 180 horses from my division. The horses are exhausted and we need to bivouac for 48 hours at Rhetel ... My outposts this morning spotted at least 60 cavalry a Corbeau heading towards Laon.

The chief of staff to General Domon, Adjutant Commandant Maureai, informed Soult that General Curely was marching to re-join the division with 154 men. He also noted the strength of the Division:[11]

> 4th Chasseurs à Cheval: 22 officers with 58 horses, 144 men with 138 horses

9th Chasseurs à Cheval: 17 officers with 39 horses, 102 men with 95 horses

12th Chasseurs à Cheval: 7 officers with 15 horses, 60 men with 56 horses.

TOTAL: 46 officers with 112 horses, 306 men with 289 horses.

Curely had been on Ney's staff at Waterloo. He had been given an active field command at the end of May 1815, but his brigade was dissolved on 6 June, and instead he was ordered to join the staff. About the retreat and his operation, General Curely notes:[12]

> During the battle [Waterloo], I carried the orders of Marshal Ney to several Army Corps. Towards evening, I was sent by the Emperor to command a brigade of Chasseurs à Cheval which had just lost its general. Upon arrival, the brigade was entirely dispersed I found 8 or 10 Chasseurs à Cheval of the 4th Regiment. I was then dragged into the crowd during the first retreat. We marched all night pell-mell, and I arrived in person at Charleroi eight o'clock in the morning. The city was crowded with guns and caissons as well as many fugitives and soon the enemy. It was about one hour in afternoon that there entered into Charleroi two or three hundred Prussian horsemen. I then took part in the to retreat and arrived near Beaumont without finding a single French soldier, as the flight was so fast. I slept that night at Grandrieu which is between Beaumont and Avesnes.
>
> On the 20th I returned to the latter place, where I found 50 Chasseurs à Cheval from the 4th regiment which I ordered to accompany me, and by the time I was at Avesnes I had 200 men from the brigade I commanded. At Avesnes Prince Jerome ordered me to send out reconnaissance patrols on the roads to Beaumont and Maubeuge. Upon my return I was honoured to dine with him along with 15 other generals. I refused to take command of the place Avesnes, as I sought to re-join my troops which were at Rocquigny heading to La Capelle, on the 21st at Aubenton and on the 22nd at Signy-le-Grand, on the 23rd at Neuchâtel sur Aisne, the 24th at Vervneuis for Pont-Arcy and finally the 25th at Soissons. Here I quitted the Chasseurs à Cheval and was given command of two regiments of Cuirassiers.[13]

General Subervie was ordered to detach the 11th Chasseurs à Cheval, and to move to Etouvelle, behind Laon, joining General Reilles 2nd Corps, who were also supported by the 1st Cavalry Division.[14]

On the night of 23 June, the army entered Soissons, where Soult began trying to regenerate the army. He ordered that all the dismounted artillery train drivers, horse artillerymen and cavalry were to leave Soissons and march directly to the general remount depot at Versailles to be remounted. These men were to be joined by those remaining in the depots that had not yet joined the army.[15] Soult also ordered that all defective muskets were to be replaced with those drawn from the Citadel of Soissons or repaired and brought back into firing condition in a 24-hour period.[16] Corps commanders were ordered to ensure that their men had sufficient cartridges and equipment, and a report on the cadre of men were to be sent to the Imperial Headquarters, as well as a report of the necessary items of equipment that each corps required.[17]

Also converging on Soissons were 4,132 men from the 1st Corps, 7,418 from the 2nd Corps, and 3,008 men from the 6th Corps, who were ordered by Marshal Soult to be broken up amongst the 1st and 2nd Corps. What remained of the 2nd Cavalry Corps mustered 879 men – a loss of 75 per cent of its effective strength. To bolster the decimated artillery, three new batteries were brought up from La Fère.[18] Also brought for the artillery of the Guard were fresh train horses and caissons, necessary to service two or three batteries.[19]

General Neigre had been ordered on 21 June to arrive on the afternoon of the 23rd at Laon with a battery of eight guns and full horse teams, as well as a second battery of six guns, manned by companies that had not served on 18 June. General Neigre had also brought with him from La Fère eleven cannon, 123 caissons with munitions, and 1,500 draught horses, of which 650 were allocated to the general artillery parc.[20]

Soult ordered General Ruty, to place the citadel of La Fère in a state of readiness to resist a siege and to send what artillery materiel he could on to Soissons.[21] Soult also ordered the troops to be issued with fresh ammunition.[22]

In order to make up heavy losses in the 1st Corps, Soult ordered the depots of the 21st, 25, 45th and 46th regiments of Line be emptied and the men dispatched to the army. The depot of the 5th Hussars was to be emptied and the men dispatched to the army also.[23]

Adjutant Dominic Fleuret of the 55th Line notes:[24]

> That evening we left Laon and marched towards Soissons. We bivouacked in front of Soissons for five days. We left Soissons and moved to Compiègne. But the English being there before us, we were received as one would expect with a discharge of artillery that were masked by a hill and, as we marched by column sections, we lost a lot of people, including a commander, who had his shoulder swept away by a ball. We threw ourselves into the great forest of Compiègne and continued to retire to Senlis … and the English abandoned the pursuit. We continued our retreat onto Paris.

113

Four leagues from Paris … we found the English and had to force our way through them with our musket fire. The English were tumbled back, and we arrived at the walls of Paris, at four in the afternoon. We passed around a small portion of Paris, and we came up and camped at the *barrière du Trône*. We remained near Paris eight days. In the meantime, I got permission to go into town to see relatives, those of my cousin Cornu, by whom I was well received. My cousin gave me money and effects worth forty francs which did me a big favour, because I lost all my effects on the battlefield of Waterloo.

Battalions of the National Guard had been mobilised to replace men in the garrisons who had deserted, and battalions from the 5th and 100th regiments of the Line had formed part of the garrison of Laon under Marshal du Camp Langeron.[25] The garrison comprised:[26]

National Guard of the Seine	100 men
Battalion of 85th Line	410
Detachment from 5th Line	300
Detachment from 100th Line	410
Battalion from 12th Light Infantry	450
Battalion of 93rd Line	350
Detachment of Engineers	50
Artillery detachment	50
Sedentary artillery	70
Sedentary National Guard	700
Total	2,890 men

Soult ensured that the 2,890-man strong garrison he was to leave behind in Soissons was fed and equipped. He also ordered on the 25th, that the Intendant General of the Army was to transport from Paris sufficient flour, bread, and biscuit for the garrison for the duration of eight to ten days. He ordered that the treasury was to be advanced 500,000 francs, the bulk of which was to pay the soldiers and feed them. Also, from this sum, 50,000 francs would be set aside to feed the garrison of Soissons and 30,000 francs for engineering works necessary to defend the place.[27]

Action at La Fère
In 1815 La Fère, as well as being the depot of the Imperial Guard Artillery, was an important crossing point, as it stood at the junction of the Oise and Seine rivers. Here also was the junction of the Sambre-Oise canal. To bolster the garrison at La Fère, Soult ordered at 16.00 hours on 25 June 1815 that nine officers and 347 men from the 64th Line

Regiment who had arrived at Soissons, were to march to La Fère. They were to be accompanied by the 5th Cavalry Division of General Subervie. If the allied troops endeavoured to stop the column reaching La Fère, they were to move instead to Coucy-le-Châteaux.[28] The men from the 64th Line Regiment were the regiment's 3rd Battalion which had taken five days to join 3rd Corps. In addition, 800 Pontoniers were ordered to La Fère.[29]

General Subervie reported to Marshal Grouchy in a letter timed at 17.00 hours, that the 11th Chasseurs à Cheval, along with 200 infantry destined for the garrison of La Fère, were ambushed at Coucy-le-Châteaux. A column of enemy cavalry had debouched from the village of Follembraye, supported by two field guns and a howitzer, the cavalry force was estimated at 1,000 sabres. Subervie notes his column had no hope of resisting this force so retreated, under an artillery barrage. Subervie withdrew to Coucy, the infantry being placed to defend the bridge at Letre and the cavalry being placed on the heights of Coucy. He was forced to retreat after a short action defending the position.[30]

General Lefebvre-Desnoëttes informed Grouchy in a letter timed 22.00 hours that the allies had occupied Coucy and he had been forced to evacuate his positions behind Laon and had moved with the Imperial Guard to Laffeaux.[31]

The bridge of Coucy was still held by General Subervie in the early hours of the 27 June by the small infantry detachment available to him. One of his cavalry regiments was placed at Crecy, and the other was placed to observe the road to Quemi, and the remaining regiment placed to observe the road to Guny[32]. The allied force opposing Subervie came from Thielmann's command, the 10th Brigade moving up to Coucy.

Grouchy

At 08.00 hours, Soult sent word to Grouchy:[33]

> The reports I have received make it known that the enemy is in Vervins, and that it is possible that his scouts will be heading towards Laon during the day. It is then of the utmost importance that you go directly by Reims to Soissons.
>
> Send me your reports to Soissons, where the headquarters will be established.

Early that morning, reports were sent into General Vallin concerning the whereabouts of enemy troops:[34]

> We have observed in the direction of La Capelle a patrol of Prussians Hussars, sometime later a body of troops of perhaps 50,000 men

was seen heading from La Capelle towards Rocroy, and from there presumably to Avesnes and Mauberge

A second dispatch reads, in part: 'A force of 25 to 30 [30,000 ed?] Prussians were in cantonments yesterday 22 June at La Capelle'[35]

Squadron Commander Fortin[36] of the 16th Dragoons sent a dispatch to Valin from Neuville timed at 03.00 hours:[37]

> I have the honour to report to you what my outposts at St Michel and Wattignies had discovered. An officer has communicated to me a letter written by the Mayor of La Capelle, and that he has discovered the English and also Prussians, that had quit different posts on the afternoon of 22 June. I enclose the certificate from the mayor of La Capelle...

At 05.00 hours General Valin sent a report to Grouchy:[38]

> I have the honour to inform you that I have at this instant received word from my patrols that the enemy army has been seen debouching at La Capelle.
>
> There has been heard a cannonade in the direction of Maubeuge and Avense.

A dispatch from Soult arrived sometime before midday:[39]

> Laon 23 June 1815. 8 o'clock in the morning
> M. Marshal,
> Reports have arrived with me that the enemy is at Vervins and it is possible they will head during the day to Laon, it is of great importance that you now move directly via Rheims to Soissons.
> Address your reports to me at Soissons

Soult sent a dispatch at 17.00 hours containing a dispatch from Davout dated 22 June.[40] Grouchy sent off his reply:[41]

> I have just received the dispatch of Your Excellency, brought to me by one of your aides-de-camp which is the duplicate of the movements orders that had been given me to yesterday evening by one of your staff officers; from talking to him, it is easy to understand the bad situation of the army and its total disorganization ...Tomorrow, the head of the right wing will arrive at Réthel, and I will still have troops at Maubert-Fontaine.
> My cavalry, which now occupies Aubenton, Rumigny and La Neuville-aux-tourers, will hold tomorrow 24th, Rosy and Moncornet, and retain Rumigny and Aubigny.
> We passed through Mézières with the major part of our artillery, Your Excellency must not consider the right wing of the army was re-united until after tomorrow when it assembles at

Réthel. If you have any orders to give me, please send them to me in this city.

Here are the latest reports I receive from my light cavalry, confined to Signy-le-Petit. If they are true, it would appear that the enemy heads to LaCapelle and Hirson.

I will know tonight if those who followed me will arrive on me by Rocroy: I do not think so.

Your Excellency must, in the rest, be better informed than I can now be from the progress of the enemy, on the road leading to Laon.

Arriving at Réthel, I will be aware of the situation of the 3rd and 4th Corps of cavalry and I shall instruct Your Excellency on the State condition which they are in.

At 16.00 hours, General Pajol forwarded news of the enemy to Grouchy:[42]

I have the honour to inform your excellency that we are established at Neuville, occupy Signy and Beauvais [?] and have a detachment at Hison [?].

The enemy were observed at LaCapelle, with a great number of infantry and cavalry, in consequence part of my cavalry were sent to Hison to report to me if they began a march to Laon.

I also wish to report that General Ameil is stationed in front of Signy.

An hour later, General Valin sent a dispatch to Grouchy:[43]

I inform you that we have arrived at Aubenton, I have written to General Kellerman to inform you of his positions and to send you news of the enemy.

I report that when we left Mézières, reports were received of the enemy army was at d'Avesnes and was heading towards LaCapelle, Vervins and Marle ... My division is guarding the road in front of d'Aubenton [illegible] and Vervins, a regiment is deployed in reverse behind this village.

In consequence, Grouchy sent the following dispatch to General Vandamme:[44]

Aubigny 23 June 1815

My dear General, here are your movement orders for tomorrow. I have received two reports, from Generals Pajol and Vial, and upon consideration of others that I have received, the enemy is headed in the direction of Laon.

The Emperor has ordered me tomorrow to march rapidly to Rheims via Soissons along with the cavalry of Excelmanns [sic] who is to travel along the roads, you are to march via Sart-à-Walhain.

The location of my new headquarters has yet to be approved, an officer has been to sent to Marshal Soult to arrange things, but unfortunately this officer of the staff has not yet returned here. The headquarters for the army is to move from Laon and will be at Soissons, where there already is a large number of our troops.

Battalion Commander Guyardin, Chief of Staff of 3rd Corps, issued the following orders:[45]

The troops of the 3rd Corps will be ready to leave their cantonments at midday and will march in the direction of Rocroi. Upon concentration at the destination, each division will be issued with its bread and water ration.

The artillery will be established on the glacis of Rocroi. General Dogureau will oversee the emplacements. The empty caissons will be sent to Laon, and it is hoped they will be returned to the army as promptly as possible.'

Later the same day Grouchy sent the following order to Vandamme from Mezieres:[46]

Lieutenant General Lemoine has communicated to me two letters containing orders &c.

Therefore, I wish your Honour to move towards Mezieres, from where I am writing to you, and since our unfortunate reverse of fortune, you and your brave army at to pass the night here, it is the only force that may redress the cruel setbacks.

However, many of the troops do not listen to orders ... But, your Honour, I have ordered General Lemoine at Mezieres to round up the fugitives from the army, and to place them under the orders of the officers from the garrison ... I have written to the Gendarmes and customs officers [Douanes] along the line of march to search the villages for fugitives, to arrest the fugitives and deserters, to take from them their horses and baggage that belongs to the army that they may have otherwise abandoned, the authorities are to deal with them [the men i.e. to be shot] and furthermore to identify which regiments they belonged to and deliver the military effects back to their regiments.

64 mules or pack horses have been gathered at Mezieres by General Balthus which has made up some of the deficit we have lost. Therefore General, which must keep good order despite it be lost ... so that the army may give yet more good service.

It is clear, Grouchy had just found out the severity of the defeat at Waterloo. He quickly realised he had to keep discipline amongst his men if his command was to be of service to France, hoping to redress the disaster that had befallen the left wing of the Armée du Nord. He urged Vandamme to collect abandoned arms, cuirasses, and equipment that were left on the road side. General Berthezene wrote to Grouchy complaining that in consequence of rumours, men were deserting from his division.[47]

At some stage on 22 June, Grouchy received news that the Emperor had abdicated. He received word via three channels:

1. Soult's dispatch was sent off at 05.00 hours on 23 June.
2. Order carried by Le Sénécal transmitting Davout's news and appeal to the soldiery to fight on under the brave eagles:[48]
3. Davout's own dispatch:[49]

Paris 22 June 1815 8 o'clock at night

To Marshal Grouchy,
   Marshal,
   I have read the reports from General Bonnemains and General Dumonceau who says you are at Dinant and Namur along with the cavalry and the 3rd and 4th Corps of Vandamme and Gérard. This news of great importance after the unfortunate events that have taken place which involved, 1st, 2nd and 6th Corps, along with the Guard at Genappe and further subsequence incidents; the certainty of your corps and cavalry is of incalculable importance at the current time. The gist of the orders to the Duke of Dalmatia will be sent to you … You with the 3rd and 4th Corps, the cavalry and artillery are to move to Laon and Mezieres. If you encounter any major enemy forces on the way from Laon you are to head via Rheims and Soissons. Please keep me frequently informed of your news.

The news was no doubt received with much consternation. Davout told Grouchy to make sure that the announcement was couched in such a way that the troops would not panic or desert, and that 'they were fighting now for the independence of the fatherland, and to entreat them to great glory.' Grouchy was also told that the provisional government was negotiating with the enemy generals for an armistice. It is clear that Davout and Grouchy were in direct contact, bypassing Soult and the regular chain of command. Grouchy penned his proclamation that night.[50] Yet we must ask, why did Soult take so long to send word to Grouchy – Soult seems to suggest at 05.00 hours that he had just received the 20.00 hours letter from Davout. This makes a journey time of nine hours compared to a mere four hours to Grouchy, who was further away. Clearly at some stage the courier to Soult got delayed. Grouchy read out the following proclamation on 23 June:[51]

Soldiers!
   The movements of the army of the Emperor have rendered necessary the painful marches that you make. But make no mistake

about their reasons or their results. You are the victors of Fleurus, Wavre, in Namur, you beat the enemy wherever you addressed them, your valour has embellished your military trophies and you can boast of not losing a single one. Together with new forces you will soon take the offensive attitude that suits you. As defenders of our beloved country, you will preserve its sacred ground and the whole of France will proclaim your rights to recognition and public adoration. I am pleased to lead you in these important circumstances where you have increased your fame by earning new laurels. I answer in your name to the country, that faithful to your oath, you will all perish rather than see it humiliated and enslaved.

Vive l'Empereur!'

Grouchy was aware that negotiating a cease fire was being considered but was kept in the dark about the timetable of these events. Soult also told Reille about the negotiations then taking place.[52]

Grouchy sent word to Soult that night, that on the following day, 24 June, the army would be at Rhetel along with the major part of his artillery, the light cavalry would be at Signy, and he would continually monitor the progress of the enemy.[53] Grouchy issued a comprehensive set of orders for 24 June:[54]

The cavalry of General Pajol at 7 o'clock in the morning is to quit Neuville-aux-[illegible]and to commence its movement to Rocroy, and to be a league to the left of General Valin who will occupy Mont-Cornet.

The cavalry of General Valin is to quite Aubertin a 9 o'clock in the morning and head to Mont-Cornet, it will pass to the left of Marle, and will have on its right the troops of General Pajol at Rocroy and will send out patrols to Vervins and in the direction of Hison.

The cavalry of General Exelmans will depart from Rumigny, tomorrow the 24th, at midday, it will move via Sogny, Aubigny, Marlemont, Frelt and the Signy-l'Abbeye which will be the headquarters of General Exelmans.

The 4th Corps will cease to occupy Aubigny and will as quickly as possible move to Rhetel, and to start this movement at 8 o'clock in the morning.

The 3rd Corps will support the 4th Corps in its movements to Rhetel … A rear guard is to be maintained to guard against enemy columns.

The Parc and artillery reserve are to be two leagues in the rear of Rhetel on the road to Rheims.

The general headquarters will be at Rhetel.

News from Paris

That morning at Laon Marshal Soult was informed of the abdication of Napoléon by a courier from Marshal Davout. He sent word to Grouchy at 05:00 hours:[55]

> Mr. Maréchal, I attach herewith a letter from the Minister of War dated June 22, at 8 p.m., which was brought to you by an aide-de-camp of His Excellency. This officer whom I met on the road, when the column was coming out of Laon, announced that the Emperor had abdicated; But he was not carrying any letters for me. It seemed so extraordinary to me that, in order to have the confirmation, I opened your dispatch, and I took a copy of it to communicate it to the generals, so that they would comply.
>
> I had to instruct you on these circumstances, to explain why the minister's letter is given to you opened.
>
> The army is starting to rally. Today it marched in very good order. The infantry is heading to Aisne, however the cavalry is on the right bank of this river, and on the line of Laon, until the enemy forces us to withdraw. I left a strong garrison at Laon; and the 3rd and 4th Cavalry Corps remained in Reims. I'm going to Soissons where the headquarters will be.

Soult informed Marshal Davout that: 'The news of the abdication of the Emperor has produced a very bad effect on the army, and some 1,000 men from the Imperial Guard have quite their posts.'[56] Soult wrote to Marshal Davout on the evening of the 23rd about the condition of the army: 'The troops have been united at Soissons, joined by the troops of Marshal Grouchy, I estimate we have 50,000 infantry and 120 pieces of cannon, but the army can be increased to 100,000 infantry, 20,000 cavalry and 300 pieces of cannon with a great effort by sending the men from that are still held in the depots.'[57]

Events in Paris were rapidly escalating as Fouché manoeuvred his way to the top. Arch manipulator Joseph Fouché duc d'Otranto and perhaps with his willing associate Marshal Davout, without reference to either Soult, Grouchy, or other army commanders decided to sack Soult as Chief of Staff. Since Napoléon had fled the army, along with his brother and Marshal Ney, Soult had provisionally taken command of what remained of the left wing of the Armée du Nord. Ably assisted by General Monthion, Soult had performed wonders, but during the evening sitting of the government on 23 June in Paris, Soult was sacked and Grouchy was named commander in chief:[58]

> Extract from the deliberations of the Commission of Government.
> Evening session of 23 June 1815 proposed by the Minister for War to the Commission of Government as law;

Article 1

The Marshal Grouchy to be named General in Chief of the Armée du Nord.

Article 2

The Minister of War is charged with the execution of this law.

Signed. The Duc d' Otranto, Carnot, Caulaincourt, Duc de Vicence, Quinette, Comte Grenier.

Davout subsequently wrote to Grouchy:[59]

> I have put in front of the Executive committee of the Government your letters of 20 and 21, it is my responsibility to let you know that you have returned to France a service that will be appreciated by all. I invite you to send me your requests for advancement and rewards for those who have given the most distinguished service.
>
> The government entrusts you with the chief command of the Northern Army, which will be divided into two bodies: the first, under the orders of Count Reille; It will be formed of the 1st, 2nd and 6th Corps, the second to comprise the 3rd and 4th Corps;
>
> The second, will be under the command of Lieutenant-General Comte Vandamme. The Comte de Valmy will command the 3rd and 4th Cavalry Corps.
>
> Lieutenant-General Vandamme will organize his body into three or four divisions.
>
> Having kept all your artillery equipment, you will send your excess to general Reille.

Amongst the thousands of archive papers relating to marshals Grouchy and Soult at Service Historique de la Défense du Armée de Terre, we can find a copy of the document of 23 June appointing Grouchy commander in chief in Grouchy's papers.[60] Alas we cannot tell when he received it, but very likely 23 June or early hours of 24 June. The Traditional histories have Soult giving up command on the evening of 25 June 1815, turning his coat once more and defecting back to the King. Clearly, Davout and the politicians in Paris sacked Soult – with Napoléon gone, Ney having fled the Army, only one man remained in any position to be found culpable for defeat- Marshal Soult.

Soult, ever since he took the position of Major-General, as with Grouchy, been the victim of character assassination. With Berthier struck off the list of marshals, the man best placed as his replacement in the function of Major-General was Marshal Soult, appointed such 9 May 1815 with General Bailly de Monthion as Chief of Staff.[62]

Soult's appointment was not confirmed till 13 May 1815.[63] In the same letter, Davout asked for the service papers of the members of the staff to be sent to him for approval.[64] The day earlier, Davout had harangued General Bertrand about Monthion and the staff, and indeed so distrustful of Monthion was Davout he asked Bertrand to, in essence, spy on him and to send all documents for the staff officers to him to be checked before they were appointed.

Soult, like Grouchy, is made the scapegoat for the disaster that befell the army. Anyone other than Napoléon was to blame for the loss at Waterloo.

Davout, the saintly darling of many Bonapartist is often cited as being the better man for the job of Major-General – yet Davout's own actions after Waterloo call his judgement and loyalty into question. Could Davout have been an able Major-General? Perhaps. He had not had direct experience of army command, and indeed he had not commanded forces beyond a Corps. He had never worked in that capacity or served directly under the Emperor. The best candidate for either Major-General or chief of staff was Monthion – but as a general he could not issue direct orders to marshals, therefore a marshal had to be in the top job, and Soult was the best candidate.

François-Gédéon Bailly de Monthion was a man of key importance to Soult as Major-General Monthion was as in previous years, ensuring the staff ran smoothly and orders got issued. He was named chief of staff on 8 April, and it is to him that we must look to as the organiser of the staff and much of the key work in the formation of the Armée du Nord. Historian Tim Clayton makes the claim that Monthion resented his demotion – yet no evidence of this resentment exists, nor was Monthion demoted. He had the same job in 1815 as he had had since 1812! Clayton also paints Soult as incompetent.[67] These claims simply don't stand up to any scrutiny and are opinion, not fact, yet again used to damn anyone other than the Emperor for the loss of Waterloo.

Be that as it may, we suppose Soult was sacked because he was seen to be at fault for the loss of campaign, but it is of course possible that other forces were involved. Someone had to take the blame for Waterloo, Soult was an easy target. As we noted earlier, Soult had performed excellently in Spain, and his campaign of 1814 against Wellington was a tactical tour de force. He was the best man to take charge of the Army and fight Wellington – he had direct experience of staff work and was the most obvious choice for chief of staff, but also the ideal man to face down Wellington after Waterloo. Soult had a proven track record of being able to rebuild the wreck of an army and get it fighting again – his achievement following Vittoria is all to his credit in getting King Joseph's demoralised army back in action.

If Soult had been given more time, could he lead a fight back? With the allies seeking peace as soon as the 23 June, Soult could be dangerous if he did rally the army and lead a fight back. What better way of demoralising the army further than to sack Soult, as his men would see this as a defection leading to further desertions and ruination of the Armée du Nord and pass command to an 'incompetent' cavalry officer who had no idea how to handle infantry, Marshal Grouchy. The nub of the issue is, Soult was sacked, either to be made the scapegoat for Waterloo, or he was a victim of Fouché and Davout's political machinations. We don't have the reasoning given in Paris or Soult's own words. We have a copy of a letter sent to Davout by Soult asking to resign, written into the Major Generals order book- but importantly, the book is a much later copy of the lost original. The letter in question is written in at last two different hands and changes tense. Without access to the original, if one exists, we cannot be sure of Soult's motives, if he had any, to resign command. When we compare it to the original letter found in the Army Archives that Soult sent to Davout, the passage about resignation is missing assuming this is indeed the original. Such are the pitfalls of historical research.

We view Waterloo as an inevitable defeat, but as far as the men of the Hundred Days were concerned, the Emperor was in power for perhaps the next fifteen or more years, and thus made plans accordingly for their own futures. Indeed, Soult's main concern as ever was money. On 5 July 1814, Soult wrote to the Minister of War concerning his owed back pay of 110,000 francs from 1812 and 1813.[70] On 20 August 1814 he was allowed to return to Paris[71] and on 31 December he submitted a request for back pay dating from 1814, some 46,800 francs, 26,000 from 1st quarter 1814, 20,800 from 2nd quarter 1814.[72]

On 11 April 1815 he pledged his honour to the Emperor,[73] and following Waterloo he wrote a cringing letter to the King on 8 August 1815, asking if before he was banished from France if he could be allowed to see his family, pledging his loyalty to the new regime and begging for clemency.[74] Soult was banished from France. He sat out his lonely exile for two years and wrote another letter to the King again on 7 November 1817 asking to see his family and pleading for clemency.[75] Hardly the act of a traitor. If Soult was an out and out Royalist who deliberately sabotaged the One Hundred Days, would Soult have needed to beg for clemency? I would say no. But for conspiracy theorists like Beckett[76], this paper trail was no doubt deliberately prepared to cover Soult's tracks. Despite his pleading in 1817, neatly three years passed before Soult was acknowledged once more as a duke and marshal on 22 January 1820 and allowed to return to France.[77] If Soult was the ultra-royalist, why did it take three years for his titles to be acknowledged? Why did he have to beg to see his family and it be refused until 1820? If he was the arch traitor, surely a five-year exile is rather long? Lefebvre-Desnoëttes was not granted clemency till 1822, so two years more than Soult; proof that Soult was let off sooner because he was a traitor? I doubt it. Or are Soult's begging letters more fabrications to hide Soult's treachery, as Beckett suggests?

Some claim Soult sent only one courier where Berthier would have sent several – we know this is simply wrong as at least four couriers were sent to Ney at Quatre-Bras all carrying the same order. Yet the myth of Waterloo says Soult did not do this – all to make him culpable for the defeat and to make Napoléon into a saint who did no wrong, and that 'it is was not for traitors, Waterloo would have been victory' is oft repeated with little substantive evidence to support this implication.

We also know Soult was frequently bypassed by the Emperor – Napoléon sent out his own aides-de-camp with orders to his field commanders, in addition to orders issued via Soult and the proper chain of command. Soult had no knowledge of these orders, and one can only assume a lot of confusion was caused by two sets of orders arriving by different couriers. Direct Imperial orders out ranked those from the staff – so what could a field commander do? Act on orders from the staff and then change plans to act on imperial orders? This duplication of transmission of orders, often with slightly different contents, lead directly to confusion amongst subordinates. Napoléon, by side-stepping the accepted chain of command was micromanaging the army and placing the staff at disadvantage. Many take this as proof that Soult was incapable as being Major-General, but Napoléon's own reasoning for this is not that Soult was an imbecile.

The character assassination of Soult and Monthion began before the Waterloo campaign. Soult could not fill Berthier's shoes, and for many historians, the great 'what if' scenario was Davout as Major-General. Davout, like Berthier, is judged through rose-tinted spectacles. Neither men could do no wrong, both led saintly lives in their devotion to the Emperor. Davout, the iron marshal for many, should have got the top job and been at Waterloo. Davout's actions in 1815 do strongly suggest he resented his desk job and made life hard for Soult. Davout it seems went out of his way to be inflexible, citing regulations from ten or more years earlier for funding for the staff that Soult was desperately trying to form for the Armée du Nord. Davout deliberately withheld funds citing regulations throughout May 1815.[78] It did not help Davout despised General de Monthion.[79] Yet it seems remarkable that Davout had such a total change of heart, as Davout had personally appointed Monthion on 8 April 1815![81] Monthion's police report states:[82]

General Monthion was on half-pay on 1st March. His dossier provides the following information on his movements before this time. He requested to be placed on the active list on 14 February, to be employed once more at his rank. This General Officer by his letter of 28 [illegible] received from Marshal Davout his letters of service as Chief of Staff [Chef d'État Major Généraux a position not to be confused with Major-General], and he carried out this function until 26 June, he then returned to Paris. He had been wounded with a severe contusion at the battle of Waterloo and on 6 July he requested to go on leave on grounds of ill health, which was agreed.

Soult, we admit, made two mistakes during the campaign, the bungling of orders on 12 June was a major error.[83] But compared to the errors Berthier made in 1809, we see that even the most gifted staff officers make mistakes. Soult bungled orders for the period 10 to 12 June yet is called a traitor, Berthier bungles the orders for the start of the campaign of 1809 yet is still seen today as a saintly figure. Why? Because the great Napoléon cannot have lost the campaign of 1815 by his own mistakes. Indeed, he was by de Bourmont on 14 June, who handed over to the allies all the orders etc. that he had. De Bourmont's defection was of vital importance to the allies staging a successful fight back.

In returning to Soult being sacked from the Army, he subsequently published a pamphlet to try and exonerate his supposed defection:[84]

> It remains for me to account for my conduct from May 11 until the day of the order requires me to be guilty.
>
> In the second period the facts are neither numerous nor likely to controversy. I was appointed Major-General of the armies, I obeyed. I signed as such an order of the day to the army and government which I obeyed. I fought the Prussians and English at Fleurus and Waterloo. If these are crimes, then I am guilty.
>
> But I trust that my conduct is not criminal, and I think it should be enough to be convinced to examine without prejudice, and not isolate it from the circumstances in which France was at that time.

Soult is blamed for being a Royalist spy, a traitor, the man who made more mistakes in 100 days than Berthier had in twenty years to quote Chandler. But none of these accusations stand up to scrutiny. No one has ever produced evidence of these mistakes. Soult went into meticulous detail in preparing the Armée du Nord for war, as well as his incredible achievement of rescuing the remains of the Armée du Nord from Waterloo, getting food and munitions issued on 19 and 20 June. He then began the process of fighting a rear guard action whilst at the same time endeavouring to rally the army, co-ordinating the distributions of food, clothing, ammunition and getting reinforcements sent from Paris. This is an incredible achievement, but one many overlook. Yet Monthion is also blamed for mistakes and sabotaging the army – again no evidence for this has ever been presented.

Soult was far from incompetent. He was an excellent administrator and workaholic as his later career testifies. He was the ultimate pragmatic realist. Whoever ran France was no concern of his in the long term, as long as the good of France and the Army was uppermost. Yes, Soult changed sides in 1815, but so did Ney, Oudinot, Jourdan Massena, Mortier, as well as other marshals and countless thousands of civil servants, officers, and soldiers. Above all else, he was a professional, and as a professional officer he did his duty well and effectively. The man who lost Waterloo was not Soult, nor Ney, and not Grouchy – that man was Napoléon. No traitors, or Royalist spies – Napoléon made more mistakes than the allies and thus lost. He was no demi-god, yet many cannot accept that he was a mortal man who made mistakes. He made mistakes at Marengo in sending off Desaix fifteen years earlier. No man is without fault, yet Napoléon for many never seems to have had any. The truth is, as commander in chief and head of state he was culpable. His decisions led to the loss of the campaign.

As well as relieving Soult of his post, the government began peace talks with the allies. As the war was fought against Napoléon and not France, the reason for war no longer existed. For the King this meant peace and stability. Soult, ever the realist and pragmatist, soon realised this could now be a war for the survival of the French nation.[85] Soult, on behalf of the Government, sounded out General Rogniat on his willingness to work for the government:[86]

> The Chamber is sending as envoys on a mission to ask of the enemy generals an end to war, above all these men need to of superior honesty, fidelity … and to work in the best interest of the fatherland.

Chapter 14

24 June 1815

At some point on 24 June, General Monthion received word that the King of Rome was now Emperor Napoléon II.[1] Monthion wrote to Grouchy about this as follows:[2]

> Mr. Marshal,
>
> I have the honour to inform you that today's monitor contains the following article:
>
> In its evening sitting of the 23rd, the House of Peers adopted the deliberations of the House of Representatives acknowledging that Napoléon II became emperor of the French, by the abdication of Napoléon 1e, and by the fact of the constitutions of the Empire
>
> Approve, etc, etc.
>
> Lieutenant-General, Chief of the General Staff.
>
> Count Monthion.

Davout sent the following letter to Grouchy:[3]

> I have the honour to send you a copy of an order from the government Commission, who appoint you as General in Chief of the Northern Army, and of another that orders the 1st, 2nd and 6th Corps of the Army of the North will be united into a single corps, under the command of Lieutenant-General Reille.
>
> Therefore, the army of the North that you command in chief, will be composed of the troops you brought with you, and from the body under the orders of General Reille. I have informed this general and prescribed him to take your orders.
>
> Give him all the instructions you deem necessary, both for the new organization of his corps, and regarding his operational movements. I beg you to correspond daily with me, and to send me as promptly as possible the exact situation status of all troops composing the Armée du Nord with their location.

Soult informed Grouchy of a letter sent from Davout regarding the treatment of officers and men who had quitted the army:[4]

> The Minister of War was instructed that generals, officers of various ranks and other military personnel that have left their posts without authorization, and had headed to Paris, are to be arrested and put on trial so that their names are doomed to dishonour.
>
> Such orders have been given to the soldiers of all ranks who have abandoned their positions and taken other directions.
>
> It is therefore ordered that the regimental commanding officers are to prepare a report about the state of the men they have under arms, any men missing are to be reported to the Minister.
>
> Lieutenant generals commanding Army Corps, will also report, if generals or staff officers under their command are in this category in order for it to be reported.
>
> As these provisions are also applicable to military administration, the lieutenant general will make the status of the Commissioners of War, medical staff and any employees who have left their positions and shall report them immediately.

At 07.00 hours, Grouchy sent orders to Pajol:[5]

> I intend to continue my movement from Réthel onto Reims, where I intend to arrive by tomorrow evening. I find you, therefore, too far away from me, and too isolated at Rosy. Go to Chaumont and make cantonments on the road, between Réthel and Castle-Porter. Send me two officers to Réthel, so I can forward orders for your movement tomorrow.
>
> Tell me what you know about the movements of the enemy, and frequently correspond with me.

Grouchy issued orders to General Valin sometime that day about his own movements:[6]

> I intend to go from Réthel to Reims. I find you too far away from me and too isolated at Moncornet. Please, therefore, march to Sevigny by this evening. You will link up with General Pajol, to whom I commanded to go to Chaumont, and you will reconnoitre all the roads that drive on Laon and try to have news of what is happening on this side of the city.
>
> Send me two officers to take my orders from Réthel and correspond as frequently as possible with me.

An hour later he sent orders to Exelmans:[7]

> It is as a result of the orders of the major-general, of which I attach a copy, that I move to Reims. I ordered the generals Pajol and Valin to move closer to Réthel, placing them in Chaumont and Sevigny. It is

appropriate, my dear general, that you move in the same direction, especially as towards Rosy and Minbréson is too exposed and too isolated from the army, and moreover, General Vandamme has only a small regiment of hussars as his rear guard.

Take yourself in the direction of Neufchatel, connecting you with Generals Pajol and Valin .... Send me reports by officers to Réthel, where I will be.

At midday, Pajol sent word to Grouchy about his operations:[8]

Rosy, 24 June 1815, noon.

Monseigneur, by the time I arrived at Rosy, I received your letter this morning. I'm going to freshen up and get started, to reach Hannogne and Bannogne.

I am going to pass orders to General Valin, to go to Sevigny, Montigny and St.-Quentin.

General Exelmans who has arrived, will taker his corps to Nizi-le-Comte, Latour, l'Or, etc.

It is useless to pass by Réthel to go to Reims, instead if we follow the path of Caesar [i.e. the Roman road ed], we will lose 4 to 5 leagues.

The enemy only pushed parties to Marlt, and a few men on Signy. I believe he only has a few hundred horses in Hirson.

It is said that he has besieged d'Avesnes, and that he attacks Maubeuge vigorously. The peasants believe they heard canon yesterday and today from the same direction: But I did not see or hear anything, which makes me believe that we could have continued our course on Laon.

I saw today the 2nd Cavalry Corps. The regiments seem to be well-mounted. There appears to be some malicious people working amongst them ... I am, etc., etc.

Lieutenant-General Count Pajol.

Clearly, for Pajol some men in the 2nd Cavalry Corps were disquieted and far from happy. With the Emperor gone, what loyalty did the men have to Grouchy and Napoléon II? As we shall see, very little indeed. At 14.00 hours, Grouchy transmitted news to Soult:[9]

I arrived here with the head of the right wing of the army. Before leaving Aubigny, one of the officers of your staff handed me your dispatch of yesterday, the 23rd instant timed at 8 a.m. My reports had informed me, as did Your Excellency, about the arrival of the enemy at Vervins. But they don't seem to have been to Marie. Anyway, tomorrow 25th June, I will arrive in Reims, and I will have my cavalry in Neufchâtel and Craonne. I wll march via Fisme on Soissons, after tomorrow.

I detained your staff officer until I arrived here: that is the cause of the delay in joining you.

At 18.00 hours, Exelmans reported into Grouchy that:[10]

It has not been possible for me to stop the movement which I had the honour inform you about, by a letter of yesterday.

I can only halt my troops in Rosy, Maimbrecy and Maimbreçon. I decided to march between Laon and Marie, before I received the Order of Your Excellency, I did so because I thought that you intended to direct me to this point. Another reason I also committed to this is the concern of the troops and the impatience they have in wanting to unite with the emperor's troops. These two things exist not only in the desires of the soldiers, but in senior officers and others.

I have the honour to ask Your Excellency to believe me that I would not have allowed myself to anticipate your intentions, if I had not been inclined to do so by the foregoing reasons. But I hope and believe that this movement on my part will have no drawbacks: I'll do everything that depends on me to achieve that.

I have the honour, etc.

Exelmans.

P. S. The enemy pushed a detachment of 60 cavalry to Hirson last night. The letters did not arrive here yesterday by mail, as is customary.

Clearly the courier system to get to Exelmans was not as efficient as could be hoped, which resulted in Exelmans doing what he thought best. In a world before modern social media, the fastest news could travel was by telegraph or galloping horse. If the courier got lost or delayed, orders did not arrive in time. Soult is damned by many for not sending multiple couriers with orders. We know he did. If a courier got lost, that was no fault of Soult's. In this case, Grouchy's couriers arrived late once Exelmans had embarked on his own plan of operations to fill a void in orders. Common sense soldiering. Yet some would say that in this case Grouchy or Exelmans were doing their best to sabotage the army, much as modern historian Beckett blames Soult for the bungling of orders and missing couriers. Mistakes happen at times of war. People are not always where they should be, horses go lame and messages arrive late or not at all. What is remarkable, is how the staff of both Grouchy and Soult with Monthion at their heads had 'bounced back' after Waterloo. This showed remarkable skill and tenacity by Soult and Monthion to get the staff working despite all the setbacks. Soult had done this before after the Battle of Vittoria. He was a man of great ability, a professional soldier, who despite major setbacks, knuckled down to work as if nothing had happened, and set too to the task in hand.

That night, Grouchy issued orders for the following day:[11]

> The division of General Valin will leave its position as Sevigny, tomorrow, 25 June, at eight o'clock in the morning, and settle in Neufchâtel, behind the Aisne, scouting along the course of this river in the direction of Soissons, and pushing their scouts on towards Corbeny and Laon.
>
> The Corps of general Pajol will leave their positions of Chaumont, tomorrow, 25 June, at 6 a.m. in the morning and will come to take a stand at Béry-au-Bac, sending scouting parties along the road to Laon, and connecting with the troops of Domon's Division, which is stationed in Corbeny.
>
> The Corps of General Exelmans will go tomorrow in the morning, from the cantonments he occupies in Châleau-Porcien, from where he will reconnoitre the road from Réthel to Reims, and make contact on his left with General Pajol, placed in Neuchâtel.
>
> The 4th Corps will leave at seven o'clock in the morning from Réthel and surrounding cantonments and come to take position near Reims.
>
> The park and the artillery reserves will move from Réthel and surrounding cantonments, at three o'clock in the morning, and will cross Reims, and go to halt on the other side of the city, on the Reims to Soissons road.
>
> These reserves will continue to be escorted by the 50th Regiment.
>
> The 3rd Corps will leave tomorrow, at 10 o'clock in the morning, the cantonments which it occupies, in front of Réthel, and will establish itself between Réthel and Reims, in the communes of Rouit, Bazamourt, Isle, Warmériville, and others on the brook beyond Suippe. Réthel,

Chapter 15

25 June 1815

Davout wrote to Grouchy at midnight, presumably in the early hours of 25 June, to warn him that when he took command of the men under Soult, that the army under Soult's orders was no longer a fighting force. Grouchy's men were all that stood in the way of the Prussians:[1]

> You will find yourselves with troops, who, unfortunately, have been in this great setback of the 18th, and which, according to all the reports, still feel it. Take all necessary steps to prevent the contagion from taking hold in your army ... Chaos reigns in the first, second and Sixth Corps. Take, as I asked you last night, strong measures, and have them write circulars in all the communes, so that we arrest the Marauders and take them to your headquarters. I have experience that once an example is made of one of them, it is enough to bring the order back.
>
> Please, Mr. Marshal, send me a detailed relation of your affairs, so that all France may know it, and appoint me the officers and soldiers for whom you ask for rewards.
>
> I made an order of the day to the generals, officers and soldiers who had abandoned their positions.

Davout repeated the point about keeping the men under check in a letter written late the same day:[2]

> Take action, Mr. Marshal, against those who would disorganize your army and excite the soldier to desert. Publish the sentences that the military laws of all countries inflict on those who are guilty of these crimes.
>
> If you can intercept any communication between the enemy, do so. You must also guard against the emissaries coming from Paris. They must only be able to reach your army with the correct passports that will be checked by your gendarmerie, who will

nevertheless monitor all those who carry it. Serve to secure your rear and stop deserters. Receive, etc, etc.

Let the situation of things also be openly known by a proclamation. Napoléon, I abdicated, and now there can be nothing more for us, than to be men of Honour and be faithful to his homeland.

The Chambers appointed the government Committee, which sent commissioners to the Allied Powers to declare that the reasons for the war no longer exist, since Napoléon abdicated, and he is no longer ruler of France. If the powers were sincere in their declarations, then peace should soon be given to Europe. If the Commissioners are not received, then our independence, our political and even individual civil liberties will be threatened, and the war will become one of national survival.

You are a man of honour, you are of good character, and I hope that it will not be in vain that the government has put its trust in you. The attitude you give to the army will suffice to make a great service to our homeland.

Grouchy had known about the abdication since late on 22 June or early hours of 23 June. Yet, it was not until 25 June that Davout authorised the army be informed of the news. Grouchy sent word of the abdication to General Valin from Rhetel at 17.00 hours:[3]

I hasten to announce that the Emperor Napoléon has just abdicated the crown. The Chambers have appointed a provisional government, and Commissioners will be sent to the Allied powers to announce this event which must remove any pretext for war. You will see by the letter, a copy of which is attached, and addressed to me by the Minister of War, the reasons for this event. Make the troops under your command aware of this news, that they must rally as strongly as ever to their eagles. Let us save the homeland in this difficult moment by our efforts, as by our Union, repel the enemy.

The positions at Laon are no longer occupied by the troops of the Duke of Dalmatia, who left only a garrison, and which is behind the Aisne, it is behind this river that the army will stop; But the cavalry will still remain on the right bank of this river.

Here is the order of the general movement of the Army for tomorrow. Send me officers to Reims to receive orders.

We don't have the movement orders, but we do have the proclamation, which in part reads:[4]

The Emperor abdicated in favour of his son, and the Chambers recognized him emperor, under the name Napoléon II
What are your duties now, soldiers?

To be faithful to the new ruler of the Empire, as you have been to his August father, to stand with your Eagles, to rally under the national banners ... Soldiers! Show yourselves such today, that you may glory in it for years to come, be worthy of the sacred cause of the homeland and its freedom, which will ensure is a triumph. Your efforts, your conduct, in this great circumstance, will ensure the tranquillity and happiness of the empire.

In Paris the Government began to slowly place Paris on the defensive and to keep seeking an armistice. Of note, Chaboulon places Soult in Paris as being directly involved with the military operations and was still in Paris in early July. As we shall see he was a realist and not a Royalist. Clearly, Soult had remained loyal to France and the state rather than fleeing immediately. Hardly the acts of a traitor. In getting back to the course of the day, he also received at midnight a second letter from Davout: [5]

I submitted the letter I sent to you last night, which was transmitted to you by my aide-de-camp Marbot[6], to the government, which approved its contents; But they instructed me to tell you that you are to avoid a general engagement. You must retire behind the cavalry; and you must with withdraw speed, as not to be not forced to give battle since your army is destined to defend the entrenchments of Paris. With the troops that are there and that we will rally, we will have, including your forces, at least 100,000 men.

With such forces, the enemy will look at it twice, and listen to proposals, in the assumption that he would have refused to listen to the extraordinary Commissioners.

I commend you, Mr. Marshal, for having Compiègne heavily garrisoned.

Due to the vagaries of history, not all the correspondence written in the fateful days of June 1815 survived. We are clearly missing letters from Grouchy to Davout as Davout refers to them, but as to the contents of the letters we have no idea. Soult sent a dispatch to Grouchy as follows:[7]

I see by the letter that you have done me the honour of writing to me at Réthel on the 24th, that today, the 25th, the cavalry at the orders of Your Excellency will be at Neuchâtel and Craonne, and that you will be with the rest of the troops in Reims, from where your intention is to you move by Fisme on Soissons.

Last night, a staff officer had been sent to you in the direction of Laon, to carry an order from the Minister of War, who informs you that the command of the Armée du Nord is entrusted to you, and that the 1st, 2nd and 6th Corps will be formed into a single army corps, under the command of Lieutenant-General Comte Reille, and that the 3rd and 4th Corps, would also form an army corps, under the command of Lieutenant-General, comte Vandamme.

According to these provisions, I have the honour to ask you, at the receipt of my letter, to go join me in Soissons, where I will give you the details of the troops gathered on this point, and after having spoken to you, I am ordered to Paris, where I have orders to surrender myself.

From Reims, you can leave the command to General Vandamme, who will finish the movement you ordered on Soissons.

I have the honour to inform you that I give orders to Mr. Le Comte de Valmy and Count Milhaud, to leave immediately at Reims, with the 3rd and 4th Cavalry Corps they command, to travel to Soissons.

I also give order to General Bom, commanding the 3rd Cavalry Division, who was in Craonne, to leave at the arrival of the cavalry that Your Excellency sent, to go to Bucy and Si Marguerite near Soissons.

I have the honour to warn you that the 1st and 2nd Cavalry divisions are still in front of Laon, and that the cavalry and infantry of the Guard, are in column behind Laon to support them. The 5th division of cavalry is at Coucy, and the 1st, 2nd and 6th Corps are at Soissons.

From this we see that Soult was ordered to leave the army, i.e. he was sacked, and placed under arrest. In reply Grouchy wrote at 17.00 hours:[8]

I arrived at Reims at this very the moment and one of the officers of your staff brought me the letter by which Your Excellency tells me that the command of the Armée du Nord is vested in me. Such a burden is too much above my ability, I do not rejoice in it. I will ask the government to take this burden from my hands.

The first troops of the right wing will only be in Reims late tonight, and those of general Vandamme will only arrive during the night. It is absolutely impossible for me, Mr Maréchal, to get to Soissons, especially since the instructions and orders of the minister, which you say have been sent to me on Laon, have not reached me and that it is essential that I confer with the General Vandamme, before leaving the right wing, where I will have to leave him detailed instructions. If it does not arrive within a few hours, do not expect me until tomorrow morning in Soissons. Approve, etc., etc.

Grouchy had the top job but did not want it. Despite the heavy burdens placed upon him, he set about the task at hand as ever the professional soldier he was. The following order was sent to Vandamme:[9]

> I inform you, my dear general, that as a result of new provisions ordered by the Government, the 3rd Corps will be united with the 4th Corps, and you are to take command. I will attach temporarily to it the division of General Valin, who will be sent his orders immediately informing him of this news.
>
> I am charged with the command of the Armée du Nord, it is placed in the following manner:
>
> The 1st and the 2nd cavalry Division are ahead to Laon, the cavalry and infantry of the guard, is behind Laon. The Corps of the general Reille is near Soissons.
>
> My intention is that your Army Corps moves to the left, and keeps the line of the Aisne, keep your left at Serneville and your right at Barbu, you will occupy Wailly. Try to be in this position by the 27th instant.
>
> General Pajol's Cavalry Corps is ordered to move tomorrow from Béry-au-Bac to Coucy.
>
> The Corps of general Exelmans will leave Château-Porcien tomorrow, to take a position at Corbeny and Craonne, and will extend his left as far as Pargny.
>
> I want you to reconnoitre the bridges on the Vesle, in case there is a need to pass on the left bank of this river.
>
> It is also necessary that you give orders for Reims to be put in a better state of defence than it is now. Please take care of this object, as it is important.
>
> Marshal Grouchy.

Battalion Commander Coudreux of the 4th Battalion, 30th Regiment of Line Infantry wrote to his brother on 25 June 1815, worrying about the future:[10]

> The first news we received from the army was distressing. Yesterday, several of our officers wounded on 19 and 20 returned to us and we had to console them. Grouchy's corps, after defeating the Prussians completely, retired in good order behind the Sambre, and we hope that the four corps that have taken fright at Waterloo will still offer quite large masses to stop the enemy. The extraordinary events that happened in Paris will undoubtedly not benefit our unhappy country! In all cases, we are determined to die to the last man for the noble cause of our independence. The inhabitants of this region are animated by the best spirit. I am delighted to have left Paris.

The 30th has lost over half its numbers: it was the vanguard of General Gérard. All senior officers were killed. I am expecting to be ordered to take command of about 500 men but we still are now commanded by a captain. I have ruined myself to mount myself properly, and I'm ready for anything.

1st Cavalry Division

Somewhere on 25 June, the 1st Cavalry Division of General Jacquinot was in action and had been for a number of previous days. It seems the 7th Hussars were used to screen the wreck of 1st Corps. The regiment was led in 1815 by Colonel Marcelin Marbot, who has left a vivid set of memoires about his military career under Napoléon. These give a picture of the Napoléonic age of warfare which for vividness and romantic interest has never been surpassed. Jean Baptiste Antoine Marcellin Marbot was born on 18 August 1782, the, son of General Jean Antoine Marbot (1754–1800), who died in the defence of Genoa under Masséna. During the Hundred Days, he was promoted general of brigade.

He was exiled at the second restoration and only returned to France in 1819. Following the revolution of 1830, he was made Maréchal-de-camp. He served during the siege of Antwerp in 1832 and was promoted lieutenant-general in 1836. From 1835 to 1840 he served in various Algerian expeditions under General d'Erlon, and in 1845 he was made a member of the Chamber of Peers. With Napoléon III establishing himself on the throne, he retired from public life, and died in 1854.[11] The regimental muster list of the regiment was not able to be consulted for writing *Waterloo Truth at Last*, but with special permission from the head for the Archive Service, the data has been collected from the muster list and is presented here in full:

MAT No. 70 Adrien Kapiot, corporal 8th company, 4th squadron, prisoner of war.

MAT No. 464 Decadi Floréal Robine, trooper, 6th company, 2nd squadron, killed in action.

MAT No. 466 Mathieu Denis, trooper, 5th squadron, 1st company, prisoner of war.

MAT No. 529 Pierre François Debeuve, trooper, 5th company, 1st squadron, prisoner of war.

MAT No. 566 Louis Jean Baptiste Alexandre Mercier, trooper 5th company, 1st squadron, missing.

MAT No. 970 Louis Besse, trooper, 4th company, 4th squadron, killed in action.

At Genappe, the regiment incurred the following loses:

MAT No. 67 Michel Muller, Adjutant Major, killed in action.

MAT No. 75 François Joseph Romer, trooper 1st company, 1st squadron, prisoner of war.

MAT No. 163 Pierre Eustache Ricard, trooper, 7th company, 3rd squadron, killed in action.

MAT No. 176 Pierre Marie Mallet, trooper, 2nd squadron, 2nd company, killed in action.

MAT No. 370 Simon Batel, trooper, 5th company, 1st squadron, killed in action.

MAT No. 411 Vincent Rougejean, trooper, 5th company, 1st squadron, killed in action.

MAT No. 414 Jean Nicolas, trooper, 2nd company, 2nd squadron, killed in action.

MAT No. 426 Joseph Royons, trooper, 8th company, 4th squadron, killed in action.

MAT No. 457 Jean Bonesse, trooper, 8th company, 47th squadron, killed in action.

MAT No. 475 Nicolas Remy, trooper, 2nd company, 2nd squadron, killed in action.

MAT No. 503 Joseph Chanalm, fourrier, 6th company, 2nd squadron, killed in action.

MAT No. 617 Louis Vangenotte, trooper, 8th company, 4th squadron, killed in action.

MAT No. 632 Hypolite Joseph Bheilly, trooper, 8th company, 4th squadron, killed in action.

MAT No. 656 Jean Baptiste Parsy, trooper, 8th company, 4th squadron, killed in action.

MAT No. 660 Alexis Dermouval, trooper, 5th company, 1st squadron, killed in action.

MAT No. 662 Jean Baptiste Beauvais, trooper, 5th company, 1st squadron, prisoner of war.

MAT No. 779 Jean Louis Richepain, trooper, 8th company, 4th squadron, killed in action.

MAT No. 1123 Jean Antoine Ymonier, trooper, 8th company, 4th squadron, killed in action.

Marbot's men were in action on 16 and 17 June. Presumably, the regiment fought at Ligny. Six men were lost that day, as well as another eighteen at Genappes, of which sixteen were killed.[12]

The loss of so many men killed at Genappe is a huge figure compared to the losses of some regiments at Waterloo of men killed in action. Clearly the fighting here was desperate and of an intensity not found at Waterloo. At Waterloo the following men were casualties:

Squadron	Killed	Deserted	Wounded	POW	Missing	TOTAL
1	6	1	0	0	0	7
2	10	0	0	0	0	10
3	17	0	0	1	0	18
4	16	0	0	2	0	18
TOTALS	49	1	0	3	0	53

The regiment records forty-nine men killed, very high when compared to other regiments in the division. The regiment was it seems also in action on 19 June, when the following men were lost:[13]

MAT No. 230 Auguste Henry Barbe, trooper 1st company, 1st squadron, reported killed in action 19 June, but clearly was POW.

MAT No. 240 Charles Auguste Edu, trooper, 8th company, 4th squadron, deserted.

MAT No. 273 Joseph Steland, trooper, 1st company, 1st squadron, killed in action.

MAT No. 283 Charles Louis Devillet, trooper, 1st company, 1st squadron, killed in action.

MAT No. 378 Joseph Regnier, trooper, 3rd company, 3rd squadron, killed in action.

MAT No. 428 Pierre Philippe Branque, trooper, 7th company, 3rd squadron, deserted.

MAT No. 1169 Korn, trooper 4th company, 4th squadron, killed in action.

Men were also lost in action on 20 June:[14]

MAT No. 122 Henry Charles Wagner, corporal, 2nd company, 2nds squadron, killed in action.

MAT No. 130 Jean Henry Sheirer, trooper, 2nd company, 2nd squadron, killed in action.

MAT No. 194 Nicolas Bertout, trooper, 2nd company, 2nd squadron, killed in action.

MAT No. 198 Antoine Motte, trooper, 2nd company, 2nd squadron, killed in action.

MAT No. 232 Pierre Devaux, trooper, 2nd company, 2nd squadron, killed in action.

MAT No. 254 Louis Castinet, corporal, 2nd company, 2nd squadron, prisoner of war, but listed killed.

MAT No. 332 Jean Baptiste LeClerc, trooper, 3rd company, 3rd squadron, killed in action.

MAT No. 480 Alexis Georges, trooper, 2nd company, 2nd squadron, killed in action.

MAT No. 517 Celestine Dromerai, trooper, 7th company, 3rd squadron, deserted.

MAT No. 571 Jean Baptiste Beaumont, trooper, 2nd company, 2nd squadron, killed in action.

MAT No. 588 François Amant Vivant, corporal, 2nd company, 2nd squadron, killed in action.

MAT No. 635 Pierre Medard Thurolhe, trooper, 7th company, 3rd squadron, deserted.

MAT No. 653 Jean Pierre Bentin, trooper, 7th company, 3rd squadron, deserted.

MAT No. 925 François Perret, trooper, 4th company, 4th squadron, killed in action.

Seven men were lost on 19 June and fourteen on 20 June, these losses are equivalent to the losses at Genappe on 17 June. In total between 16 and 20 June, the regiment lost ninety-nine men. The regiment seems have then enjoyed two days of relative peace and quiet, presumably they had given the Prussian pursuers the slip. The respite was short lived as the regiment was in action on 23 June:[15]

MAT No. 104 Etienne Lamache, trooper, killed in action.

MAT No. 204 Michel Blondot, trooper 1st company, killed in action.

MAT No. 407 Valentin Leininger, trooper 5th company, killed in action.

MAT No. 693 Henry Mousset, trooper 1st company, killed in action.

Again, two days passed before the regiment exchanged blows with the Prussians once more on 25 June:[16]

MAT No. 341 Antoine Pistatout, sergeant, 2nd company, killed in action.

MAT No. 723 Jean François Riche, trooper, 1st company, killed in action.

Oddly, the rest of the division suffered no recorded losses in the time frame, so clearly the 7th Hussars bore the brunt of the fighting, presumably as the rear guard. We do acknowledge that the 4th Lancers had a major desertion problem, with seventeen men being declared AWOL 20 to 25 June.[17]

In a report dated 26 June, General Delcambre, chief of staff of 1st Corps, reported to Marshal Davout that the light cavalry division attached to the Corps had been detached to serve with the Imperial Guard, and that the corps had a single battery of six field guns and a single caisson. He also reported the corps mustered 310 officers and 4,333 men. Shockingly the 25th Line was down to seventy-eight men.[18]

The Heavy Cavalry
The 1st Cuirassiers seem to have run into trouble on 25th June:[19]

Squadron	Killed	Deserted	Wounded & POW	POW	Missing	TOTAL
TOTALS	0	5	2	0	0	7

The regiment lost 109 men at Waterloo and eight at Genappe, making 117 men lost in action. The regiment began the campaign with eighty-one officers and 423 other ranks, losing 27 per cent of effective strength at Waterloo. Even so the regiment still had a theoretical strength of 300 on 19 June. Since Waterloo nineteen men were lost, one man was wounded and three deserted on 21 June, another man was wounded on 26 June. Clearly, the regiment was still involved in spasmodic fighting after Waterloo.

The 12th cuirassiers was also in action on 25 June. The regiment had mustered 234 men on 1 June:[20]

Squadron	Killed	Deserted	Wounded	POW	Missing	TOTAL
TOTALS	0	47	0	2	0	49

The regimental records a total of 119 men lost at Waterloo, far exceeding the eighty-five men claimed in the regimental history, and no men were officially lost at Ligny. Therefore, the regimental history seems very suspect when tested against documents from the period. Whatever happened to the 12th Cuirassiers, it seems to have been a mass panic.

In returning to the narrative of the day's events, sometime late on 25 June, General Monthion issued the following order:[21]

> The Provisional Government has named M. Maréchal Grouchy as commander in chief to the Armée du Nord.
>
> M. Lieuteant General Comte Reille, commander in chief of the 1st, 2nd and 6th Corps is to be retained at his post.
>
> M. Lieutenant General Comte Vandamme commander in chief of 3rd and 4th Corps is to remain at his post.

Henceforth Grouchy was now defacto commander in chief of the Armée du Nord. This was his last field command. The letter also shows that Monthion remained ever faithful to the cause of France. Delcambre, who had caused so much delay to 1st Corps, arrival at Quatre-Bras on 16 June, was now it seems on the army staff. Who was running the wreck of 1st Corps staff cannot be determined other than the possibility that all functions of the staff of 1st and 6th Corps were entirely handled by Reille.

Chapter 16

26 June 1815

History tells us that on 26 June the Duke d'Otranto, backed by General Carnot and M. Quinette, declared that the government of France was to be conducted in the name of the people. Napoléon II who reigned for a mere three days had been replaced by the machinations of Fouché as a prelude to the return of King Louis. Ironically, the same day General Guyardin published a proclamation urging the army to fight for Napoléon II.[1] This proclamation was out of date when it was published and read aloud to the army, such was the pace at which politics swept along. It was signed by Grouchy and also Guyardin. Attached to the proclamation was an order from Soult regarding the prevention of officers and men quitting ranks and dishonouring their flags. Soult also issued orders to Davout asking for money to be sent to pay the men, and also issued a proclamation telling the officers and men that they would be paid their owed pay. Soult was not stupid, and indeed he comments that telling the men they would get paid if they remained in ranks was a ploy to keep as many men with the army as possible. Soult informed Davout, who probably already knew that:[2]

> I have the honour to inform Your Excellency that that Lieutenant General Count Morand wrote to me from Urcel at half past eleven last night, to inform me that Marshal Blücher refused to suspend all hostilities.

Blücher demanded Napoléon be surrendered to him as a condition for cease-fire. This was clearly never going to happen. Blücher was clearly stalling for time. Wellington was opposed to the execution of Napoléon or his surrender to the Prussians and negotiated Napoléon be handed over to the British. Rather than make the handover of Napoléon a primary condition for the acceptance of the cease-fire, Wellington demanded the return of Louis XVIII. In this goal, Wellington was supported by Fouché and Davout. Thus, Fouché and Davout in the next twenty-four hours drafted a new memorandum for the cease-fire, the transmission of which to the allies would cost Grouchy his command, as we shall see.

But returning to the narration of the day of 26 June, Grouchy informed Davout of his meeting with Soult and the state of the Army at Soissons at 08.00 hours:[3]

> However, honoured I am, Mr. Marshal, of the command entrusted to me, I am too devoted to my country, not take on this duty, but it is above my abilities at this present time, and above all, the disorganization of the left wing of the army substantially weakens the moral of the troops I bring back with me. The bad example set by the debris of the Emperor's army, make us lose many men through desertion. The right wing consists of only 20,000 infantry men, 5,000 horses.
>
> I doubt that what is here is a mass of more than 25,000 men.

Grouchy had the top job but did not want it or feel capable of it. About Soult's departure Grouchy complained to Marshal Davout that:[4]

> The departure of the Duc de Dalmatie has totally disrupted and disorganised the officer personnel of the staff of the army. They are all trying to compete against each other in getting to Paris first, using the excuse that he had given them permission to do so. Please send to me General Guillaminot to act as chief-of-staff, and he must bring staff officers and clerks with him.

Clearly Soult's staff was missing a lot of key personnel for Grouchy to have requested them to join his own staff. Grouchy further noted that the Imperial Guard was agitating the troops in the area to desert and to march to Paris to aid Napoléon:[5]

> The disorganisation of the army that we are trying to reform here is still very depressing. No matter what orders I give, no matter the measures I take, I cannot prevent the soldiers leaving the colours and carrying out the most damaging acts. The Imperial Guard is also leaving, inflamed by rabble-rousers who are endeavouring to tell the men that they can best serve the Emperor's interest in Paris, they are using this as an excuse to quit their ranks and rush to the capitol.
>
> The troops at Soissons do not appear capable of fighting, though the cavalry is in better mood than the infantry and one can still get some service from them. It is impossible to use such demoralised infantry in combat.

Grouchy sent orders that the local gendarmerie was to be called out to stem the tide of deserters flooding to Paris both from the army and mobilised cohorts of the National Guard. Without Soult's guiding hand, or perhaps more importantly with the Emperor gone, what was left to fight for? The troops at Soissons, it seems, had begun to drift away from the army, and the work Soult had done over the previous ten days to rally the army and consolidate it was undone. Langeron, the garrison commander at Laon, despaired at being able to hold the place without regular soldiers being sent to bolster the garrison, either sent from Paris or detached from the Armée du Nord.[6]

However, Grouchy was able to report that Jacquinot's light cavalry was established in the suburbs of Laon, the Imperial Guard infantry and cavalry were between Soissons and Laon, Exelmans was between Craonne and Corbeny, Pajol's light cavalry was behind Coucy while 1st, 2nd and 6th Corps, under Reille, were at Soissons. Parts of 1st Corps were marching to Compiègne under the orders of General Comte d'Erlon. The cavalry of Kellerman and Milhaud were at Senlis.[7]

Furthermore, Grouchy reported to Marshal Davout that the allies had begun to concentrate at Laon, and in an action the line of communication with La Fère had been cut, despite the best efforts of General Pajol.[8]

The local newspaper announced that:[9]

> Soissons 26 June. The army is reunited under our walls. After many prodigies of valour at Mont-Saint-Jean, the enemy occupied positions that were impenetrable, and we attacked with an army of inferior numbers. We now have around 30,000 men. The Marshal Grouchy, who this morning was named commander in chief of the Armée du Nord. We have 100 pieces of cannon, all of them, manned.
>
> The Imperial Guard is placed in echelon along the road to Laon. The communications with this town are perfectly open. We are able to put up a strong defence. On the 22nd there was united at Chavignon and Laon, 5,000 men of the of the infantry of the Old Guard, and 2,000 cavalry of the same. It is obvious that they have not been massacred contrary to various announcements.
>
> At the moment, the troops of the 1st, 2nd and 6th Corps are all united under the command of General Reille and have received the order to move to Compiègne. The other troops are in position at Meaux. The 3rd and 4th Corps commanded by the General Vandamme will replace the corps of General Reille. General Corbineau, who is here, works with great zeal in reorganising the army.
>
> The Marshal duke of Dalmatia, Major-General, has left this morning for Paris.

Grouchy set about the task of re-organising the wreck of the Armée du Nord. The same day he took formal command, he authorised rations to be distributed. Vandamme, meanwhile, kept Grouchy informed of his situation in a dispatch timed at 05.30 hours:[10]

> Until now, there has not been anything new to report to you in the entire area occupied by the 3rd and 4th Corps, the latter will take position today, the 26th, from Junchery to Fisme. Early tomorrow morning, the three divisions will be returned to Barbu, Vailly, and Sermoise.
>
> Of the divisions of the 3rd Corps; one occupies Rheims, one is in front on Vitry, and the 4th is behind at Muizon.
>
> A rear-guard of hussars remained at Réthel to watch for the enemy moving from Vervins, Mézières and Sedan. Tomorrow all the troops of this Corps will be in Fisme, having only a rear guard in Reims. I think, Mr Marshal, that you will judge it wise to leave a battalion there, if only the Swiss. The National Guard are not able to do much, and it would be shameful if a cavalry party took this place; I'll wait for Your Excellency's orders.
>
> I will be in Soissons tomorrow, but I need to remain in Reims all this day.
>
> General Valin who sent me to ask for orders, will remain today where he is, in Neufchâtel.
>
> Our troops are paid and fed. They will fight well if they have to. They are like us, wanting to defend the fatherland.

Clearly in the chaos of the retreat, Vandamme had managed to keep his men fed and paid. This was vital in keeping the men under arms. Vandamme, in maintaining the 3rd and 4th Corps as an effective fighting force, had clearly made sure that despite the situation he kept the welfare of his men upmost in his mind. Subervie sent a dispatch to Grouchy from Crécy-au-Mont timed at 17.00 hours:[11]

> What I had expected has happened: the enemy has just pushed me back from Coucy-le-Château. At the receipt of your letter, I had manoeuvred to this town, with the 200 infantrymen, whom Marshal Duc de Dalmatie had sent me, to form the garrison of the latter. I was busy placing my posts in front of the place, when a cavalry column emerged from the village of Follembraye. I had with me the 11th Chasseurs à Cheval. As I was holding the enemy in check, the enemy put into battery two cannon and a howitzer, and deployed his column into line of battle, which I judged be 1,000 men strong. I could not resist this force, and having behind me a march 3/4 leagues on a paved road, in the middle of two marshes, I ordered the retreat to the regiments that were still at this place, and I ordered my entire cavalry corps on the height of Crécy-au-Mont. I had the infantry take position behind Létre.

While I was conducting my retreat under the fire from the enemy artillery, I saw a second column on the road from Chauhan to Nogent, to move to Coucy. We were able to continue to retreat.

As I had the honour to inform Your Excellency before, it was necessary to occupy Coucy, with infantry and artillery. The cavalry can do nothing here; they are useless.

In consequence I occupied the bridge over the Létre with 200 infantrymen, and all my cavalry is on the height of Crécy, which would still have to be defended with infantry and artillery, so that the enemy could [illegible] He may well turn the position from afar, but his artillery would still be forced to follow the road.

Lieutenant-General Subervie

P. S. General Trommelin arrives, I have sent one of my aides-de-camp to him to ask if the enemy force had any infantry.

Three hours later, General Domon sent a report to Grouchy from Craonne: [12]

An hour before the receipt of your order dated June 26th which ordered me to stay in Craonne until the arrival of General Exelmans, I received from His Excellency the Duke of Dalmatie, an order dated Soissons from June 25, at 10 o'clock in the evening, sent from Bussy, near Soissons, where it was assumed that I was, that I was to move to Compiègne, following the great road which passes to the left bank of the Aisne, etc., etc.

I have just learned that 200 Prussian cavalry have just arrived in Fétieux, between Laon and Corbeny. I still do not know if it is a reconnaissance patrol or the head of a column. In any case, I am on the defensive, I have informed General Jacquinot in Laon of this threat.

I think I have to give notice to Your Excellency that the General Orders are badly dispatched or miss handled. The proof is that I just received by one of my aides-de-camp, who has just left the post office at Soissons with orders for all the cavalry generals of your former Army Corps in Craonne.

Command and control were starting to break down. It is clear the order for Domon from the 25 June had not arrived with him till 26 June, and in consequence he had acted upon Soult's now out of date orders and not Grouchy's. With Soult and Grouchy issuing orders as commander in chief, often contradicting each other due to orders arriving in the wrong order, field commanders no doubt tried to do what they thought was best. Is this yet more treason by Soult and Monthion, or (as is more reasonable) was the staff slowly imploding? Lack of sleep, lack of 'down time', lack of food for horses and men would all contribute to the collapse of the staff corps, as would Prussian pickets ambushing couriers.

That night General Subervie sent news to Grouchy that Prussian columns were approaching his position at Coucy. He reported he had attempted to hold the bridge which he barricaded and with dismounted cavalry troopers endeavoured to hold off the Prussians. But faced with infantry he had no option other than to withdraw.[13]

Chapter 17

27 June 1815

In the morning of 27 June, the Prussian advanced guard of lancers arrived at Soissons. Grouchy began evacuating the place. At some point on 27 June, Marshal Grouchy ordered General Morand to unite his command of the infantry of the Guard with the light cavalry of the Guard under Lefèbvre-Desnoëttes at Villiers-Cotterêts, along with the 1st and 2nd Cavalry Brigades commanded by General Jacquinot. From Paris, several provisional regiments of cavalry were dispatched to the front from Saint-Denis:[1]

1st provisional regiment of Chasseurs à Cheval
1st Chasseurs à Cheval: 131 men
3rd Chasseurs à Cheval: 100 men
4th Chasseurs à Cheval: 105 men
8th Chasseurs à Cheval: 143 men
9th Chasseurs à Cheval: 40 men
12th Chasseurs à Cheval: 200 men
Total: 719 men and horses

1st Provisional regiment of Hussars
3rd Hussars: 150 men
7th Hussars: 150 men
Total: 300 men and horses

1st Marching cavalry regiment
1st Lancers: 83 men
13th Dragoons: 60 men

Total men from Saint-Denis: 1,162.

Furthermore, a mixed force of 400 men from the 2nd Carabiniers, 2nd and 11th Cuirassiers, and the 2nd Dragoons would arrive at Paris on 2 July.[2] They were to take up position by 14.00 hours.[3] The order

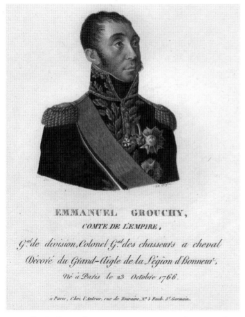

Marshal Grouchy, commander in chief of the right wing of the army from 16 to 26 June and then commander in chief of the army 26 June to 30 June.

General Gerard, commander of 4th Army Corps. He was wounded at Wavre on 18 June 1815.

General Vandamme, commander of 3rd Army Corps. He took command of 4th corps with Gerard's wounding.

Marshal Jean de Dieu Soult, Chief of Staff to the Armee du Nord, and titular head of the Army from 19 to 26 June. Following the restoration of the monarchy he was banished from France for 5 years.

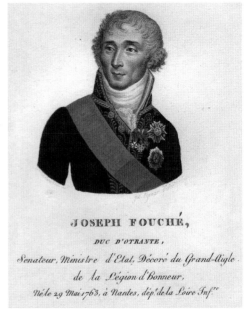

Marshal Nicolas Davout, Minister of War and acolyte of Comte d'Otranto. As Minister of War he sought to micro-manage the Armee du Nord from his desk in Paris and override Soult's orders.

Joseph Fouché, he led France following the abdication of Napoleon and sought peace at virtually any price to restore the monarchy.

General Drouot, nominal head of the Imperial Guard, following Waterloo he quit his command, and on pain of being shot as a deserter, he was complicit with Grouchy in peace negotiations with the Prussians.

General Exelmans led the 2nd Cavalry Corps throughout the 100 days. His lack of initiative on 18 June had major repercussions on the fate of the French army that day.

FRANÇOIS-ETIENNE KELLERMANN,
COMTE DE VALMY,
Général de Division, Commandeur de la Couronne de Fer,
Grand-Officier de la Légion d'Honneur,
Né le 4 Aout 1770 à Metz Dep.t de la Moselle.

General Kellerman led 3rd cavalry corps.
It was his men who sought to defend
Compiegne in the last days of June 1815.

General of Brigade Andre Burthe led the
1st brigade of General of Divisions Strolz
9th Cavalry Division, part of 2nd Cavalry Corps.

The farm at Sart-a-Walhain where Grouchy
heard the guns of Wavre

General of Division Louis Pierre Aime
Chastel led the 10th Cavalry Division
throughout the 100 days.

The entrance gateway under which Grouchy rode on 18 June to head to Wavre to fight the Prussians. It is a very evocative place to visit.

An 18th century map of Namur, the vital strong point that General Teste defended on 20-21 June 1815.

A late 19th century image of the defences of Namur.

A modern-day image of the last vestiges of the walls that once encircled Namur and the Brussels Gate.

The monument commemorating the French defenders of the Brussels gate. (Dominique Timmermans)

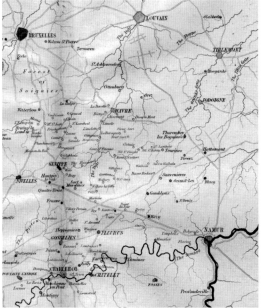

Map showing Namur in relation to Wavre, the river Sambre and Charleroi. Louvain, where an eye-witness states Grouchy was to be on 18 June is in the top centre of the map.

Paris as mapped in 1800. The city wall can be clearly seen as well as the numerous gates.

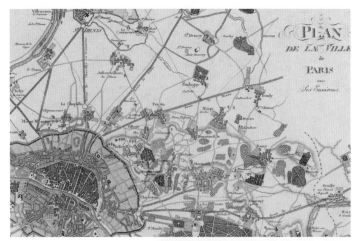

Map of the north east quarter of Paris in 1800, with Saint Denis in the top left.

Map of the south east quarter of Paris, centred on Vincennes, as drawn in 1800.

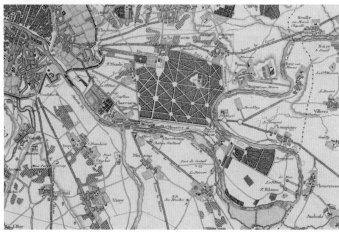

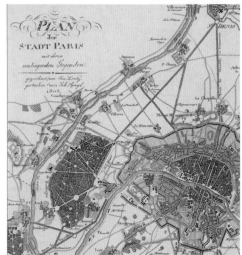

The south west quarter of Paris as mapped in 1800. In the centre is the plain of Grenelle, where the last battle of the Napoleonic wars took place.

The north west quarter of Paris, centred upon Neuilly, the scene of bitter fighting in July 1815.

77. COURBEVOIE — Le Pont de Neuilly

The old bridge of Neuilly which was contested over the course of 30 June to 3 July betwixt the French and Prussian armies.

The old bridge at Pecq, the control of which was of key strategic importance in the first days of July 1815.

46. - SAINT-CLOUD. — Le Pont - Vue générale
The Bridge - General View.

The old bridge at Saint Cloud, of strategic importance and the scene of bitter fighting.

The Bridge at Sevres, defended by the 2nd regiment of Line Infantry on 2-3 July 1815.

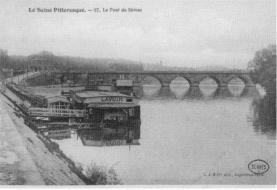

La Seine Pittoresque. — 97. Le Pont de Sèvres

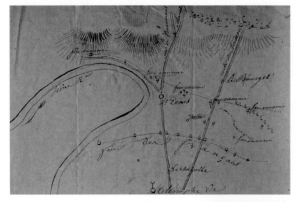

Incredibly rare hand drawn map of the defences of the north of Paris drawn on 1 July 1815.

Detailed map pf Rocquencourt made in 1792. It was in these streets that Exelmans cavalry ambushed the Prussian troops commanded by Von Sohr.

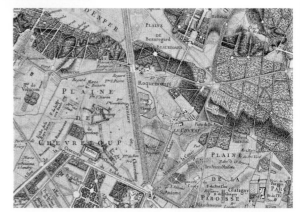

The memorial in Place Exelmans situated in Rocquencourt that commemorates the action on 1 July 1815.

Marshal Andre Massena. The 'dear child of victory' was given command of the Army of Paris on 3 July 1815. This was his last military command. He had been placed in command of the National Guard during the 100days, but was elevated once more to high command on the orders of Fouche when Davout was sacked. (Musee de l'Armee).

to Lefebvre-Desnoëttes was written from Soissons sometime after 08.00 hours, and read:[4]

> You have done very well, my dear general, to bring your troops to the position of Laffeaux, as this was only ordered by my letter of 2 o'clock in the morning. You must stay in this position until further orders which you will receive during the day. I beg you, in the meantime, to keep in contact with General Subervie, who was still at 2 in the morning at Puits-au-Mont, and, therefore, will be able to support you.
>
> When you make your retrograde move, you must inform General Subervie of this, so that he will follow you.

Sometime around 10.00 hours, Grouchy sent orders to Exelmans:[5]

> Please, general, leave with your army corps the position of Fisme, which you had to occupy yesterday, and go by Tradconois and Oulchyle-Château, onto Ferté-Milon, where you will take up positions, and where I will send you new orders.
>
> From La Ferté-Milon, you will return, after tomorrow on the road from Paris to Nanteuil, whereas we shall go to great steps on the capital, to defend it from the enemy which is at Compiègne. As you will not arrive until very late, tomorrow, in La Ferté-Milon, this is where I shall send you new orders

At around 14.00 hours, Grouchy wrote to Davout, informing him that the Guard was at that moment arriving and was to be based at his headquarters. General Reille was expected to arrive in the evening.[6] Grouchy's order to Reille can be found in the French Army Archives regarding his move to Nanteuil, via Crépy and Versigny.[7] Likewise, so does Grouchy's far more complete order to Vandamme:[8]

> My dear General,
>
> The enemy continues its moves to the capital, and it is indispensable that you reach their at great haste. They are massing towards Soissons. I shall be leaving the place by two o'clock and will head to Senlis and Paris via Villiers-Cotterêts and Crépy.
>
> I have already sent to Senlis, passing by Compiègne, the Comte d'Erlon with the 1st Corps of Infantry as well as the 3rd and 4th Cavalry Corps. You are to defile towards Senlis with your two corps, the others I am sending on the road to Nanteuil, where I desire them to be position by tomorrow, if this is not possible however, I will write to you with new orders.
>
> The Corps of General Exelmans is headed to La Ferté-Milon.
>
> The Corps of General Pajol will stand this evening on the heights of Villiers-Cotterêts along with the Infantry and Cavalry of the Guard.

The Infantry Corps will be at Nateuil this evening and Dammartin tomorrow.

I will give you new orders tomorrow from Nanteuil, where you are to send your reports. My headquarters will be this evening at Villiers-Cotterêts.

Further, the Comte d'Erlon endeavoured to hold Compiègne and re take the positions the enemy had captured from us – you can well imagine our embarrassment. The enemy are heading from Compiègne to Verbery and one of their corps is headed to Crépy…[illegible] Order the Division of Valin. that the Division of Domon as soon as it enters Villiers-Cotterêts will no longer be the rear-guard cavalry.

At 15.00 hours, Grouchy sent orders to Vandamme:[9]

My dear General,

The Division of Vichery has arrived here at 8 o'clock in the morning, I have ordered them to depart here this evening and head to Villiers-Cotterêts, from where they should arrive tomorrow morning to occupy Crépy in good time. I have received no news from Compiègne … [remainder illegible]

Sometime after 15.00 hours Grouchy received word about the enemy and its move to Paris. In response, Grouchy sent more orders to Vandamme. One can feel Grouchy's desperation that the capital might fall before he could arrive with the army:[10]

My Dear General,

The movement to Paris becomes ever more urgent, as every moment passes. The enemy is heading to cross the l'Oise and gain the capital. [illegible and crossed out] send your corps to La Ferté-Milon, Ary and Dammartin, lose not a minute in your movement …

I will leave here at 5 o'clock and head straight to Villiers-Cotterêts and thence to Dammartin.

You are to give orders that the Division of Vichery will form the rear guard as soon as it gains Villiers-Cotterêts. You are to give the same order to the Cavalry of General Valin, which is part of your Army Corps; they will be reinforced by General Exelmans who will be at La Ferté-Milon.

On the evening of 27 June, around 19.00 hours, the Guard cavalry and elements of the Guard infantry, under the command of General Reille, as well as the troops of Marshal Grouchy, occupied the town of Villiers-Cotterêts. Grouchy sent news to Vandamme that evening about d'Erlon's failure:[11]

I send to you my dear General copies of reports that I have received from General d'Erlon that have I have just received. Lose not a

minute in your movements to Paris and make your march as fast
as possible. I am leaving here tomorrow at 2 in the morning along
with the Imperial Guard to head to Dammartin, to arrive later that
day when I hope you shall also arrive at Nanteuil with your Corps.

Vandamme noted that at 02.00 hours on the 28th, he, with 2nd Corps
and the Imperial Guard, left the place, with the cavalry of General
Domon in support, and headed to Dammartin.[12]

Action at Soissons

On the morning of 27 June, the Prussian advanced guard of lancers
arrived at Soissons. Grouchy began evacuating the place. Blücher, notes
Grouchy, was at Noyon, preventing him from establishing a strong
force at Compiègne. As a result, 1st Corps, along with the cavalry of
Kellerman and Milhaud was ordered to move to Senlis. General Reille
with 2nd and 6th Corps was ordered to move to Nanteuil and hold
the position whilst Grouchy himself and the Imperial Guard was to
move to Villiers-Cotterêts, hoping to arrive on the evening of the 27th.
General Vandamme with 3rd and 4th Corps was ordered to form the
rear guard and continue his movement to Paris.

According to the Prussian writer Damitz, what remained of the
French 2nd Corps under Reille was attacked at Nanteuil by the
troops of Prussian General Zieten. The cavalry screen of 2nd Corps,
comprising it seems of dragoons of the Imperial Guard and some
lancers, were attacked by the 1st Silesian Hussars. A battery of guns
from the Imperial Guard Horse Artillery had been established on
the left of the main road, and were quickly overrun, losing two guns.
The Prussians pursued the French beyond Nanteuil and onto Paris.[13]
Clearly, Reille at some stage, ran into trouble that day. The 5th Lancers
lost a considerable number of men on 28 June as well as men through
attrition as POW:[14]

	1st Co.	2nd Co.	3rd Co.	4th Co.	5th Co.	6th Co.	7th Co.	8th Co.	Total
Presumed POW	2	2	0	1	0	0	1	0	6
POW	9	1	7	3	4	3	1	1	29
Deserted	0	0	0	2	0	0	1	2	5
Missing	0	1	0	0	0	0	0	0	1
Killed	0	0	0	0	1	0	0	0	1
Total	11	4	7	6	5	3	3	3	42

Clearly, the 5th Lancers ran into trouble on 28 June. In comparison the regiment lost forty-eight men at Waterloo. At the time of disbandment on 5 December 1815, the regiment recorded seventeen men wounded and 264 men missing, either prisoners, deserted, or killed since 18 June 1815 and 1 July. In comparison, we can use the parade states of 10 June and 24 June to give total losses for the regiment in the intervening fourteen days. On 10 June, the regiment mustered forty-three officers and 543 other ranks. Kellerman informed Marshal Soult on 24 June that the regiment the mustered twenty-four officers with thirty-five horses, and 301 other ranks with 299 horses.[15] This represents a loss of 242 other ranks, or 44 per cent of the effective strength being lost between the 10 and 24 June 1815. The brigaded 6th Lancers lost no men.[16] This is perhaps understandable when one aligns the casualty data from Quatre-Bras and two reports made by General Wathiez. The regimental muster list is presented here in full for Quatre-Bras:[17]

Squadron	Killed	Deserted	Wounded	Wounded POW	Missing	TOTAL
1	4	0	8	0	0	12
2	1	0	10	0	0	11
3	3	0	11	2	0	16
4	4	0	6	0	1	11
Etat Major	1	0	2	0	0	3
TOTALS	13	0	37	2	1	53

Seven officers were either killed or wounded and in terms of other ranks lost, fifty-two men were killed, wounded or made prisoner, and perhaps as many as 104 horses. No men are recorded lost at Waterloo.

Clearly, Wathiez's brigade sat out the action at Waterloo. Wathiez reports to Davout that in the regiment, Colonel Galbois was wounded and had left the regiment, and not a single squadron commander remained in post. To this end, command of the regiment had devolved upon Captain Mathonet who Wathiez recommended be promoted to squadron commander.[18] Mathonet served as commanding officer of 2nd company, to which he had been appointed on 23 August 1809.[19] With the regiment losing fifty-three men and perhaps as many as 160 horses, from a total of 347 present on 1 June, we see 43 per cent of the regiment was out of action after Quatre-Bras. Coupled with all the senior officers being dead or wounded, we can see why the regiment took no part in any fighting. Wathiez also informed Davout that Squadron Commander Milet of the 5th Lancers had quit the regiment for anti-French sentiments; Captain Maradan was his temporary replacement.[20] In a second dispatch, Wathiez informed Davout that the wounded men and horses of the 2nd Cavalry Division had been sent to their depots. He notes his chief of staff was also wounded.[21] Oddly he only talks of the battle of 16 June 1815. Was it possible the entire brigade sat out Waterloo? Yes.

Due to a combination of exhaustion, the total lack of any rations being issued since the morning of the 18th, or at Soissons, the army was starving, and men were deserting home, feeling that without Napoléon, they had no obligation to remain under arms.

Action at Villiers-Cotterêts: 27 to 28 June 1815

Marshal Grouchy ordered General Morand to unit his command of the Infantry of the Guard with the Light Cavalry of the Guard under Lefebvre-Desnoëttes at Villiers-Cotterêts, along with the 1st and 2nd cavalry brigades commanded by General Jacquinot. They were to take up position by 14.00 hours.[22]

At around that time, Grouchy wrote to Davout, informing him that the Guard was at that moment arriving and was to be based at his headquarters. General Reille was expected to arrive in the evening.[23]

During the evening, around 19.00 hours, the Guard Cavalry together with elements of the Guard Infantry, and the troops of General Reille and Marshal Grouchy, occupied the town of Villiers-Cotterêts. General Vandamme noted that at 02.00 hours on 28 June, he, with 2nd Corps and the Imperial Guard left the place with the cavalry of General Domont in support and headed to Dammartin.[24] About the attack Clausewitz noted:[25]

> Toward evening on the 27th the utterly exhausted troops of Marshal Grouchy's 4th Corps arrived at Villers-Cotterêts, and those of the 3rd at Soissons. He quartered his troops in the nearby villages, in order to provide them with essential food and rest as quickly as possible and decided at two o'clock the following morning to continue the march to Nanteuil. Since he must have received news at Villers-Cotterêts of the battle that had taken place that morning at Compiègne, it was very risky for him to continue the march on the Soissons road. It would have been more sensible to turn immediately toward Meaux, via La Ferté-Milon, for at Nanteuil he could have run into three Prussian corps and been destroyed within sight of Paris. Most probably the thought of taking his weary troops on a new detour over terrible roads repelled him, and the hope of still getting through on a good quality and straight major road attracted him. He did not in fact achieve his goal, for he still

had to abandon the road, but he also did not suffer the catastrophe that had threatened him. This is because the Prussian forces were not sufficiently concentrated to mount a concerted attack on him.

As we have already said, General Pirch and his 2nd Brigade were detached toward Villers-Cotterêts and on the night of the 27th-28th reached Longpré, about an hour away, at 01.00 hours. He allowed his troops some rest and broke camp again at 02.00 hours. He initially ran into a train of French horse artillery, consisting of fourteen guns and twenty munitions wagons, which were trying to reach the highway from their camps at Viviers, Montgobert, and Puiseux, and were moving with virtually no escort; they were thus captured immediately. After this General Pirch advanced to attack Villers-Cotterêts itself.

Grouchy assembled his troops, 9,000 strong (presumably Gérard's corps), and offered resistance. On the other side Vandamme came up from Soissons with the French 3rd Corps. Although the sound of cannon fire on the Paris highway immediately caused a kind of panic-stricken terror to set in, as cries that they might be cut off led most of the troops there to strike out at once by way of La Ferté-Milon for Meaux, Vandamme, nevertheless, succeeded in advancing up the road with about 2,000 men and came to Marshal Grouchy's assistance.

General Pirch had only five under-strength battalions, five squadrons of cavalry, and thirteen cannon; General Zieten and most of the Prussian 1st Corps were on the march from Gilicourt to Crépy, around three hours away, and were not near enough to provide support. Vandamme advanced against Pirch's left flank, Grouchy manoeuvred against his right, and under these circumstances General Pirch correctly decided a bold assault was ill-advised and so began to retreat toward Compiègne, from which he later turned toward Crépy by way of Fresnoy. General Zieten had not yet assembled his troops at Crépy, so when the French corps passed by, he could move against the highway with only the 3rd Brigade and half the reserve cavalry. The village of Levignen, through which the French passed, was shelled and the rear guard pursued to Nanteuil, where two cannon were taken.

At some stage in the action, the 2nd regiment of West Prussian Dragoons charged the French, but were pushed back, and then attacked in the flank by the regiment of Light Horse Lancers of the Imperial Guard, supported by the 1st and 5th Hussars, according to an eyewitness in the latter regiment.[26]

We have just arrived at the camp near Meaux. The enemy followed us from Villers-Cotterets until we reached a village three leagues beyond. His scouts approached and we were recognized. As we followed along the high road, he sent us numerous volleys of cannon, which did no harm to us. As his skirmishers flanked us from very close range, I was detached with a platoon to scout the right of the column. Scarcely had I time to skirmish for few minutes, when I saw emerge from the wood five squadrons of Hussars and two squadrons of Lancers, who arrived at full gallop.

The 1st Hussars was formed immediately to receive the charge, but finding themselves turned by their left, they dispersed almost immediately. Our regiment which was a hundred yards behind, was not yet formed. Colonel Liegeard charged at the head of two pelotons who were assembled. When I saw the Colonel move forward, I threw myself on the enemy's right flank, with the few skirmishers who wanted to follow me. The Hussars had not followed the movement of Colonel; they had dispersed so we found ourselves fighting with the enemy, with only the officers of the regiment and the few soldiers who would not abandon us.

I did not think it is possible to see such a melee: nearly all the Prussians were drunk so they could only carry their sabres very poorly and struck almost all blows with the flat of the sabre. I received three, including one on the head … The Colonel would have had his head split had he been without his shako, but it slightly grazed his cheek. His arms and shoulders were covered with strokes from the flat of the sabres. However, he was slashing vigorously.

The officers fought despite it being hopeless. I cut down five or six, including one officer who came upon me enraged and touched the head of my mare with the tip of his sword. I gave him a blow on the forehead with mine. He fell away from his horse and his blood splashed onto me. We were dealing with the Hussars of Brandenburg and Pomerania, and the Lancers. Against all odds, we lost very few people, I believe that the enemy took a number killed or wounded. We were obliged to withdraw and, during the next two leagues and a half, we were unable to rally the troops. The enemy pursued us until two leagues from Meaux, and we arrived at seven o'clock in the evening, abysmally tired.

According to Captain Jean Roche Coignet of the Imperial Headquarters, the Prussians attacked the town, and once the town had been taken, the Prussians followed the tide of retreating French troops.

The attack proper came later that morning outside the town of Villiers-Cotterêts. Prussian General Roder with the Reserve Cavalry ran into 800 or so Cuirassiers that remained under the orders of General Milhaud. Prussian General Zestow, at the head of the 2nd Regiment of West Prussian Dragoons and the Brandenburg Uhlans, charged the

French, but were pushed back, and then attacked in the flank by the regiment of Light Horse Lancers of the Imperial Guard.[27]

Sergeant-Major Chevalier of the Chasseurs à Cheval of the Imperial Guard notes that the ambush in the woods took place when horses had been taken to water:[28]

> It was getting dark and we formed our camp and some shelters. Our horses had been off-saddled, and we had gone to water them at the large gully through which a small river flows and was more than one mile from the camp. During these times, we were all on guard, as a large number of skirmishers had invested the forest.
>
> They surrounded us, advancing themselves into the wood and thickets, and rained on us a hail of bullets. Nothing is more stupid than a rider without a horse. However, we opened fire with our carbines, and we made concerted efforts to prevent them from slipping into the brush with the cut grain for our horses. Our Chasseurs à Cheval à Cheval came back at the gallop, having heard the shooting. We were obliged to leave the camp, a very bad place for us, and to establish ourselves the other side of the ravine which we could easily guard.

General Guyot wrote:[29]

> I passed Villiers-Cotterêts at mid-night, at 02:00 on the 28th. 400 or 500 Prussians entered Villiers-Cotterêts, and surprised the Marshal Grouchy, who escaped by running through the gardens. A parc of artillery comprising 12 canon and their caissons were captured. The occupation of Villiers-Cotterêts impeded our movement of retreat ...
>
> 28th June. At four o'clock in the morning a strong enemy reconnaissance patrol entered Crépy and forced us to mount our horses, we rested in our position until around seven o'clock in the evening. At this time, M. General Drouot, who had been newly placed in command of the Imperial Guard, ordered me to begin my march towards Dammartin, and we would on the route unit with the light cavalry of the Guard under the orders of M. General Lefebvre-Desnoëttes. It was towards midday that this retrograde movement began.

In the retreat to Dammartin, it seems that the Chasseurs à Cheval ambushed the Prussians on 29 June, and wrought their revenge:[30]

> The next day we marched quietly along the road to Dammartin, marching by platoons, as we had spent all night on the alert, whilst everyone else was asleep. The platoons were very close and only a little distant from each other. But suddenly, we were pleasantly

and suddenly awakened by a charming Hooray, we made upon the Prussian cavalry, which threw us against its head, tail and on the sides, charging all at once. They were quickly awoken up and were soon assembled charging around our head and rear. They were soon routed and tumbled back and we learned to respect another a little better.

1st Cavalry Division
In the chaos many of the cavalry regiments became scattered and lost heavily. The regimental muster is presented here in full:[31]

Squadron	Killed	Deserted	Wounded	POW	Missing	TOTAL
TOTALS	2	13	1	5	0	21

The brigaded 4th Lancers also lost men. The regimental muster list is presented here in full:[32]

Squadron	Killed	Deserted	Wounded	POW	Missing	TOTAL
TOTALS	0	11	0	1	1	13

Colonel Bro's regiment lost eighty-six men at Waterloo with a further twelve men being recorded missing on 20 June and two men listed missing on 21 June. Presumably these men were dismounted and left behind during the retreat. Ten men had been lost on 17 June at Ligny. This makes a total loss of 110 men 17 to 20 June.[33] In the same division was the 7th Hussars, which recorded just two men having deserted:[34]

Chapter 18

Action at Compiègne 26 to 28 June 1815

The Prussian juggernaut was rolling remorselessly to Paris. Important bridges at La Fère and Compiègne had to be taken if they were to be stopped. Compiègne had been occupied by the advanced guard of the Prussian I Corps, and the whole of Jagow's brigade deployed in the defence of the town by 05.00 hours on 27 June. It was here that Grouchy planned to attack the Prussians.

D'Erlon's 1st Corps was placed between Soissons and Compiègne, with the cavalry of General Delort providing a screen. The 5th Cuirassiers were at Montigny, the 10th Cuirassiers at Haute-Fontaine, and the 6th were at Jaubry with Delort's staff,[1] The cavalry of Domon, Kellerman, and Milhaud were to march to Compiègne in support of d'Erlon and 1st Corps, which had been dispatched to undertake this flank attack.[2] This was a large-scale operation, which if it would have succeeded would have delayed the Prussian army, and given Vandamme with 3rd and 4th Corps more time to get to Paris, along with Reille with the remains of 2nd and 6th Corps. The daring plan however did not bank on the fact that 1st Corps would not fight. Grouchy should have known this, but clearly, he was clutching at straws by using what turned out to be overwhelming French forces against the Prussians.

The French, even in the most dispirited state, could have one a small victory over the Prussian advance guard which was headed by the 1st Silesian Hussars, but Major Von Engelhardt entered the town at 20.00 hours unhindered, by the French:[3]

> I wish to report to your excellency that I have just arrived here. I immediately went to the town hall, where the sub-prefect presented me with a letter from the commandant of Soissons. In the

letter, he states he surrenders the town and has provisions for 10,000 men. Despite the letter, preparations for its defence are being taken. The mood of the inhabitants here seems to be very good. All were shouting 'Vive le Roi!'.

Early that morning reports came in from field commanders to Grouchy's headquarters. At 06.00 hours General Milhaud sent in his report to Headquarters, it read:[4]

I sent Delort the order to proceed on the way to Compiègne and I warned him that we had to execute all the orders of General Comte d'Erlon. I'll follow as closely as possible, with the Division of General Wathier.

I have informed General Comte de Valmy of my movements, and of the enemy on Compiègne, so that he will be able to support us and hasten his movement, until he receives orders.

Likewise, General Subervie sent reconnaissance reports to Grouchy from Crécy-au-Mont, which read as follows:[5]

The enemy does not make any dispositions before me. I continually observe the different roads.

I have had the honour to inform you that General Blücher's headquarters are in Chanin.

A patrol returned from Blerancourt told me that the peasants there had seen the day before yesterday move from Noyon, a column of 8.000 men heading for Compiègne. It is likely that this movement continued today.

We heard the cannon all night in the direction of Guise.

Grouchy issued orders to General Domon about 08.00 hours:[6]

Please, my dear general, leave immediately from the position you occupy in Rucy, repassing Soissons, and go and settle in the villages of Mont-Ghazal and Rivière, on the right of the road from Soissons to Villers-Cotterets. My headquarters will be in Villers-Cotterets tonight, where you'll send me two officers to receive orders for tomorrow. You will establish yourself and keeping your guard The government did not know that you were here when it amalgamated your Corps with that of General Reille and general Comte de Lobau. Since this provision is quite contrary to the good of the service, I think I have to suspend its execution, I will report this to the minister.

Please, my dear general, take the 1st Corps to Compiègne, where you will take up position: I want you to be established their tomorrow. I put under your command the 3rd and 4th Corps of cavalry, commanded by Generals Kellerman and Milhaud. They are, both on the road from Soissons to Compiègne, the 1st in Ambleny, and the 2nd in the village of Châtellet. You will send them orders and dispose of them to along the roads of Noyon, Mondidier and others, culminating in Compiègne.

You will restore the defensive work that had been done last year, for the defence of this city, you will order that preparations are undertaken to blow up the bridge of Compiègne and you will make a reconnaissance along the right bank of the Oise, taking a position at the intersection of paths from Compiègne to Clermont, and from Pont-St-Maxence to Roye. By keeping this point continually monitored, we will be assured if the enemy is on the Oise, and manoeuvres on our left flank, as various reports announce.

I wish, my dear general, that you destroy all the boats that can be found on the Aisne, from Soissons, to Compiègne. Please also ensure that bridge over the river, at the of the village of Attigny is destroyed

Finally, my dear general, I defer to your judgement, as to movement of the left wing of the army, and urge you to keep me well informed of everything you learn about the movements of the enemy in the direction of Compiègne where the enemy is.

At the same time as the Prussians were heading to Compiègne, Grouchy dispatched orders to d'Erlon at 07.00 hours:[7]

General Delort reported to his corps commander, General Milhaud, at 20.00 hours on 26 June, which Milhaud forward to Grouchy at 06.00 hours on 27 June:[8]

I have the honour to inform you that my division is established as follows:

The 5th regiment in Montigny; 10th at Haute-Fontaine, and 6th in Jaubry, with my staff.

All the boats have been sunk, from Soissons, to Compiègne. Consequently, I could not send a reconnaissance patrol of cuirassiers to the right bank of the Aisne; But I have instructed the mayor of Jaulzy, to interrogate the peasants at Àulrèche and Audignecourt.

I will send you their reports, as soon as they have reached me.

The 1st Infantry Corps is placed in front of me and left here a brigade.

The country is poor, it is difficult to buy oats.

We are assured that the enemy is in Noyon, but I think he did not come in force.

The report was transmitted by General Milhaud at 06.00 hours on 27 June. Where were the 9th Cuirassiers? They had been under Delort's command, but clearly had become separated from the Division.

Clearly also, a now lost dispatch arrived with Grouchy, the contents of which he passed onto Davout:[9]

> I have the honour to inform your excellency that the Prussian Army is marching to Noyon and Compiègne. The headquarters of General Blücher last night were at Noyon. Orders were issued to occupy Compiègne but have not been able to be carried out. Prussian lancers have already seized the place about half past eight last night. The officer I sent arrived at the same time as them. The Comte d'Erlon had marched with his corps and two corps of cavalry with orders to move to Senlis and occupy the position.
>
> The other corps of the Armée du Nord are heading towards Paris, the corps of General Comte Reille, is to head to Nateuil and occupy the place. Also taking part in this movement will be the Corps of the Guard, which will depart Soissons and Laon and move via Villiers-Cotterêts, which is where I will probably establish my headquarters this evening.
>
> The Corps of General Vandamme is the in rear and is moving to Soissons; he is forming the rear guard and will continue his movement to Paris.
>
> I attach a report for your excellency on the movements the enemy are making on Paris and are in pursuit we are lost if the army is not rallied army and the government takes no steps towards the defence of Paris.
>
> M. Marshal, please accept my assurances for you
>
> The Marshal Comte de Grouchy
>
> P.S. Enemy lancers last night were distributing white cockades and encouraging the population of Compiègne to shout, 'Vie le Roi'.

In addition, as we have seen, between writing to d'Erlon at 07.00 hours, the reports of Domon, Milhaud and Delort had arrived at headquarters. Clearly, troops had not arrived in time to occupy the place. An eye-witness to these events was General Kellerman who felt it was a huge mistake not to send troops on 26 June:[10]

> Marshal Soult on first hearing the news of the enemy's approach had retreated to Soissons, Marshal Grouchy replaced him, and arrived there at 4 o'clock in the morning of the 27th. The danger was pressing and there was no time to be lost in gaining the bridges over the Aisne or Oise. He should, on the 26th or at least early on the 27th, have occupied Compiègne which the enemy entered at 7 o'clock in the evening of the same day.
>
> The Comte d'Erlon was sent on the following, day, the 28th, but could not entre and had to retire into the forest. The Comte de Valmy and the Comte Milhaud also went to this place, but the place had already been occupied.

Kellerman is writing very much after the fact. Kellerman is wrong that d'Erlon was not sent till 28 June, he was ordered there on 27 June. He also blames Grouchy for the lack of initiative to take Compiègne, but again gets the date on which Grouchy arrived wrong, for Grouchy was with Soult on 25 June.

Getting back to our narrative, in response to the reports he had received, Grouchy sent new orders to d'Erlon at 08.00 hours:[11]

> My dear general,
>   I sent you two orders, the 1st at 3:00 a.m., the 2nd at 5:00. This one will clarify ones you have received. By the reports that come to me, it seems to me that the movement of the enemy on Compiègne is conducted only with cavalry.
>   If that is the case, there is no downside to the movement on Compiègne that you are undertaking. If not, and the enemy does indeed have infantry, which may not as yet have arrived, it would announce the enemy's intention to advance from this point. In this situation you must go from where you currently are to Senlis, or through the forest of Compiègne, or by running along its edge. You will occupy as quickly as possible the bridges at Verbery and Pont-St-Maxence. The reports I'll receive from you will determine the movement I'll make with the army.

Early on the 27th, d'Erlon's corps observed elements of the Prussian I Army Corps around 03.30 hours, and d'Erlon duly occupied the bridges of Verbie and Pont-Saint-Maxence. D'Erlon attacked at around 06.00 hours but failed to prevent the Prussians occupying Compiègne in force and began to withdraw to Gilicourt. The bridges were to be occupied and then destroyed to secure Vandamme's flank. The Prussians were in position by 05.00 hours, by which time d'Erlon's columns had already been observed. A single battery of Prussian artillery reportedly opened fire and the advance stalled.[12] How could 1st Corps, and two corps of cavalry have been so easily pushed back by just four artillery pieces? Simply put, the moral of 1st Corps was so shattered that a few salvos of artillery fire sent the corps running for cover in the Bois du Compiègne. A force of just seventy Prussian cavalry cleared the wood. The men of Waterloo no longer had any desire to fight.

This gave the Prussians time for the entire I Corps to arrive at Compiègne. The Prussians were as equally exhausted as the French but could still fight. If d'Erlon had been able to fight, he would have found Compiègne occupied only by the Prussian 29th Infantry Regiment and 2nd West Prussian Infantry Regiment supported by the 1st Silesian Hussars, a force of no more than 3,000 men. In comparison, d'Erlon had roughly 4,500 infantry and 4,000 cavalry.[13]

With Compiègne already occupied by the Prussians, d'Erlon, ever cautious and not desiring to press home his overwhelming numerical advantage, retreated towards Senlis. Clearly d'Erlon knew his men had no stomach to fight, but the importance of this fact does not seem to have been transmitted sufficiently clearly to Grouchy to make him understand that the 1st Corps could no longer be counted upon as an effective and cohesive element of the Armée du Nord. The only troops capable of fighting were Vandamme's 3rd and 4th Corps, supported by the cavalry of Pajol and Exelmans, and from 27 June, Vandamme regained Vallin's and Domon's cavalry. At some time before 14.00 hours on 27 June, d'Erlon sent word to Grouchy.[14]

> As we arrived at the positions the enemy had taken in front of Compiègne, we were greeted by a cannonade from the far bank of the river. As the road to Soissons leads to the Châteauxx Terrasse which is too strong to be attacked from the front, I took care of the means of outflanking it by moving along the Paris road. It was then that I received the order of Your Excellency to move to Senlis. I will execute this movement, masking it as much as I can and I will make sure to occupy Verberic and Pont-St.-Maxence. But I'm afraid it may already be too late to do so.

At 15.00 hours d'Erlon wrote once more to Grouchy:[15]

> On the heights of Gilicourt, on 27 June 1815, 3 o'clock in afternoon.
> Mr. Maréchal, I have already had the honour of reporting to Your Excellency that I received the order this morning to move to Senlis. I also received your second letter as well as the one written to me by General Monthion.
> There is no doubt that the enemy heads to Compiègne. There was already this night in this city 4 or 5000 infantry, and we saw a more considerable column coming from Noyon.
> I therefore believe, Mr. Maréchal, that there is no time to lose for Your Excellency to execute your movement.
> I'm here with my infantry and general Milhaud. I had given orders to General Kellerman, but he has not yet arrived. I'm going to go to Néry. When Mr. General Kellerman arrives, I will order him to send scouting parties to Verberic and Pont-St-Maximin.

This letter is important in two ways. It describes d'Erlon's operations, but more interestingly, it shows that Monthion was still doing his job, that of Chef d'État Major Généraux, i.e. running the head-quarters staff. He sent out couriers with orders, getting copies written up of verbal or written orders and then sending them to where they were needed. Of interest, when Soult had left Soissons on 26 June, Monthion had apparently travelled with him. But it seems that Monthion was still very much part of the military machine that kept the Armée du Nord running. Was he still running Soult's former headquarters? Yes, it seems to be the case based on the evidence of Monthion transmitting orders. We assume therefore that Guillaminot took over the running of Grouchy's staff.

About the action at Compiègne, General Curely, in command of a brigade of Chasseurs à Cheval reported that:[16]

> The 27 June, a portion of the army which was held at Soissons, marched to Compiègne to occupy this important position and hold the line of the Aisne, but the enemy we were warned and occupied Compiègne and we had to make a move to the left for us to withdraw through the wood of Senlis. After a very difficult march, we arrived at ten o'clock at Senlis. A brigade of cuirassiers of General Kellerman's corps, to which I belonged, crossed the city to withdraw by the road to Paris. My brigade, the head of which was with me, General Kellerman and General Roussel, commander of the division to which it belonged, set off to follow the first, and we entered Senlis. We arrived at about the middle of the city, which was illuminated so that one could see as plain as day, when five or six shots were fired suddenly from a small street leading to the one we followed, and a bullet struck the knee of a squadron leader of cuirassiers.
>
> We continued to advance to reach the exit of the town, but when we arrived near the Paris Gate, I saw under the gate a group of men. I advanced to try to recognize them, and when I was ten paces from them, I was greeted by a volley directed at me and the head of the column. It was the enemy which had seized the gate. As they continued to shoot, it became impossible to leave by the Paris Gate and we fell back in disorder towards the Compiègne Gate, but found it also occupied by enemy infantry, so that three generals and two regiments of cuirassiers were stranded in the town of Senlis. There was no middle way, it was necessary to make ourselves prisoners or ride over the enemy, there was no hesitation, we took the road by which we returned and we retired that night to Borest, our loss was confined to a general's hat and some wounded men.

Kellerman himself wrote:[17]

> The Comte d'Erlon forced his march to gain Senlis and Crépy. We assumed that the enemy troops that were at Compiègne were heading directly to Senlis … there was no time to lose. The 4th cavalry corps, a force of some 1500 cavalry, marched to Crépy where it halted at 2 o'clock in the afternoon at the insistence of

Comte d'Erlon. Because of this, it had not been possible to keep due diligence on the advance of the enemy on Senlis and to the right bank of the l'Oise. The Comte de Valmy was in support on the road to this town, but it too had already been occupied. The news was of great surprise as he had been assured the road from Compiègne to Senlis was free. In response he had to change direction to gain Louvres, and had to pass through a wood and returned to Senlis with a force of 500 cavalry, where it was supposed he would arrive on the rear of the army corps that had captured the place. It was about 9 o'clock that he arrived at the gates of Senlis ... he ordered the attack. The brigade commanded by General Picquet charged through the town.

Rigau, colonel of the 2nd Dragoons which, along with the 7th Dragoons, formed a brigade commanded by General Picquet, takes up the story:[18]

General Kellerman retired with his regiments, artillery and wounded on Paris. Before arriving at Senlis, he gave me two squadrons of my brave regiment to act as the vanguard, for two hours ahead of the troops of his cavalry corps, instructing me to press my march in order to forestall the enemy, and keep me there until his arrival. I learned, half a league from this city, that the enemy had been there several hours. I immediately sent an officer with the news to the general for orders, he sent me word to go and try to push back the vanguard that was there. He assumed it was weak, when in reality it was an entire corps. I left a reserve squadron with orders to await the arrival of the General, I put myself with the other, and at the gallop entered Senlis ... Our cries of 'Vive l'Empereur!' cast terror among the Prussians but with the rapid arrival of night it was difficult to see what was happening.

Arriving at the outskirts of Senlis, which I entered by the main street, I had to stop to discover the whereabouts of the enemy camp. The horsemen who had fled before us, and who had thrown themselves into the streets or alleys adjacent, believed that this their moment to try and stop us by force. They began to fire on the flanks of the squadron, which, believing itself to be facing serious resistance, returned to join the squadron which had remained outside the city: the squadron was easily misled by the darkness. Left alone with six men, and soon surrounded, we were unable to return through the main street. I threw myself into the interior of the town and arrived near a small place where there were few trees. I stopped to listen, and I heard the alert that I had just given all the troops ... I went with my six men in a house with a carriage entrance, to avoid the many patrols that began to circulate, I passed the night there ... At daybreak, the enemy's army continued its march and I left the city at eleven o'clock.

Adjutant Fleuret of the 55th Line noted:[19]

> We bivouacked at Soissons for five days, and we left to go to Compiègne, but the enemy had arrived there before us, and opened fire on us with their artillery which they had concealed behind a ridge. We marched in column by section, so we lost many men including a commandant who had his shoulder taken off by a cannon ball. We were thrown back into the great forest of Compiègne.

It is easy to understand how d'Erlon's men, marching in column were very easy targets for the Prussian artillery, and how quickly the moral of men, which was already at a very low ebb, would send the officers and men into panic and render the 1st Corps null and void as a combat force. About the failure of d'Erlon, Grouchy sent word to Davout at 22.00 hours that:[20]

> Mr. Maréchal, I have the honour to pass on to you the two reports I received from General Comte d'Erlon on my arrival here. You will see that the enemy was in force at Compiègne when he appeared before this city. He was only able to head to Senlis by crossing through the forest. I ordered him to go during the night to Senlis. It is of the greatest importance that he arrives there before the enemy. Occupying the place would delay the enemy in their movement from Compiègne to Paris. Without this delay, the Anglo-Prussian army will arrive at Paris before I can.
>
> I request again, Mr. Maréchal, that all the available troops that you have in Paris be sent to Senlis to support D'Erlon. It is necessary that he be supported by some new soldiers, as the troops he has with him no longer want to fight, and the march of the enemy does not allow me to move via Crépy to Senlis, as I proposed, and indeed the Corps of General Vandamme can only leave tomorrow morning from Soissons.
>
> In the position that I am in, there is nothing left for me to do but to press on with my move on Paris. The Corps of general Reille will arrive tomorrow, I hope, at Gonesse.
>
> The guard and my headquarters will be at Dammartin, and if General Vandamme is not attacked, he will arrive at Nanteuil.
>
> I'll write to you as soon as I'm at Dammartin.

The following day d'Erlon wrote once more to Grouchy:[21]

> I was not able to occupy Senlis yesterday evening. General Kellerman made contact with the enemy there in a small clash. As a result of this I endeavoured to gather my entire force at Borest. The men were totally exhausted.

D'Erlon added bitterly:[22]

> Because most of the train drivers have deserted, my artillery is useless, as there are no drivers. I have had to have the infantry pull the guns. If I cannot pass at la Patte d'Ore, then I shall endeavour to move to the road from le Bourget via Tremblay. I only have a few men remaining and cannot rely upon them.

The situation of 1st Corps was made clear to Davout:[23]

> The Troops I have here of the Comte d'Erlon are so demoralised that they would scatter at the first musket shot. We lost 12 artillery pieces on the march and six in action … I consider it my duty to inform you in all haste of this tragic situation.

Chapter 19

28 June 1815

Events in Paris

An eye-witness wrote of the mood in the city:[1]

> The Duke of Otranto, who feared the calamity which might await the city by attempting its defence, received, it is said, positive assurances, that no battle should be fought within its walls.
>
> In the middle of the day, no firing being heard, there was a rumour of a capitulation; but so strictly are the barriers guarded, and so secret are all the measures, both of the government and the generals of the army, that the inhabitants are in utter ignorance of what is passing within two miles of the town. It is a fact that as two regiments of cavalry were passing along the boulevards, about two o'clock, with drawn swords, the people who were standing near me, looking at them, in the Rue Mont Blanc, did not know whether they were Prussians or French; some of my neighbours were positive that they were the former. These troops passed in silence. I have since learnt that they were a portion of Vandamme's corps, which has unexpectedly arrived, and that they were going to take up a position on Mont Rouge, under the Bicetre, in consequence of the Duke of Wellington having crossed the Seine, at Meulan, where some English cavalry are said to have been drowned. No capitulation has taken place; distant cannonading is still heard at intervals.

The government in Paris declared Paris under a state of siege and ordered back from the Vendée two regiments of the Young Guard.[2]

> The terrible truth is revealed. Paris is to be saved, if it can be saved, only by a battle, to be fought under its walls. The law declaring the city in a state of siege is announced, as is an order from the government commanding the Armée du Nord to repair without delay to the capital ... But care has been taken to show that only

the approaches to the capital shall be defended, and by the troops of the line only, encamped without the walls, and seconded by the skirmishers of the national guard. The guard itself is not to be employed ... Besides these notices, which appeared as an order of the day from the minister of war, dispositions have been made for a battle to be fought tomorrow morning, so says the report, at day-break.

Those dispositions were as follows:

All the soldiers at this moment in Paris, armed or not, will move immediately. Those of the first, second, and sixth corps shall place themselves in front of the height of Cinq Moulins, near the butt Montmartre, and the village la Chapelle; those of the cavalry, mounted or not mounted, upon the road to St. Denis, to the crossroads of Clichy.

Those of the third and the fourth corps, to the telegraph upon the height of Belleville.

Those of the infantry of the guard, commanded by General Deriot, upon the road to Vincennes, near Petit Charonne.

The general officers, and those of the staff, belonging to these different corps, will take themselves to the posts respectively assigned.

The general officers of the staff, who have no destination, will repair to the head of the village of Lavallette, near the canal of L'Ourq, where the general headquarters is fixed.

It is expressly forbidden, under the severest penalties, to give asylum to soldiers not wounded, who shall not repair to the post to which they are called by the call of honour, and of their country.

There shall be established, in each place above assigned, a depot of 4000 arms. General Desforneaux for the first, second and sixth corps; General Fully for all the cavalry, mounted or not mounted; General Beaumont for the third and fourth corps, and General Deriot for the guard, are charged to review their respective troops, armed or not armed, to take cognisance of the number of arms wanting, and to expedite an order, with which the officer of artillery, appointed by General Evam, at each of the depots, will take care to comply.

That eye-witness continued:

It is not to be doubted but that considerable alarm is entertained by such of the Parisians as are known to be attached to the royalist cause, many of whom now say that all their hopes for the preservation of Paris lay with Fouché: the other members of the commission are forgotten; and his house alone, at the demand of the national guard, is protected by a guard of honour. Yet I find the Tuilleries' gardens, and the boulevards, as full of company as usual ... It may seem

171

strange to you ... when you consider that the Square Vendome, close by, is covered at one corner with wounded men, lying on straw, at the other with the waggons carrying all the property of the villagers, driven in by the enemy; and that a battle is to be fought tomorrow, for the honour and independence of France, with the last relics of the army, under the walls of the city. More singular still may it appear to you, that the whole plain under Montmartre is crowded by men, women and children, straggling about, to visit their comrades and acquaintance in the French camp; and that the barriers towards that quarter are choked up with carts and coaches, going to, and returning from, the expected scene of tomorrow's battle. Although it is the more common opinion on the whole, that there will be no fighting in the town itself ...

There are two royalist reports on this subject: one is, that the whole hostile movement is but a semblance on the part of Fouché, to keep quiet the army and the suburbs, until the force of the enemy shall be so overwhelming as to make all opposition fruitless and justify a surrender; the other spreads the notion, that the remainder of the army is to be sacrificed tomorrow, to secure the repose of the capital, and of France. The latter report finds encouragement even with the army; it came to me first through an officer of the imperial guard. The Prince of Eckmuhl [Davout] has taken the command of the whole army, which is now close to Paris, Marshal Grouchy's corps arrived this morning.

The army as a whole numbered 55,000 infantry, 15,000 cavalry and 500 guns; the Imperial Guard mustered 458 officers and 9,200 men, of which 3,392 were cavalry, 1,401 artillery and train as well as 460 engineers and sailors. Some 300 guardsmen from Paris, along with fifty Empress Dragoons and twenty-five lancers had arrived from the depots by this date.[3] Arrayed against them were 62,000 Prussians accompanied by 30,000 British troops.

Grouchy

At 04.00 hours Grouchy sent word to Vandamme that three strong enemy columns had left Compiègne, one heading to Crépy, the second to Villiers-Cotterêts, and the last to Senlis. In consequence, Vandamme was to head to Paris via Ferté-Milon and Meaux[4]

General Monthion transmitted the following order to Vandamme:[5]

Claye 28 June 5 o'clock
General, M. The Marshal, the commander in chief has the honour that you are to continue to move towards Meaux. As soon as you take up lodgings you are to make contact with the grand-quartier-general which is located in this town. If, however the enemy have

taken this place, the Marshal orders that you are to continue your movement via Gousses, along with the Guard, to Claye. In order to reach Paris more speedily, the Marshal requests you make no halts. If you find the enemy you are to attack.

The Grenadiers à Cheval and Empress Dragoons were at Claye by 19.00 hours on 28 June. General Guyot notes that the weather was extremely hot. At 23.00 hours the Grenadiers à Cheval and Empress Dragoons bivouacked in the suburbs of La Chapelle, outside the walls of Paris.[6] The Chasseurs à Cheval also arrived on the 29th.[7] Clearly, the Guard cavalry had marched in three separate columns. Late that night, Pajol sent news to Grouchy:[8]

Monseigneur, the enemy is too close, and the post of Curcy [sic I assume he means Coucy] is too much in sight so that I may have to withdraw from the place before nightfall without compromising the infantry and cavalry. I will therefore only make my move at 9 o'clock, and will not return to Danivet, where I beg you to send me your orders until 1 o'clock tomorrow morning.

According to the information and reports of the peasants, it seems that the enemy had sent out all his cavalry, and that he advances with great caution: he fears the right wing of the Armée du Nord [i.e. the French 3rd and 4th Corps], and I believe that he will only deploy when he is well supported.

The Guard disorganizes everything that it meets. General Subervie writes to me that the 11th Chasseurs à Cheval and the 2nd Dragons have been perverted by the Guard, and that he had a lot of trouble holding them back. The indiscipline is at its height, and if we do not rigorously fight against all these rascals, they will cause everything to be lost. I'm going to bring your order into force, and I'll have the first offender shot. The guard will compromise us and is no longer able to fight. It is astonishing how many officers and soldiers allow themselves to act inappropriately.

Bad news indeed for Grouchy. But it was perhaps not unexpected. The army of 1815 was fragile and bore little semblance to the army that Napoléon had commanded in previous years. The rank and file, like many officers, were war weary and did not want to fight in some cases, for example the 45th and 46th Line. Other regiments were ready to fight and wanted to fight, such as the 10th Line, but on the whole, this was not a feeling shared by some senior officers and the public at large in France. France was sick of fifteen years of war. The country was bankrupt and needed stability. Napoléon had marched to war knowing full well that any setback would result in the collapse of his power. At the other end of the scale, none of the higher-level formations had any experience or had conducted any brigade or divisional exercises. Commanders and staff were still joining their divisions as the campaign started. General Allix, for example, did not take up his appointment in 1st Corps as he did not get to Paris in time to join the army. Colonel Arnaud Rogé of the 1st Carabiniers was on honeymoon as his regiment marched to war but did join them in time to serve in the campaign. Rogé had been an aide-de-camp to Marshal Grouchy since 7 January 1812 and had no recent command experience, He had never commanded a regiment, let alone served as a squadron commander! Not a man best suited to command a heavy cavalry regiment. His last field command was as a lieutenant in the 8th Chasseurs à Cheval in 1811.[9] He was promoted beyond his own competence to a field command, a situation which was not unique amongst the senior officers in the army.

Napoléon's top table of officers were hardly a dream team. D'Erlon, at the head of 1st Corps, was not a great soldier, Vandamme was the architect of the disasters at Kulm in 1813, Reille was capable, as were Mouton and Gérard. Ney and Soult were considered traitors but had taken posts out of political expediency. Donzelot had no field command experience whatsoever, Durutte was out of his depth commanding a division, let alone a brigade. Charles Esdaile remarks that the Armée du Nord was nothing like the Grande Armée, and was less likely to win battles or to be able to sustain defeat.[10] How right he is.

Prussian General Bülow attacked Grouchy on the road from Claye to Paris, and pushed the French troops over the river Marne at a cost of 500 captured French troops. The remnants of the French army retired in such haste that they were not overtaken by the pursuing Prussians until about midway between Levignon and Nanteuil; here they halted their rear-guard, which made a stand against the Prussians. On coming up with the French rear-guard, two squadrons of the 2nd West Prussian Dragoons charged; but they were repulsed and attacked in the flank by a French lancer regiment. The French then advanced, with the hope of completely routing the Prussian cavalry. This attempt failed in consequence of a most successful attack by the 1st Silesian Hussars, by which the French were put to flight, and two of their guns captured. A battery of horse artillery drew up at the same time on the left of the high road and poured fire on the flying French who were pursued by the Prussian cavalry beyond Nanteuil. The Imperial Guard cavalry and infantry, alongside the 6th Corps who were under the more immediate orders of Grouchy, had formed the column that retired through Villers Cotterets in the morning, reaching Levignon after Zieten had passed through it in pursuit of Reille's troops to Nanteuil. The Prussian army, therefore, had succeeded in cutting off the line of retreat of the French troops by the Soissons high road, compelling the greater portion of them to disperse. The Prussians then occupied both the high roads leading from Senlis and Soissons and had their advanced posts in front of the French 4th Corps, within five miles of Paris.

After this rear-guard action, the bulk of the French troops entered Paris. In Paris the Guard joined up with the troops from the various military depots in the city, the French forces numbering perhaps 50,000 men.

Chapter 20

The mission of Charles de Le Sénécal

Early that morning, 29 June, Grouchy sent word to Davout that:[1]

> I have the honour to report that I am at Claye with 4,000 infantrymen and 1,800 horses of the Guard, the division of Jacquinot, the 2nd Cavalry Division and two of the regiments of the corps of General Pajol. The rest of this corps could not deploy at Nanteuil and could not reach me. General Vandamme has deployed on La Ferté-Milon and will certainly not be able to arrive until tomorrow in Paris.
>
> General d'Erlon is with the debris of his corps at Bondi. This corps consists of only 1,500 men in infantry and cavalry.
>
> The troops I have with me, and those of d'Erlon are in such a state of demoralization, that at the first gunshot they hear, they run away… It results from this state of affairs, that the Government can count for the defence of Paris, only on a very weak army, which has no desire to fight, and one that is completely disorganized.
>
> I believe it is my duty to educate you in haste about this sad situation, so that the government will not be deluded by the means it has to defend Paris, which I will lead.
>
> I will be in Paris at midnight having the enemy on my flank at Tremblay.
>
> I very much regret not being able to be joined by General Vandamme but he can only arrive 24 hours after me, even assuming that he is not defeated on the other side of the Marne, by the forces he has arrayed against him.

The political situation, however, was rapidly unravelling. Throughout the last days of June, the government was in secret negotiations with Blücher for an armistice. The previous day Davout ordered that:[2]

> Mr. Laloy will immediately go to the headquarters of Mr. Marshal Grouchy, to give him the attached letter from the Chairman of

the Government Commission, which must be sent forthwith to the plenipotentiaries. He will inform him of the road that the plenipotentiaries will have taken, and if they had not headed to the headquarters of Mr. Marshal Grouchy, he would follow the same route as them to try to join them and give them the dispatch of which he is carrying.

Paris, June 28th, 3:00 a.m. The Minister of War.

The letter in question came from Fouché. Did Davout know its contents? Perhaps no as we shall see. But clearly, he knew peace negotiations were under way, and had been since 23 June.

The letter read:[3]

Letter from the Duke of Otranto
    To the plenipotentiaries.
    Gentlemen, according to the news communicated to me by the Minister of war, it seems that the enemy is advancing in forced marches on Paris and that nothing stands in their way. I invite you to conclude immediately an armistice with Marshal Prince Blücher. It is better to sacrifice a few places if it is necessary, than to sacrifice Paris. You will be accountable to the government for what you have been able to do in this regard.

The letter seems very clear cut. Fouché reasoned that with Blücher arriving at Paris before Vandamme with 3rd and 4th corps along with 1st and 2nd cavalry corps, the war was lost and Paris would be attacked and over-run by Prussians seeking revenge for all that they had suffered at the hands of the French. To prevent the sack of Paris, Fouché ever the realist, ordered that:

a)   An immediate ceasefire be concluded.
b)   Paris was to be saved, and other places that held out like Soissons, Laon, La Fère could be sacrificed for the greater good

But, on what terms was a ceasefire to be agreed? Fouché seemingly left that very vague. In basic terms, the leading plenipotentiary, Laloy, was authorised to seek an immediate ceasefire, and to do so by any means. The gist was that Soissons and other garrisons were to be allowed to fall and be sacked to save Paris. What was to happen to Grouchy's forces was not mentioned. Was Grouchy's army a bargaining chip?

If Fouché realised the war was over, so did Grouchy.

Grouchy knew that the wreck of the army from Waterloo could not fight, and 3rd and 4th corps would arrive at Paris after the Prussians. Grouchy realised the game was up. France had lost. Grouchy took the only pragmatic and only realistic option open to him – to act on the contents of the letter, believing to be empowered to do so by the

177

President, and to end the war as soon as possible. Grouchy, after speaking with General Drouot, considered it the best option to open negotiations directly with Blücher. Grouchy and Drouot wrote a second dispatch to Blücher concerning the peace negotiations, and the letter was carried by Colonel de Le Sénécal. Drouot recalls:[4]

> After the abdication of the Emperor, the government commission having given me command of the Imperial Guard, I left Paris in the last days of June 1815, to return to the army. I joined the headquarters of Mr. Marshal Grouchy in Villers-Cotterets. During the march from Villers-Cotterets to Paris, the Marshal received a dispatch from the government which prescribed him to negotiate a suspension of hostilities with the enemy generals. Mr. Marshal begged me to write a draft letter according to the basic facts and the indications he gave me. I descended from my horse and seated myself on the edge of a ditch, I wrote hastily on my knees the minutiae of a letter. I presented it unsigned to the marshal who had stayed on horseback, read it, approved it, and a few moments later he sent the letter. I do not know if Mr. Marshal kept the note I had written very hastily.

The letter to Blücher read:[5]

> I have the honour to report to Your Highness that I have been authorised by the French government to negotiate a ceasefire on the basis of the demands the Allied powers have made to the French envoys. I have the honour Your Highness to request that you send me an officer with whom I can establish the conditions for such a cease fire. I further request Your Highness to halt the march of your troops and to end all hostilities. Continued fighting would be pointless as the wishes of the Allied powers have already been fulfilled. I do not doubt that Your Highness will make haste to permit my request and thus void any further bloodshed. The glory that Your Highness has achieved can only be made greater by the cessation of hostilities.

Both Laloy and Le Sénécal were sent with the letter from Grouchy as well as that from Fouché. Upon the arrival of the French delegation with Blücher he ordered Bülow's aide-de-camp, Von Nositz, to commence negotiations with the French. Nositz, based on Grouchy's letter, and aware of Prussian intentions, drafted his own memorandum:[6]

1. The cease-fire is between the Prussian Army and the Corps of Marshal Grouchy. It applies only to those troops under the command of the Marshal.

2. The Corps of Marshal Grouchy is to march without halting to the far bank of the Loire, where the Marshal has the option of either taking positions or sending his troops to cantonments.
3. Marshal Grouchy agrees that the march to the Loire is to be undertaken as fast as possible from Paris. Both parties are to appoint officers to agree the details.
4. Marshal Grouchy agrees on his word of honour to provide no assistance to the defence of Paris, nor place any obstacles in the way of the operations of the Prussian Army.
5. Marshal Grouchy is to hand over Laon, La Fère and Soissons which are held by his Corps.
6. Hostilities may recommence three days after both parties have given notice of such.

The ceasefire would have neutralised the only troops the French had that realistically could put up opposition to the Prussians as they advanced upon Paris. A copy of the document created by Nositz was sent to Grouchy for ratification.

Grouchy and Drouot, via Laloy and Le Sénécal, had achieved Fouché's aim of an immediate ceasefire. Paris was saved from the Prussians at the cost of other garrisons, just as Fouché allowed for, and the bargaining chip to prevent the sack of Paris was Grouchy's army retreating behind the Loire. Fouché at no stage had mentioned how the ceasefire was to be achieved. Did this give Grouchy et al free rein? Perhaps it did. Was this deliberate? Did Fouché assume the Prussians would simply say 'ok' to them taking Soissons, La Fère etc to save Paris? I doubt he was that naïve. I suspect he understood that the key to success would be getting Grouchy's troops away from Paris. This understanding was not written into the orders it would appear, as it seemed the obvious solution to the problem, and furthermore if the plan failed, or indeed succeeded, no blame would fall on him. Fouché could state in all honesty that Grouchy, in surrendering his army, was a traitor, acting with no orders. The vagueness allowed freedom of action for Grouchy et al, yet at the same freedom of action could be used as a weapon against them. I suspect also that Grouchy knew this. Le Sénécal certainly did.

Le Sénécal went with Nositz to Louvres. Here, Le Sénécal encountered a group of Royalists claiming that they were acting on behalf of the Provisional Government. They stated that Louis XVIII had been proclaimed King. Le Sénécal questioned this, claiming that he had not, nor would he ever, recognise Louis as monarch. Both men headed to Chenevieres, to meet the French negotiators, who rejected Blücher's demands. General Gneisenau, on the other hand, ratified the deal with Grouchy. Tragically, at that moment, news of the action at Villiers-Cotterêts arrived; the agreement had been broken before it had begun. Gneisenau, Nositz and Le Sénécal returned to the Prussian lines. From there, Le Sénécal and Major von Brunneck headed to Paris in a coach. The coach was intercepted by the 1st Chasseurs à Cheval, who on finding out the reason for a Prussian to be heading to Paris, attacked the coach. Le Sénécal and von Brunneck had to be rescued by General Exelmans, who wrote of this to Davout:[7]

> I have the honour to tell Your Highness that I arrived here in the evening. I would have hastened to pay my respects to Y. H. had I not been prevented from doing so by certain reasons relating to my service. I must have the honour to announce to Y. H. what befell general Sénécal this morning as he was passing through my column of troops. This officer was recognised as travelling in a cabriolet with a Prussian officer. I did what depended of me to protect general Sénécal from the fury of the soldiers, and I had him come here with the Prussian officer.

Brunneck himself wrote about the incident to Davout:[8]

> It was on June 29th, at one o'clock in the morning, that I received the order from Prince Marshal of Blücher Wahlstadt to bring my person to the post house, in order to escort French general Senegal [le Sénécal] to Marshal Grouchy from whom he had been sent in the morning, after our troops had attacked the Marshal's corps near Villers-Cotterêts …
>
> The Marshal Prince Blücher, who was trying to use the situation to his advantage without having to push his troops too far on he left, requested of me to tell Marshal Grouchy that he was favourable to a cessation of hostilities should he be willing to take a position behind the river Marne or the river Seine with his army corps, without attempting a link-up with the troops in Paris. Should the marshal agree upon this condition, I was to notify our outposts and make the hostilities end.
>
> During my journey to Dammartin via the road to Senlis, I had General Sénégal guarded by an escort of our cavalry until we reached our most advanced outposts. I then dismissed the escort on account of the great distance we would have to travel from the outposts, being convinced moreover that I could not have had a better safeguard than that of a French general. As I could not find Marshal Grouchy in Meaux, I followed the movement of his army via Lagny and Chaumes. Barely had I entered the columns of his rear-guard cavalry however, then suspicion was already beginning to be harboured about General Sénégal and I. General Watier, who was leading, as I think, the 1st Regiment of Chasseurs à Cheval,

had General Sénégal dismount and started interrogating him while I remained seated in the coach.

I was immediately given an escort. I began being treated as a prisoner and not as an envoy.

An officer from the Chasseurs à Cheval claimed he saw General Sénégal conceal a paper as he was getting off the coach, although the General gave his word of honour that this was not true. As far as I'm concerned, I could swear on my word of honour and on everything that is dearest to me in the world that I did not see the paper. Meanwhile more and more Chasseurs à Cheval were gathering around my coach and began insulting General Sénégal in such a manner that he had to jump from the coach and beg the generals to provide justice for him. It is to the senior officers and especially Lieutenant-General Exelmans, who treated me with such kindness, that I owe my escaping being harmed, if not cut down perhaps by the Chasseurs à Cheval.

After General Exelmans had made himself acquainted with all the particulars, he had the kindness to invite me to dinner in Vincennes and to allow me one of his own horses for my return journey, giving me his chief of staff for safeguard. As the situation of the army of Marshal Grouchy has much changed in the last twenty-four hours, I thought I needed not make propositions for a ceasefire to Marshal Grouchy any longer. This is why I haven't had the honour to speak to him. Yet I thought it my duty to make my report about my errand to His Highness the Minister of War, Prince of Eckmühl.

Unfortunately, once in Exelmans care, Brunneck was treated as a prisoner of war and arrested. Indeed, General Bülow's chief of Staff, Major Royer, requested Davout hand him over.[9] Grouchy had also explained the situation to Fouché:[10]

I have the honour to send to you general Le Sénécal whom I had sent yesterday, with a letter to General Blücher, to consider entering into talks in connection with an armistice. He brought with him a Prussian major, who said he had sufficient powers, to suspend hostilities. I urge you to receive him as soon as it has been brought to you by my aide-de-camp, and to give his overtures the response you deem fit.

At some stage, Davout no doubt went apoplectic. Grouchy had agreed a ceasefire without his knowledge, despite having ordered Grouchy to conduct such a ceasefire! For Davout to change his mind entirely on this issue, we wonder at his actual motivations for sending orders to Grouchy. Be that as it may, for Davout, Grouchy had surrendered his army like Marmont had. He sacked Grouchy on the spot.

As soon as Le Sénécal had finished his meeting with Fouché, he was arrested on Davout's orders. This is where the story gets tricky. Fouché and Davout both knew that the war was over, they had ordered Grouchy to assist in the negotiations for a cease fire. Laloy, Le Sénécal, Drouot and Grouchy were complicit in the ceasefire agreement written by Drouot, yet Grouchy took the blame! Grouchy ranted to Davout that:[11]

> As a result of his mission, he brought back a Prussian major, responsible for making known the demands made by the enemy. The Prussian Major not wanting to enter into Paris, General Le Sénécal left him at Vincennes in the custody of a squadron commander of Chasseurs à Cheval whom Lieutenant-General Exelmans had provided for his escort. He came to find me in Paris. I sent him to the President of the Government Committee at the moment he arrived with me, with a letter in which I urged him to call upon the Prussian major. The president met General Sénécal the next day at 11:00 a.m. He returned home at this hour, and it was upon his release from the president of the Government Commission, that General Sénécal was arrested by your orders. I beg you, Mr. Marshal, to end such an astonishing arrest, and to make a public witness to the conduct of General Sénécal who, in this circumstance as in all others, has never strayed from the line of his duties.

Comment

Clearly, Davout had found out about the initiative before Grouchy got his news to Fouché. Both Grouchy and Drouot felt they were acting on orders from Fouché and for the best outcome they could expect for France. They had hoped no doubt that Paris would not be besieged and the war would end. Exelmans, Drouot and Grouchy were acting in the best interest of France. Drouot denied his involvement until 1840. Indeed, a day earlier Drouot told the government that Grouchy was responsible for the defeat at Waterloo:[12]

> Meantime, the Prussian corps which had joined the left of the English placed itself *en potence* upon our right flank and began to attack about half-past five in the afternoon. The 6th Corps, which had taken no part in the battle of the 16th, was placed to oppose them, and was supported by a division of the Young Guard and some battalions of the Guard. Towards seven "clock we perceived in the distance, towards our right, a fire of artillery and musketry. It was not doubted that Marshal Grouchy had followed the movement of the Prussians and was coming to take part in the victory.

Drouot writes in the immediate aftermath of defeat, and it seems is the originator of the story of Grouchy losing the battle. Did Drouot know of orders for Grouchy to head to Waterloo which made him think this, and that any trace of such an order is lost? Perhaps, but without a shred of evidence at all to vindicate Drouot, it seems he was making Grouchy a scapegoat. Of interest, Drouot is also the originator of the theory that mud delayed the start of the battle, which can be categorically shown to be wrong. Drouot, therefore, seems to have been clutching at straws to explain the defeat, rather than face facts that Wellington and Blücher made fewer mistakes in the campaign when it mattered, and were able to concentrate their forces at the crucial time, winning Waterloo and the campaign. The Emperor sent Grouchy off on a mission that could not succeed, and based on evidence, knew Grouchy was not coming to Waterloo. Did Grouchy know this? Was Drouot being 'two-faced'? If Grouchy knew this, then he harboured no grudge with Drouot. What was Drouot's motivation? Was his speech in Paris an emotional uncontrolled rant to find reasons other than the Emperor making huge mistakes for the loss of the battle, or was it a deliberate and calculated oration to damn Grouchy? If the latter, what was then his motivation on 28 June? Was this a cynical ploy to get Grouchy stripped of his command, imprisoned, or shot?

One option is that Drouot realised the war was over and did what was best for France regardless. As we have seen, Drouot clearly had issues with Grouchy, but was he out to do his best to destroy Grouchy? The same question hangs over Exelmans. Exelmans was a key person in getting Brunneck to Paris. Yet in later life he denied he had ever had any involvement, and indeed joined the war faction with Davout on 30 June, taking a leading part as we shall see in later chapters in defending Paris. Did Exelmans tip off Davout about Sénécal and his mission? Yes. Was he two-faced and said one thing to Grouchy and another to Davout? His later actions suggest he did not believe the war was over, but yet he took an active role in the peace negotiations. Exelmans never admitted any involvement and painted himself as a proud Bonapartist to the end of his life. Yet history says otherwise. Was Exelmans culpable for the loss of Waterloo? His cavalry corps did nothing on 18 June. He explained this by claiming his men were too exhausted to take part in fighting. We have very little idea of what 2nd Cavalry Corps did on 18 June. Grouchy, in not using the corps offensively, committed a great error, but if Exelmans was such an ardent Bonapartist, why did he not act more proactively? Rather than urging Grouchy march to Waterloo early on 18 June, he insisted the Emperor's orders to march away from Waterloo to be adhered to and agreed with Grouchy. Either way, both men were at fault on 18 June. Grouchy's biggest mistake was not using his resources better. Exelmans later in life deliberately fictionalised his role in the campaign. Rather than supporting Grouchy in marching to Wavres, Exelmans paints a picture of a skilled general stifled by a buffoon, an incompetent, who ignored his advice to march to Waterloo via different route. Documents from 18 to 20 June 1815, which are undoubtedly genuine documents, paint a very different picture of Exelmans making the decision about whether or not to head to Waterloo. It was Exelmans that agreed with Grouchy to head to Wavre and not follow Gérard's pleadings. Exelmans deliberately hid his actions in 1815, which would have been believed had it not been for finding more archive resources at the French Army Archives, which reveal his true motives in 1815.

Drouot had abandoned his command on 18 June. As nominal commander-in-chief of the Imperial Guard since Marshal Mortier had absented himself on 13 June, his duty was to be with his command and not to run as fast as he could to Paris. Drouot, the sage of the 'grande armée' had left his post. He had deserted just like the Emperor, just like Ney, not like Soult or Grouchy. When Davout issued his order about having officers who left their posts shot, Drouot headed out from Paris on 27 June to find the Imperial Guard – abandoning his post could have meant him being shot for desertion. No doubt he realised the game was up and moved to try and save his own neck.

If Soult is maligned for supposedly abandoning the army, why is Drouot's reputation never in doubt? Simply put, because for many Soult was an incompetent that lost Waterloo, and Drouot, like Berthier and Davout, were unimpeachable saints who could do no wrong. The truth is that Drouot deserted. With the Emperor's second abdication, his Bonpartist zeal changed to one of realism and pragmatism. On learning of the failure of d'Erlon's move to Compiègne, and like Grouchy, realising that the Prussians would get to Paris before Vandamme with the only portion of the army able to fight, he knew the war was lost, and would soon be over with total defeat. Ergo, rather than making the defeat far worse, and more men needlessly being killed, he supported Grouchy's aim for a cease-fire. If Grouchy is to be dragged through the mire for this, Drouot and Davout deserve the same fate.

Exelmans never acknowledged his involvement in the peace negotiations. Grouchy was condemned in 1815 and throughout his life for this act. It is odd that only Grouchy was sacked and Drouot and Exelmans were let off the hook. Davout ordered Grouchy to assist in a ceasefire, so why was he sacked for obeying orders? Fouché was two-faced, he was the arch politician who schemed for the betterment of himself, just like Talleyrand. Fouché's double dealing is understandable, but was Davout totally ignorant of the contents of the letter from Fouché he dispatched to Grouchy via Laloy? His reaction at finding out the news of what had happened suggests so, yet he knew peace negotiations were underway. Either he was somewhat naïve, or he knew what was going on. Fouché's letter makes it evident that Davout and Fouché were in communication about the military situation, it is clear that Fouché was convinced the war was lost and no time could be wasted to save Paris. The fact Davout sent his own ADC implies that he was well aware of his master's views, as well as the ongoing peace negotiations as well as the military situation. Did Davout really have no idea what was going on? He told Grouchy several times about the peace negations, so did he really not know of Fouché's intentions? I doubt it. If he did, he clearly failed to grasp the situation that France was actually in.

Grouchy is usually blamed for squandering his resources, because he outnumbered the Prussians under Thielemann, but this is probably not the case. Thielemann had at his disposal, on 18 June, 19,500 infantry, 3,450 cavalry and forty guns. Grouchy is said to have commanded 35,000 men. This is simply not true. Grouchy commanded 27,000 men, of whom 23,000 were infantry, thus the two forces were approximately equal. However, this belies the fact that until Gérard's 4th Corps arrived about 18.00 hours, followed by Teste's command sometime later, Grouchy was outnumbered at Wavre, Bas-Wavre and Bièrges by almost two-to-one. Only with the full arrival of all his troops in the evening of the 18th did Grouchy obtain numerical superiority.

When one takes into consideration the losses sustained by Vandamme's men in the first stage of the action from around 14.00 to 19.00 on 18 June, Gérard's men perhaps did not overtly tip the action in favour of the French numerically. However they provide fresh troops to go into action against weary Prussians who had received no reinforcements, other than the troops of General Borcke's brigade, which was sucked into the action of 19 June near Neuf Cabaret. The two forces that faced each other over the River Dyle were about equal, Grouchy did not have overwhelming troop superiority, neither did he have at Wavre and Bas-Wavre an opportunity to follow up the early success. This was due to the bottleneck of feeding men over the Dyle onto the northern bank, where Thielemann could operate virtually unmolested and march reinforcements to check Vandamme far quicker than Vandamme could feed men into the action, neither of which are directly attributable to failings of Marshal Grouchy.

Not outflanking Thielemann further south by crossing the Dyle at Moustier does not seem to have been a considered option, assuming Grouchy was aware of this bridge. To reach the bridge, his troops would have either had to fight their way past Thielemann at Wavre to head south or retreat south to Mont-Saint-Gilbert and then head to Moustier, which would have taken time – a full-frontal, headlong assault, it seems, was the only initial option Grouchy explored, and only later did he pin down Thielemann at Wavre and send Gérard and Teste south to outflank Wavre and head to Brussels, where Grouchy was convinced the Prussians were heading until he received Napoléon's summons around 19.00 hours. Napoléon seems to have been totally ignorant of the situation Grouchy was in. A quick glance at either the Ferraris map of 1777 or Le Capitaine map of 1789, both of which were used in the campaign, shows the terrain Grouchy had to fight over. Napoléon knew very well the nature of the terrain between Waterloo and Wavre, and yet he still ordered Grouchy to Wavre, knowing that when Grouchy went into action with the Prussians, it was not as simple as he thought to break off the action, pin down and control the Prussians and then send men to Waterloo. Napoléon was asking the impossible.

Grouchy chose to try and fight his way to Saint-Lambert, with Vandamme heading off to Brussels via Louvain on 19 June, and Vichery, with 4th and 6th corps, heading to Rixensart in the direction of the field of Waterloo. With Napoléon's news received about 19.00 hours, of the three Prussian columns, Grouchy had one in front of him at Wavre, one facing Napoléon, and the third was either heading to Brussels or was linking with Wellington, which history tells us it did. Grouchy's mission-blindness in heading to Brussels, it seems, had clouded his objective judgement, but in heading to Brussels he was executing Napoléon's orders, and when new orders did arrive, it was far too late for Grouchy to change his modus opperandi. Napoléon and Grouchy were equally culpable, Napoléon more so for issuing vague and unrealistic orders.

Finally, the ultimate blame for the mistakes made during the campaign must lie with the commander-in-chief: Napoléon. He foolishly divided his army, so that a river and a dense forest separated the two wings, impeding communication and slowing down any effort to join up. Grouchy was far from an ideal choice as commander of the detached force, but he was severely hampered by errors made by Napoléon. Napoléon lost the Battle of Waterloo due to mistakes of his own making.

Grouchy, however, bears some responsibility. He repeatedly threw Vandamme's 3rd Corps into Wavre, rather than using his cavalry force to find a ford either up or downstream of the Dyle, which he would be able to cross unmolested and out-flank the Prussians. The fact this did not happen is a failure on behalf of Grouchy and directly contributed to his forces getting bogged down in Wavre. Exelmans should have been sent off to reconnoitre both flanks of the Prussians, find a river crossing, and to make contact with Napoléon.

Exelmans, on 18 June, appears to have contributed very little to the action at Wavre. He could, and should, have been ordered to move to Waterloo by Grouchy. Instead, an entire cavalry corps was uselessly tied down, just as with d'Erlon's 1st Corps on 16 June. Lack of initiative by Grouchy, and from Exelmans, was a major contributing factor to the outcome of 18 June for the right wing. In defence of Grouchy, he did eventually come to his senses and sent Pajol off to reconnoitre for a river crossing, supported by infantry. This could, and should, have happened much earlier in the day, and the fact that it was left too late falls totally with Grouchy. Exelmans' corps should then have been sent off round the flank of the Prussians to Waterloo – we can only speculate about the outcome of the battle if his men came charging into the rear of Bülow!

Grouchy, even if he crossed the Dyle at 15.00 hours, still could not have got to Waterloo with his infantry and artillery until the battle had been lost. It would have been impossible to get to Waterloo and intervene decisively in the battle. As it was, he did not get the order until 18.00 to 19.00 hours.

Either Napoléon believed that only a small portion of the Prussian army had eluded Grouchy (hardly surprising given the lead they had over the marshal), or he was over-confident in his chances of success against Wellington and the Prussians. Napoléon's judgement on both scenarios was horribly wrong.

For a fact, Napoléon knew from 14.00 hours that he faced both Wellington and Blücher, and that Grouchy was not marching to his aid, regardless of what later French and Anglophone writers have stated. Grouchy's own actions at Wavre were a major concern for the Prussians. Rather than as traditional history tells us, his attacks were not feeble.

Did Napoléon really believe that Grouchy could simply break off the action at Wavre and head to Waterloo? He was experienced enough to realise the difficulty of breaking contact with the enemy once action had begun, as at Eylau in 1807. How could Grouchy break off action until he had reached unmerical parity with the Prussians? He could not. Only with the arrival of 4th Corps could he make a decisive blow against the Prussians, and even then, Grouchy, unless he left Wavre before 10.00 hours on 18 June, could not have got to Waterloo to intervene in the action. Robbed of his 'eyes and ears' by Napoléon on 17 June, he had no idea where the Prussians were that day until Pajol and Exelmans found them. Even then, until the infantry caught up there was little Pajol or Exelmans could do to initiate a major cavalry attack.

By early evening, Thielemann sent a request to Gneisenau for reinforcements, and had Prussian troops been sent back to Wavre, Waterloo may have had a different outcome. As it was, Grouchy tied down all of Thielemann's command. Grouchy's action at Wavre was vitally important, as it prevented the defeat at Waterloo being far worse than it was.

What, then, can we say of Grouchy? His track record in the years before 1815, and during the campaign, was faultless. His retreat from 19 June was an almost perfect fighting retreat. Grouchy has often been lambasted for not being fit for independent command, but his actions in the campaign clearly show he was, and far more competent than Ney. Yet, since 18 June 1815, the blame for the defeat of the army had been squarely placed with Ney, Soult and Grouchy. Grouchy cannot take blame for what happened. All of Grouchy's reconnaissance reports indicated a Prussian retreat to Louvain, which is of course where Prussian 4th Corps were going before they headed west. As Grouchy was moving north-east, the body of troops Milhaud had found were moving north to join Wellington. In assuming the Prussians could not fight was a blunder of immense proportions made by Napoléon alone.

In returning to the events of 28 to 30 June, despite the realities of the situation, Davout declared Paris to be in a stage of siege. History shows that Blücher had acted dishonestly with Grouchy. In peace talks on 2 July, Blücher changed his bargaining position – he would only accept a ceasefire if his troops were in Paris. Getting Grouchy out of the way without losing men made his task far easier of getting into Paris. However, Wellington, Gneisenau, Muffling and Bülow endeavoured to 'pull the rug' from under Blücher's feet. Wellington did so by negotiating with Davout personally on 3 July. Davout imprisoned Grouchy and Le Sénécal for negotiating a ceasefire, under orders from Fouché, and yet here is the same Davout undertaking direct peace negotiations with Wellington.

Chapter 21

Davout takes command

Grouchy, ever the honourable man, did his duty in sending Le Sénécal and Major Brunneck to Fouché, and pleaded with Davout for the release of Le Sénécal once he had been arrested. At no stage did Grouchy question, it seems, being placed under house arrest. Other officers may have been indignant at being sacked, but Grouchy appears to have taken the news well, and based on extant letters, Grouchy was far more concerned about others than himself. In many regards, at this crisis point, Grouchy acquitted himself with dignity. Yet in his own memoires Grouchy totally ignores this unhappy episode, stating he:[1]

> Left command of the army under Paris in the evening of 29th June, not wanting to serve under the orders of Davout, who was minister of war, and had command of all the troops and whose intentions were the most malevolent for the Emperor and his dynasty. The Prince d'Eckmühl indeed, in conjunction with the Duc d'Otranto prepared everything for a second restoration. Marshal Grouchy did not want to do anything to associated himself with the projects of the two men.

Here Grouchy is lying. He was involved in Fouché's schemes and he was prepared to negotiate an armistice, the only obvious conclusion to which was a restoration of the Bourbons. Only by uncovering the archive documents about the case can we prove Grouchy is not telling us the truth. General Pajol reports the same fabrcation:[2]

> On arriving in Paris, Grouchy had seen Davout. He found him looking to gain a different cause to victory; a loyal soldier, he resigned his command. Fouché made overtures to Grouchy.

189

The marshal refused to be a negotiator for a second restoration and retired.

Clearly, the whole unhappy episode, a scheme of Fouché and Davout's, was hastily buried by all those who took part, yet Fleury de Chaboulon reported that Grouchy had indeed been involved in the plotting of Fouché, and had been prepared to surrender his army:[3]

> It appears certain, that Marshal Grouchy had held parleys with the allies, and that an arrangement on the plan of the Duke of Ragusa was about to be signed, when General Excelmanns [sic] arrested the Prussian colonel, who was sent to the marshal, to conclude the treaty already agreed upon.

Clearly, General de Flahaut, who communicated this information to de Chaboulon, was telling the truth about the unusual case of Charles Le Sénécal. Yet how strange it seems that Davout and Drouot are not censored, just Grouchy? How easy it must have been to blame all the ills of the campaign on one man. So well covered up is the whole affair, that it is missing from nearly all histories of the post-Waterloo period. Be that as it may, Grouchy was under house arrest and stripped of command. Davout was now commander-in-chief. Davout informed Vandamme of this in a long rambling letter and hid the news about Grouchy in the second paragraph of the second page of a three-page missive:[4]

> I must also inform you my General that the Government Commission has confided in me the command of the 3rd and 4th Corps as well as the cavalry. In consequence you are to cease your correspondence with Marshal Grouchy.

The almost casual way in which the news was hidden belies the reality of the situation. With the stroke of a pen Grouchy's career was over. He had fought his last battle. He had extracted 3rd and 4th corps along with the 1st and 2nd cavalry corps from the grips of the Prussians who could have destroyed his entire force. His rear-guard action was text-book perfect. His actions saved the wreck of the 1st, 2nd and 6th Corps. He got his army to Paris, only to face the ignominy of being sacked.

The same day that Grouchy was sacked, Blücher ordered General Bülow to attack Saint-Denis, and seized the bridge over the Seine at Saint-Germain.[5] Davout declared Paris in a state of siege.

Throughout the capital were various detachments of men. At Versailles, General Margerand had a small cavalry force comprising nine officers fifty-eight other ranks of the 4th Chasseurs à Cheval, three officers and 143 other ranks of the 6th Hussars, and four officers and ninety-seven other ranks from the 1st Carabiniers.[6] Paris and the immediate area held just 1,254 cavalry men with 1,331 horses:[7]

1st Hussars, fifty-seven men, fifty-seven horses, sent to Lavallette
3rd Hussars, 152 men, 156 horses, sent to Lavallette
7th Hussars, 144 men, 148 horses sent to Belleville
1st Chasseurs à Cheval, 122 men, 143 horses sent to Mont Rouge
3rd Chasseurs à Cheval, ninety-two men, ninety-three horses sent to Belleville
4th Chasseurs à Cheval, 110 men, 112 horses, sent to Montrouge
8th Chasseurs à Cheval 149 men, 151 horses, sent to Montrouge
9th Chasseurs à Cheval, sixty-five men, sixty-five horses sent to Lavallette to link with 3rd Hussars
12th Chasseurs à Cheval, 217men, 240 horses, sent to Montrouge
1st Lancers, eighty-five men, ninety-one horses sent to Lavallette
13th Dragoons, sixty-five men, seventy horses sent to Montrouge

Marchand wrote to Vandamme, informing him that his troops would by joined the 1st, 4th, 8th, 12th chasseurs à cheval and 13th Dragoons.[8]

General Mouton-Duvernet was given command of the men in the infantry depots around Paris:[9]

39th Line, sixty-two officers, 243 men
103rd Line, forty-six officers, 205 men
6th Light Infantry, twenty-five officers and 338 men
9th Light Infantry, fifty officers, 321 men
111th Line, thirty-seven officers, 183 men
59th Line, forty-seven officers, 158 men
57th Line, 478 officers, 215 men

Davout also placed under his command twenty officers and 532 men of the 1st Battalion of the Elite National Guard of the Department of Indre-Loire[10]. General Guillaminot, Chief of Staff to Davout, ordered Mouton-Duvernet to defend the Paris district of Saint-Germain.[11] For taking command of these men and his involvement in the Hundred Days he was executed by the returning Bourbons. General Deriot, aide-major of the Imperial Guard, reported to Davout about the men of the Guard in barracks in Paris able to take the field:[12]

Chasseurs à a Pied, three officers, seventy-one men
Voltigeurs, six officers, 180 men
Grenadiers à Pied, fifty-four men

7th Tirailleur, seven officers, forty-five men
Grenadiers a Cheval, two officers, eighty-four men
Dragoons, three officers, 105 men
Chasseurs à Cheval, twenty-five officers, 584 men
Lancers, eight officers, 210 men

This made a total of 350 infantry and 983 cavalry. Independently, Lefebvre-Desnoëttes reported that he had brought to Paris some 400 men under arms and well mounted and had bivouacked at the bridge of Neuilly.[13] Squadron Commander Schmidt reported that the light cavalry of the guard had been merged into a single regiment, with squadrons placed as follows:[14]

1st, Squadron formed of Lancers, commanded by Captain de Brack at Neuilly

2nd Squadron formed of Lancers, Chasseurs à Cheval and Mamelukes at Saint Cloud

3rd Squadron formed of Chasseurs à Cheval at the bridge of Sèvres and along the Versailles road, commanded by Captain de Kleinenberg

As a whole, the Old Guard mustered on 30 June:[15]

Infantry: 199 Officers, 4,258 other ranks (gained sixty-one officers and 1,688 other ranks since 23 June)

Cavalry: 176 Officers and 3,216 other ranks

Artillery: 64 Officers, 1,337 other ranks (gained twelve officers and thirty men since 21 June)

Engineers: 4 officers, 125 other ranks (gained one officer and thirty-six men since 23 June)

Sailors: 4 Officers, 118 other ranks (gained two officers and forty-one men since 23 June)

Administration Battalion and Ambulances: eight officers and 201 other ranks

Total: 458 officers and 9,211 other ranks.

The Guard infantry had received a reinforcement of 1,710 men through casualties and deserters returning to ranks, and the men of the depot battalions being sent to the field, which for the Old Guard comprised five officers and 1,911 men.[16] The Imperial Guard based at Villiers was under the command of General Drouot with Deriot as aide-major. The 4th Grenadiers were disbanded on 30 June, the men under arms from the 4th regiment were to be merged with the survivors of the 3rd regiment on the orders of Drouot.[17]

Furthermore, the Young Guard Infantry division mustered 1,353 men all ranks. The Young Guard artillery mustered 203 men.[18] On 23 May 1815, the Young Guard artillery mustered two officers, twenty-nine sub-officers and ninety-five other ranks, whilst on the 3 June four officers are listed, one sergeant major, four sergeants, two corporal-quartermasters, two drummers, and 124 gunners. Clearly the increase to 203 men shows that the company was still being recruited during the campaign, as were all the regiments of the Imperial Guard, and this number included, no doubt, the artillery train drivers of the Young Guard, of which twenty-one drivers were with the company by the end of June 1815.

In addition to the Imperial Guard were the various army corps from the Armée du Nord and reserve formations. The table below shows the relative strength of the Army and its location around Paris for the defence of the city:[19]

Infantry

Formation	Commander	Head-Quarters	Strength 29th June	Notes
1st Corps	d'Erlon	Belleville		
1st Division			1116	133 gunners
2nd Division			1312	
3rd Division			699	
4th Division			1182	
2nd Corps	Reille	La Chapelle		
5th Division			1340	513 gunners. None from former 6th Corps
6th Division			2092	
7th Division			2064	
9th Division			1561	
19th Division			1829	
20th Division			961	
3rd Corps	Vandamme	Petit-Montrouge		
8th Division			2742	No gunners
10th Division			2896	
11th Division			2671	
21st Division			1546	
4th Corps	Vichery	Vaugirard		
12th Division			2719	No gunners
13th Division			2117	
14th Division			2550	
Total			**31469**	

Cavalry

Corps	Commander	Head-quarters	29th June	Notes
1st Division	D'Erlon	Belleville	1064	
2nd Division	Reille	La Chapelle	1248	
3rd Division	Vandamme	Petit-Montrouge	600	
4th Division	Vichery	Vaugirard	1200	
1st Cavalry Corps	Pajol	Vilette	1991	No gunners
2nd Cavalry Corps	Exelmans	Montrouge	2000	No gunners
3rd Cavalry Corps	Kellerman	Neuilly	1641	111 gunners
4th Cavalry Corps	Milhaud	Auteuil	1127	No gunners
Total			10871	

Reserves

These men came from three sources:

1. Veterans.
2. Men who returned to Paris and formed into regiments du marche, i.e. temporary formations.
3. Men from the various depots in Paris.

In addition, a further 10,00 National Guardsmen would have joined these troops on 3 July, making the total number of French troops in Paris some 80,000 men. The location of the reserves on 29 June 1815 were as follows:[20]

Commander	Head-Quarters	Infantry	Cavalry	Artillery	Notes
Beaumont	Belleville	1683	0	0	375 veterans from Seine et Marne
Tilly	Bercy	492	0	58	5 guns
Ambert	Vilette	3209	0	84	8 guns. Infantry formed into two divisions commanded by Generals Cambriels and Meunier. Formed from men returned to Paris separately to their regiment
Meunier	Aubervilliers	1939	0	0	
Pully	Bois du Boulogne	2031	334	0	1st Polish foreign Infantry regiment, 7th regiment of Light Horse Lancers (Polish)
Allix	Saint-Denis	1848	0	483	50 guns
Totals		11202	334	625	

Thus, by 30 June 1815, Davout had over 4,053 officers and 69,495 men available to defend Paris.[21] Indeed, this number would continue to swell as mobilised National Guardsmen made their way to Paris and the command of General Lamarque returned from the Vendée. The army had in twelve days found a new sense of confidence and was ready and able to fight.

If these men could inflict a major defeat on either Wellington or Blücher, just maybe the balance of power could shift back to the French and the defeat of Waterloo nullified under the walls of Paris. However, the political machinations of Fouché and also those of Marshal Davout, as we shall see, rendered these hopes null and void.

Of interest, the army that was drawn up in Paris contained a high number of 'foreign regiments'. The decree of 11 and 15 April 1815 created six foreign regiments, their role being mainly to spread pro-Bonapartist propaganda in the frontier regions. The existing foreign regiments were retained, but were consolidated, so that the four Swiss regiments provided the cadre for a single regiment, the 2nd Foreign regiment (Swiss). The 3rd Foreign Regiment, the 'Legion Irlandais' was retained. The officers were to be recruited from the foreign officers living in France, as were the other ranks. Crucially, deserters from the fledgling Dutch-Belgian Army, as well as from former Confederation of the Rhine States were allowed to be enlisted as 'volunteers'.[22] Napoléon was trying to weld back to the Empire, the former allied states, who were now arrayed against him, most notably Russian-occupied Poland, and Prussian-controlled Saxony. In previous years Napoléon had relied upon troops from allied and satellite states to bolster his troop numbers, something he endeavoured to do again in 1815. The Poles formed three regiments in 1815, one infantry, one line cavalry and a squadron of lancers in the Imperial Guard. The Belgians were, for the second time, made to feel part of the empire as a distinct people with the foreign regiment and the 16th Chasseurs à Cheval. Before this, the only distinctly Belgian regiment in the Grande Armée had been the 27th Chasseurs à Cheval d'Arenberg. By once more honouring the Belgians, and allowing deserters to join his cause, Napoléon was hoping to attract large elements from the Dutch-Belgian Army, perhaps in a limited way to cause discontent between the Dutch and the Belgians, and to try and draw the Belgians, who had been part of the French Empire for far longer than the Dutch, back into the French sphere of influence.

The 31st Light Infantry, formed in Piedmont, and primarily manned by Piedmontese citizens, was reformed as the 1st Foreign Regiment. A second Italian peninsular regiment was raised with the decree of

20 May and was to comprise former soldiers from the Kingdom of Italy and other provinces, excluding the Piedmontese.[23]

The 1st Foreign Regiment, formed from the cadre of the disbanded 31st Light Infantry, was commanded in 1815 by Colonel Esprit Cacherano de Bricherasio, assisted by Adjutant-Commander Martinet. Major Bourbaki commanded the 1st regiment bis, formed outside of the official decree, by former members of the 31st Light Infantry keen to fight for Napoléon once more. By 1 May the cadre of three battalions was some 217 other ranks, increasing to 281 by 28 May.

Each of the eight infantry regiments was, in theory, to comprise some 1,000 men, and was to be organised as a standard Line Infantry regiment. A further two regular army units were formed, the 7th regiment of Light Horse Lancers, from the former 7th, 8th and 9th Light Horse Lancer regiments which had been disbanded in 1814, and the 16th Chasseurs à Cheval which was made up entirely of Belgian volunteers. By 15 June, the number of foreign soldiers exceeded 4,000 officers and men, some of whom saw service in the fighting of 1815. In 1815 Napoléon was faced with a lack of experienced soldiers. The 'Corps Francs' filled out with volunteers, the Battalions of Retired Soldiers, the 'Fédérés' and these 'Foreign' troops were all part of Napoléon's bid to attract experienced soldiers back to his 'Eagles' at a time when money, horses, muskets, gun-powder and experienced soldiers were lacking. Like a lot of the projects of 1815 (the projected three lancer regiments for the Imperial Guard were never raised, and the Young Guard Artillery and Cavalry were barely more than skeletal cadres by the time of Napoléon's abdication), these regiments never reached full strength and many were never involved in any fighting. They were overall a net drain of resources. However, when viewed as part of Napoléon's wider ambitions once he had defeated the allies, he clearly aimed to draw back to him from the Allies, the Belgians, northern Italians, and many other former allied states. These non-French troops have often been overlooked by many historians, but this shows that in 1815 the war was not simply France verses the Allies, but actually France and her supporters against the Allies which also included Frenchmen. France was not dominated solely by Napoléon, as many French men chose to fight for the King, just as many Poles, Saxons, Italians and some Portuguese and Spanish fought for Napoléon.

Chapter 22

30 June 1815

A resident of the French capital wrote the following on 30 June:[1]

At three o'clock this morning a cannonading was heard, sometimes loudly, sometimes faintly, which continued till five. The fire of distant musquetry was also heard, in the direction of St. Denis; but at eight o'clock neither cannon nor small arms were distinguishable; and an officer of engineers assured me at nine o'clock, that he had received permission to quit his post at La Villette – a suspension of arms having been agreed upon with the allies. Other reports said that the battle was still raging, and that the Prussians were beaten and in flight.

Walking into the town, I found, for the first time, the shops shut, and large patrols of the national guards parading the streets, in every direction; many soldiers of the line were loitering about, singly, and in small parties of three and four, which did not give cause to suspect that the decisive battle had taken place. The Tuilleries' gardens and boulevards are crowded with well-dressed people, chiefly ladies; but there is not the slightest show of any disturbance: however, two men were killed yesterday for crying *Vive le Roi*. An address from the prefect of the Seine, Count Bondy, to the inhabitants of Paris, is placarded, and tells them distinctly: 'It is not you who are called upon to pronounce upon the great interests of the nation; distrust then all those who may advise you to take too active a part in the important determinations, in which your concurrence can be of no service.' Order and tranquillity are all that is demanded of them; all rallying signs, all acclamations of every kind, are forbidden. [...]

Napoléon did leave Malmaison at four o'clock yesterday afternoon, which was announced by General Beker, intrusted with the escort of the ex-Emperor.

197

About the army the same writer notes:[2]

> The last hopes of France are now ranged under the walls of the capital. General Laguette Mornai and M. Garat reported that at ten o'clock on the evening before they had visited the lines under arms from La Vilette to St. Denis, and had seen the divisions Lambert, Meunier, Alix, and the corps of General Reille. Marshal Grouchy had recovered his alarm, and the Prince of Eckmuhl regained all his confidence, by the arrival of General Vandamme, which, he said, had rendered the defence of Paris much less difficult; not a single man had deserted from the corps of General Reille; and of the 15,000 deserters returned from the army to the capital, nearly the whole would be immediately brought again into the field. When the commissaries mentioned the enthusiasm with which the army repeated the cries of '*Vive Napoléon II*'. A similar acclamation was heard in many parts of the assembly. General Mouton Duvernet moved, that the chamber should open a subscription for the relief of the wounded in the capital; when the whole assembly arose, without hearing his proposal in form, carried the measure by acclamation, and instantly appointed commissaries to examine the hospitals.

Round 1 at Aubervilliers

The guns heard in Paris were those under the command of Marshal Davout whose headquarters were at Aubervilliers. The Saint Denis and L'Ourq canals provided the first line of defence for the north east of the city. The Saint Denis canal linked Saint Denis and Villette and formed the primary line of defence. The L'Ourq canal ran almost due north east from Villette as far as the town of Bondy. The two canals funnelled the Allied armies to Vilette. If Vilette fell, the allies would have easy access to Paris. The L'Ourq canal was in reality the L'Ourq river which had been canalised through the efforts of Napoléon as First Consul in 1802. It was also he who ordered the construction of the Saint Denis canal. The L'Ourq as well as defending Paris's north-eastern quarter, also diverted allied troops to the south of the city. Vilette had to be held at all costs.

The first attack against the north east of Paris came in the early hours of 1 July. Prussian forces headed by Generals Bülow and Sydow attacked the French defensive line from Saint-Denis to Aubervilliers. The L'Ourq Canal was hastily flooded, despite not being completed, and was to be the principal line of defence. If the Prussians were to take Paris, they had to take key bridges. The villages of Vertus and Vilette acted as bastions for the French, with buildings being loopholed.

At Saint-Denis was General Allix. He had a composite command. It comprised: [3]

2nd Line: twenty officers, 505 men

69th Line: thirty-three officers, 261 men

76th Line: forty officers, 202 men

1st Polish Infantry: twenty-seven officers, 419 men

16th Company, 1st Foot Artillery: three officers, fifty-eight men

3rd Company, 4th Foot Artillery: three officers, fifty-seven men

4th Company, 2nd Battalion Marine Artillery: three officers, 102 men

2nd battalion of Engineers: seventeen officers, 194 men

10th company, 8th squadron of artillery train: one officer, fifty-three men, eighty-nine horses.

TOTAL: 147 officers, 1851 men, 89 horses

His cavalry force was the 4th Hussars, which mustered twenty-six officers and 346 men. [4]

General Joachim Ambert was placed in command of the 1st Division at La Villette: [5]

5th Voltigeurs of the Guard: twenty-eight officers, 950 men

National Guard of Paris: six officers, sixty-six men

1st Light Infantry: fifty officers 635 men

4th Light Infantry: forty-seven officers, 293 men

Artillery: six officers, seventy-six men, eight guns

Engineers: sixty-seven officers, 1069 men

General Meunier commanded the 2nd Division at la Villette, centred on Aubervilliers, his troops comprised: [6]

7th Voltigeurs: sixteen officers, 417 men

8th Voltigeurs: sixteen officers, 128 men

Grenadiers à Pied de la Garde: two officers sixty-six men

5th Tirailleurs: fifteen officers, 608 men

Voltigeurs Young Guard: six officers, 169 men

Tirailleurs Young Guard: eleven officers, 338 men

8th Line: twenty officers and 127 men

TOTAL: eighty-six officers, 1853 men

The cavalry command comprised:

1st Hussars: three-six officers, 489 men

5th Hussars: twenty-nine officers, 391 men

General Jamin, with what remained of 20th Infantry Division, was deployed along the Saint Denis canal:[7]

5th Light Infantry: twenty-nine officers, 340 men
107th Line: twenty-six officers, 195 men
10th Line: thirty officers, 341 men.
Total: eighty-five officers, 876 men.

The action on 30 July was duly reported by General Delort on 1 July, written in the third person:[8]

> On June 30, 1815, Lieutenant General Delort was ordered by Marshal Grouchy, then the army commander, to cover his retreat, from the cross-roads to the Barrière de la Villette. He formed the 5th 10th, 6th and 9th Cuirassiers in echelon on the main road supported by an infantry battalion at his disposal. These were able to save a large number of men that scattered and fled and effected their retreat in the best order to the barrier of La Villette.
>
> They stopped, by their bravery and firmness, a vanguard with numerous infantry, cavalry and artillery which was often attacked, and which threatened to charge several times but did not dare approach the cuirassiers who remained steadfast in the midst of the strongest fusillade of grapeshot and musketry: so that the infantry corps of general Reille and d'Erlon managed, unmolested, to affect their retreat into the walls of Paris. By an unheard-of happiness, the cuirassiers exposed for more than two hours to fire the most vivid and closely followed by the sharpshooters of the enemy, both infantry as horsemen did not experience any loss.

General Pierre Soult's Division of Cavalry, the 1st, 4th and 5th Hussars, were moved up to Villette in support to replace Milhaud's command which was deployed to Saint Cloud, where it took up position by daybreak on 1 July.[9]

Action at Pecq

The defence of the bridges at Pecq and Saint-Germain was entrusted to what remained of the 1st Corps commanded by General Allix. The bridge at Pecq was defended by the 66-year-old veteran officer Jacques-Denis Boivin. He was born in Paris in 1748 and had served in the army as a dragoon from 1771 to 1779. He joined the volunteers in 1789 and progressed to the rank of battalion commander in 1795. Named general in 1804, he retired in 1814 before re-joining upon the return of Napoléon.[10] Boivin wrote:[11]

> I left the headquarters at a quarter-past five o'clock in the evening, and I went to establish myself at Saint-Germain-en-Laye, I did

not arrive until half an hour after midnight due to difficulties I encountered. When I arrived, my first duty was to find the mayor who was sent to search for the officer commanding the troops ... I learnt that the colonel had arrived earlier at nine o'clock the same evening, and after a short conference with the commanding officer of the 95th Regiment of the Line who, due to excessive fatigue, had withdrawn to sleep. I ordered him brought to me so we could discuss the situation of the enemy. He arrived at half past one o'clock in the morning.

The bridge itself, noted Boivin, was guarded by fifty or sixty men. The action began around 22.00 hours when the Prussians debouched from a nearby wood, the advance guard being formed by 180 to 200 sharpshooters, which we are told maintained a lively and effective fusillade. The Prussian force, Boivin tells us, was 300 to 400 infantry and 400 to 500 cavalry.[12] The senior officer noted by Boivin as absent was Colonel Regeaud. He writes as follows about the strength of the French defences:[13]

I have the honour to observe your excellency that I was at Saint-Germain with a battalion of the 95th Regiment of the Line, numbering no more than 180 men, and a sergeant of gendarmerie, and two gendarmes, who were also dismounted, who were all our cavalry.

Your excellency will realise that with so few men, it became very difficult to maintain this place, especially as it was open on all sides. For this post to be held, at least one battalion of 500 men is needed. Also needed would be at least twenty-five cavalrymen to reconnoitre the roads from Saint-Germain to Poissy as well as other roads.

The 3rd and 4th Battalions of the 46th Regiment of Line Infantry, only 109 men strong, were established at Poissy to guard the bridge.

Due to lack of munitions, the men of the 95th Regiment of the Line had only five cartridges each.[14] This lack of munitions, let alone being only 180 strong, meant that the 95th were unable to hold the position against an enemy column of 900 men[15], and retreated towards Saint-Cloud.[16] A detachment of 450 men from the 95th Regiment commanded by General Porson quit Versailles at 02.30 hours on the morning of 1 July and established themselves in defensive positions at the Bridges at Marly and Versailles.[17]

Jacques Bosse of the 95th Regiment left us this narration:[18]

The Fédérés occupied the Butte Chaumont to the right of the barrier of Pantin which I was responsible for defending with 2 artillery pieces and 300 men who remained in the 95th, and it was well into the night which preceded the capitulation, when they plundered the food stores, broke wine barrels and those of spirits that had been gathered on the hill, and descended in the greatest disorder, passed under the barrier that I occupied, firing at will and into the air their muskets. They then moved to the Faubourg Saint-Martin and the boulevard and began shouting and spreading alarm and confusion as they were all drunk having consumed the wine and spirits and it was these wretches we are told had defended Paris during the invasion ... I was obliged to put my soldiers in the redoubt to shelter from the musket balls fired by these drunks.

General Allix recounted the difficulties he had in demolishing the bridge at Saint-Germain:[19]

The Prussian army, after four or five days of fruitless efforts at Saint-Denis, where I commanded (I had the second and third line divisions of Jannin and Reille), and were determined to carry Saint-Germain and to cross the Seine. As soon as I gave notice of this movement to Marshal Davout, who was at La Villette, the marshal gave the orders to blow up the bridge, but the agents of the enemy, who were so active in Paris, had knowledge of this order, and they sent emissaries to Blücher, to give him warning of this. One of these emissaries was sent from Martainville with the White Flag, and the other was a man of no importance. I went to my posts before Saint-Denis in broad daylight, dressed in military uniform and decorated with the Legion of Honour, and he recognised me instantly, but already the emissary was out of sight. Blücher then sent a regiment of cavalry, who drove off the workers employed to mine the bridge.

Chapter 23

1 July 1815

The mood of Paris and the events of the day are summed up by an eyewitness:[1]

No disturbance took place in the city last night; and the wounded and the peasants' carts being removed from the square Vendome, this quarter of the town appears more in its usual state than it did yesterday. The number of national guards on duty amount to 12,000. The steps of the palace of the representatives are covered with troops, who are on duty all night.

The grenadiers of the eleventh legion petitioned the chamber today to order that such of the guard as wished to serve might have the requisite posts assigned them; the chamber referred this petition to the government. The popular journals complain, that no measures are taken to arm the fédérés, and, indeed, Count Thibaudeau, in the house of peers, two days ago, hinted that this measure was advisable, and would be adopted, were it not for certain pusillanimous inclinations which had crept into the government and the chambers. Could it be ascertained that the first victims of these irregular levies would not be the royalists, whom the events of the last fifteen months have but too well designated, one might be allowed to wonder that this extremity has not been adopted. M. Bory de St. Vincent made, this morning, a report of his visit to the army yesterday, and concluded a long speech, containing the most assuring details of the state and dispositions of the troops, by moving that the national guards should be called upon to serve with their brothers in arms upon the heights, and that their efforts should not be paralysed; also, that five representatives should be in constant attendance upon the army.

In his speech he declared, that if the fédérés were armed, the capital might be saved. He disclaimed all wish of seeing a battle fought in the streets, but said, that Paris should take a menacing, not a suppliant attitude. The speech is to be printed, sent to the departments, and placarded; but no step is taken as to the project itself. The chamber has adopted an address to the nation similar to M. Manuel's, but in which are the words, 'his son (of Napoléon) is called to the empire.'

It has also heard a report from the hospitals, by which it appears that 2838 wounded soldiers have been already received in nine different places, and that preparations are making for nine or ten thousand more. The gift of 30,650 francs from the chamber, and an immense quantity of presents of all kinds from the inhabitants, have been handed to the troops.

The army has replied to the address of the chambers in a letter, which begins thus: 'Representatives of the people – we are in the presence of our enemies: we swear to you, and in the face of the world, to defend to our last sigh the cause of our independence and of the national honour. They would impose upon us the Bourbons, and these princes are rejected by the immense majority of the French.' And it concludes in these terms: 'The inexorable voice of history will one day recount what the Bourbons have done to reinstate themselves on the throne of France. It will recount, also, the conduct of the army, of this army essentially national, and posterity will decide which of the two has the better claim to the esteem of the world.' The letter was read and read twice with unmixed applause.

No message has yet been sent from the government to the chambers; and so great is the anxiety which prevails on that account, that a M. Saussey has accused the executive of a criminal delay in forbearing to tell them one word of the operations of the armies, or of the success of their negotiators at the allied camp. 'I have this instant,' said M. Saussey, 'met a lieutenant colonel who has been just wounded, and I can contain myself no longer.'

In truth, nothing is known but that the movement to the left of the enemies' line continues, and that some partial affairs have taken place in the neighbourhood of Versailles, and the course of the Seine, so that the great attack may be expected from the left bank of the river. Marshal the Prince of Eckmuhl, commander in chief of the army, has written a letter to Lord Wellington, demanding a cessation of hostilities until the decision of congress shall be known, and enclosing the armistice concluded between Marshal Suchet and General Bubna. No cannonading has been heard in the neighbourhood of Paris, but wounded men and horses continue to arrive. In the chamber of peers, this day, Marshal Grouchy vindicated himself from the charge of having given too dispiriting an account of the corps under his command and begged his colleagues to appreciate the merit of having brought 40,000 men twenty-eight leagues in thirty hours, from the Dyle to the Seine, with his flank exposed for eighteen hours to a victorious enemy, who were nearer the capital than himself. The marshall has resigned, as he says, from a just diffidence of his abilities to conduct the defence of Paris. Very little is known of the state of the country; it appears the allies are advancing rapidly. La Meurthe is occupied entirely; the sovereigns are said to have arrived at Nancy, forty posts from Paris.

Clearly in Paris, the mood of the population was fluctuating between war and peace, as well as between the ideal of Napoléon, the Republic and the Royalists. Many in the army sought only Napoléon. The army became to feel increasing disenfranchised by events.

At Belleville General d'Erlon conducted a complete reorganisation of 1st Corps. General Donzelot was placed in command of the 1st Division, General Quiot now headed the 1st Brigade which comprised the 28th, 54th, 55th and 105th Line, and General Schmitz headed the 2nd Brigade, namely the 13th Light Infantry, 17th Line, 19th Line and 51st Line. General Marcognet commanded the 2nd Division, with General Pégot commanding the 1st Brigade which comprised the 21st, 46th, 25th and 45th Line and General Brue headed the 2nd Brigade comprising the 8th, 29th, 85th and 95th Line. Donzelot was assisted by Adjutant-Commandants Durosnel and Kohorn, and Marcognet by Adjutant-Commander Bruyere and General Grenier.[2]

In a subsequent order, Marcognet was ordered to take the 2nd Division to Belleville where it was to be united with the 1st Division.[3] A second order was sent sometime later. In it, d'Erlon ordered that the 8th Line was to relieve a battalion of the Young Guard at Pantrin and would have the 7th Hussars in support. The 29th Line was to relieve the Lyon Volunteer Battalion at Romainville. A company was to be placed to guard the bridge, the others deployed to guard the valley, particularly on the right side. The 95th Line was sent to the gate at Pantrin and occupy a bastion. The rest of the division was ordered to be established behind Belleville in reserve.[4] A third order was sent off to Marcognet, in response to a now lost report from Marcognet. D'Erlon requested that Marcognet take up position by 13.00 hours and was to transmit a copy of his movement order to Donzelot.[5]

General Jamin, with what remained of 20th Infantry Division, was at Saint-Denis and sent off a hurried observation report to Davout. In his dispatch he noted a column of 15,000 troops heading to Saint-Denis using the roads of Montmorency, Pontoise and were in the rear of Argenteuil. The troops began their movement to Saint-Denis around 09.00 hours and arrived at Pierrefitte at 15.00 hours. An English cavalry regiment had been observed in the same location along with a column of 30,000 men at Bourget. Jamin also reported that General Reille had observed the arrival of an English column heading in the direction of Bouqueval with a cavalry screen at the head of column. Jamin reports furthermore that Reille had observed another column that had left the main road in the rear of Bourget and was headed to Saint-Denis, where it arrived on the heights at 16.00 hours. The head of column was formed of lancers, with more cavalry, infantry, and artillery, amongst which he observed not one red uniform.[6]

General Allix sent a hurriedly written dispatch from Saint-Denis to Davout sometime on 1 July. He reported that he had ordered one of his aides-de-camp to carry out a renaissance patrol on the road to Pierrefitte. He reported that he saw a line of vedettes along the Epernay road to Pierrefitte and that a large body of infantry was also in the area. Enemy sharpshooters and cavalry prevented the patrol getting close enough to establish the strength of the enemy forces.[7] Sometime later he sent word to Davout that the enemy were debouching from Pierrefitte Saint-Denis.[8]

General Milhaud at the head of the 4th Cavalry Corps reported to Davout from Auteuil that his cuirassiers had that evening arrived at the bridges of Sèvres and Saint Cloud, where General Pully was established with infantry and had taken steps to make the bridge impassable to infantry. The cuirassiers had expended all their carbine ammunition in defence of the bridge. Milhaud also noted that General Pully was desperately short of powder and needed the assistance of engineers and an officer of engineers. He noted the position was of great of importance, and if it fell to the enemy would be much to their advantage as they could cross the Seine. He added that it was important that more infantry was sent to defend the bridges as well as artillery if the advance of the enemy was to be retarded. In a very pointed and critical postscript, Milhaud censored Davout for not fully grasping the situation. He commented furthermore that 30,000 fédérés were in Paris, and he asked why they were not deployed.[9]

Round 2 at Aubervilliers

Delort's cuirassiers had been bolstered by the arrival of Soult's light cavalry and elements of the Young Guard, which comprised:

1st Brigade:

- The 4th Tirailleur mustered ten officers and 326 other ranks commanded by George Albert who had been appointed 13 April 1815. The battalion commanders were Savinien Lours appointed 1 April 1815 and Baron Joseph Nicholas Ritter. Three officers came from the Elban Flanqueur's, Captain Salvini and lieutenants Bozio and Negroni. Others included lieutenants Monet and Jean Baptiste Lechenaux formerly, of the Fusilier-Grenadiers.

- The 4th Voltigeurs, twenty-nine officers and 585 other ranks. The regiment was commanded by Jean-François Teyssere.

2nd Brigade, Adjutant-Commandant LaForest:

- The 5th Tirailleur mustered twenty officers and 167 other ranks under the orders of Colonel Dorsenne. Edme Charles Louis Le Paige Dorsenne was the older brother of the famous Jean Marie Pierre François Le Paige Dorsenne of the Imperial Guard. Battalion commanders were Louis Ranchon and Rene Urbain Jegu.
- The 5th Voltigeurs, twenty-eight officers and 203 other ranks. The regiment was commanded by Joseph Leclerc. This senior officer had received the order of Marshal Davout to take command of the village of the Vertus, near Saint-Denis on the outskirts of Paris, to join 167 men of the 5th Tirailleurs of Young Guard, under the orders of Colonel Dorsenne, who were already there.

At 03.00 hours, the Prussians, led by General Bülow and General Sydow with an infantry battalion and two regiments of cavalry, numbering perhaps 3,000, made an attack on the village of Vertus, cutting off any line of retreat to the French garrison, who had entrenched themselves there. In a second assault General Sydow led four battalions in columns under the command of Colonel Letzow; five other battalions were in support. He cleared the barricades and captured 200 of the 1,000-man strong garrison. With the village captured, and the L'Ourq canal seized, the 3rd Battalion of the Pomeranian Landwehr Regiment and the 10th Hussars spread out on reconnaissance.[10]

Despite the initial set back, seizing the initiative, Adjutant-commander Laforest:[11]

> sounded the charge and led forward his brigade to within the range of the Prussian pistols, released a volley of musket fire and crushed them with a bayonet charge. He broke through the village and moved up to the church. There, he still found himself having to cut his way through the lances of the Cossacks who had met at this point, while climbing, under the sharpest fire, the barricades ... Then, he formed his small troop in square, crossed the plain between the canal and the village of Vertus, and had the good fortune due to his rapid fire, to bring back most of his men to a redoubt raised in Villette.

The French artillery and sharpshooters along the canal kept up a constant fire against the Prussians. Bülow's 14th Brigade was badly shaken by the French resistance and artillery bombardment and could do little else until more Allied troops had arrived. In response to the French taking back Aubervilliers, the allies sent fresh troops to the attack. Sir Neil Campbell led forward three companies from the 51st Regiment of Foot.[12] According to Siborne, Campbell's men captured houses closest to the Allied lines, and rather than fighting to the death, a truce was agreed. LaForest's gains had been short-lived.

The attack, it seems, was a tentative measure to probe the French defences. Blücher chose to attack Paris from the South which was relatively undefended. This action acted as a screen to hide the bulk of the Prussian army heading south.[13] Pierre Soult's command was involved in the action. In the 1st Hussars, two men were wounded and 6 reported missing.[14]

Action at Villacoublay

On the 1st July, the French counter-attacked the Prussians and British at Vertus but were pushed back by Prussian sharpshooters and artillery fire. That afternoon at Villacoublay, General Exelmans at the head of the 5th, 15th and 20th dragoons (some 3,000 men), moved against the Prussians, whilst the division of General Piré, comprising the 5th and 6th Lancers, the 1st and 6th Chasseurs à Cheval, supported by the 33rd Regiment of Line Infantry, attacked the Prussian forces assembled on the road to Sèvres. Elsewhere around Paris, small actions took place at Versailles and Cheney.[15]

From here, Exelmans headed towards Versailles.

Action at Rocquencourt

The Battle of Rocquencourt was a cavalry action fought on 1 July 1815 in and around the villages of Rocquencourt and Le Chesney. A Prussian brigade of hussars under the command of Lieutenant Colonel Eston von Sohr was destroyed by men under Exelmans' command. Rumginy, who we met earlier, had this to say about the defence there:[16]

> Marshal Davoust then gave me a command at La Villette. Among the men I had to command were 1,800 *fédéras*, which were rather ardent, but not disciplined. I did not do much, although we struggled for a few days against the Prussians. They had made the mistake of separating, and a corps of 30,000 men had set out to Versailles.
>
> A council of war was held at La Villette, where Marshal Davoust had his headquarters. It was agreed that the troops encamped in front of Montrouge under the orders of General Exelmans should attack Sèvres and attack the Prussians. 12,000 men of the guard were to form the head of the column which would leave by the old Neuilly to march on Saint-Germain, the rest of the army was to follow and threaten the left of the enemies.

Marshal Davoust ordered me to take charge of General Gérard's corps, as he was wounded and not yet fit to ride. I went to Montrouge and followed the troops when they were on the march. General Exelmans was in the vanguard with the cavalry. He met the Prussians at Sevres, cut them up them, and arrived at Versailles, where a regiment of Brandenburg hussars was obliged to lay down their arms. The Versailles Gate, which blocks the road to St. Germain, was closed, so that the enemy regiment could not make its way. The rest of the army did not move. Naturally, the hussars and Prussian prisoners were taken along the boulevard, where all the Parisians could see them. This little success inflamed the ardour of some national guards, but it was too late; the nation had lost its chief, the speeches of some deputies threw discouragement and that led to nothing.

The French were commanded by General Exelmans, who was in charge of the French forces on the south of Paris and led forward the 5th and 15th regiments of dragoons, with Colonel de Briqueville leading his 20th Dragoons along with the 6th Hussars in reserve, a force of 3,000 men, to head out along the road from Montrouge towards Plessis-Piquet. The regimental history of the 5th Dragoons adds considerably to the back story of what occurred:[17]

On 1st July, General Pire was ordered to move to the village of Issy and with the 1st and 6th Chasseurs à Cheval, along with the 44th Line via Vill d'Avrey and Rocquencourt, and to conceal their movement from the enemy until they had passed this place. General Exelmans moved to the village Villesse with the intention of gaining Versailles by three routes. Near the wood of Verrieres he encountered an enemy force of 1,500 cavalry which were advancing rapidly with cries of 'Paris! Paris!'. The 5th and 6th dragoons which formed the head of column, charged the Prussians with great audacity, whilst the 6th Hussars and 20th Dragoons charged the Prussian flank. Pushed back on all points, the Prussian cavalry quitted the road to Versailles, leaving many dead and wounded covering the road.

During this time, General Piré executed his move on Rocquencourt. The Prussian column, being vigorously pursued by the 5th, 6th and 20th dragons as well as the 6th Hussars, came headlong into the general's ambush and point-blank fire from the 44th Line.

Lieutenant Henckens, of the 6th Chasseurs à Cheval, adds that Exelmans:[18]

Had in his bivouacs his dragoons as well as the 1st and 6th Chasseurs à Cheval, and Soult's Hussars, as well as the 44th Line. He, sent, under the command of General Hubert, the two regiments of Chasseurs à Cheval, with a battalion of the 44th Line via the wood of Meudon and Ville d'Avray, which are situated on the Versailles to Saint-Germain-en-Laye road, with the order to place them in an advantageous position for an ambush to cut the retreat of the Prussians that General Exelmans would try and push back with the dragoons and hussars in the direction of the location of the ambush.

Our regiment knew the terrain well, have been in garrison at Saint-Germain-en-Laye, and knew the area was ideal for an ambush.

General Hubert placed us close to the Rocquencourt, ordering the 6th to attack from the front whilst the 1st were to assail themselves upon the infantry ... General Exelmans led an all-out charge with the four regiments under his command, forced the Prussians to retreat towards Saint-Germain-en-Laye, and onwards to the ambush where three quarters of it was massacred, the commander was killed and the remainder were made prisoners. The Prussian infantry that accompanied the cavalry would have also been thrown back to Saint-Germain had not Marshal Davout sent orders to General Exelmans to return to the bivouac at Montrouge when they had just arrived at Marly, and General Vandamme had moved up in support.

General Delort noted:[19]

in approaching Paris several corps were already reorganized, some platoons of the division of cuirassiers of General Delort had sufficed to hold for three leagues all the enemy's vanguard, but a few days after General Exelmans with his division of dragons defeated and exterminated several regiments of Prussian cavalry, near Versailles, and the infantry encamped in the plain of Grenelle had repelled several attacks of combined Anglo-Prussians.

Concerning the 44th Line, General Hulot commented:[20]

On 1st July General Exelmans had sent me one of his officers to inform me that he was to make a move with his cavalry to Versailles and enquired from me if I had received an order to support him. I had actually received orders to the opposite, that I was not to leave my positions, but seeing how useful some infantry could be to this expedition, I took it upon myself to give orders to Colonel Paulini commanding the 44th Line to move along the road from Sèvres to Versailles, and to take and execute any orders he received from General Exelmans.'

An eyewitness to these events wrote on the night of the Sunday 2 July 1815:[21]

The affair of General Exelmans at Versailles yesterday appears to have been more considerable than was supposed. The town has been retaken by the French, and two regiments of Prussian cavalry

210

destroyed. This was announced to the chambers by a message from the Tuilleries.

In the immediate environs of the action, the 5th and 6th lancers marched along the Sèvres road upon Viroflay; the 6th Chasseurs à Cheval proceeded to occupy the crossroads connecting Sèvres with the northern portion of Versailles; the 1st Chasseurs à Cheval moved by Sèvres towards Rocquencourt, about three miles from Versailles, on the road to Saint-Germain; the 44th Line followed this movement sometime later. Both the latter regiments were destined to cut off the retreat of the Prussian cavalry, should it be driven back by Exelmans.[22]

According to General Piré himself, the first Prussian squadron came under fire at the entrance of Rocquencourt; outnumbered, it attempted to escape through the fields. It was forced into a small, narrow street in Le Chesney where many were killed or captured. The Prussians then fell back upon Versailles, pursued by the French; who vainly endeavoured to force an entrance into the town, at the gate of which a gallant resistance was made by the Prussians. The short time that was gained by this resistance sufficed to allow the main body of the brigade to collect on the open space at the outlet leading to Saint-Germain, towards which point it might have retreated through the park; but having received information of the advance of Prussian III Corps commanded by Johann von Thielmann, and expecting every moment to receive support, Lieutenant Colonel Sohr retired by the more direct road through Rocquencourt.[23]

Later the same day, about 19.00 hours, the Prussian hussars were fired upon by the National Guard from the barrier. It was then that the 1st Chasseurs à Cheval attacked the Prussians but, with the mortal wounding of squadron commander Rambourgt from a pistol shot, the regiment fell back and was pursued by Prussian cavalry. Two companies of the 3rd Battalion of the 44th Line, posted behind some hedges near Le Chesney, opened fire on the Prussians. The hussars, reacting to the musket fire, turned tail and rode hell for leather back to the Prussian lines.[24]

The official army bulletin of the 2 July 1815 read:[25]

General Exelmans defended the gate in the afternoon, with a party of cavalry at Versailles. The enemy occupied the town with 1,500 cavalry. General Exelmans formed, in order to capture the place, in consequence, ordered Lieutenant General Piré with the 1st and 6th Chasseurs à Cheval and the 44th infantry, to move to Ville-d'Avray and Rocquencourt, and their recommended that they ambush the enemy at that place. In person, Lieutenant General

Exelmans reached the gate of the road from Montrouge to Velisy, with the intention of entering Versailles at three places. He had reconnoitred the heights and wood of Verrieres, where there was a strong enemy column.

The 5th and the 15th Dragoons, the latter at the head, charged the enemy with rare intrepidity. The 6th Hussars and 20th Dragoons pierced the enemy flank. The enemy was pushed back on all points, and were forced to leave Versailles, the road being blocked with their dead and wounded.

During these times, Lieutenant General Piré executed his movement to Rocquencourt with much vigour and intelligence, the Prussian column which was pursued by General Exelmans, fell against the corps of General Piré. They were received by a fusillade from the 44th regiment and charged by the 1st and 6th Chasseurs à Cheval, and also by the 6th Hussars and 5th Dragoons, and were pursued beyond Versailles.

The result of these great affairs was the entire destruction of the two hussar regiments, Brandenburg and Pomerania, the best of the Prussian Army.

The French troops, infantry, and cavalry were unrivalled with their courage … A government commission has been charged by the Minister of War, to pay a dividend to the officers, sub-officers and soldiers who were the most distinguished in the affair.

In these two good affairs, a number of prisoners had been taken and horses captured.

In the attack, the following losses are recorded by the French, oddly no mention is ever made of the 8th Chasseurs à Cheval being involved in the action beyond the colonel being wounded, but the regiment was clearly involved:

Regiment	Killed		Wounded		Missing		Total
	Officers	Men	Officers	Men	Officers	Men	
5th Hussars[26]	0	0	2	0	0	2	4
6th Hussars[27]	0	2	1	5	0	12	20
1st Chasseurs à Cheval	No meaningful data recorded						
6th Chasseurs à Cheval	No meaningful data recorded						
8th Chasseurs à Cheval[28]	0	5	6	1	0	12	24
5th Dragoons[29]	0	0	3	1	0	2	6
15th Dragoons[30]	0	0	1	0	0	17	18
20th Dragoons[31]	0	0	7	0	0	0	7
Total	0	7	20	7	0	45	79

The Prussians were clearly not push-overs, as the casualty reports attest. Colonel Simonneau of the 1st Chasseurs à Cheval was promoted to Marechal du Camp for his actions on 3 July 1815.

Despite crushing the Prussians, the attack faltered. Many officers felt the advantage that Exelmans had gained over the Prussians was squandered. Henckens, an officer with the 6th Chasseurs à Cheval, writing after the fact, commented that Davout had in essence sabotaged Exelmans, daring plan by halting the advance of Vandamme. General Allix noted that:[32]

> Vandamme intended to attack the Prussian army, and had detached Exelmans towards Versailles, where Exelmans met four regiments of Prussian cavalry which he utterly destroyed but was stopped suddenly at Issy by an order of Fouché.

Which were the four regiments referred to by Allix, we ask? Von Sohr's brigade lost:

Regiment	Killed		Wounded		Missing		Total
	Officers	Men	Officers	Men	Officers	Men	
Brandenburg Hussars	1	15	7	36	0	4	63 men and 248 horses
Pomeranian Hussars	1	57	4	77	0	0	139 men and 324 horses

The 9th Prussian Brigade in addition suffered seven dead, one officer and seventy-four men wounded, and twenty-two missing. The French claimed 437 hussars as prisoners, but which other cavalry regiments did Exelmans face? The 1st as well as the 2nd squadron 3rd Kurmark Landwehr cavalry were with 9th Brigade. Are these two units those referred to by Henckens? Presumably so. Yet despite inflicting huge losses, the attack was not followed up.

General Pajol suspected he knew what was going on:[33]

> The French Army, which originally was to have marched almost entirely, did not move. At the instigation of Fouché, who wanted no further fighting at any cost, Davout had given a counter order. A government council was called at 10 AM.
>
> At the council, which included several marshals, there was much talking, but nothing was decided, the question of defending Paris was assessed by a council of war which was composed of the same army men that Davout had called together the night before at his headquarters at La Vilette ... It seemed that someone was fearful of doing too much harm to the enemy. Pajol, who re-entered the lines

before being able to set his men in motion, was very irritated; he understood what was happening … Pajol violently resisted the idea of a capitulation … Davout wrote up what had been said, and stated resistance was useless and impossible.

Fleury de Chaboulon, former secretary to the Emperor, adds with hindsight in 1820:[34]

The whole army, generals, officers, soldiers, were still animated with a devotion, that nothing could rebut. Proud of the confidence placed in them by the national representatives, they had answered their appeal by an address full of spirit and patriotism. They had sworn to each other to die in defence of the honour and independence of the nation, and they were impatient, to fulfil their oaths.

General Excelmanns was sent after the Prussians with six thousand men. A corps of fifteen thousand infantry, under the command of General Vichery, was to follow him by the bridge of Sèvres, and connect its movements with six thousand foot of the 1st Corps, and ten thousand chosen horse, who were to march by the bridge of Neuilly. But at the moment of executing these movements, the success of which would unquestionably have ensured the destruction of the Prussian army, counter-orders were issued by the Prince of Eckmuhl, from what motives I know not. General Excelmanns alone continued to fight. He attacked the enemy in front of Versailles, drove them into an ambuscade, cut them to pieces, and took from them their arms, baggage, and horses. Generals Strolz, Piré, Burthe, and Vincent, colonels Briqueville, Faudoas, St. Amand, Chaillou, Simonnet, Schmid, Paolini, and their brave regiments, performed prodigies of valour, and were intrepidly seconded by the citizens of the neighbouring communes, who had preceded as 'skirmishers' before the arrival of our troops on the field of battle, and during the battle proved themselves worthy to fight by their side.

This victory filled the Parisian patriots with hope and joy. It inspired them with the noble desire of imitating the fine example that had just been set them. But when it was known, that a general engagement had been unanimously desired and agreed upon and that the enemy, had it not been for counter-orders, surprised and cut off, would have been annihilated, this intoxication was changed into depression, and a cry was raised on all hands of infamy and treason.

Excelmanns and his brave men, not being supported, were obliged to retreat. The Prussians advanced and the English moved out to support them. They formed a junction and came and encamped together on the heights of Meudon.'

Council of War

Perhaps in endeavouring to spread the burden of command, Davout organised a round-table conference of all senior officers. For those present, it seemed more to be an exercise in limiting culpability and doing nothing. Fleury de Chaboulon again:[35]

> Count Carnot, who had been to examine our positions and those of the enemy in company with General Grenier, made a report on the situation of Paris to the assembly. He stated: 'That the fortifications erected on the right bank of the Seine appeared sufficient to secure Paris against any assault on that side. But that the left bank was entirely open and presented a spacious field to the enemy's attempts. That the English and Prussian generals had moved the greater part of their armies to this vulnerable point with impunity, and appeared disposed to attempt an attack with that force. That, if they failed the first time, they might return to the charge a second, and renew their attempts till they rendered themselves masters of the capital. That they would have fresh troops, to oppose to us continually, while ours, obliged to be constantly on their guard, would soon be exhausted with fatigue. That the arrival of subsistence was becoming difficult, and that a corps of sixty thousand Bavarians would apparently block up the way between the Seine and Marne in the course of a few days. That the enemy, already masters of the heights of Meudon and the best surrounding positions, might entrench themselves there, cut off our retreat, and reduce Paris and the army, to surrender at discretion.
>
> The president of the committee, after having called the attention of the members of the assembly to these serious considerations, requested them to give their opinions. It was observed to him that it appeared necessary to make known the present state of the negotiations. This the committee did not refuse: but the communication having brought on a discussion respecting the Bourbons, the committee reminded them that they ought to confine themselves to the military question; and that the point was, purely and simply to decide, whether it was advisable or possible, to defend Paris.
>
> The Prince of Essling, being called upon, said that this city would be impregnable if the inhabitants would make of it a second Saragossa. But there was not sufficient harmony in their sentiments, to think of a resolute resistance; and the most prudent part would be to obtain a suspension of hostilities at any price. The Duke of Dantzic declared, that he did not think it impossible to prolong their defence by rapidly accelerating the works begun in the plains of Montrouge. The Duke of Dalmatia maintained, that the left bank of the Seine was not tenable; that it was even very hazardous, since the occupation of Aubervilliers, to remain on the right side. That

if the line of the canal, that joins St. Denis to Lavallette, should be forced, the enemy might enter by the barrier of St. Denis pell-mell with our troops. Some of the members, agreeing in opinion with the Duke of Dantzic, demanded, that positive information should be procured respecting the possibility of putting the left bank into a state of defence, before coming to a decision. In fine, after some debate, it was decided, that the assembly was not competent to determine such a question and that it should be submitted to the examination and decision of a council of war, which the Prince of Eckmuhl should convene for the following night...

The council of war assembled on the night of the 1st of July at the headquarters at Lavallette, under the presidentship of the Prince of Eckmuhl. Care was taken, it appeared, to keep away some suspected generals, and not to neglect calling those officers, whose principles, moderation, or weakness, was known. All the marshals present in the capital were admitted...

The committee, in order to prevent all political discussion, had stated the questions, to which the members of the council were to confine their deliberations: but this precaution, as might be supposed, did not prevent their entering familiarly into the moral and political considerations, that might influence the defence or surrender of the city. Marshal Soult pleaded the cause of Louis XVIII, and was eagerly seconded by other marshals, and several generals who, though they entered into the council under the national colours, would willingly have gone out of it with the white cockade.

It is impossible, to recapitulate the opinions, given in turn or confusedly by the fifty persons, who were called to take a share in this great and important deliberation ... These considerations, the force of which was generally felt, were unanimously approved. It was acknowledged that it would be unquestionably most prudent not to expose the capital to the consequences and dangers of a siege, or of being taken by assault. It was acknowledged, too, at least by implication, that, the return of the Bourbons being inevitable, it was better to recall them voluntarily, under good conditions, than to leave to the allies the act of restoring them. But the members did not think proper, to explain themselves on this delicate subject; and accordingly confined themselves to laconic answers of the questions proposed by the committee.

Questions proposed by the Committee of Government to the Council of War, assembled at la Villette, 1 July 1815, and answered by Davout at 03.00 hours on 2 July are as follows:

1st. What is the state of the intrenchments raised for the defence of Paris?

Answer: The state of the intrenchments, and their supply of ordnance on the right bank of the Seine, though incomplete is, in general, satisfactory enough. On the left bank the intrenchments may be considered as null.

2nd. The army, can it cover and defend Paris?

Answer: It may, but not indefinitely. It ought not to expose itself to a want of provision, or to have its retreat cut off.

3rd. If the army was attacked on all points, could it prevent the enemy from penetrating into Paris on one side or the other?

Answer: It would be difficult for the army to be attacked on all points at once, but should this happen, there would be little hope of resistance.

4th. In case of a defeat, could the commander-in-chief reserve, or collect, sufficient means to oppose a forcible entry?

Answer: No general can answer for the consequences of a battle.

5th. Is there sufficient ammunition for several battles?

Answer. Yes.

6th. In fine, can you answer for the fate of the capital? and for how long a time?

Answer: We can warrant nothing on this head.

The answers were transmitted immediately to the Tuileries, and they became the subject of a long and profound deliberation. There were advantages and dangers of a protracted defence, and it was thought that Paris, without hope of succour and surrounded on all sides, would either be taken by assault, or forced to surrender at discretion. It was also understood that the army, without any means of retreat, would find itself perhaps reduced to choose between the disgrace of surrendering or of burying themselves under the ruins of the capital. The committee, therefore, decided unanimously, that Paris should not be defended, and that they would submit to deliver it into the hands of the allies, since the allies would not suspend hostilities at any other price.

General Zieten, who commanded Prince Blücher's advanced guard, was informed of this decision by Davout. Zieten sent the following reply on 2 July:

> General Revest has communicated to me verbally, that you demand an armistice, to treat the surrender of Paris. In consequence, M. General, I have to inform you, that I am in no way authorized to accept an armistice. I dare not even announce this demand to his Highness Marshal Prince Blücher: but however, if the deputies

of the government declare to my aide-de-camp, Count Westphalen, that they will surrender the city, and that the French army will surrender itself also, I will accept a suspension of hostilities. I will then communicate it to his highness Prince Blücher.

General Berthezene was savvy enough to know what had taken place:[36]

On the 30th, the enemy passed on the left bank of the Seine by the Pont du Pecq, where he found no obstacle. It is not possible to think that the Prussian general would have dared to risk such a rash operation in the presence of an army of 80,000 men, had he not been certain that nothing would be done against him. At the sight of this manoeuvre, Napoléon, who was still in Paris, sure of beating the enemy, asked the Provisional Government for permission to attack, declaring that he would restore power after having rendered his service to his country; but Fouché, whose betrayal was patent, took care not to allow it. Instead of acting and taking advantage of the imprudence of the Prussians, the ardour of the troops, and the good disposition of the Parisian volunteers, the marshals held at La Villette a council of war, where it was discussed whether Paris should to be defended. When one does not wish to fight, the best way to hide one's responsibility is to assemble a council of war where the most prudent advice always has the majority, and this is what happened at La Villette.

Chapter 24

2 July 1815

After General Piré's victory at Rocquencourt on the morning of 2 July, Marshal Blücher moved to Versailles with the 9th Brigade from Thielmann's 3rd Corps. The Prussian army was in motion towards the south side of Paris, where they intended taking possession of the advantageous position comprising the Heights of Meudon and Chatillon, and their immediate vicinity. The bulk of the Prussian 3rd Corps itself halted two hours at Rocquencourt to wait for the arrival of Zieten's Corps. As the latter corps advanced, it threw out a Detachment to its left, consisting of the 1st Battalion of the 1st West Prussian Regiment, two pieces of horse artillery, and a squadron of cavalry. This force was under the command of Captain Krensky who was directed to proceed by Malmaison towards St Cloud. Krensky communicated with Major Colomb, who had already been detached with his force towards the Bridge of Neuilly; they kept a look out on the direct road to Paris.

At about 15.00 hours, Zieten's 1st Brigade, under Steinmetz, arrived at Sèvres. This was followed by the 2nd and 4th brigades which advanced towards the heights of Meudon. The Reserve Cavalry of the corps followed the 1st Brigade, in support. The 4th Brigade occupied Sèvres. The leading elements of what remained of the French 1st Corps moved via Saint-Germain to the bridges at Saint-Cloud.

An eyewitness to the movements of the enemy on Meudon was Captain of Topographical Engineers Charbonnel. He was stationed in the tower of the Cathedral of Saint-Suplice and reported that at 05.06 hours on the morning of 2 July, the enemy occupied the mill at Meudon and had deployed three artillery pieces and caissons.[1]

According to Baron Louis Sebastian Grundler (1774-1833), when Kellerman's cuirassiers and carabiniers arrived in Paris, they began a spree of pillaging, and the 7th Cuirassiers had crossed the River Seine to maraud and pillage on the opposite bank to the carabiniers. He further notes to Marshal Davout in his letter dated Neuilly 2 July, that part of the Grenadiers à Pied was at Suresnes, whilst some were at the Bois de Boulogne and had pillaged Neuilly mercilessly. He requested a lieutenant general be appointed to restore discipline.[2]

In a similar vein, General Donzelot reported that due to lack of pay, fire wood and food, 4,000 men had deserted from 1st, 2nd and 3rd corps as well as the barracks in Paris. The army was slipping away.[3]

Sometime that day, Reille reported to Davout that Vandamme had observed the head of a column of Blücher's army arrive at Versailles. At the same time at Petit Mont Rouge, Reille noted that the Imperial Guard commanded by Drouot had debouched to the left of the place. Kellerman with his cavalry corps along with the 1st Hussars headed by General Clary, had crossed the Seine at St Ouen and that the 7th Hussars had passed the Seine at Lavallette.[4]

Action at Neuilly

The French garrison at Neuilly was commanded by Baron Grundler. In a very scathing report to Davout, Grundler complained that the bridge there was insufficiently defended by four small calibre artillery pieces. He reported that the Prussians opposite him had thirty or forty cannon. He asked if General Kellerman could move from Chaillot with a battery of 12-pounders. General Bachelu, at the head of General Soye's brigade from 2nd Corps, was flung out along the river banks and was ordered to open fire on any movement observed on the far bank.[5] In a second dispatch, this time sent to General Guillaminot, he reported that in the twenty-four hours since his last report (i.e. 1 July) a battery of 8 x 12-pounder field guns had arrived with him, and that Kellerman was soon to arrive with eight more 12-pounders and two companies from the Young Guard – but he feared these men with no experience of battle or any training would be more of a hinderance than a help. He asked Guillaminot why all the heavy artillery was in the lines at Vilette or at Chaumont and Montmartre and not where they were needed. He complained bitterly to Guillaminot that he lacked the guns and men he needed to defend Neuilly, and in consequence he had mined the bridge, which would be detonated as soon as the enemy moved. He blamed Davout for the poor defence of the city.[6]

Kellerman sent an order from Neuilly to General Haxo sometime on 2 July. He requested that Haxo send an officer of engineers and some miners to Neuilly as fast as was possible to detonate the bridges.[7]

Action at Sèvres.

The defence of the Southern side of the capital was led by General Pully, who was bolstered by the infantry of the Imperial Guard. Charles Joseph Randon de Malboissière Pully (1751-1832) was a colonel of cavalry in 1792, promoted to general of division 8 March 1793. He was made count of the empire on 15 August 1809. He was a veteran cavalry officer whose fighting days had been over a decade before. His force comprised: [8]

Lancers of the Guard: four officers, 104 men
Chasseurs à Cheval of the Guard: six officers, 220 men
105th Line: thirty-seven officers, fifty-nine men
13th Light Infantry: eleven officers, seventy-three men
85th Line: thirty-three officers, fifty men
40th Line: ten officers, 194 men
21st Line: seventy-six officers, 130 men
Belgian Chasseurs à Cheval: thirty officers, 350 men
Polish Infantry: four officers, 120 men
2nd Line: twenty officers, 500 men
TOTAL: 231 officers, 1800 men

The bridge itself at Saint-Cloud was defended by the 2nd Regiment of Line Infantry and the 7th Regiment of Light Horse Lancers, which were recruited exclusively from Poles. [9]

General Hulot with part of 4th Corps was ordered to Sèvres: [10]

> I received an order from General Vandamme to move with the 3rd Division to the Châteaux of Bellevue and to establish myself there. After having executed this movement I reconnoitred the position, I judged it a bad one, and I requested to move the greater part of my men to be in front of the woods in the direction of Versailles in order to better cover numerous approaches which come from this place, or alternatively to leave just two battalions at Bellevue and to take up positions with the rest on the heights that exist behind Sèvres and Meudon. These heights, which were planted with vines, offered me an excellent fighting position, whereas at Bellevue I would not have been able to manoeuvre well due to the steep slopes of the hill towards the Seine. However, I received an order to remain at Bellevue. I therefore deployed my line from the main road at Sèvres, which I guarded with a battalion, and to beyond the Châteaux of Meudon ... towards 8 o'clock the skirmishers of General Vandamme's corps, coming from Issy and Vanves, advanced along the left bank in order to make a diversion for the attack on Sèvres, and warmly engaged the enemy on their flank and rear. The fighting continued until ten o'clock at night.

Versailles had been occupied in force by the enemy during the night. All the information that came to me confirmed this offensive movement on us. I made a report to and sent it to General Toussaint with part of his brigade and all our artillery to the rear of the valley and the Sèvres and Meudon road and awaited the enemy. All my advanced posts were attacked towards midday. The 111th Line had a battalion which covered the front of Sèvres was assailed with determination. I only held the position long enough for our advanced posts to be collected from the trackways in front of the wood, making sure to leave no one behind, suffering only a few men wounded from the 111th.

As I retired my body of men to where General Toussaint was established in echelon, I received an order from General Vichery to take a position to the left of the road in front of Vaugirard that was occupied by his division, which was then commanded by General Morio de l'Issel, and that he was moving to the heights above Issy which was being attacked by the enemy. After a stubborn resistance the division was forced to retire during the night and reformed at Vaugirard. The enemy had seized Issy.

General Vichery himself sent a dispatch to an unknown general, presumably one under his command, stating that one of the inhabitants of Meux had informed him that he was to be attacked by 15 to 20,000 enemy troops which were heading from Meux to Sèvres.[11] A second dispatch read that enemy scouts were heading to the brides of Sèvres and Versailles, and that a column of 6,000 men was heading to Versailles and was comprised primarily of English and Prussian cavalry. In response therefore they had to retreat to Vaurirard.[12]

Captain Robinaux, commanding 5th Company 2nd Battalion 2nd Regiment of Line Infantry, described the events he witnessed from his position between the bridges of Saint Cloud and Sèvres:[13]

> The enemy having manoeuvred on our left and headed towards Versailles, we were obliged to leave our positions on the banks of the Seine and move to Neuilly, Saint-Cloud and Sèvres; our regiment occupied this place betwixt the stone bridge to the wooden bridges called the 'nets of Saint-Cloud'. There was a small detachment of Poles between the stone bridge and Saint-Cloud. Marshal Davout, being Minister for War, came to our position and ordered that two arches of the stone bridge were to be loaded with straw, covered over with planks and then covered with tar. I was ordered to lead this expedition. I took thirty soldiers for the task and I took the planks that I found here and there along the river and spread them on the bridge above the two arches, and with a barrel of tar that someone had sent, covered everything with it, putting the rest of the combustible in the middle.

The Marshal arrived at that moment and told me to complete work as quickly as was possible, as he said the Prussians would appear on the Sèvres heights in a quarter of an hour. Immediately I set fire to the bridge in the presence of the Marshal and in less than a quarter of an hour the structure of the bridge was burning and the two arches, which were almost blocked, fell into the river. It was less than ten minutes after the bridge had collapsed that the Prussians arrived on the Sèvres heights with four artillery pieces supported by infantry and a small cavalry force. They descended into the town of Sèvres, taking positions on the banks of the Seine, and opened fire. They had come with the intention of re-establishing the bridge; if they had arrived in time they would have crossed it, as due to our inferiority we would not have been able to stop them … the firefight became heavy between the Prussians and one of our companies which were entrenched in some of the houses that were at the head of the old wooden bridge which the Prussians wanted to re-establish, as we had cut the closes bridge to Sèvres. We were obliged to send the 3rd Company to take up positions on little tongue of land between the two bridges, about 500m long between the two arms of the river, in order to defend it from the Prussians. They wanted to capture the wooden bridge, but as soon as our troops were in position the fire of musketry became heavy and continuous. The firing had started about 2pm; for four hours our troops were under fire from the enemy who were hidden in the houses on the other side of the river and our artillery was not able to reply successfully to the enemy guns which were in position on the heights and concealed by a thick wood. The 3rd company was being eviscerated by canister fire, musketry and shells which never ceased to rain down upon them; it was necessary to go to them in support because they were so much weakened by loss that they could not hold their position.

My colonel ordered my company to leave our column that was concealed behind a high wall and some houses and to set off to support the 3rd Company on the island. I immediately set off with my troop of 137 men. To get onto the island I had to the cross the wooden bridge closest to Paris, the entry to which was on our left. As soon as the enemy observed us, all their fire was directed onto the bridge we were crossing. When Marshal Davout saw me from a far on the bridge he cried out 'Run! Run!'. We were immediately struck by a heavy volley of cannister fire and musketry that cut down a dozen of my men as well as my lieutenant who fell dead with a musket ball to the head.

We immediately broke into a run and threw ourselves onto the island where I started to position my men as sharpshooters, we fired until 10PM; I lost only 30 men because they were well positioned. We had two or three positions that we well covered which saved many men, for the amount of fire we were under was astonishing.

The enemy force was about 1,500 strong and his losses were considerable. At 10 o'clock the firing ceased along the whole line and the enemy descended the heights onto the bank of the Seine where they took new positions, placed sentries and moved a large column into the village facing the end of the island that I occupied. I followed their movements to better identify their new positions.

General Pully wrote:[14]

The fire from the enemy artillery batteries ceased at Sèvres at 10 o'clock in the evening. The fire of musketry lasted longer where I am until half past 10 in the evening. Of the 1,100 men under the orders of Colonel Tripe for the defence of this place, 700 have been engaged, with a lively fire of musketry, conducted with great merit. The enemy attacked the post with four regiments of infantry. We lost around 150 wounded and 50 killed, which included an officer of the 2nd Regiment of Line Infantry and an officer of the 7th Regiment of Light Horse Lancers. Colonel Tripe[15] acted in the most brave and intrepid manner as did the men under his command ... It is urgent you send without delay a company of engineers to the bridge at Sèvres to complete the destruction of the bridge before it can be taken by the enemy ... They attacked at the same time the bridge at Saint-Cloud. Exchanges of musketry commenced on both side at one o'clock and has not yet fully ceased. We have had 21 wounded.

General Pully further noted in his dispatch to Davout that his men needed the support of an additional battalion of infantry and more ammunition as his men had fired all the rounds that they had, explaining that thanks to the tremendous expenditure of munitions, they had killed or wounded 600 to 700 Prussian troops.[16] No more munition or men arrived, no doubt as Davout and Fouché would have been furious at Pully inflicting such large losses Prussian troops whilst delicate peace negotiations were going on to secure an armistice. Losses in the 2nd Line at the bridge of Sèvres are in the table below:[17]

2nd regiment of Line Infantry					
Battalion	Wounded	Wounded & Pow	POW	Killed	Missing
1st	8	0	0	1	0
2nd	5	0	0	0	0
3rd	8	1	0	0	1
4th	3	0	0	0	0
Total	24	1	0	1	1

Despite Fouché's and Davout's machinations, at some stage Kellermans cuirassiers clattered along the road and charged enemy troops to relieve Pully's beleaguered men.[18]

Despite the best efforts of the Prussians, General Pully still occupied and held the bridges at Sèvres and Saint-Cloud on the morning of 3 July 1815. General Pully notes:[19]

> The artillery barrage and fusillade from the enemy infantry began at the break of day against the bridge at Sèvres, I had ensured that the cartridges I had ordered be sent this important point had arrived in sufficient number ... Our brave men had put up an obstinate resistance and are very fatigued and it is my opinion that they can no longer take part in opposition to the enemy ... it is essential we hold the two bridges at Sèvres and Saint-Cloud.

Captain Robinaux again:[20]

> In the morning, 3rd July, we were in the same positions as the previous day, and the sun had appeared before any shots were fired. I was in a position on the side of the river and hidden by a high bank opposite a grand house situated on the heights on the other side of the river where the Prussians were.

General Pully was unaware of the political machinations of his masters, as a day later the bridges would be handed over to the allies.

Comment

From reading the letters and dispatches written during the battle for Paris, it is clear that Davout had lost the trust of a large section of the army. Many of his subordinate commanders were openly questioning Davout's motives and actions. It was evident to men like Grundler, Kellerman, Milhaud, Allix, Pully and others that Davout was, in essence, sabotaging the defence of the city.

Davout was clearly torn between his own judgement and instincts as a soldier, and also the will of the government and his master, Fouché, in wanting peace. Peace had been the stated gaol of the French Government since 22 June. Davout therefore squandered the resources available to field commanders and prevented any major fightback by Vandamme and others. Why? If peace was to be declared in a few days, it boded well not to fight back too strongly. It would not look very good to Fouché and the peace envoys if suddenly Vandamme led the French army to victory and defeated the exhausted Allied troops. Peace would be achieved at any cost, even if it meant compromising the defence of the city, notably at Sèvres and Neuilly. Davout deliberately left the bridge with an inadequate garrison so that, on the surface, it would look like the garrison had been overwhelmed, the bridge had fallen, and the way into Paris was open. But as we have seen, General Milhaud and others had guessed Davout's game. Despite what the politicians were planning, Vandamme and others wanted to give the allies a bloody nose.

Chapter 25

3 July 1815

Before dawn on 3 July, sometime around 03.00 hours, the ever irascible General Vandamme, hoping to build on the victory at Rocquencourt, ordered his troops to the attack. His infantry force comprised fifteen battalions drawn from 2nd, 3rd and 4th corps, supported by cavalry. His goal was to retake the ground lost on the previous day.

Vandamme placed his cavalry between Vaugirard and the Seine, flanked by an artillery battery advantageously posted near Auteuil on the right bank of the river.

The action commenced with the French guns opening fire. Vandamme hoped to take the village of Issy. In the village, the Prussians had constructed some barricades, and other defences, during the night; but these were of little protection from the French guns. The Prussian garrison comprised the 12th and 24th Prussian regiments, and the 2nd Westphalian Landwehr, supported by a half battery of 12-pounders. General Revest, chief of staff to Vandamme in a dispatch timed at 03.00 hours adds much detail to the events as they unfolded. He notes the 8th Infantry Division led by General Lefol debouched from Mont-Rouge, supported by the cavalry of General Domon. General Berthezene with the 10th and 11th infantry divisions deployed to the right of the 8th. Lefol had ordered out companies of voltigeurs to act as skirmishers to cover the French advance, which only began when General Exelmans with the 2nd Cavalry Corps arrived, which Reverts notes, pushed back the enemy skirmish line. As Exelmans' men trotted forward into Prussian musketry and artillery fire, General Vichery with the 13th Infantry Division from 4th Corps rapidly advanced and occupied the Prussian positions.[1]

As Exelmans men charged the Prussians, trooper MAT No. 236 Antoine Chataignier of the 5th Dragoons was mortally wounded.[2] He was possibly the last French soldier to die in the defence of the city until the Franco-Prussia war.

Reverst in his lengthy report added, that by 05.00 hours General Drouot had moved to Mont-Rouge with 10,000 men of the Old Guard and had deployed them along the main road leading from Mont-Rouge. He further comments that Kellerman with the 3rd and 4th cavalry corps was by this time in the field, and his command was deployed on the plain of Grenelle. Exelmans command was by now bolstered by Domon's and Vallin's commands.[3] Confirming Reverts dispatch was General Guyot, who commanded the heavy cavalry of the Imperial Guard:[4]

> 3rd July, at 5 o'clock in the morning we moved 1 league. All the cavalry of the Guard and the infantry of the Guard were assembled on the Champ de Mars, along with the artillery, and it was expected we would give battle to the enemy which had taken post on the heights of Meudon, and where a strong engagement had been ongoing since 9 o'clock last night.

In essence, here was the last showdown of the Napoléonic wars. Every man in the French Army that could fire a musket and not run away when the enemy opened fire, as had happened so many times before, was there. The army was itching for a fight. The army had a score to settle with the Prussians and to avenge Waterloo. This was to be no mere display of sabre rattling. The army wanted blood, preferably Prussian.

General Milhaud reported to Davout that he had taken advantageous positions on the Plain of Grenelle. In his dispatch he informed Davout that the Prussians had occupied the village of Issy and placed in support a regiment of lancers and one of dragoons. But he concluded, that after a short artillery barrage from the guns with his cavalry corps, he ordered his cuirassiers to charge, took the Prussians in the flank and swept them off the plain of Grenelle.[5] The scene was set for a much larger battle to push back the Prussians from the walls of Paris.

General Teste, Commanding the 21st Infantry Division part of 6th Corps and comprised the 8th Light Infantry Regiment, the 75th Regiment of Line Infantry and 1st Battalion of the 65th Regiment of Line Infantry noted:[6]

> The whole army deployed ready to fight. My division occupied the 'Grande Montrouge' and the park. The exits of the village were quickly barricaded, the garden walls loop-holed; the 65th Line defended the exists of the village on the side of the plain and the 2nd battalion of the 8th Light those on the side of the Orleans road. The 1st battalion of the same regiment and the 75th Line were placed in the park with the artillery which had several guns in battery on its edge.

General Lefol's division was formed in line to the rear of Montrouge covering the Orleans road. The Prussian and English armies had separated in crossing the Seine and were marching on Meudon. We were going to give them a famous lesson; profiting from the position of our troops and of the anger that inspired the entire army that had passed through Paris. We could now fall on the enemy that had taken up a poor position.

We went quickly to General Vandamme's headquarters who commanded the area. We would wipe out the Prussians. They offered us this great opportunity. Myself and ten general officers, amongst whom were Exelmans, Flahaut, Lefol explained to Vandamme in a few words of the pressing need to submit to our wishes.

Captain Beraud, who fought at Waterloo with the 4th Grenadiers, and then the 3rd Grenadiers of the Imperial Guard wrote:[7]

We fought every day around Paris; in the environs of Sèvres, on the slopes of Meudon, in the vineyards of Clamart, in those of Chatillon, at Nanterre, in the plain of the Vertus, daily combats and skirmishes took place. Two bridges of boats had been established by the French for their communications; one above the Austerlitz bridge on the side of the Garre, the other below and at a short distance from the bridge of Jena; but the Chatou Bridge had been restored by the enemies.

A part of the Army of the West, which was under the orders of the generals Lamarque and Travot, had been recalled by the government, and returned to join the army of Paris.

The English and Prussians were eager to join forces, and to take up positions to start a general battle. The repeated attacks of the French were intended to hinder the union of the two armies, and to dispute the positions. In these little actions the French showed themselves ardently, and always gained some advantages; Amongst these small battles we remember the splendid act of arms of General Excelmanns [sic], who, although much inferior in number, beat a Prussian corps completely near Versailles, and made a great number of prisoners. The enemy, in all his movements, showed uncertainty.

At last, on the 3d of July, at eight o'clock in the morning, the French army and that of the allies found themselves in each other's presence; ours in the plain of Grenelle, that of the enemies in the plain below Meudon.

The Duke of Wellington's army was composed of Englishmen, Hanoverians, Brunswickers and Belgians, that of Marshal Blücher, Prussians, Saxons, and Hessians. No Russian had yet arrived but some Bavarians had arrived. As for the Austrians, we saw that they were on the side of Lyons, where they had consented to an armistice.

On both sides the arrangements were finished at midday; already a few gun shots had been exchanged. Our skirmishers had already made the Prussians suffer a great deal.

For Beraud, here was the final showdown between the French and allied armies. The French Army looked certain to push the Prussians back and break out. Alas, this was not to be. The action at Issy was the final attempt of the French Army to defend Paris and, with this defeat, all hope of holding Paris faded. An eyewitness to these events wrote on the night of the 3 July 1815:[8]

It was known early this morning that there had been partial actions yesterday at Nanterre, at Sèvres, and upon different points on the right bank of the Seine, between Neuilly and Argenteuil, that Versailles had been retaken, and the bridge of Choissy occupied by the Prussians. The Prussians and English passed the night in intrenching themselves in the wood of Meudon and Verviers, and advanced early this morning to the villages of Vauvres and Issy, as in preparation for a general attack of the combined armies on the capital. At eight o'clock the two armies were facing each other; the French in the plain of Grenelle, and the allies in the plain beneath Meudon. Firing had been heard and seen the whole night from the heights of Chaillot, which were crowded by people with telescopes. A portion of the cavalry of the guard, which was stationed in the Champ de Mars, rode off at eleven o'clock along the left bank of the Seine, and were the last to take up their positions, which, at twelve o'clock, seemed concluded, and left the two armies in the line of battle.

Some corps of infantry, amongst which were two battalions from the higher Marne, joined the army to-day. The corps of Generals Lamarque and Travot are on their march to the capital. It was commonly reported, early in the afternoon, that a general action was on the point of being fought. The throng and the silence, and the eager looks of the multitudes in the gardens and boulevards, the groups collected round, and trailing after two or three straggling dragoons, leading their wounded horses, or carrying orders to the head-quarters of the Square Vendome – the dead, unsocial solemnity of the heavy patrols parading the streets without music – the doors of the houses and courts all shut, the upper windows opened every now and then, and occupied by female faces, as the clattering horse of a *gend'arme* announced the expectation of intelligence – every appearance of anxiety and apprehension, unusual even since the commencement of the siege, was to be recognized, at the first glance, for an hour or two after it was known that the two armies were in each other's presence. More than once crowds rushed towards the elevated spots of the gardens and squares, at the exclamation of individuals, who announced the opening cannonade.

At four o'clock the battle had not begun. I called on your friend Madame and found her in tears. I was thunderstruck with the news. Her son, the lieutenant general, had just left the army; all was lost – Paris had surrendered, with a devoted army of 80,000 soldiers before her walls. He was determined to denounce the treason and the traitors that night in the house of peers. Leaving the house, I soon heard the intelligence confirmed, both relating to the capitulation and the expected denunciation. Indeed, the artillery and some of the troops are now filing through Paris in their retreat.'

The Last Charge

Forgotten by history, cavalry trumpets sounded the charge in the early hours of 3 July. A squadron of Polish Lancers sallied forth at Sèvres and charged into history. This was the last cavalry charge of the Napoleonic Wars. About the action here, a writer in 1821 commented:[9]

The enemy had established three batteries, one on the heights of the park of Saint Cloud, firing against the new and the old bridge of Sèvres; the second was at the house of Coislin providing enfilade fire against the great road from Paris to Versailles; the third, on the heights of Bellevue, firing at the wooded island of the Seine, at the end of which is the old bridge of Sèvres. The skirmishers engaged at the same time as the cannon. The Prussians occupying the positions of the natural amphitheatre of the left bank, which was good for the defence, but it lost the enemy this advantage by approaching the river, either to attack the bridges, or to try to cross by boat. The French troops, enjoying cover from the undulations of the ground, the copses of the island, as well as shelter from houses and walls of enclosures that had been crenelated. On the right bank, the deadliest fire came from the enemy as soon as he wished to bombard houses and alleys of Sèvres.

Deceived by barricades which had been deliberately placed on the new bridge, the Prussians attacked believing that the bridge was intact; they recognized their mistake, when the well-directed fire of their adversaries had already caused them great losses, to free themselves from the obstacles which encumbered this defile.

Towards eight o'clock, skirmishers of General Vandamme's corps, coming from Issy and Vanvres, advanced on the left bank, in order to divert the attack on Sèvres, and harried the enemy on his flank and on its rear. The fight was sustained until ten o'clock, when both parties ceased their fire.

On July 3, the Prussians began weak attacks on the two bridges at Sèvres, when the armistice which had just concluded ended hostilities. Then the communications between the two armies were established by a bridge which the Duke of Wellington had sent to Argenteuil.

An English corps had already passed on the left bank of the Seine, occupying Nanterre, and the fine position of Mount Valerian.

Captain François of the 30th Line, part of 4th Corps, was an eyewitness to the action:[10]

> Towards 3 AM we heard a lively fusillade to the left of Sèvres. We took up arms and passing through Saint-Cloud took up positions on the plain of Grenelle with our right close to the left bank of the Seine. In our march, we found the road covered in detachments escorting Prussian cavalrymen that been made prisoners at Versailles ... Towards 6 Am I took command of a picket consisting of 150 men. About 7 Am we heard a lively fusillade towards Sèvres. After a short time, we observed our men dropping back in skirmish order on both sides of the Sèvres road, retiring, running over the mounds as far as the Orleans road ... I received orders to move forward 1500 paces from the line of battle formed by the divisions of the corps. Hardly had I arrived at my new position when I observed the enemy descending into the plain of Grenelle. I formed my line and my soldiers began to skirmish with the enemy; cavalry as well as infantry. Our line of skirmishers stretched from the left bank of the Seine to the Orleans road.

Into this melee thundered the Polish Lancers. The mounted contingent of the 7th Lancers, which were under the orders of Adjutant-Commandant Carrion de Nisas, took to the field riding from the Bois de Boulogne. If an account from 1862 is to be believed, between Ville-d'Avray and the bridge at Sèvres, the lancers encountered two Prussian cavalry regiments and attacked, and cut the Prussians 'to pieces'. This implies the regiment had crossed the river Seine and were attacking the Prussian left wing at Belle Vue. The bridge at Sèvres was the extreme right of Vandamme's line at Grenelle, and this attack needs to be seen as part of the last gasp of the Napoléonic state until Napoléon III was crowned Emperor.

Losses in the 7th Lancers were as follows:[11]

7th Regiment of Light Horse Lancers					
squadron	Wounded	Wounded & Pow	POW	Killed	Missing
1st	0	21	0	9	30
2nd	0	4	0	7	11
3rd	0	1	0	3	4
4th	0	1	0	0	1
Total	0	27	0	19	36

Total losses were nineteen killed and twenty-seven wounded, with one man being taken prisoner. This regiment had been in in the Bois de Boulogne on 1 July and mustered 334 all ranks. From the high losses, it is clear the regiment was heavily engaged at Sèvres on the morning of 3 July 1815. The bulk of the fighting fell on 1st squadron. Men had been lost from desertion in the days leading up to the battle in Paris. The regiment had been raised at Soissons and on the march to Paris, men had fallen by the wayside, no doubt in the chaotic evacuation of the town which we commented upon earlier:[12]

The regiment had been formed from the Poles who had remained in France with the disbanding of the Polish Lancers of the Guard, and the 7th, 8th and 9th lancer regiments of the Line. These were all veteran troopers, with eighteen months or more experience. On paper, this was one of the best regiments in the French Army. The Poles had learned their trade in Spain and in the 1814 campaign of France. Lack of training for over a year, lack of cohesion and team bonding probably affected combat readiness of the unit, but the men fought well, and despite being grossly outnumbered, outfought the Prussian cavalry.

We can imagine the lancers in their blue uniforms faced yellow clattering through the streets, the trumpeters sounding the charge, and the regiment falling pell-mell onto the Prussians. According to *Le Moniteur de l'armée* of 1862, the lancers charged against two Prussian regiments, the Brandenburg Hussars and the Pomeranian Hussars. This is perhaps confused as Von Sohr's brigade was rendered *hors de combat* at Rocquencourt on 1 July, unless it was back in the field on 3 July. It is more likely that the cavalry encountered by the Poles came from Ziethen's I corps. Ziethen's 1st Brigade had been at Sèvres since 2 July, and the 3rd Brigade was headed to Saint Cloud. Only the 1st Brigade had cavalry, the 1st Silesian Hussars some four squadrons strong. Presumably it was these hussars that the lancers encountered.

This was the last cavalry charge of the Napoléonic Wars. It has been, until the details were teased out from the mass of paper work in the French Army Archives, totally forgotten about.

Armistice and peace

With the French forces pushing the Prussians back, victory seemed possible. However, the empire would never strike back. Politics had now taken centre stage. The realists sold out the army for the good of France. The army howled with rage that it had been betrayed. Indeed, it had. If the Prussians had been defeated under the walls of Paris, then what? The British army was close at hand, with the Russians and Austrians not far behind. What good would the victory have done?

The war was lost and prolonging the fighting would have prolonged the killing for no reason.

As we have seen, Davout and Grouchy were involved in peace negotiations from 27 June, and peace had been the stated objective of the Provisional Government. In trying to continue the peace negotiations after the Charles Le Sénécal debacle, Davout had sent a peace overture on 30 June to Wellington and Blücher. Wellington took a conciliatory tone in his reply of 1 July. All the French had do was make a declaration for the return of Louis XVIII and the war would be over. On 2 July Blücher acknowledged that his men were too exhausted to push on and face bitter hand to hand fighting to get into Paris.

Yet, despite Vandamme's success at Grenelle and Grundler's attack against Wellington at Neuilly, after four hours fighting with victory seemingly assured, Davout sent word to Wellington that he had agreed the terms of the cease fire as had been brokered. In consequence, rather than leading 3rd Corps to victory, General Reverst at 07.00 hours under a white flag of parley offered the surrender of Paris to General Zieten.[13]

Fouché issued the following proclamation:[14]

> Frenchmen,
>
> Under the difficult circumstances, in which the reins of government were entrusted to us, it was not in our power to master the course of events and repel every danger; but it was our duty, to protect the interests of the people, and of the army, equally compromised in the cause of a prince, abandoned by fortune and by the national will.
>
> It was our duty, to preserve to our country the precious remains of those brave legions, whose courage is superior to misfortune, and who have been the victims of a devotion, which their country now claims.
>
> It was our duty, to save the capital from the horrors of a siege, or the chances of a battle; to maintain the public tranquillity amid the tumults and agitations of war, to support the hopes of the friends of liberty, amid the fears and anxieties of a suspicious foresight. It was above all our duty to stop the useless effusion of blood. We had to choose between a secure national existence or run the risk of exposing our country and its citizens to a general convulsion, that would leave behind it neither hope, nor a future.
>
> None of the means of defence, that time and our resources permitted, nothing that the service of the camps or of the city required, have we neglected. While the pacification of the West was concluding, plenipotentiaries went to meet the allied powers; and all the papers relative to this negotiation have been laid before our representatives.

The fate of the capital is regulated by a convention: its inhabitants, whose firmness, courage, and perseverance, are above all praise, will retain the guarding of it. The declarations of the sovereigns of Europe must inspire too great confidence, their promises have been too solemn for us to entertain any fears of our liberties, and of our dearest interests, being sacrificed to victory.

At length we shall receive guarantees, that will prevent the alternate and transient triumphs of the factions, by which we have been agitated these five and twenty years, that will terminate our revolutions and melt down under one common protection all the parties, to which they have given rise, and all those against which they have contended.

Those guarantees, which have hitherto existed only in our principles and in our courage, we shall find in our laws, in our constitution, in our representative system. For whatever may be the intelligence, the virtues, the personal qualities of a monarch, these can never suffice to render the people secure against the oppressions of power, the prejudices of pride, the injustice of courts, and the ambition of courtiers.

Frenchmen, peace is necessary to your commerce, to your arts, to the improvement of your morals, to the development of the resources remaining to you: be united, and you are at the end of your calamities. The repose of Europe is inseparable from yours. Europe is interested in your tranquillity, and in your happiness.

Officers were dumbstruck with the news. General Gougaurd:[15]

The armies were soon in the presence of each other, and the Provisional Government signed a capitulation, in which nothing was stipulated either for the rights of the nation or the interests of the army; the latter was bound to evacuate Paris, and retire behind the Loire, thus abandoning the capital without resistance to an army of equal force, for the Austrian and Russian armies were still at a distance of more than fifteen days' march. This is without doubt one of the most shameful transactions, which history records. What worse could have happened after having fought and lost a battle, than thus to deliver up Paris without any stipulations? But the Provisional Government displayed neither talent, nor patriotism, nor energy.

When the enemy's army extended itself from St. Denis to St. Cloud, had its strength been double that of ours, its ruin was certain, as has before been observed, by debouching on it by St. Denis. But after the moment for executing this manoeuvre was past (a manoeuvre which ought to have been obvious even to the lowest soldier), the possession of Paris might still have been retained with the fédérés and the national guard; which would have raised our force to upwards of one hundred and twenty thousand men. Conditions advantageous for the army, and which would have guaranteed the rights of the people, might then have been obtained. But it may truly be said, that after the departure of Napoléon the army lost all its zeal; the Marshals were divided in opinion, and no one among them had enough strength of character for such a crisis. The Provisional Government and the Chambers had, through the whole proceedings, been betrayed by Fouché and the party which maintained intelligence with the enemy. Carnot acted an upright part; but he allowed himself to be easily deceived.

Such was the infatuation of the Chambers, that at this important period they wasted their time in vain discussions on constitutional principles. Posterity will scarcely credit, that they carried their blindness so far as to imagine that the execution of their decrees would be guaranteed and ensured by Prussian battalions. The national guard, inspired with the same blind confidence, declared, that they would maintain the national colours; and, in the meantime, the allies entered Paris.

All illusion was soon at an end. The day after this declaration, the King ordered the dissolution of the two Chambers, which were already surrounded by Prussian bayonets, and on the 8th of July he made his entry into the capital. The members of the Chamber of Deputies, driven from their place of assembly, met at the house of their President, Lanjuinais, and all ended in vain and powerless protests.

It was either now or earlier in the day that Davout had been stripped of command by Fouché. The wily old Prince of Essling, Marshal Massena, was named commander-in-chief of French forces defending the city of Paris, and was to organise the evacuation of the army.[16] The document was signed by Fouché, Caulaincourt, Carnot and Quinette. This was the proud marshal's last military service to the French state.

The army had not yet come to terms with defeat in 1814 and now they felt that they had been sold out by their political masters. Sometime that morning Davout sent a hurried note to Guillaminot that a ceasefire was to start at 09.00 hours.[17] Berthezene captured the mood of the army at this time:[18]

> The Provisional Government pretended to give them [the troops] satisfaction; arrangements were made and everything seemed to be preparing for a battle, but on the 3d of July, just as we were going to attack, a counter-order suspended everything and three commissioners were sent to deal with Blücher with the surrender of Paris. At the same moment, General Trommelin, Fouché's agent, was returning from the Prussian camp ... a new, though

superfluous, proof of the infamy of this provisional head of the State. The announcement of this sudden and unforeseen resolution revived the murmurs of the army, and as soon as the convention was known, the fermentation reached its height. Soldiers and lower officers complained … They shouted on all sides that their leaders betrayed them and were corrupted by dint of gold … and [even] the austere probity of Marshal Davout could not escape their suspicions.

The generals and superior officers exhausted themselves in vain efforts to restore them to order; they succeeded only in preventing more serious excesses … as soon as the army was united under Paris, Davout took the command. One might expect some energetic act on the part of the victor Auerstädt but it was not so; he saw no salvation save in submission and undertook to obtain it.

Beraud was indignant:[19]

Our army begged to attack the enemy more seriously, when it learned that a suspension of arms had just been agreed upon, and negotiations had a begun. A few hours later, we received the order to return to the Seine at the Austerlitz bridge. Hardly had the convention made with the enemy generals been made known to our brave soldiers, when they uttered cries of fury … they highly accused the government of perfidy, and the chambers of incompetence and weakness. But finally, we managed to maintain order.

However, General Kellerman felt Davout had made the right decision:[20]

It was on the 29th of June that the army entered the lines of Paris; it was only on the 1st of July that Marshal Grouchy's corps re-joined; Marshal Davout took command. His first care was to send a detachment of 300 cavalry to St. Germain, to guard this point, and to ensure destruction of the Pont du Pecq, and all the roads from the Seine to Mantes; but in the meantime, a Prussian detachment had appeared ahead of him. The occupation of this important point, which opened to the enemy a passage over the Seine, decided the enemy's general movement in this direction. They found there the double advantage of outflanking our positions at Montmartre, and of taking Paris from the rear if the enemy decided to force its way into Paris.

The enemy also obtained strong positions on the heights of Meudon, Saint-Cloud, Saint-Germain. If we look at these positions it is easy to understand that the French army was not in a position to dislodge the enemy from them. Marshal Davout was censored for not having taken advantage of this movement, to fall on the flank of the enemy upon them leaving Saint-Denis, and thus having missed the opportunity to crush the enemy.

But with tired, demoralized soldiers could such a decisive action have been attempted? and when could this attempt have been made? But the general-in-chief of the French army was dominated by a single over-riding thought, that of preserving Paris from disaster occasioned by a direct assault; he could not sacrifice the capital for the hope of a triumph without purpose, and one probably of only a feeble result.

The passage of the Seine, and the establishment of the bulk of the enemy army on the heights of Meudon and Chatenai, had rendered the situation of Paris and that of the French army more critical. The latter had had to return in great haste to the left bank, to cover the capital which was entirely undefended on this side. The army was disposed to fight and to defend the city with desperate resolution, but the enemy generals were very careful not to risk an untimely attack against troops determined to fight to the death, and they changed their plans to delay their entry into Paris. They took up a position on the formidable heights of Saint-Cloud and Meudon, extending their right towards the Orleans road, with the intention of encircling the French army and starving the capital.

And besides, was the French army and its leaders well assured of the disposition of the population? The royalist party, overwhelmed by the events of the 20th of March, had awakened at the sound of the defeat of Waterloo. The Emperor had left Paris and left his most pronounced partisans without hope and without defence. As early as the 22nd, the minister became head of the Provisional Government and communicated with the Bourbons; the second restoration could not be avoided. In short, there was talk of treason, but there was none in the army. There were three desertions on the evening of the 17th, but these desertions had no influence on events. We talked about mistakes. There were many, but the principal mistakes belonged to the Emperor; it has been argued that the generals had been weak and undecided, that their weakness and indecision paralyzed the soldiers' devotion and enthusiasm. In this allegation, there is truth and falsehood. It cannot be said that the generals Count Lobau, Count de Valmy, Duhesme, Foy, and others, had been weak and indecisive. But there was little enthusiasm in the army. The generals, for the most part, fatigued by constant war, dared not risk anything, because they no longer found in their soldiers, the self-possession and coolness of the old regiments destroyed in Russia and in the campaign of 1813.

In the interior there have been betrayals, I have no doubt. I mentioned that of the Pont du Pecq, whose author is well known; there were still others: the enemy generals would not have risked their direct movement on Paris, if they had not been called there. Fouché, a clever man, had perfectly understood the dangers of the situation of the Emperor; he had foreseen the outcome of his attempt to take power, and had abandoned it to spare his future. But these betrayals themselves served little for the enemy, who did not need it.

To find the truth about the catastrophe of 1815, we must always return to the same point. Success required a miracle and fortune was tired of doing it for us.'

What, then, would have been the point of more bloodshed? Far from accusing Marshal Davout, and without paying too much attention to his private thoughts, we should be grateful for him not having yielded to the puerile vanity of risking a battle which might have added something to his military glory, but which, supposing a brilliant success, would not have prolonged the end of the struggle by more than eight days.

Upon hearing the news of capitulation, rioting broke out across Paris. The *Journal de l'Empire* reported on 4 July 1815 that gangs roamed the streets from the heights of Montmartre to the barrier of Saint-Antoine. Paris was not ready to accept the fact that France had lost the war. The peaceful resignation of a year earlier was not repeated. The Parisian National Guard under the orders of Marshal Massena cried 'we have been sold off like beasts'.[21] Could the army, the National Guard and the fédérés have fought on? Yes perhaps. Certainly, Massena had over 100,000 men under his orders with more men making his force stronger by the day in both moral and man power.

However, peace had been the goal of the Provisional Government since the day it had been formed, and they wanted peace at any cost. The war could have ended sooner politically. As it was the French army, which for fifteen years had come to dominate Napoléon's political actions, found that it had no influence over the course of events and was increasingly marginalised. War for Napoléon had been diplomacy by other means. In 1815 diplomacy ruled. Consequently, during the night of 3 July 1815, provisions were made to evacuate the lines, which still protected Paris, and to deliver them to the enemy.

Chapter 26

Royalist or Realist?

The armistice began at 08.00 hours on Tuesday 4 July 1815, with the French army being ordered to move behind the river Loire. Paris had fallen, the army had been vanquished and the Emperor was in exile.[1] France had lost the war. An eyewitness to these events writes on the night of the Tuesday 4 July about the mood of the Parisians:[2]

> A persuasion of treachery has become very prevalent this afternoon, and some movement was then expected on the part of the troops and the fédérés.
>
> I just hear that the whole national guard are put under arms. Single muskets shots have been heard in various parts of the city and on the bridges, the boulevards, the squares, parties of men are running through the back streets, shouting *'Vive l'Empereur!'* A cannon or two have been fired from Montmartre. I saw a carriage stopped in my presence, in the rue St. Honore, by two men, who insisted on knowing whether any of the government were in it. The movement began at three o'clock, when many groups were formed in the gardens and streets, listening to harangues and denunciations. At six o'clock the doors and windows were shut, and the whole of the national guard received orders to hold themselves in readiness to act at a moment's warning. The women disappeared from the streets, and preparations were made in the interior of many houses for a defence against massacre and pillage ... no actual insurrection has yet broken out, or any violence been attempted. The tumult in the town now seems to subside – the guards have everywhere been doubled.

The defeat of Napoléon and the restoration to the throne of France of the Bourbons once more had been the goals of the allies, and indeed had been the view of some ministers who served Napoléon. For a second, perhaps third time in eighteen months the people of France had a new government imposed on them. With such rapid change it is little wonder that many officers and soldiers switched sides equally rapidly – change being the constant theme throughout 1814 and 1815. Change would come again in 1830 and 1848.

The French army wanted to keep fighting, and by the start of July, it had over 150,000 men to continue the fight against the invading allies and liberate France from the yoke of the oppressors. Elements did continue to resist, and the brutal repression of Bonapartists was urged by the English press, most notably the *Morning Post*. The newspaper, which was supported by many influential Tory peers, welcomed the Bonapartist uprisings and claimed that the Royalist backlash was justified to prevent a civil war and future European war. The newspaper, along with *The Times*, blamed the excesses on the harmful influence on the king by marshals Ney, Soult and Massena. The *Morning Post* blamed the arch intriguer Fouché.[3] The Whig or Liberal newspaper the *Morning Chronicle* abhorred the arrest for treason of Marshall Ney and declared that Napoleon was not a blood thirsty tyrant.[4] Having removed Napoléon, the allies' primary war aim, they, it seems, turned a blind eye to the Bourbons' vengeful retributions. Indeed some English politicians felt that with France defeated it was the time to avenge the battle of New Orleans in America. Lord Castlereagh was accused of turning a blind eye to genocide.[5]

The war aims of removing Napoléon and restoring the Bourbons to the throne of France had been achieved, but it seems the implications of this upon France had not been taken into consideration. The allies occupied Paris and Louis 'The Inevitable' was restored to his throne. The king entered Paris on 8 July 1815. The army was disbanded. Captain Leon-Michel Routier explains:[6]

> The government wanted to make a whole different kind of army than that which existed, both in its composition and names. As a result, new frameworks for the infantry corps were created … and placed at their head, of course, were emigrant royalists which the government thought more reliable, and finally some deserters from the imperial cause … It would be difficult to imagine what we had to suffer during the early years of the second restoration of the Bourbons. We were placed under the supervision of the police and all our actions were spied on by snitches. We suffered this impropriety and had been made forget our rank and our services until we were put under the spotlight, by each of our respective mayors, and then we had to submit to a ridiculous and humiliating interrogation. A tricolour cockade, buttons, or plaques bearing the eagle and other ornaments that formed part of the uniform under the empire, were

enough to transform the poor officer on half pay to a conspirator that was dismissed from the army, through this unfortunate attachment to objects and memoires. They took a sacrilegious hand to us for six years holding from us half of our pensions, and the injustice of this theft has not yet been repaired despite the constant claims made since that time. Finally, a ministerial decision ordered all officers on half pay to go to the place of their birth and remain there. We easily conceived the iniquity of this new measure and how it caused much consternation. It put us on the same level as the convicts who were released from prison and returned to their homes and were to remain under the supervision of the police and that it was forbidden for them to break their parole; our position was absolutely the same!

When Napoléon left Paris on 10 June 1815, he had left behind him a country in turmoil. Napoléon needed a victory to secure his position. Indeed, it seems political scheming by Talleyrand and Fouché had commenced as soon as their master had left Paris, judging by the speed in which the hastily re-erected Napoléonic state imploded. Napoléon's grip on power and France during the Hundred Days was shaky, as had been the loyalty of his generals, ministers and large elements of the French populous.

With Napoléon's return to France, he faced, in essence, civil war. The Vendée and the departments of the north were in open rebellion against the imperial faction. In 1814 the choice faced by many officers, men and ministers of state was the same in spring 1815; men who had sworn fidelity to the king had done so out of the reality of the situation, army officers and civil servants still needed an income, and they put the reality of the situation before the politics involved. In 1815 the same choice had to be made. The king represented stability, prosperity, and peace, the Emperor represented instability and war. Who knew how long the Emperor was back in power upon his return to France? For many it seemed a *fait accompli* and it was better to come to terms with the new government. Many though stuck to their convictions in support of the monarchy. Out and out Bonapartists were few and far between in 1815. Vandamme and Exelmans were certainly men of conviction for the Emperor, but amongst the higher echelons of the officer corps, they were perhaps an exception. Many hundreds, if not thousands, of officers were realists, from the marshallate down to lowly sous-lieutenant. These realists are often condemned by rabid Bonapartists, then and now, as traitors, as if somehow anyone who was not 100 per cent with the Emperor was a traitor and working against the empire. The army and the French state were neither

Royalist or Bonapartist, they were realists. It did not matter who ran the government, what mattered was earning enough money to pay the bills and feed the family. The peasants in the fields, the millers, farmhands, factory workers, career soldiers, just got on with their day-to-day existence. Who was in charge did not matter. Governments change, what remains the same was the mayor, the tax collector, the mundane nitty gritty boring aspects of everyday life.

Marshal Soult, branded by many as a traitor on no grounds whatsoever, was a career soldier. He served the Republic, the Consul, the Empire, the monarchy, the July Monarchy, the Republic and Empire, just like any politician and soldier. You 'cut your cloth' to suit the conditions. In 1815, he reluctantly sided with the Emperor. As the professional soldier, he did the best he could do with the resources he had as Major-General. The army of 1815 was not the army of old, it was reluctant to fight and lacked the spirit, drive and devotion to the Emperor that it once had, like the men who commanded it.

Grouchy, the man who for many lost Waterloo, fought a text book retreat to Paris. Once he realised that his army would not get to Paris before the Prussian juggernaut, he knew that the fate of the empire was over. He faced two options, fight on for a cause that was lost and let many thousands be killed or wounded, or accept defeat and do his best to bring the war to an end. He chose the second option, along with General Drouot, and supported the plans of Fouché.

Davout in Paris, though, was a man of divided loyalties. As a professional soldier, he had to obey the edicts of his superiors. Fouché wanted peace and, therefore, Davout the good soldier followed the party line. Clearly this left him torn between loyalties. Once the wreck of the Armée du Nord was in Paris at the end of June, morale among the troops began to rise, and men like Vandamme and Exelmans wanted to go down fighting. They also felt that they could change the situation that faced France and cripple the Prussians and British, who were now outnumbered by a resurgent French army. Davout must have been wracked with indecision. Go down fighting, or keep in line with Fouché?

Many officers at the time felt that Davout sabotaged their attempts to defend Paris and to fight back; they were quite correct. Peace was inevitable, so why antagonise the soon-to-be occupiers and allies. Time and time again, on 1 and 2 July, Davout stopped the army taking the offensive. He prevented the movement of troops and munitions. Was he a Royalist? No, he was a realist, like Soult and Grouchy, yet from a pro-Bonapartist view point, he was very much a traitor. He knew the war was lost, the government wanted peace, and he had to temper the mood of the army sufficiently, even by rescinding orders, to allow the peace negotiations to take place. So yes, he was a traitor to the Bonapartist cause in a very simplistic manner. Yet on 3 July, we see a man torn by conscience. He was at the head of the French Army and had a good chance to knock out the Prussians on the Plain of Grenelle. The attack went ahead – clearly with Davout's backing as Vandamme did not have the authority to set the army in motion. Davout as Commander-in-Chief had the authority to order the Imperial Guard into action and the two reserve cavalry corps of Milhaud and Kellerman. Sometime that morning Fouché had Davout sacked and replaced by Massena. Was Davout sacked because he had disobeyed Fouché's orders and gone on the offensive? Perhaps so. We do not know why Davout was sacked, but it is an intriguing possibility that his desire not to see France humbled and Paris fall to the allies without a fight overcame his realism, and he set the army in motion only to be sacked for his sense of duty.

Men like Vandamme and Exelmans were few and far between. Exelmans, indignance at Grouchy acting on Fouché's peace negotiations and arresting the Prussian envoy shows how much he detested the ideals of Fouché and the government. Yet this devotion to the Emperor stands full in the face of his total inaction on 18 June 1815. What did he do with 2nd Cavalry Corps for a period of twenty-four to thirty-six hours? It seems nothing at all. If he had been more proactive, and blame for this also falls on Grouchy, then the situation that France faced could have been averted. Just imagine what impact 2nd Cavalry Corps could have had if they fell on the rear of Bülow? Waterloo may have been a French victory. Be that as it may, Exelmans, record in 1815 is dubious. Lacking initiative, he was no longer a dynamic and forceful general, but rather timid in his actions, and yet in the last page of the last chapter of the 1st French Empire, Exelmans was forceful and aggressive, despite all the overwhelming evidence that the empire was doomed to fall.

This brings us back to Grouchy. For men like Vandamme and Exelmans, his shift from Bonapartism to realism when faced with the true reality of the situation he found himself in, smacked of treason. For these men it was better to go down fighting for a lost cause than to try and save lives and admit defeat. Grouchy's dealings with Fouché, became yet another 'stick' with which to batter at his reputation. In later life, Exelmans and Vandamme both invented scenarios to blacken Grouchy's name and used his dealings with Fouché as proof he was always a Royalist. Into this mix, Napoléon's own accusations and those of Gérard, fed the denigration of an honest man's reputation which has never recovered. Marmont and Augereau are dammed for their actions in 1814, in being realists, and so is Grouchy. Yes, the army could have fought back on 3 July, but what would have it achieved? With the Russian and Austrian armies heading to Paris, any victory outside Paris was going to be short term. If Davout had won, then what? A new *coup d'état*? A new military dictatorship to oust the Chambers of Representatives?

The Bonapartists had no long-term strategy or vision in 1815. Napoléon made no plans beyond army reconstruction. What were his aims for the economy? For the development of the state and education? As ever, nothing. The Napoléonic state was based on immediate reactionary policies of an army attached to a country. The long-term stability of France was sadly, never possible while the Emperor refused to accept compromise. His nephew Napoléon III managed this far better and created a government that worked for the state rather than just feeding the military machine. France, after twenty-five years of war, needed peace and stability to allow the economy and country to recover. It had to deal with the huge economic imbalance that war had placed on the French people. The monarchy offered this, Napoléon did not, and never had done once he became Emperor.

The key players in the drama of 1815 were not Napoléon and his inner circle. The politicians held the real power. Napoléon and his acolytes were incredibly naïve in 1815 – when the news of Waterloo reached Paris, many hoped that the government would rally to the colours to save France. They were badly disappointed. The French government and its key players, Fouché and Talleyrand, knew that the loss of the battle meant a return to the monarchy, as the monarchy in 1815, just as it had done in 1814, represented peace and stability.

Grouchy and Soult were no traitors, they were realists. Davout also falls into this camp. His actions show that he knew the cause of the Emperor after Waterloo was lost and did his best to allow the peace negotiations to go ahead, and yes, he did his best to stop the army fighting. If being a realist and knowing the 'game was up' makes Davout a traitor to the Emperor, then he is guilty as charged, like Soult and Grouchy. The king however treated Davout less harshly than Soult. Soult was exiled until 22 January 1820, Davout was home with his wife on 21 June 1816, and was elected Peer of France 5 March 1819. Why was Davout home four years before Soult? If Soult was the traitor and Royalist agent some says he was, surely he would have returned to France sooner? I suspect the truth is Davout had played ball with Fouché, holding back the more Bonapartist elements of the army, much to their chagrin, and easing the way for return of the king.

He had submitted the army to the king on 14 July 1815. In essence, he got time off for good behaviour.

Objectively, the Hundred Days were doomed to fail: with all of Europe ranged against the Emperor, France riven by civil war, virtually bankrupt, it was a foolhardy gamble that certainly was not guaranteed success. This was not another Brumaire coup – the allies refused to let it become one –and when the events are viewed dispassionately with the eye of the realist, it was always bound to fail. But looking at the events passionately, the Hundred Days represents a great 'what if' scenario, into which it is easy to place men as traitors to explain the failure, the story of the little man against all the odds is always appealing, indeed it is the story of Napoléon's life. He was the outsider, the nobody, who became Emperor of France on his talent of winning battles. He inspires almost religious devotion, both then and today, which clouds any true objective judgement of the man and his life. I can be guilty of this. We all have our own bias.

In this book, I hope to have explored how the Hundred Days campaign ended and the empire fell, not through treason, but by men who had taken an objective overview and had taken the most realistic option available to them. Napoléon wanted blind obedience to his plans, what Grouchy, Soult and perhaps Davout did in 1815 was to think for themselves and see the bigger picture objectively, taking actions according to the reality that faced them.

Grouchy, is remembered for the loss of a battle he could never have affected the outcome of, a man slandered for doing Fouche's bidding by those who tried to hide their own complicity in doing so, a man slandered by his colleagues – he is the 'whipping boy' of Waterloo, the man to blame for the defeat of 1815. Soult is also charged with treason by some so called historians, as the man who sabotaged the campaign. Yet what I hope this book has done, is to show that in Grouchy's case none of the accusations and lies spread by former colleagues and promulgated by historians are based in fact. None of the charges which Grouch faced stand up to scrutiny using documents from those June days of over 200 years ago. The charges levied against Soult don't stand up, but many historians and acolytes are so desperate to make Napoleon a great man who made no mistakes, that sadly hard facts get in the way and tend to be edited out. In my book, *Waterloo Truth at Last*, I have demonstrated that the French Army ran away at Waterloo or were made prisoners of war, especially the Imperial Guard, but the data is disputed and derided, and conclusions challenged because it threatens how for 200 years the battle has been understood. The Imperial Guard being made prisoners undermines many cherished

British Army myths and this upsets a lot of people; just like Sergeant Ewart of the Scots Greys not capturing the eagle of the 45th Line. In many ways, any author and researcher who tries earnestly to present 'the alternative' facts, as some would say, is never going to win approval, despite presenting rigorous academic research using previously unused archive sources. Just as with Waterloo, my research on Grouchy is unpopular. It shifts the blame squarely on the Emperor for the loss of Waterloo. The review of the events post-Waterloo presented here shows that Waterloo was not the end, but the beginning of the end. My research has also exposed the two huge tensions in the army; fight for the Emperor as exemplified by Vandamme, Exelmans and many senior officers like Pajol, or do the best for France, which in real terms means the return of the king. Davout was torn between his loyalty to the Emperor and to France. Ultimately, he sided for king and country, much to the chagrin of those who served under him.

By going through the extant paper archive in France that has previously not been used to study the fighting post-Waterloo, we can also see from his own records and of those around him that Grouchy was a capable soldier, a skilled administrator, just as Soult was. Grouchy's retreat was masterful and showed the true brilliance of the man. Sadly, the mass of material concerning his military operations before 14 June 1815 will perhaps never see the light of day in print, especially his own journal about his actions in the Vendée.

Again, by analysing the paperwork Soult generated in 1815, Soult's energy in rallying the wreck of the army and trying to get the men fed, new munitions issued and sending reinforcements to the front, show Soult at his best. Tired and demoralised he may have been, but he worked tirelessly to re-organise the army, not the mark of a traitor in my view. If both men are guilty of anything, it's of being realists and not 'unto death' Bonapartists or Royalists. Their crimes, if they can be described as such, were to end the war, to save lives, and do what was best for France. 1815, in the end, was a victory of realism.

Bibliography

Archive Sources
Archives Nationales, Paris:
AFIV 1938
AFIV 1939 Registre d'Ordres du Major General 13 Juin au 26 Juin 1815
AFIV 1940 Garde Impériale 1815
LH 1438/54, LH/2385/67, LH/2385/69, LH 910/54, LH/2189/1, LH/95/62, LH/1859/43, LH/86/25, LH/2773/22, LH/1012/69, LH/144/19, LH/1594/40, LH/2285/62, LH 2397/31, LH 62/73, LH/2251/19, LH/2316/18, LH 747/48, LH/1003/7, LH/1723/42, LH 274/9, LH 2630/86

Service Historique Armée du Terre, Paris:
Memoires
GR 1M 717–729
GD 2M 1135

Personal record boxes
SHDDT GR 6Yd 46 Remy Exelmans
SHDDT 6yd 6 Jean Soult
SHDDT GR 6Yd 26 Emmanuel Grouchy
SHDDT GR 7Yd 863 Bonnemains
SHDDT GR 7Yd 557 Bailly de Monthion
SHDDT GR 7 YD 1145 Jean Baptiste Antoine Marcelin Marbot
SHDDT GR 8yd 1279 Burthe
SHDDT GR 8 YD 2805 Arnault Rogé

Officers records
GR 2 Yb 105 Contrôle Nominatif Officer 2e Ligne
GR 2 Yb 87 2e regiment de chevau-legers lancers de la Garde Impériale. Contrôle Nominatif Officer
GR 2 Yb 422 Contrôle Nominatif Officier 7e Hussards 9 Septembre 1814 a 12 Aout 1815

Regimental record boxes
Xb 392 21e de Ligne 1812 a 1815. Dossier 1815
Xc 183. Dossier 6e Lanciers
Xab 74

Correspondence Hundred Days

C15 3 Correspondence Armée du Nord 21e Mai au 31e Mai 1815

C 15 4 Correspondence Armée du Nord 1e au 10 Juin 1815

C15 5 Correspondence Armée du Nord 11e Juin au 21 Juin 1815

C15 6 Correspondence Armée du Nord 22e Juin au 3 Juillet 1815

C 15 20 registre d'ordres du 2e regiment des Chasseurs à Pied de la Garde Impériale 22 Avril au 27 Aout 1815

C15 34 Situations Garde Impériale 1815

C 15 35 Situations Armée du Nord 1815

C15 39 Decrets Cent-Jours

C16 11

C16 20 Correspondence Militaire General 1er Juin au 7 Juin 1815

C16 21 Correspondence Militaire General 8e Juin au 18Juin 1815

C16 22 Correspondence Militaire General 19e Juin au 25 Juin 1815

C16 23 Correspondence Militaire General 26e Juin au 6 Juillet 1815

C37 15 Correspondence MInistre de Guerre

Line infantry muster lists

GR 21 YC 19 2e régiment d'infanterie de ligne dit régiment de la Reine, 20 mai 1814–21 août 1814 (matricules 1 à 2 997)

GR 21 YC 202e régiment d'infanterie de ligne dit régiment de la Reine, 9 septembre 1814–6 juin 1815 (matricules 3 000 à 4 723)

GR 21 YC 279 30e régiment d'infanterie de ligne, 21 juillet 1814–6 juillet 1815

GR 21 YC 726 80e régiment d'infanterie de ligne (ex 96e régiment d'infanterie de ligne), 2 février 1815–16 août 1815

Line cavalry regimental muster lists

GR 24 Yc 9 Régiment du Roi organisation 1814

GR 24 YC 16 1e Cuirassier Juin 1814 a 24 Décembre 1815

GR 24YC 21 Regiment de Reine organisation 1814 – 29 Juillet 1815

GR 24 YC26 Regiment du Dauphin organisation 1814 – Juin 1815

GR 24YC 36 5e Cuirassier 1814 a 2 Juillet 1815

GR24 YC 41 Contrôle Nominatif Troupe 6e Cuirassiers 9 Aout 1814 a 6 Aout 1815

GR24 YC 46 Contrôle Nominatif Troupe 7e Cuirassiers 9 Aout 1814 a 6 Aout 1815

GR 24YC 50 Contrôle Nominatif Troupe 8e Cuirassiers 9 Aout 1814 a 6 Aout 1815

GR24 YC 55 Contrôle Nominatif Troupe 9e Cuirassiers 9 Aout 1814 a 6 Aout 1815

GR24 YC 60 Contrôle Nominatif Troupe 10e Cuirassiers 15 Avril 1815 a 27 Juillet 1815 organisation 1814

GR24 YC 64 Contrôle Nominatif Troupe 11e Cuirassiers 15 Avril 1815 a 27 Juillet 1815 organisation 1814

GR 24 YC 69 12e Cuirassier 1814 a 20 Juin 1815

Gr 24 YC 96 Lanciers du Roi 1814–1815

GR 24YC 102 2e Lanciers de Reine 1814–1815

GR 24YC 107 3e Lanciers du Dauphin 1814–1815

GR 24YC 114 Monsieur 4e Lanciers 1814–1815

GR 24YC 121 regiment Angouleme 1814–1815

GR 24 YC 129 7e Lanciers 1815

GR 24 YC 138 2e régiment de dragons (ex. Condé 1790). 21 juin 1814-1er septembre 1815 (1er régiment du roi 1814, 1er régiment de dragons)

GR 24YC 143 4e dragon 1814–1815

GR 24 YC 148 5e dragons

GR 24 YC 253 6e dragons

GR24 YC 158 Contrôle Nominatif Troupe 7e dragons 15 Avril 1815 a 27 Juillet 1815 organisation 1814

GR 24 YC 169 12e dragon 26 Aout 1814 a 31 Aout 1815

GR 24YC 174 10 juillet 1814–4 août 1815 (8e régiment de Condé 1814)

GR 24 YC 180 10 août 1814–23 décembre 1815 (9e régiment de dragons, 1814)

GR 24 YC 185 Août 1814–6 août 1815 (10e régiment de dragons, 1814)

GR 24 YC 190 21 août 1814–10 septembre 1815 (11e régiment de dragons 1814)

GR 24YC 195 17e dragon 21 Juillet 1814 a 28 Juin 1815

GR 24 YC 213 29 juillet 1814–12 août 1815 (15e régiment de dragons, 1814)

GR 24YC 254 Contrôle Nominatif regiment du Roi organisation 1814

GR24 YC 264 Contrôle Nominatif Troupe 3e Chasseurs à Cheval organisation 1814

GR24 YC 274 Contrôle Nominatif Troupe 4e Chasseurs à Cheval organisation 1814

GR 24 YC 282 Contrôle Nominatif Troupe 6e Chasseurs à Cheval organisation 1814

GR 24 YC 293 8e Chasseurs à Cheval 1 Juillet 1814 a 26 Septembre 1815

GR24 YC 299 Contrôle Nominatif Troupe 9e Chasseurs à Cheval organisation 1814

GR24 YC 309 Contrôle Nominatif Troupe 11e Chasseurs à Cheval organisation 1814

GR 24 YC 326 14e regiment Chasseurs à Cheval 1 Octobre 1814 – 30 Octobre 1815

GR 24 YC 383 1e Hussar 20 Octobre 1813 a 20 Mai 1815

GR 24 YC 384 1e Hussard 20 Mai 1815 a 12 Octobre 1815

GR 24 YC 389 2e régiment de Hussards (Chamborant an VI). 16 juillet 1814–21 août 1815 (la reine)

GR 24 YC 402 4e Hussard Juillet 1814 a 3 Mai 1815

GR 24 YC 403 4 Hussard Mai 1815 a 28 Octobre 1815

GR 24 YC 409 5e Hussard 11 Aout 1814 a 25 Septembre 1815

GR 24 YC 414 6e Hussard

GR 24 YC 415 6e Hussard 10 Mai 1815 a 16 Octobre 1815

GR 24 YC 422 7e Hussard 1814 a 12 Aout 1815

Printed sources

Anon (1815) *Porte-feuille de Buonaparte: pris à Charleroi le 18 juin 1815,* The Hague: De L'imprimiere Belgique

Anon *Lettre d'un Combattant de Waterloo* in Feuilles d'Histoire No. 6, 1911

Anon La Souvenir Napoléonien No. 337 September 1984

Anon Carnet de la Sabretache 1912

General Allix 'Souvenirs Militaires et Politique' in *Journal des Sciences Militaires* Vol. 26 January 1832

André Eugène (1898) *Le maréchal Exelmans (1775–1852)* Impr. de Comte-Jacquet, Bar-le-Duc

A. F. Becke (1995), *Napoléon and Waterloo: The Emperor's Campaign with the Armée du Nord, 1815*, Greenhill Books, London

Beckett Stephen (2015) *Waterloo Betrayed. The Secret treachery that defeated Napoléon.* Mapleflower House. Kindle edition

Beraud Antoine Nicolas (1829) *Histoire de Napoléon*, Brussels, de Kock

Pierre Berthezène (1855), *Souvenirs militaires de la République et de l'Empire*, J. Dumaine, Paris

Berton Jean Baptiste (1818), *Précis historique, militaire et critique des batailles de Fleurus et de Waterloo, dans la campagne de Flandres, en juin 1815*, J. S. Wallez, La Haye

Booth John (1817), *The Battle of Waterloo, also of Ligny, and Quarter-Bras*, London

Broughton John Cam Hobhouse (1816) *The Substance of some letters written by an Englishman resident at Paris during the reign of the Emperor Napoléon* M Thomas Philadelphia

de Chaboulon Pierre Alexandre Edouard baron Fleury (1820) *Memoirs of the Private Life, Return, and Reign of Napoléon in 1815* John Murray London, 2 volumes

Clayton Tim (2014), *Waterloo: Four Days that Changed Europe's Destiny*, Little, Brown, London

Coates John, (2012) *The Hour Between Dog and Wolf*, Fourth Estate, London

Cornwell Bernard (2014) *Waterloo. The History of Four Days.* William Collins London

Dallas Gregor (1996), *1815: The Roads to Waterloo*, Pimlico, London

Damitz (1838) Geschichte *des Feldzuges von 1815 in den Niederlanden und Frankreich* 2 volumes. Berlin

Dawson Paul (2005) *Wakefield Memories*, Sutton Publishing, Stroud

Dawson Paul (2017) *Napoléon and Grouchy.* Frontline, Barnsley

Lemonnier-Delafosse Marie Jean Baptiste (1850) '*Campagnes de 1810 a 1815: souvenirs militaires*, Harve: Commerce

Deville George, '*Grouchy a Waterloo*' in *Revolution Français*, No. 53, 1907

Delort, *Notice sur la batailles de Fleurus et de Mont Saint Jean* in Revue Hebdomadaire Juin 1896

Dulaure Jacques-Antoine (1834) *Histoire des Cent-Jours.* Paris

Esdaile Charles (2008) Napoléon's *Wars*, Penguin, London

Esdaile Charles (2016*) Napoléon, France and Waterloo: The Eagle Rejected* Pen & Sword, Barnsley

Ferryman (1913*) The life of a regimental officer during the great war, 1793–1815 comp. from the correspondence of Colonel Samuel Rice, C.B., K.H. 51st light infantry, and from other sources.* Blackwood & Sons, London

François (Capitaine) (1904), *Journal, 1792–1830, publié d'après le manuscrit original par Charles Grolleau*, Paris

Fleuret Ferdinand (1929) *Description des Passages de Dominique Fleuret.* Firmin Diderot, Paris

Fussell Paul (1975), *The Great War and Modern Memory*, Oxford University Press, Oxford

Gérard Etienne Maurice (1829) *Quelques documens sur la bataille de Waterloo.* Paris

Gerbet Philippe (1866), *Souvenirs d'un officier sur la campagne de Belgique en 1815*, Émile Javal, Arbois

Green Anna and Troup Kathleen (1999) *The Houses of History*, Manchester University Press, Manchester

Gougaurd Gaspard (1818) *Campagne de 1815*, P Mongie, Paris

Grouchy Emmanuel (1819) *Observations sur la relation de la campagne de 1815 publiee par le general Gourgaud.* Chez Chaumerot Jeune

Grouchy Emmanuel (1840) *Fragments historiques réunis pour* établir *le fait de calomnie répandue dans un libelle du général Berthezène, publié en date du 27 mai 1840: campagne de 1815 (2e éd., augmentée de documents inédits jusqu'à ce jour) par le maréchal E. de Grouchy.* Impr. de F. Poisson (Caen)

Grouchy Emmanuel (1874) *Memoires du Maréchal Grouchy* 4 vols. E Dentu Paris.

Guyot (1999) *Carnets de la Campagne du General Comte Guyot 1792–1815.* Teissèdre

Guverich, The French Historical Revolution: The Annales School, in Hodder et al, *Interpreting Archaeology*, Routledge, London, 1995, pp. 158–61

Henckens (Lieutenant), (1910) Mémoires *se rapportant à son service militaire au 6e régiment de Chasseurs à Cheval à cheval Français de février 1803 à août 1816.* La Haye

Hooper George, (1862) *Waterloo, the Downfall of the First Napoléon*, Smith, Elder, London

Houssaye Henry, (1903)*1815 Waterloo*, Paris

Kelly William Hyde (1905), *The Battle of Wavre and Grouchy's Retreat*, John Murray, London

Hulot, Souvenirs Militaire du General Baron Hulot in *Le Spectateur Militaire* Vol 27, 1884, 4th Series

Lavisse and Rambaud, *Histoire* Générale

Lefol (1854) *Souvenirs sur le prytanée de Saint-Cyr, sur la campagne de 1814, le retour de l'Empereur Napoléon de l'île d'Elbe et la campagne de 1815, pendant les Cent-jours* Montalant-Bougleux, Versailles

von Lettow-Vorbeck Hans Oskar (1904) *Napoléons Untergang 1815*, Mittler, Berlin.

Octave Levavasseur (2001) *Souvenirs militaires, 1800–1815.* A la Librairie des Deux Empires

Martin Jacques François (1867), *Souvenirs d'un ex-officier 1812–1815*, Paris

Mistler Jean and Michaud Helene (1970) *Lieutenant Chevalier: Souvenirs des Guerres Napoléonienne*, Hachette, Paris

Miot-Putigny Hubert (1950), *Putigny, Grogrnard d'Empire*, Gallimard, Paris,

Morris Thomas (1845) *Recollections of Military Service in 1813, 1815 and 1815.* James Madden & Co, London

des Odoards Louis Florimond Fantin (1895), *Journal du général Fantin des Odoards*, E. Plon, Nourit et Cie, Paris

von Ollech Karl Rudolf (1876), *Geschichte des Feldzuges von 1815 nach archivalischen quellen*, E. S. Mittler und Sohn, Berlin

Pajol (1874) *General en Chef*, Firmin Didot, Paris

Perrot (1821) *Histoire de l'ex-garde, depuis sa formation jusqu'à son licenciement, comprenant les faits généraux des campagnes de 1805 à 1815, son organisation, sa solde, ses indemnités, le rang, le service, la discipline, les uniformes de ses divers corps, terminée par une biographie des chefs supérieurs de la garde.* Delaunay, Paris

Pétiet Auguste-Louis, (1844) *Souvenirs militaires de l'histoire contemporaine*, Dumaine, Paris

von Pflug-Harttung Julius (1908), *Von Wavre bis Belle-Alliance (18 Juni 1815)*, Berlin,

Extrait des Souvenirs historiques de Théobald Puvis., in la *Revue historique des Armées*, 1997, n° 3, pp. 101–129

Rigau (1846), *Souvenirs des guerres de l'Empire*, Garnier Freres Paris

Robinaux Capitaine (1908) *Journal de route (1803–1832)*. Publié par Gustave Schlumberger Plon, Paris

Ropes John Codman (1892), *The Campaign of Waterloo*, C. Scribner's Sons, New York

Routier Leon-Michel (2001) *Recit d'un Soldat de la Republique et de l'Empire 1792 – 1830* Editions du Grenadier

Rumigny Marie Theodore Gueulluy (1921) *Souvenirs du général comte de Rumigny, aide de camp du roi Louis-Philippe, 1789–1860*. Paris, Émile-Paul

Saint Just (1891) *Historique du 5eme regiment de Dragons*. Paris, Librairie Hacette

Schlumberger Gustave (1908) *Soldats de Napoléon Lettres du commandant Coudreux à son frère (1804–1815)* Librairie Plon Paris

Le Sénécal Charles (1840*) Réponse, au nom de la mémoire du général baron Le Sénécal, à la calomnie publiée par M. le baron Berthezène, dans un libelle en date du 27 mai 1840.* Impr. de E.-B. Delanchy Paris

de Dieu Soult Nicolas-Jean (1815) *Mémoire justificatif de M. le maréchal Soult, duc de Dalmatie* Chaumerot Jeune Paris

Siborne William, (1900) *The Waterloo Campaign 1815*, A. Constable

Thoumas Charles Antoine (1887) *Le General Curely*, Paris Berger-Levault

Thoumas Charles Antoine (1891) *Le maréchal Exelmans* Berger-Levrault Paris

Tissot Pierre François (1833) *Histoire de Napoléon, rédigée d'après les papiers d'état, les documents officiels, les mémoires et les notes secrètes de ses contemporains, suivie d'un précis sur la famille Bonaparte. L'ouvrage, orné de portraits et plans, est précédé de réflexions générales sur Napoléon* 2 vols. Delange-Taffin Paris

Thayer M. Russell (1873), *The Life, Character and Writings of Francis Lieber*, Collins, Philadelphia

Voss (1906) *Napoléon Untergang 1815*. 2 Volumes Berlin. Volume 2 Von Belle-Alliance diz zu Napoléon Tot

Weltzien Karl (1857) *Memoiren des Konglichen Preussichen Genes der Infanterie Ludwig von reiche*. Leipzig

de Zenowicz Georges de Despots (1848), *Waterloo: déposition sur les quatre journées de la campagne de 1815*, Ledoyen, Paris

Newspapers
French
Journal de l'Empire,
Journal de Rouen
Journal de Toulouse
Journal des débats politiques et littéraires
Journal Militaire
Revue Retrospective

BIBLIOGRAPHY

British
Cobbett's Political Register
Morning Chronicle
Morning Post
Leeds Mercury
The Times

Dutch
Niederländischer Staatscourant

Lecture notes
Paul Lindsay Dawson (2015) *Benjamin Gaskell*, lecture presented to mark the
bicentenary of the Battle of Waterloo

Online sources
https://www.cairn.info/revue-materiaux-pour-l-histoire-de-notre-temps-2014-1-
page-110.htm
www.waterloo-campagne.nl. Preamble p.17 accessed 17/12/2017 @ 19:35
http://www.clausewitz.com/readings/1815/five40-49.htm.
http://www.frenchempire.net/articles/reprisals/ accessed 29 March 2018

Notes

Introduction

1. John Coates, (2012) *The Hour Between Dog and Wolf,* Fourth Estate, London.
2. Guverich, *The French Historical Revolution: The Annales School,* in Hodder et al, *Interpreting Archaeology,* Routledge, London, 1995, pp. 158–61. This short paper offers a good introduction to the notion and concept of the Annales School for those unfamiliar with the theory of history.
3. Paul Fussell (1975), *The Great War and Modern Memory,* Oxford University Press, Oxford, 1975 p. 311.
4. Anna Green and Kathleen Troup (1999) *The Houses of History,* Manchester University Press, Manchester p. 231.
5. https://www.cairn.info/revue-materiaux-pour-l-histoire-de-notre-temps-2014-1-page-110.htm
6. Fussell p. 311.

Chapter 1

1. Gregor Dallas, *1815: The Roads to Waterloo,* Pimlico, London, 1996, p. 313.
2. Dallas, p. 315.
3. Dallas, p. 323.
4. The *Morning Chronicle,* 18 March 1815.
5. Journal Militaire 2e semester 1814 p. 28.
6. Charles Esdaile (2008) *Napoléon's Wars,* Penguin, London p. 554

Chapter 2

1. Journal des débats politiques et littéraires 11 April 1815 p.3.
2. SHDDT GR 6Yd 46 Remy Exelmans.
3. SHDDT GR 8yd 1279 Burthe.
4. SHDDT GR 7Yd 863 Bonnemains.
5. SHDDT C15 5 Dossier 15 Juin 1815. Order du Jour 14 Juin 1815.
6. Pierre Alexandre Edouard baron Fleury de Chaboulon (1820) *Memoirs of the Private Life, Return, and Reign of Napoléon in 1815* John Murray London, 2 volumes. Vol. 2 pp.168–170.
7. Chaboulon (1820), pp.177–178.

Chapter 3

1. SHDDT C15 6 Dossier 20 Juin 1815. Unknown letter 20 Juin 1815.
2. Marie Theodore Gueulluy Rumigny born 12 March 1789. Awarded Legion of Honour 20 August 1812, made Officer of the Legion of Honour 28 September 1813 whilst aid-de-camp to General Gérard. AN LH/1225/8.

3. Marie Theodore Gueulluy Rumigny (1921) *Souvenirs du général comte de Rumigny, aide de camp du roi Louis-Philippe, 1789–1860*. Paris, Émile-Paul. pp.99–103.

4. Maurice Louis Saint-Rémy born 11 April 1769, died 31 October 1841. Colonel Chief of Staff to 4th Corps. AN LH/2442/29.

5. SHDT C15 5 Correspondence Armée du Nord 11 au 22 Juin 1815, Dossier 17 Juin, Grouchy to Soult 17 June 1815.

6. Error, General Girard according to Thomas Aubry.

7. Berton, p. 15.

8. ibid.

9. SHDDT GR 24 YC 414 6e Hussard. See also SHDDT GR 24 YC 415 6e Hussard.

10. SHDDT GR 24 YC 293 8e Chasseurs.

11. SHDDT GR 24 YC 253 6e Dragons.

12. SHDDT GR 24 YC 190 16e Dragons.

13. Rumigny, pp.103–104.

14. Etienne Maurice Gérard (1829) *Quelques documens sur la bataille de Waterloo*. Paris p. 12.

15. Lefol (1854) *Souvenirs sur le prytanée de Saint-Cyr, sur la campagne de 1814, le retour de l'Empereur Napoléon de l'île d'Elbe et la campagne de 1815, pendant les Cent-jours* Montalant-Bougleux, Versailles pp. 59–60.

16. Etienne Maurice Gérard (1829) *Quelques documens sur la bataille de Waterloo*. Paris.

17. François (Capitaine) (1904), *Journal, 1792–1830, publié d'après le manuscrit original par Charles Grolleau*, Paris.

Chapter 4

1. ibid.

2. Chaboulon Vol. 2 p.254.

3. SHDDT: C15 5. Dossier 17 June 1815. Soult to Grouchy. This is the original, handwritten order from 17 June 1815.

4. John Franklin personal communication.

5. ibid.

6. Emmanuel Grouchy (1819) *Observations sur la relation de la campagne de 1815 publiee par le general Gourgaud*. Chez Chaumerot Jeune, Paris, no page.

7. AN: LH 1438/54. Hilaire Noël Taurin La Fresnaye was born on 3 September 1789 and was listed as a second lieutenant in the 2nd Cuirassiers on 1 June 1808. He left the regiment on 18 May 1810 and died in 1879.

8. SHDDT: C15 5. Dossier 18 Juin 1815. Grouchy to Napoléon, timed at 11.00. Copy made by Comte du Casse in June 1865. See also: Hans Oskar von Lettow-Vorbeck, *Napoléons Untergang 1815*, Mittler, Berlin, 1904, Vol. 8, p. 390, who states that the letter was sent at 10.00. In Grouchy's register, the letter has no time. See also: Grouchy, *Relation succincte de la campagne de 1815*, Vol. 4, p. 28.

9. Grouchy, *Relation succincte de la campagne de 1815*, Vol. 4, pp. 136–7.

10. Charles Thoumas (1891) *Le maréchal Exelmans* Berger-Levrault Paris p. 53.

11. AN: LH/2385/67.

12. AN: LH/2385/69.

13. SHDDT Xb 392 21e de Ligne 1812 a 1815. Dossier 1815.

14. Fussell p. 311.

15. AN: LH 910/54. Alexander Cesar Louis d'Estourmel was born in Paris on 29 March 1780 and in 1799 volunteered with the 'Legion Franks', serving in Egypt. He was promoted to sub-lieutenant in 1800, to captain of the elite company of the 27th Chasseurs à Cheval in 1806, to adjutant in 1808, to the headquarters staff, and to squadron-commander on 1 November 1814. He was attached to the Duke of Berry

on 10 March 1815 and went with the King to Ostend on 25 March 1815. He was then attached to the staff of the 1st Military Division on 9 July 1815. He states he did not serve in the Hundred Days campaign, remaining with the King, which if true, suggests he never carried an order to Exelmans.

16. Henry Houssaye, (1903) *1815 Waterloo*, Paris, p.169
17. Grouchy 1819 no page number.
18. ibid.
19. SHDDT: GR 21 YC 798 *90e régiment d'infanterie de ligne (ex 111e régiment d'infanterie de ligne), 1 Août 1814–7 Mai 1815 (matricules 1 à 1,800)*.
20. Jean Marie Joseph Deville, born at Tarbes 3 February 1787. Volunteered to the army 1803. Discharged 1815. 1830 commandant of the Tarbes National Guard. Discharged 1833. Entered politics in 1848. Died 19 May 1853.
21. George Deville, 'Grouchy a Waterloo' in *Revolution Français*, No. 53, 1907, pp. 281–4.
22. AN AFIV 1939 Registre d'Ordres du Major General 13 Juin au 26 Juin 1815 pp. 56–59.
23. SHDDT: GR 21 YC 798.
24. Grouchy 1819, no page.
25. SHDDT: C15 *Registre d'Ordres et de correspondance du major-general a partir du 13 Juin jusqu'au 26 Juin au Maréchal Grouchy*, p. 30. See also: SHDDT: C15 5. Dossier 18 Juin 1815. Soult to Grouchy, timed at 13.00. Copy of the original order made by Comte du Casse in June 1863. Du Casse either copied Grouchy's version of the letter, or had access to a duplicate set of material. This order is missing from the correspondence register of Marshal Soult.
26. Etienne-Maurice Gérard, *Quelques documents sur la bataille de Waterloo*, Paris, 1829.
27. Eugène André(1898) *Le maréchal Exelmans (1775–1852)* impr. de Comte-Jacquet, Bar-le-Duc, pp.87–88.
28. Tim Clayton (2014), *Waterloo: Four Days that Changed Europe's Destiny*, Little, Brown, London, p. 48.
29. SHDDT C15 5 Dossier 17 Juin 1815 Soult to Grouchy. This is the original hand-written order from 17 June 1815.

Chapter 5

1. AN LH/2189/1. See also AN AFIV 1939 Registre d'Ordres du Major General 13 Juin au 26 Juin 1815.
2. AN: AFIV 1939, pp. 49–50. See also: SHDDT: C15 5. Dossier 18 Juin 1815. Soult to Grouchy, timed at 13.00. Copy of the original order made by Comte du Casse in June 1863. Du Casse either copied Soult's version of the letter or had access to a duplicate set of material. A third version exists, published in 1826. This order is missing from Marshal Grouchy's correspondence register, however.
3. SHDDT: C15 *Registre d'Ordres et de correspondance du major-general a partir du 13 Juin jusqu'au 26 Juin au Maréchal Grouchy*, p. 30. See also: SHDDT: C15 5. Dossier 18 Juin 1815. Soult to Grouchy, timed at 13.00. Copy of the original order made by Comte du Casse in June 1863. Du Casse either copied Grouchy's version of the letter, or had access to a duplicate set of material. This order is missing from the correspondence register of Marshal Soult.
4. Georges de Despots de Zenowicz (1848), *Waterloo: déposition sur les quatre journées de la campagne de 1815*, Ledoyen, Paris.
5. Gérard (1829) pp. 41–42.
6. Paul Dawson (2017) *Napoléon and Grouchy*. Frontline, Barnsley pp. 237–239.
7. Chaboulon p.180.

8. AN AFIV 1939 Registre d'Ordres du Major General 13 Juin au 26 Juin 1815 pp. 56–59. The original dispatch cannot be found in the French Army Archives.

9. Charles de Beauveau Lieutenant Aide-de-Camp to General Gérard. His other aides-de-camp were Colonel de Rumigny, Captain Gérard, Lieutenant Bolin and Sous-Lieutenant Vaulerberg. SHDDT C15 35. Grouchy reports that de Beauveau indeed had been to report to Soult and returned to his own headquarters on the 20 June. See Grouchy to Napoléon, Rocroy 20 Juin 1815. SHDDT C15 16 Dossier 20 Juin 1815. Clearly, here is independent substantiation and or corroboration that the letter from Soult is authentic, and that Grouchy did indeed give orders to head to Waterloo, and that fighting had indeed taken place at Saint-Lambert. These two documents have been in the French Archives for over 200 years and prove Grouchy did obey orders to send at least some of his force to Waterloo as they were at Saint Lambert, as this is reported by two independent witnesses, Rumigny and Beauveau.

10. Jean Baptiste Berton, *Précis historique, militaire et critique des batailles de Fleurus et de Waterloo, dans la campagne de Flandres, en juin 1815*, J. S. Wallez, La Haye, 1818, pp. 49–50.

11. Pierre François Tissot (1833) *Histoire de Napoléon, rédigée d'après les papiers d'état, les documents officiels, les mémoires et les notes secrètes de ses contemporains, suivie d'un précis sur la famille Bonaparte. L'ouvrage, orné de portraits et plans, est précédé de réflexions générales sur Napoléon* 2 vols. Delange-Taffin Paris Vol. 2 pp. 272–273.

12. Grouchy, vol 4.

13. John Booth (1817), *The Battle of Waterloo, also of Ligny, and Quarter-Bras*, London, p. 251.

14. Grouchy (1819) no page.

15. G. Zenowicz, Waterloo (1848), *Deposition sur les quatre journées de la campagne de 1815*, Paris.

16. SHDDT 6yd 6 Jean Soult. Décret 9 Mai 1815.

17. SHDDT 6yd 6 Jean Soult. Davout to Soult 13 Mai 1815.

18. Bernard Cornwell (2014) *Waterloo. The History of Four Days*. William Collins London.

19. See the author's *Napoléon and Grouchy, the Last Great Waterloo Mystery Unravelled*, Frontline, Barnsley, 2017) for a full assessment of Grouchy in the campaign.

20. www.waterloo-campagne.nl. Preamble p.17 accessed 17/12/2017 @ 19.35 hours.

21. Stephen Beckett (2015) *Waterloo Betrayed. The Secret treachery that defeated Napoléon*. Mapleflower House.

22. AN: LH/95/62.

23. AN: LH/1859/43.

24. AN: LH/86/25.

25. AN: LH/2773/22.

26. AN: LH/1012/69.

27. AN: LH/144/19.

28. AN: LH/1594/40.

29. AN: LH/2285/62.

30. Anon (1815) *Porte-feuille de Buonaparte: pris à Charleroi le 18 juin 1815*, The Hague: De L'imprimiere Belgique p.125.

31. SHDDT GR 8yd 6 Jean Soult. Soult to Davout 19 Mai 1815.

32. SHDDT GR 8yd 6 Jean Soult. Soult to Davout 19 Mai 1815.

33. SHDDT GR 8yd 6 Jean Soult. Davout to Napoléon 19 Mai 1815.

34. SHDDT GR 8yd 6 Jean Soult, Davout to Soult 23 Mai 1815.

35. ibid, Soult to Napoléon 23 Mai 1815 Face.

36. ibid, Jean Soult, Soult to Napoléon 23 Mai 1815. Obverse.
37. AN/AF/IV/ 1940 Davout to Bertrand 8 Mai 1815.
38. www.waterloo-campagne.nl. Preamble p.17 accessed 17/12/2017 @ 19.35 hours.
39. Paul Dawson (2005) *Wakefield Memories*, Sutton Publishing, Stroud. p.100.
40. Grouchy (1819) no page.
41. George Hooper, (1862) *Waterloo, the Downfall of the First Napoléon*, Smith, Elder, London, pp. 343–4.

Chapter 6

1. Bellina Kupieski was born in 1778 and began his army career in 1797 with the rank of sergeant. He was promoted to sergeant-major on 31 May 1799 in the Italian-Polish Legion and was promoted to 2nd lieutenant on 24 April 1802. Promoted to 1st lieutenant in the Vistula Legion on 24 July 1812, he was named interpreter to the Grande Armée on 2 May 1813. Attached to 12th Corps as captain-adjutant-major from 7 July 1813. Named squadron commander of the 7th regiment of Line Lancers on 1 January 1814, he accompanied Napoléon to the Island of Elba and was promoted colonel on 15 May 1815. Following Waterloo, he emigrated to the United Sates on 12 August 1816.
2. SHDDT C15 fol 5. Dossier 23 Juin 1815. Kupieski to Davout 23 Juin 1815.
3. Maréchal du Camp Antoine Joseph Claude Le Bel was assistant chief of staff on the Imperial Headquarters. He was born in Paris on 6 January 1765. He had joined the Royalist Army on 28 April 1784 and was promoted to 2nd lieutenant on 1 September 1791, and was then promoted to lieutenant on the 17 June 1792 in the 7th Dragoon regiment. Promotion to squadron-commander came on 5 December 1793. From 23 September 1805 he was aide-de-camp to Marshal Kellerman, and from 23 September 1806 he was aide-de-camp to General Watier. He served with the general during the first years of the Peninsular War and the Austrian campaign of 1809 and served again in Spain from 12 December 1809 as aide to General Loision. He participated in the Russian campaign and served in Germany in 1813 with the staff of the 3rd Corps of Reserve Cavalry. Promotion to adjutant-commandant came on 23 January 1813. He was captured by Cossacks on 21 October 1813 and was returned to Paris in July 1814. He rallied to Napoléon in April 1815. He was wounded at Charleroi on the night of the 18 June.
4. Roul was born on 9 June 1775 at Le Villard. He was admitted to the 13th regiment of Hussars on 22 March 1793, he served as a Guide to General Bonaparte from 3 May 1796 and was admitted to the Chasseurs à Cheval of the Consular Guard on 3 January 1800 with the rank of corporal. In 1805 he was promoted lieutenant, wounded at the battle of Eylau in February 1807 and served in Spain in 1808. He retired in 1810 from the regiment. Re-called in 1813 to command a company of Gendarmes, he was attached to the staff of General Sebastiani in January 1814. He served on the Island of Elba with Napoléon and was named squadron commander in the Light Horse Lancers of the Imperial Guard on 14 April 1815. Promotion to colonel followed on 1 May 1815 with the function of Orderly Officer to the Emperor. He was captured at Waterloo. AN: LH 2397/31.
5. Charles Esdaile (2016) *Napoléon, France and Waterloo: The Eagle Rejected* Pen & Sword, Barnsley p.70.
6. *The Times*, 13 July 1815.

Chapter 7

1. AN AFIV 1939 Registre d'Ordres du Major General 13 Juin au 26 Juin 1815 pp. 54–55.
2. ibid, pp. 55–57.
3. Grouchy, *Observations sur la relation de la campagne de 1815*, pp. 20–2.
4. Bassford, Moran, Pedlow, *The Campaign of 1815 Chapters 40–49*, On Waterloo, available at http://www.clausewitz.com/readings/1815/five40-49.htm.
5. Lettow-Vorbeck, pp. 460–1.
6. Maurice Fleury (1901), *Souvenirs anecdotiques et militaires du colonel Biot*, Henri Vivien, Paris, p.235.
7. SHDDT GR 24 YC 383.
8. ibid, 403.
9. Berton, p. 67.
10. Grouchy, *Observations sur la relation de la campagne de 1815*, pp. 20–2.
11. Grouchy, *Relation succincte de la campagne de 1815*, Vol. 4, pp. 146–51.
12. AN: LH 62/73.
13. SHDDT: C15 23, p. 333.
14. This order exists in a number of original transcripts:

    1 SHDDT: C15 5. Dossier 19 Juin. Soult to Grouchy 19 Juin 1815. This is the original order in Soult's handwriting.
    2 AN: AFIV 1939, p. 52.
    3 SHDDT: C15 *Registre d'Ordres et de correspondance du major-general a partir du 13 Juin jusqu'au 26 Juin au Maréchal Grouchy*, p. 30. This is Grouchy's receipt of the order.
    4 SHDDT: C15 23 p. 32. This is a transcript by Vandamme noting he received the order.

15. SHDDT: C15 5. Dossier 19 Juin 1815. Soult to Grouchy. Copy of the original order made by Comte du Casse in June 1865.
16. SHDDT: C15 *Registre d'Ordres et de correspondance du major-general a partir du 13 Juin jusqu'au 26 Juin au Maréchal Grouchy*, p. 27. See also: SHDDT: C15 23, p. 32.
17. Louis Florimond Fantin des Odoards (1895), *Journal du général Fantin des Odoards*, E. Plon, Nourit et Cie, Paris, p. 446.
18. SHDDT: C15 *Registre d'Ordres et de correspondance du major-general a partir du 13 Juin jusqu'au 26 Juin au Maréchal Grouchy*, p. 32. See also: SHDDT: C15 5. Dossier 19 Juin 1815. Grouchy to Vichery; see also SHDDT C15 6 Dossier 19 Juin Grouchy to Vichery for a copy of the original order made in June 1865 by Comte du Casse.
19. Grouchy, *Mémoires du Maréchal de Grouchy*, 1874, Vol. 4, pp. 60–1.
20. SHDDT GR 24 YC 414 6e Hussard. See also GR 24 YC 415 6e Hussard.
21. SHDDT GR 24 YC 293 8e Chasseurs.
22. SHDDT Gr 24 YV 253 6e Dragons.
23. SHDDT Gr 24 YC 190 16e Dragons.

Chapter 8

1. SHDDT C15 6 Dossier 20 Juin 1815. Grouchy to Vandamme 20 Juin 1815.
2. Grouchy, *Observations sur la relation de la campagne de 1815*, pp. 20–2.
3. Lefol, pp. 59–60.
4. Gérard, *Dernières observations*, pp. 25–6. See also: SHDDT: C15 5. Dossier 18 Juin. Exelmans to Gérard, 1 February 1830.
5. Julius von Pflug-Harttung, *Von Wavre bis Belle-Alliance (18 Juni 1815)*, Berlin, 1908, p. 616.

6. Berton, p. 64.
7. Clayton, p. 48.
8. William Hyde Kelly (1905), *The Battle of Wavre and Grouchy's Retreat*, John Murray, London.
9. A. F. Becke (1995), *Napoléon and Waterloo: The Emperor's Campaign with the Armée du Nord, 1815*, Greenhill Books, London.
10. Berton, p. 56.
11. Grouchy, *Mémoires du Maréchal de Grouchy*, 1874, Vol. 4, pp. 60–1.
12. Booth, 1817, p. 251.
13. Grouchy, *Observations sur la relation de la campagne de 1815*, pp. 15–16.
14. SHDDT: C15 5. Dossier 18 Juie1815. Handwritten statement from Blocqueville to Grouchy, no date.
15. Booth (1817) pp. 251.
16. Berton p. 64.
17. SHDDT GR 24 YC 148 5e dragons.
18. SHDDT GR 24YC 174 10 Juillet 1814–4 Août 1815 (8e régiment de Condé 1814).
19. SHDDT GR 24 YC 185 Août 1814–6 Août 1815 (10e régiment de dragons, 1814).
20. SHDDT GR 24 YC 213 29 Juillet 1814–12 Août 1815 (15e régiment de dragons, 1814).
21. AN LH/2251/19.
22. SHDDT GR 24YC 143 4e dragon 1814–1815.
23. SHDDT GR 24 YC 169 12e dragon 26 Août 1814 a 31 Août 1815.
24. SHDDT GR 24 YC 180 10 Août 1814–23 Décembre 1815 (9e régiment de dragons, 1814).
25. SHDDT GR 24YC 195 17e dragon 21 Juillet 1814 a 28 Juin 1815.
26. SHDDT GR 24 YC 148 5e dragons.
27. SHDDT GR 24YC 174 10 Juillet 1814–4 Août 1815 (8e régiment de Condé 1814).
28. SHDDT GR 24 YC 185 Août 1814–6 Août 1815 (10e régiment de dragons, 1814).
29. SHDDT GR 24 YC 213 29 Juillet 1814–12 Août 1815 (15e régiment de dragons, 1814).
30. SHDDT GR 24YC 143 4e dragon 1814–1815.
31. SHDDT GR 24 YC 169 12e dragon 26 Août 1814 a 31 Août 1815.
32. SHDDT GR 24 YC 180 10 Août 1814–23 Décembre 1815 (9e régiment de dragons, 1814).
33. SHDDT GR 24YC 195 17e dragon 21 Juillet 1814 a 28 Juin 1815.
34. Berton, pp. 68–70.
35. *Journal de l'Empire*, 22 Juin 1815, p. 2.
36. ibid.
37. SHDDT: C15 5. Dossier 20 Juin. Bonnemains to Bourke, 20 Juin 1815.
38. ibid, Dossier 20 Juin 1815. Bonnemains to Chastel 20 Juin 1815. The original handwritten order is difficult to read in many places, the translation is a gist understanding, as Bonnemains own handwriting is not clear enough to read, not helped by his editing of the letter as he was composing it.
39. SHDDT: C15 5. Dossier 20 Juin 1815, Bonnemains to Bourke no date.
40. ibid, Vincent to Napoléon. 20 Juin 1815 The original handwritten order is difficult to read in many places.
41. SHDDT GR 24 YC 148 5e dragons.
42. ibid, 174 10 Juillet 1814–4 Août 1815 (8e régiment de Condé 1814).
43. ibid, 185 Août 1814–6 Août 1815 (10e régiment de dragons, 1814).
44. ibid, 213 29 Juillet 1814–12 Août 1815 (15e régiment de dragons, 1814).
45. ibid, 143 4e dragon 1814–1815.
46. ibid, 169 12e dragon 26 Août 1814 a 31 Août 1815.

47. SHDDT GR 24 YC 180 10 Août 1814–23 Décembre 1815 (9e régiment de dragons, 1814).
48. SHDDT GR 24YC 195 17e dragon 21 Juillet 1814 a 28 Juin 1815.
49. *Niederländischer Staatscourant*, 27 June 1815. Transcript by Erwin Muilwijk.
50. Fantin des Odoards, pp. 437–8.
51. Hubert Miot-Putigny (1950), *Putigny, grognard d'Empire*, Gallimard, Paris, pp. 245–6.
52. Philippe Gerbet (1866), *Souvenirs d'un officier sur la campagne de Belgique en 1815*, Émile Javal, Arbois, pp. 21–3.
53. AN: LH 747/48.
54. SHDDT GR 21 YC 279 30e régiment d'infanterie de ligne, 21 Juillet 1814–6 Juillet 1815.
55. SHDDT GR 21 YC 726 80e régiment d'infanterie de ligne (ex 96e régiment d'infanterie de ligne), 2 février 1815–16 Août 1815.
56. SHDDT: C15 *Registre d'Ordres et de correspondance du major-general a partir du 13 Juin jusqu'au 26 Juin au Maréchal Grouchy*, p. 34.
57. M. Russell Thayer (1873), *The Life, Character and Writings of Francis Lieber*, Collins, Philadelphia, pp. 9–10.
58. SHDDT: C15 *Registre d'Ordres et de correspondance du major-general a partir du 13 Juin jusqu'au 26 Juin au Maréchal Grouchy*, p. 26.
59. SHDDT: C15 *Registre d'Ordres et de correspondance du major-general a partir du 13 Juin jusqu'au 26 Juin au Maréchal Grouchy*, p. 28. See also: SHDDT: C15 5. Dossier 19 Juin 1815. Grouchy to Napoléon. Copy of the original order made by Comte du Casse in June 1865. See also: *Le Moniteur*, No. 175, 24 June 1815. In the archives of the Service Historique Armée de Térre in Paris, six copies of reports of Grouchy to the Emperor dated 19 June 1815 can be found. In themselves they could have their interest, was it not for the fact that they contain a huge amount of overlap and that it is therefore very hard to assess how they relate to each other. However, of these orders, only the order cited here, and a much shorter note written on 19 June at Dinant which did not reach Soult, can be considered authentic, as only these orders appear in Grouchy's own register of correspondence, providing a cross-reference. We note that none of the six orders in the dossier at Vincennes are originals, all are copes by Comte de Casse in 1865 of the now lost originals, except in two cases.
60. SHDDT: C15 *Registre d'Ordres et de correspondance du major-general a partir du 13 Juin jusqu'au 26 Juin au Maréchal Grouchy*, p. 28.
61. ibid, p. 34. See also SHDDT C15 6 Dossier 20 Juin. Grouchy Ordre du Jour 20 Juin 1815 timed at 23.00 hours. This is the original document.
62. SHDDT C15 6 Dossier 20 Juin 1815. Dumonceau to Davout 20 Juin 1815.
63. ibid, 1 Juillet 1815. Gobrecht to Davout 1 Juillet 1815.

Chapter 9

1. AN AFIV 1939 Registre d'Ordres du Major General 13 Juin au 26 Juin 1815 pp. 55–59.
2. ibid.
3. Puvis pp. 101–129.
4. Anon *Lettre d'un Combattant de Waterloo* in Feuilles d'Histoire No. 6 1911 pp. 441–445.
5. ibid.
6. http://www.clausewitz.com/readings/1815/five50-58.htm#Ch50.

Chapter 10

1. AN AFIV 1939 Registre d'Ordres du Major General 13 Juin au 26 Juin 1815 pp. 55–59.
2. ibid.
3. SHDDT C15 5. Dossier 23 Juin Kupieski to Davout 23 Juin 1815.
4. SHDDT C15 5 Dossier 22 Juin. Dejean to Davout 21 Juin 1815.
5. SHDDT C15 5 Dossier 22 Juin, Soult to Tancarville 22 Juin 1815.
6. SHDDT C15 5. Dossier 21 Juin, Foy to Soult 21 Juin 1815.
7. Puvis pp. 101–129.
8. SHDDT Xab 74 Situation report Artillerie a Pied de la Garde Impériale 21 Juin 1815.
9. SHDDDT C 15 5 Dossier 21 Juin. Grouchy to Vandamme 21 Juin 1815 A.
10. ibid, Vandamme Movement orders 21 Juin 1815.
11. ibid, Grouchy to Vandamme, Givet 21 Juin 1815 B.
12. SHDDT C15 5 Dossier 21 Juin, Bourke to Davout 21 Juin.
13. SHDDT C15 *Registre d'Ordres et de correspondance du major-general a partir du 13 Juin jusqu'au 26 Juin au Maréchal Grouchy*, p. 44. See also: SHDDT C15 15. Dossier 21 Juin. Grouchy to Soult. This is the original handwritten document sent to Soult.

Chapter 11

1. SHDDT: C15 *Registre d'Ordres et de correspondance du major-general a partir du 13 Juin jusqu'au 26 Juin au Maréchal Grouchy*, p. 44.
2. SHDDT C15 5 Dossier 22 Juin. Ordre de Mouvement 22 Juin 1815. This is the original document. See also: SHDDT: C15 *Registre d'Ordres et de correspondance du major-general a partir du 13 Juin jusqu'au 26 Juin au Maréchal Grouchy*, p. 44.
3. ibid pp. 51–3. See also SHDDT C15 6 Dossier 22 Juin 1815. Davout to Grouchy 22 Juin 1815. This is the original document.
4. SHDDT C15 5 Dossier 22 Juin. Le Sénécal to Vandamme 22 Juin 1815.
5. AN AFIV 1939 Registre d'Ordres du Major General 13 Juin au 26 Juin 1815 pp. 55–59. See also SHDDT C15 6 Dossier 22 Juin 1815. Soult to Napoléon 22 Juin timed at 07.00 hours. This is the original letter sent from Soult to Napoléon. The copy in the Major General's order book is a word for word transcript.
6. AN AFIV 1939 Registre d'Ordres du Major General 13 Juin au 26 Juin 1815 pp. 55–59. See also SHDDT C 15 6 Soult to Napoléon 22 Juin 1815. This is a copy of the order book of the Major General made by Comte de Casse in Juin 1865. In no way does this copy provide corroboration for the contents of the now lost original order book and lost original letters.
7. SHDDT C15 Registre d'Ordres et de correspondance du major-general a partir du 13 Juin jusqu'au 26 Juin au Marechal Grouchy p. 44.
8. SHDDT C15 5 Dossier 23 Juin. Kupieski to Davout 23 Juin 1815.
9. AN AFIV 1939 Registre d'Ordres du Major General 13 Juin au 26 Juin 1815 p. 91.
10. Fleuret p. 150.
11. Puvis pp. 101–129.

Chapter 12

1. John Cam Hobhouse Broughton (1816) *The Substance of some letters written by an Englishman resident at Paris during the reign of the Emperor Napoléon* M Thomas Philadelphia pp. 241–247.
2. Broughton pp. 250–251.

3. Jacques-Antoine Dulaure (1834) *Histoire des Cent-Jours.* Paris p. 205 citing Armand Jean Flotard of the 4th Lancers.
4. Leon-Michel Routier (2001) *Recit d'un Soldat de la Republique et de l'Empire 1792 – 1830* Editions du Grenadier.

Chapter 13

1. AN AFIV 1939 Registre d'Ordres du Major General 13 Juin au 26 Juin 1815 p. 91.
2. ibid, p. 93. See Also SHDDT C15 6 Soult to Reille 23 Juin 1815 A; SHDDT C 15 6 Dossier 23 Juin 1815 Soult to Reille 23 Juin 1815 B See Also SHDDT C15 6 Dossier 23 Juin Soult to Reille 23 Juin 1815 timed at 10.30 hours.
3. AN AFIV 1939 Registre d'Ordres du Major General 13 Juin au 26 Juin 1815 p. 96 See Also SHDDT C15 6 Dossier 23 Juin Soult to d'Erlon 23 Juin 1815.
4. ibid, pp.99–100.
5. SHDDT C15 6 Dossier 23 Juin 1815 Watthiez to Reille 23 Juin 1815 timed at 01:00. This is the original document sent to Davout. See also SHDDT C15 6 Dossier 23 Juin 1815 Wathiez to Reille 23 Juin timed at 01:00. This is the original document sent to Reille.
6. AN AFIV 1939 Registre d'Ordres du Major General 13 Juin au 26 Juin 1815 p. 101. See Also SHDDT C15 6 Soult to Davout 23 Juin concerning Wathiez [sic]. See Also SHDDT C15 6 Dossier 23 Juin 1815 Soult to Davout 23 Juin 1815 copy of report from Watthiez [sic] To Reille; SHDDT C15 6 Dossier 23 Juin 1815 Wathiez to Reille 23 Juin timed at 01.00 hours.
7. AN AFIV 1939 Registre d'Ordres du Major General 13 Juin au 26 Juin 1815 p. 101.
8. ibid, p. 102.
9. SHDDT C15 6 Dossier 23 Juin 1815. Soult to Kellerman 23 Juin 1815 timed at 00.00 hours.
10. SHDDT C15 6 Dossier 23 Juin 1815 Domon to Soult 23 Juin 1815.
11. ibid, Maureai to Soult Craon 23 Juin 1815.
12. Charles Antoine Thoumas (1887) *Le General Curely,* Paris Berger-Levault pp. 419–420.
13. Curely took command of Donop's cuirassier brigade. Ian Smith pers comm 1 October 2018.
14. AN AFIV 1939 Registre d'Ordres du Major General 13 Juin au 26 Juin 1815 pp. 103–104.
15. ibid, pp. 115–116.
16. ibid, p. 116.
17. ibid, p. 117.
18. SHDDT Xab 74 Situation report 21 Juin 1815.
19. AN AFIV 1939 Registre d'Ordres du Major General 13 Juin au 26 Juin 1815 p. 91.
20. ibid, p 73.
21. ibid, p. 75.
22. ibid, p. 91. See Also SHDDT C15 6 Dossier 23 Juin 1815 Soult to Ruty 23 Juin 1815. This is the original copy of this document.
23. AN AFIV 1939 Registre d'Ordres du Major General 13 Juin au 26 Juin 1815 p. 79.
24. Fleuret pp. 155–157.
25. AN AFIV 1939 Registre d'Ordres du Major General 13 Juin au 26 Juin 1815 p. 116.
26. SHDDT C15 6 Dossier 23 Juin 1815 Soult to Reille, Laon 23 Juin 1815.
27. AN AFIV 1939 Registre d'Ordres du Major General 13 Juin au 26 Juin 1815 p. 123.
28. ibid, p. 129.
29. ibid, p. 130.
30. SHDDT C15 fol 6 Subervie to Grouchy 26 Juin 1815 timed at 17.00 hours.

31. ibid, timed at 22.00 hours.
32. SHDDT C15 6 Dossier 27 Juin 1815 Subervie to Grouchy 27 Juin 1815 timed at 04.00 hours.
33. SHDDT C15 6 Dossier 23 Juin 1815 Soult to Grouchy 23 Juin timed at 08.00 hours.
34. SHDDT C15 6 Anonymous to Anonymous Colonel. This letter is included in the dispatch from Fortin to Vallin. Possibly an officer of the 16th Dragoons reporting to Fortin who was acting Colonel. The letter is signed by [?] Hesson.
35. SHDDT C15 6 Anonymous dispatch dated 22 Juin. This letter is included in the dispatch from Fortin to Vallin. Is this the letter from the Mayor of La Capelle Fortin mentions?
36. AN LH/1003/7 Daniel Fortin, born 24 August 1772. Admitted to 15th Line Regiment on 12 October 1789, promoted corporal 15 December 1791, passed to Legion of the North 13 March 1793, passed to 16th Dragoons 30 March 1794. Promoted sergeant 20 August 1794, sergeant-major 8 December 1794, sub-lieutenant 21 April 1800, lieutenant 8 December 1806, adjutant-major 16 September 1808, captain-adjutant-major 16 March 1810, captain 17 May 1813, squadron-commander 21 June 1813. Discharged from the army 14 December 1815. Died 19 September 1825.
37. SHDDT C15 6. Dossier 23 Juin 1815 Fortin to Vallin 23 Juin 1815 timed at 03.00 hours.
38. SHDDT C15 6. Dossier 23 Juin 1815 Valin to Grouchy 23 Juin 1815 timed at 05.00 hours. The attached letter is missing, but Davout also sent the same dispatch directly to Grouchy, cited later.
39. ibid, timed at 08.00 hours.
40. ibid, timed at 17.00 hours.
41. ibid, Grouchy to Soult 23 Juin.
42. SHDDT C15 6. Dossier 23 Juin 1815 La Neuville[?] 23 Juin timed at 16.00 hours.
43. ibid, Valin to Grouchy 23 Juin 1815 timed at 17.00 hours.
44. ibid, Grouchy to Vandamme at Aubigny.
45. ibid, Ordre du Jour et de Mouvement 23 Juin 1815.
46. ibid, Grouchy to Vandamme at Mezieres.
47. SHDDT C15 6. Dossier 23 Juin 1815 Berthezene to Grouchy 23 Juin 1815.
48. ibid, Le Sénécal to Grouchy.
49. ibid, Soult to Grouchy 23 Juin 1815 timed at midnight 22 Juin. Does this mean it arrived with Grouchy at midnight?
50. SHDDT C15 5 Dossier 22 Juin. Ordre du Jour 22 Juin 1815 sent on the behalf of Grouchy by Guyardin. See also SHDDT C15 5 Dossier 22 Juin, Order de Jour, Charlemont 22 Juin for Grouchy's own hand written first proof of the proclamation.
51. SHDDT: C15 *Registre d'Ordres et de correspondance du major-general a partir du 13 Juin jusqu'au 26 Juin au Maréchal Grouchy*, p. 58. See also SHDDT C15 6 Ordre du jour 22 Juin 1815. Soult only informed Grouchy of the abdication on the morning of 23 Juin at 05:00, yet this original document is dated 22 Juin, and obverse are orders dated 22 Juin to Vandamme.
52. SHDDT C15 6. Dossier 23 Juin 1815 Soult to Reille 23 Juin 1815.
53. ibid, Grouchy to Soult 23 Juin 1815.
54. ibid, Grouchy Ordre du Mouvement pour le 24 Juin 1815.
55. SHDDT C15 6 Dossier 23 Juin 1815. Soult a Grouchy 23 Juin 1815 timed at 17.00 hours.
56. AN AFIV 1939 Registre d'Ordres du Major General 13 Juin au 26 Juin 1815 p. 116.
57. ibid pp. 105–109.
58. SHDDT C15 6 Le Commissions du Gouvernement, Arrette nomant le Marechal Grouchy Gal. ed Chef de l'Armée du Nord le 23 Juin. Soult is supposedly to have resigned command on 23 June, but that letter cannot be found amongst the paperwork of the French Army Archives. It is of course not impossible that Soult

did resign his command, turn his coat and flee, but no evidence can be found by the present writer using documents from June 1815 to confirm this. We must remember the order book of the Major-General cited in this work, is a copy made by Marshal Grouchy of the lost original, so we cannot be certain what orders are original, edited or omitted – or what Soult added later, or indeed others may have added. Clearly the book is not an accurate copy as an order to Vandamme dated 28 June at Claye is found amongst the orders dated 18 June. Therefore, we have no idea what is missing or added. In many cases however, where the original orders can be found and compared to the order book the copies by Grouchy are word for word. But we do not know what Grouchy may have added or edited out as the extant paper work at the French Army Archives does not provide in loose paper form an exact duplicate of this book. A resignation can be found in the pages of the Major-Generals order book [AN: AFIV 1939, p. 123.] It is written in the third and first person which seems strange. Secondly it seems impossible for the order to have reached to Paris in time for the Government to debate the order and act upon. On 22 June, Davout sent word to Soult at 20.00, it took nine hours to reach him travelling from Paris to Laon, a distance of 86 miles. Soissons is roughly 70 miles from Paris, a journey on horseback taking at least six hours distant assuming no breaks, it is likely the order took more than six hours. The letter to which the resignation paragraphs are attached was sent from Soissons. Soult arrived at Soissons on the evening of 23 June. Even if the government met at midnight on 23 June, it was impossible for the letter to get to Davout, and for Davout to convene the council and act upon Soult's orders. Unless the original order can be found, I consider the letter of resignation to be suspect. If so, who did the deed? Would Grouchy have anything to gain by adding this material? Not really. Would Soult? Possibly to cover up the shame of being sacked? Certainly, Soult was aggrieved by the events of 26 June, that would later be used to tarnish his career, much like Grouchy's named was tarnished by the events of 18 and 19 June. Or is it added by unknown person? Grouchy by 1830 admits to having the order book. But where was it before then? General Vaudoncourt certainly had sight of it in 1825–1826. But how it became to handled by Vaudoncourt and then in the possession of Grouchy we know not. Of course, we accept the possibility that the order is genuine and by an amazing feat of horsemanship the letter did get to Davout very late on 23 June, but on balance of evidence this does seem unlikely. Certainly, Grouchy took command from Soult on 26 June, but the true reason for Soult leaving the army and handing over command are open to question. My hypothesis fits the evidence as I see it. Readers are of free to make their own judgements.

59. Grouchy (1840) *Fragments historiques réunis pour* établir *le fait de calomnie répandue dans un libelle du général Berthezène, publié en date du 27 mai 1840: campagne de 1815 (2e éd., augmentée de documents inédits jusqu'à ce jour) par le maréchal E. de Grouchy.* Impr. de F. Poisson (Caen) pp. 11–12.
60. SHDDT GR 6Yd 26 Emmanuel Grouchy.
61. AN AFIV 1939, p. 123.
62. SHDDT 6yd 6 Jean Soult. Décret 9 Mai 1815.
63. SHDDT 6yd 6 Jean Soult. Davout to Soult 13 Mai 1815, p. 1.
64. ibid, p. 2.
65. Clayton, p. 42.
66. SHDDT GR 6yd 6 Jean Soult, Soult 5 Juillet 1814.
67. ibid, Dupont to Soult 20 Août 1814.
68. ibid, Arête de Liquidation 31 Décembre 1814.
69. ibid, Soult to Davout 11 Avril 1815.

70. ibid, Soult to Minister of War 8 Août 1815.
71. ibid, Soult to Minister of War 7 Novembre 1817.
72. S Beckett (2015).
73. SHDDT GR 6yd Minister of War to Soult 24 Janvier 1820.
74. SHDDT GR 8yd 6 Jean Soult. Davout to Napoléon 19 Mai 1815. See also SHDDT 8yd 6 Jean Soult. Davout to Soult 23 Mai 1815.
75. AN AFIV 1940 Davout to Bertrand 8 Mai 1815.
76. ibid.
77. SHDDT GR 7yd 557 Bailly de Monthion. Rapport 23 Décembre 1815.
78. ibid.
79. www.waterloo-campagne.nl. Preamble p.17 accessed 17/12/2017 @ 19.35 hours.
80. Nicolas-Jean de Dieu Soult (1815) *Mémoire justificatif de M. le maréchal Soult, duc de Dalmatie* Chaumerot Jeune Paris pp. 34–35.
81. SHDDT C15 6. Dossier 23 Juin 1815, Soult to Rogniat 23 Juin 1815.
82. ibid.

Chapter 14

1. SHDDT C15 Dossier 24 Juin 1815, Monthion 24 Juin 1815.
2. ibid, Monthion to Grouchy 24 Juin 1815.
3. ibid, Davout to Grouchy 24 Juin 1815.
4. ibid, Grouchy to Pajol 24 Juin 1815 timed at 07.00 hours.
5. ibid, Soult to Grouchy 24 Juin 1815.
6. ibid, Grouchy to Vallin 24 Juin 1815.
7. ibid, Grouchy to Exelmans 24 Juin 1815 timed at 08.00 hours.
8. ibid, Pajol to Grouchy 24 Juin 1815 timed at 12.00 hours.
9. ibid, Grouchy to Soult 24 Juin 1815 timed at 14.00 hours.
10. SHDDT C15 6 Dossier 24 Juin 1815. Exelmans to Grouchy 24 Juin 1815 timed at 18.00 hours.
11. ibid, Order du de Mouvement.

Chapter 15

1. SHDDT C15 6 Dossier 25 Juin 1815. Davout to Grouchy 25 Juin 1815 timed at 08.00 hours.
2. ibid, timed at midday.
3. ibid,Grouchy to Vallin 25 Juin 1815 timed at 17.00 hours.
4. SHDDT C15 6 Dossier 25 Juin 1815, Proclamation.
5. ibid, Davout to Grouchy 25 Juin 1815 timed at midnight.
6. Antoine Adolphe Marcelin Marbot, born 22 March 1781. Elder brother of Colonel Marbot of the 7th Hussars. Admitted to 21st Chasseurs a Cheval in June 1797, promoted sous-lieutenant in the 2nd Battalion of Volunteers of the Seine 1799, passed as aide-de-camp to General Bernadotte 1 June 1800, transferred to the 49th demi-brigade as lieutenant 1 August 1802, passed as captain aide-de-camp to General Duaen 20 June 1803, passed to the staff of the Army of Batavia 8 October 1803, passed as captain of 1st Chasseurs 20 May 1804. Attached to the staff of Marshal Augereau September 1806, he was posted as captain-adjutant to the staff of 7th Corps 31 October 1806. Nominated for the Legion of Honour 12 January 1807 he was made Augereau's aide-de-camp once more on 15 January 1807. Passed to the staff of 5th Corps 11 April 1807, named aide-de-camp to Marshal Massena 30 June 1807, passed as aide-de-camp to Marshal Lannes 1 October 1808 and then passed to Marshal Berthier as aide-de-camp 4 December 1808. In Berthier's service he was promoted squadron commander 21 April 1810 and

passed back to Massena's service as aide-des-camp 21 April 1810. Transferred to the 16th Chasseurs a Cheval 1 October 1811. Passed to the Military Staff of Paris 10 October 1814, awarded Order of Saint Louis 3 November 1814. Passed to the staff of the 1st Military Division 20 January 1815, named aide-des-camp to Marshal Davout 11 May 1815. Discharged from the army 4 August 1815. He died June 1844; see AN LH/1723/42.

7. SHDDTC 15 6 Dossier 25 Juin, Soult to Grouchy 25 Juin 1815.
8. ibid, Grouchy to Soult 25 Juin 1815 timed at 17.00 hours.
9. ibid, Grouchy to Vandamme 25 Juin 1815.
10. Gustave Schlumberger (1908) *Soldats de Napoléon Lettres du commandant Coudreux à son frère (1804–1815)* Librairie Plon, Paris.
11. SHDDT GR 7 YD 1145, Jean Baptiste Antoine Marcelin Marbot.
12. SHDDT GR 24 YC 422.
13. ibid.
14. ibid.
15. ibid.
16. ibid.
17. SHDDT GR 24 YC 114 Lanciers de Monsieur.
18. SHDDT C15 6. Dossier 26 Juin 1815. Delcambre to Davout 26 Juin.
19. SHDDT 24YC 16 1e Cuirassier.
20. SHDDT 24YC 69 12e Cuirassier
21. SHDDT C15 6 Dossier 26 Juin 1815, Ordre du Jour 26 Juin 1815.

Chapter 16

1. SHDDT C15 6 Dossier 26 Juin, Order du Jour 26 Juin.
2. ibid, Soult to Davout 26 Juin timed at 05.00 hours.
3. ibid, Grouchy to Davout, 26 Juin 1815 timed at 08.00 hours.
4. ibid, timed at 5.30 hours.
5. ibid.
6. ibid, 05.30 hours.
7. ibid.
8. ibid.
9. Journal de Rouen 29 Juin 1815 p. 1.
10. SHDDT C15 6 Dossier 26 Juin, Vandamme to Grouchy 26 Juin 1815 timed at 05.30 hours.
11. SHDDT C15 6 Dossier 26 Juin, Subervie to Grouchy 26 Juin 1815 timed at 17.00 hours.
12. ibid, Domon to Grouchy 26 Juin 1815 timed at 20.00 hours.
13. ibid, Subervie to Grouchy 26 Juin 1815 timed at 22.30 hours.

Chapter 17

1. SHDDT C15 6. Dossier 27 Juin, rapport 27 Juin 1815.
2. ibid.
3. ibid, Grouchy to Morand, Soissons 27 Juin 1815.
4. ibid, Grouchy to Lefebvre-Desnoëttes 27 Juin.
5. ibid, Grouchy to Exelmans 27 Juin timed at 10.00 hours.
6. ibid, Grouchy to Davout 27 Juin timed at 14.00 hours.
7. ibid, Grouchy to Reille 27 Juin 1815 written at Soissons.
8. ibid, Grouchy to Vandamme 27 Juin 1815 written at Soissons.
9. ibid, Grouchy to Vandamme 27 Juin 1815 timed at 15.00 hours.
10. ibid, timed after 15.00 hours.

11. SHDDT C15 6. Dossier 27 Juin, Grouchy to Vandamme 27 Juin timed at 19.00 hours.
12. Karl Rudolf von Ollech (1876), *Geschichte des Feldzuges von 1815 nach archivalischen quellen*, E. S. Mittler und Sohn, Berlin, p. 324.
13. Damitz (1838) Geschichte *des Feldzuges von 1815 in den Niederlanden und Frankreich* 2 volumes. Berlin. Vol. 2. p. 157.
14. SHDDT GR 24 YC 121.
15. SHDDT C15 34 Situations Garde Impériale 3e Corps du Cavalerie, Situations du 24 Juin 1815.
16. SHDDT GR 24 YC 126 6e Lanciers.
17. ibid.
18. SHDDT C15 6 Dossier 26 Juin 1815, Wathiez to Davout 26 Juin 1815 A.
19. SHDDT Xc 183, Dossier 6e Lanciers.
20. SHDDT C15 6 Dossier 26 Juin 1815, Wathiez to Davout 26 Juin 1815 A.
21. ibid, Wathiez to Davout 26 Juin 1815 B.
22. ibid, Grouchy to Morand Soissons 27 Juin 1815.
23. ibid, Grouchy to Davout 27 Juin 1815 timed at 14.00 hours.
24. Ollech p. 324.
25. http://www.clausewitz.com/readings/1815/five50-58.htm#Ch50.
26. Revue retrospective 1884 Paris, pp. 365–367.
27. Ollech (1876) Geschichte *des Feldzuges von 1815 nach archivalischen quellen* Berlin p. 324.
28. Jean Mistler and Helene Michaud (1970) *Lieutenant Chevalier: Souvenirs des Guerres Napoléonienne*, Hachette, Paris. pp. 328–329.
29. Guyot (1999) *Carnets de la Campagne du General Comte Guyot 1792–1815*. Teissèdre p. 301.
30. Chevalier, pp. 328–329.
31. SHDDT Gr 24 YC 107 3e Lanciers.
32. SHDDT GR 24 YC 114 Lanciers de Monsieur.
33. ibid.
34. SHDDT GR 24 YC 422.

Chapter 18

1. SHDDT C15 fol 6 Dossier 26 Juin 1815, Delort to Grouchy 26 Juin 1815 timed at 20.00 hours.
2. ibid, Grouchy to Davout 26 Juin 1805 timed at 05.30 hours.
3. Voss (1906) *Napoléon Untergang 1815*. 2 Volumes Berlin. Volume 2 Von Belle-Alliance diz zu Napoléon Tot pp 35–36.
4. SHDDT: C15 6. Dossier 27 Juin. Milhaud to Grouchy 27 Juin 1815 timed at 06.00 hours.
5. Ibid, Subervie to Grouchy 27 Juin 1815.
6. SHDDT: C15 6. Dossier 27 Juin, Grouchy to Domon 27 Juin.
7. ibid, Grouchy to d'Erlon, 27 Juin 1815 timed at 07.00 hours.
8. ibid, Milhaud to Grouchy 27 Juin 1815 timed at 06.00 hours.
9. SHDDT C15 6. Dossier 27 Juin, Grouchy to Davout 27 Juin timed at 08.00 hours.
10. SHDDT MR 718 Relation Campagne 1815 par le Duc de Valmy p. 32.
11. SHDDT C15 6 Dossier 27 Juin 1815, Grouchy to d'Erlon 27 Juin 1815 timed at 08.00 hours.
12. Karl Weltzien (1857) *Memoiren des Konglichen Preussichen Genes der Infanterie Ludwig von reiche*. Leipzig., Vol 2 p.249.
13. AN AFIV 1140 Situation report 29- 30 Juin 1815.
14. SHDDT C15 6 Dossier 27 Juin 1815. D'Erlon to Grouchy at the Bridge of De Benne.
15. ibid, D'Erlon to Grouchy 27 Juin 1815, timed at 15.00 hours.

16. Charles Antoine Thoumas (1887) *Le General Curely*, Paris Berger-Levault pp. 421–422.
17. SHDDT MR 718 *Relation Campagne 1815 par le Duc de Valmy* p. 32.
18. Rigau (1846), *Souvenirs des guerres de l'Empire*, Garnier Freres Paris, pp. 116–118.
19. Fleuret pp 155–156.
20. SHDDT C15 6 Dossier 27 Juin 1815. Grouchy to Davout 27 Juin timed at 22.00 hours.
21. SHDDT C15 6. Dossier 28 Juin 1815, d'Erlon to Grouchy 28 Juin 1815.
22. ibid.
23. ibid, Grouchy to Davout 29 Juin 1815.

Chapter 19

1. Broughton p. 286.
2. ibid pp. 270–273.
3. SHDDT C2 Situation report 26–27 Juin 1815.
4. SHDDT C15 6 Dossier 28 Juin. Grouchy to Vandamme 28 Juin timed at 04.00 hours.
5. This order exists in two forms. The original hand-written order by Monthion can be found in SHDDT C15 6 Dossier 28 Juin, Monthion to Vandamme timed at 05.00 hours. The second version can be found in C15 23 Registre d'Ordres et de correspondance du major-général à 3e Corps d'Armée pp.32–33. Of note is that the order is dated 18 Juin. This is impossible and it likely however to be an error on the part of the copyist of the original document.
6. Guyot p. 302.
7. Chevalier p. 329.
8. SHDDT C15 6 Dossier 29 Juin. Pajol to Grouchy 29 Juin 1815 timed at 20.00 hours.
9. SHDDT GR 8 YD 2805.
10. Charles Esdaile, *Napoléon, France and Waterloo: The Eagle Rejected*, Pen & Sword, Barnsley, 2016, p.70.

Chapter 20

1. SHDDT C15 6 Dossier 29 Juin, Grouchy to Davout 29 Juin 1815. Copy made by Comte du Cases.
2. ibid, Ordre Davout 28 Juin 03.00 hours.
3. ibid, Fouché 28 Juin 1815.
4. Charles Le Sénécal (1840*) Réponse, au nom de la mémoire du général baron Le Sénécal, à la calomnie publiée par M. le baron Berthezène, dans un libelle en date du 27 mai 1840.* Impr. de E.-B. Delanchy, Paris p.13.
5. Voss pp 131–132.
6. ibid.
7. SHDDT C15 6 Dossier 29 Juin 1815, Exelmans to Davout 29 Juin 1815.
8. ibid, Brunneck to Davout [?] 30 Juin 1815.
9. SHDDT C15 6 Dossier 30 Jui,. Royer to Davout 30 Juin 1815.
10. SHDDT C15 6 Dossier 29 Juin, Grouchy to Fouché. Copy made 1865 by Comte du Cases.
11. ibid, Grouchy to Davout 29 Juin 1815.
12. *Journal de l'Empire*, 27 Juin 1815, pp. 1–2.

Chapter 21

1. Grouchy Vol. 5 pp.1–2.
2. Pajol (1874) *General en Chef*, Firmin Didot, Paris p.262.
3. Chaboulon pp. 207–208.
4. SHDDT C15 6 Dossier 29 Juin 1815. Davout to Vandamme 29 Juin 1815.

5. Damitz, Vol. 2, pp. 180.
6. SHDDT C15 6 Dossier 30 Juin 1815, Margerand to Davout 30 Juin 1815 timed at 05.00 hours.
7. ibid, Marchand [?] to Davout 30 Juin 1815.
8. ibid, Marchand to Vandamme 30 Juin 1815.
9. ibid, Marchand to Mouton-Duvernet 30 Juin 1815.
10. ibid.
11. ibid, Guillaminot to Mouton-Duvernet 30 Juin 1815.
12. ibid, Deriot to Davout 30 Juin 1815 time at 10.00 hours.
13. SHDDT C15 6 Dossier 30 Juin 1815, Lefebvre-Desnoëttes to Davout 30 Juin 1815.
14. ibid, Schmidt to Davout 30 Juin 1815.
15. AN AFIV 1140 Situation rapport 29- 30 Juin 1815.
16. AN AF IV 1940 Garde Impériale 200.
17. SHDDT C15 6. Dossier 30 Juin 1815, Order du Jour 30 Juin 1815 signee Comte Roguet.
18. An AfIV 1140 Situation report 29- 30 Juin 1815.
19. ibid.
20. ibid.
21. SHDDT C15 35 Situation Rapport Armée du Paris 1 Juillet 1815.
22. SHDDT 15 C4 Rapport Avril 1815.
23. ibid, Décret 20 Mai 1815.

Chapter 22

1. Broughton pp. 277–279.
2. ibid, p. 282.
3. SHDDT C15 35 Situation Rapport Armée du Paris 1 Juillet 1815.
4. ibid.
5. ibid.
6. ibid.
7. SHDDT C15 35 Situation Rapport Armée du Paris 1 Juillet 1815.
8. Delort, *Notice sur la batailles de Fleurus et de Mont Saint Jean* in Revue Hebdomadaire Juin 1896 p. 382.
9. SHDDT C15 35 Situation Rapport Armée du Paris 1 Juillet 1815.
10. AN LH 274/9.
11. SHDDT C15 6 Dossier 30 Juin 1815. Maréchal du Camp Boivin to Marshal Davout 30 Juin 1815.
12. SHDDT C15 6 Dossier 30 Juin 1815, Maréchal du Camp Boivin to Marshal Davout 30 Juin 1815.
13. ibid, Colonel Regeaud to Marshal Davout 30 Juin 1815 timed at 20.30 hours.
14. ibid, Colonel Regeaud to Marshal Davout 30 Juin 1815 timed at 20.30 hours.
15. ibid, Colonel Regeaud to Marshal Davout 1 Juillet 1815 timed at 03. 00 hours.
16. ibid, Maréchal du Camp Boivin to Marshal Davout 30 Juin 1815.
17. ibid, 1 Juillet 1815, Colonel Regeaud to Marshal Davout 1 Juillet 1815 timed at 03.00 hours.
18. Anon La Souvenir Napoléonien No. 337 September 1984.
19. General Allix 'Souvenirs Militaires et Politique' in *Journal des Sciences Militaires* Vol. 26 January 1832 p. 313.

Chapter 23

1. Broughton (1816) p. 286.
2. SHDDT C15 6 Dossier 1 Juillet 1815, Ordre du Jour 1 Juillet 1815.

3. ibid, d'Erlon to Marcognet 1 Juillet 1815 A.
4. ibid, d'Erlon to Marcognet 1 Juillet 1815 B.
5. ibid, d'Erlon to Marcognet 1 Juillet 1815 C.
6. ibid, Jamin to Davout 1 Juillet 1815.
7. ibid, Allix to Davout 1 Juillet 1815.
8. ibid, Allix to Davout 1 Juillet 1815 timed at 16.30 hours.
9. ibid, Milhaud to Davout 1 Juillet 1815.
10. Damitz (1838) Geschichte *des Feldzuges von 1815 in den Niederlanden und Frankreich* 2 volumes, Berlin. Vol. 2. pp. 178–179.
11. Perrot (1821) *Histoire de l'ex-garde, depuis sa formation jusqu'à son licenciement, comprenant les faits généraux des campagnes de 1805 à 1815, son organisation, sa solde, ses indemnités, le rang, le service, la discipline, les uniformes de ses divers corps, terminée par une biographie des chefs supérieurs de la garde.* Delaunay, Paris, pp.242–243.
12. Ferryman (1913*) The life of a regimental officer during the great war, 1793–1815 comp. from the correspondence of Colonel Samuel Rice, C.B., K.H. 51st light infantry, and from other sources.* Blackwood & Sons, London pp. 298–299.
13. Damitz, Vol. 2. pp. 176–180.
14. SHDDT GR 24 YC 383.
15. Damitz, Vol. 2. p.p. 285–300.
16. Rumigny, pp. 112–114.
17. Saint Just (1891) *Historique du 5eme regiment de Dragons.* Paris, Librairie Hacette pp. 322–323.
18. Henckens (Lieutenant), (1910) Mémoires *se rapportant à son service militaire au 6e régiment de chasseurs à cheval Français de février 1803 à Août 1816.* La Haye pp. 246–247.
19. Delort, p. 264.
20. Hulot, Souvenirs Militaire du General Baron Hulot in *Le Spectateur Militaire* Vol 27, 1884, 4th Series p.218.
21. Broughton p. 286.
22. SHDDT C15 6 Dossier 1 Juillet 1815 Rectification relative au rapport insere dans le Moniteur du 3 Juillet 1815 concernant les combats de Versailles et de Rocquencourt. See also SHDDT GR 1M717 – 729 Campagne 1815 reconnaissance de Champ de Bataille Rocquencourt.
23. ibid.
24. SHDDT C15 6 Dossier 1 Juillet 1815 Rectification relative au rapport insere dans le Moniteur du 3 Juillet 1815 concernant les combats de Versailles et de Rocquencourt. See also SHDDT GR 1m 717 – 729 Campagne 1815 reconnaissance de Champ de Bataille Rocquencourt.
25. Journal des débats politiques et littéraires 3 Juillet 1815 pp. 1–2.
26. SHDDT GR 24 YC 409 5e Hussard, 11 Août 1814 a 25 Septembre 1815.
27. SHDDT GR 24 YC 414 6e Hussard. See also GR 24 YC 415 6e Hussard.
28. ibid, YC 293 8e Chasseurs.
29. ibid, YC 148 5e Dragons.
30. ibid, YC 185 Août 1814–6 Août 1815 (10e régiment de dragons, 1814).
31. ibid, C 213 29 Juillet 1814–12 Août 1815 (15e régiment de dragons, 1814).
32. General Allix p. 313.
33. Pajol, pp. 267–268.
34. Chaboulon, pp. 368–372.
35. Chaboulon pp. 371–386.
36. Pierre Berthezène (1855), *Souvenirs militaires de la République et de l'Empire,* J. Dumaine, Paris, p. 404.

Chapter 24

1. SHDDT C15 6 Dossier 2 Juillet 1815, Charbonnel to Davout no date timed at 05.06 hours.
2. ibid, Grundler to Davout 2 Juillet 1815.
3. ibid, Donzelot to Davout 2 Juillet 1815.
4. ibid, Reille to Davout 2 Juillet 1815.
5. ibid.
6. SHDDT C15 6 Dossier 2 Juillet 1815, Grundler to Guillaminot 2 Juillet 1815.
7. ibid, Kellerman to Haxo 2 Juillet 1815.
8. SHDDT C15 35 Situation Rapport Armée du Paris 1 Juillet 1815.
9. SHDDT C15 fol 42 Situation Rapport 30 Juin 1815.
10. Hulot p.218.
11. SHDDT C15 6 Dossier 2 Juillet. Vichery to unknown general 2 Juillet 1815 A.
12. ibid, Vichery to unknown general 2 Juillet 1815 B.
13. Capitaine Robinaux (1908) *Journal de route (1803–1832)*. Publié par Gustave Schlumberger Plon, Paris pp.216–219.
14. SHDDT C15 6 Dossier 2 Juillet, General Pully to Marshal Davout 2 Juillet 1815 timed at 23.00 hours.
15. AN LH 2630/86 Colonel Louis Jean Tripe was the commanding officer of the 2nd Regiment of Line Infantry.
16. SHDDT C15 6 Dossier 3 Juillet 1815, General Pully to Marshal Davout 2 Juillet 1815 timed at 23.00 hours.
17. SHDDT GR 21 YC 19 2e régiment d'infanterie de ligne dit régiment de la Reine, 20 mai 1814–21 Août 1814 (matricules 1 à 2 997). See Also SHDDT GR 21 YC 202e régiment d'infanterie de ligne dit régiment de la Reine, 9 septembre 1814–6 juin 1815 (matricules 3 000 à 4 723).
18. SHDDT C15 6 Dossier 3 Juillet 1815, Ordre de Mouvement.
19. ibid, General Pully to Imperial Headquarters, 3 Juillet 1815.
20. Robinaux pp.216–219.

Chapter 25

1. SHDDT C15 6 Dossier 3 Juillet 1815. Reverst to Drouot 3 Juillet 1815 timed at 03:00. Given the letters contents, it must have been added to after 03.00 hours and sent much later in the morning.
2. SHDDT GR 24 YC 148.
3. SHDDT C15 6 Dossier 3 Juillet 1815. Reverst to Drouot 3 Juillet 1815 timed at 03.00 hours.
4. Guyot p.302.
5. SHDDT C15 6 Dossier 3 Juillet 1815, Milhaud to Davout 3 Juillet 1815.
6. *Carnet de la Sabretache* 1912 pp.248 and 290.
7. Antoine Nicolas Beraud (1829) *Histoire de Napoléon*, Brussels, de Kock pp.340–341
8. Broughton p. 288.
9. Author's collection.
10. François, p.898.
11. SHDDT GR 24 YC 129 7e Lanciers 1815.
12. ibid.
13. Damitz Vol. 2. p. 307.
14. Chaboulon pp. 396–397.
15. Gaspard Gougaurd (1818) *Campagne de 1815*, P Mongie, Paris pp.163–167.

16. SHDDT C15 6 Dossier 3 Juillet 1815, Extrait des Minutes de la Secretairerie d'État.
17. ibid, Davout to Guillaminot 3 Juillet 1815.
18. Berthezene pp.404–405.
19. Beraud p. 341.
20. SHDDT MR 717, Observations sur la Campagne du 1815.
21. Journal de l'Empire 4th Juillet 1815 p. 2.

Chapter 26

1. Damitz. Vol. 2. pp. 314–316.
2. Broughton (1816) p. 286.
3. *Morning Post*, Friday 28th July 1815. See also the *Morning Post* of Thursday 24th August 1815. and Monday 29th August 1815.
4. *Morning Chronicle* Thursday 31st August 1815.
5. *Cobbett's Weekly Political Register*, Saturday 9th September 1815.
6. Leon-Michel Routier (2001) *Recits d'un Soldat de la Republique et de l'Empire 1792 – 1830* Editions du Grenadier.

Index